Sand Chronicles

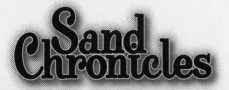

Shojo Beat

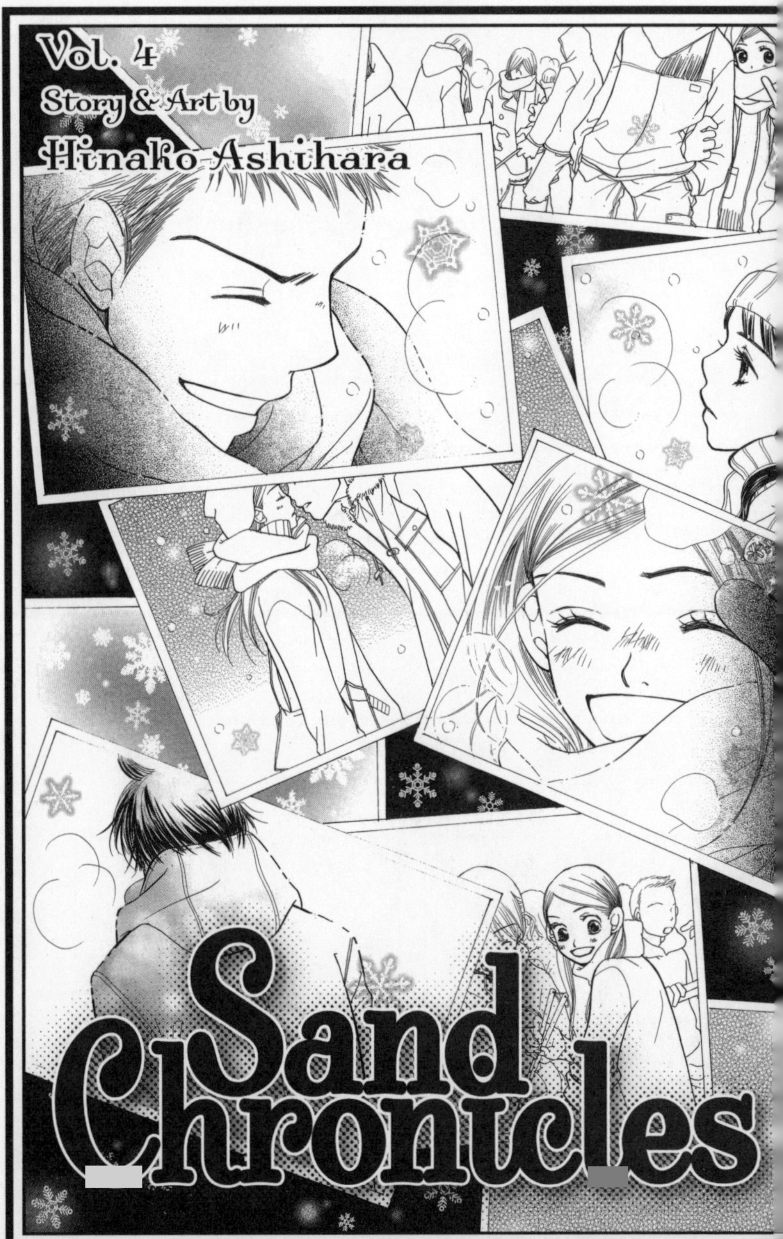
Vol. 4
Story & Art by
Hinako Ashihara
Sand Chronicles

Sand Chronicles

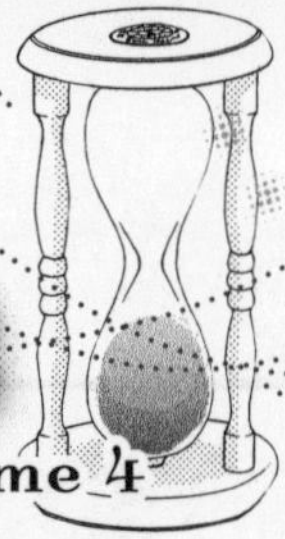

Volume 4

Contents

Story thus far...

After her parents' divorce, Ann moves to rural Shimane with her mother. At first, Ann doesn't like living in the country, but then she makes friends with a boy named Daigo and wealthy brother and sister Fuji and Shika.

After Ann's mother commits suicide, Daigo is a great support to her. But then Ann moves back to Tokyo to live with her father. Now she and Daigo struggle to maintain a long-distance relationship.

Meanwhile, Fuji and Shika try to unravel the secret surrounding their birth. Then, suddenly, without a word to anyone, Fuji disappears...

Main characters

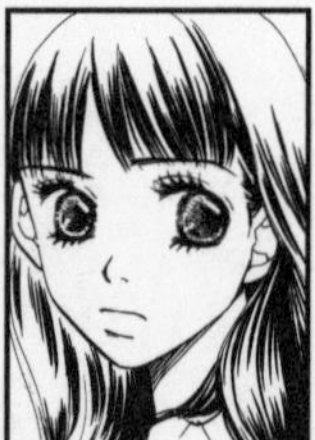

Shika Tsukishima
Fuji's shy and attractive younger sister.

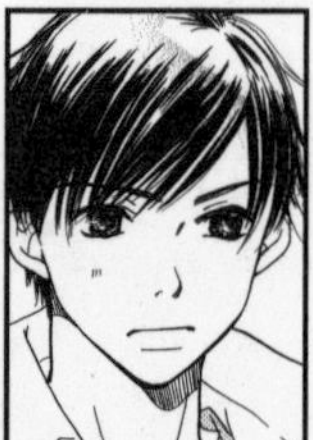

Fuji Tsukishima
The son of an important family. A loner.

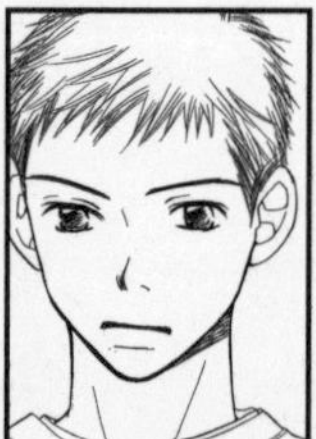

Daigo Kitamura
Boyish and gruff, but kind.

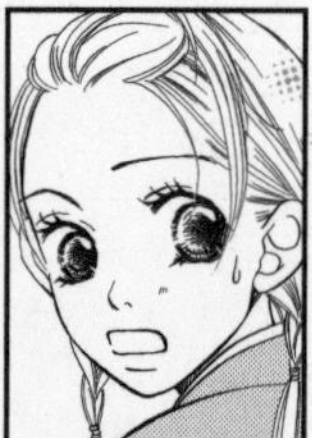

Ann Uekusa
Confident, but sensitive like her mother.

WINTER, AGE 16: SNOWS OF REMEMBRANCE

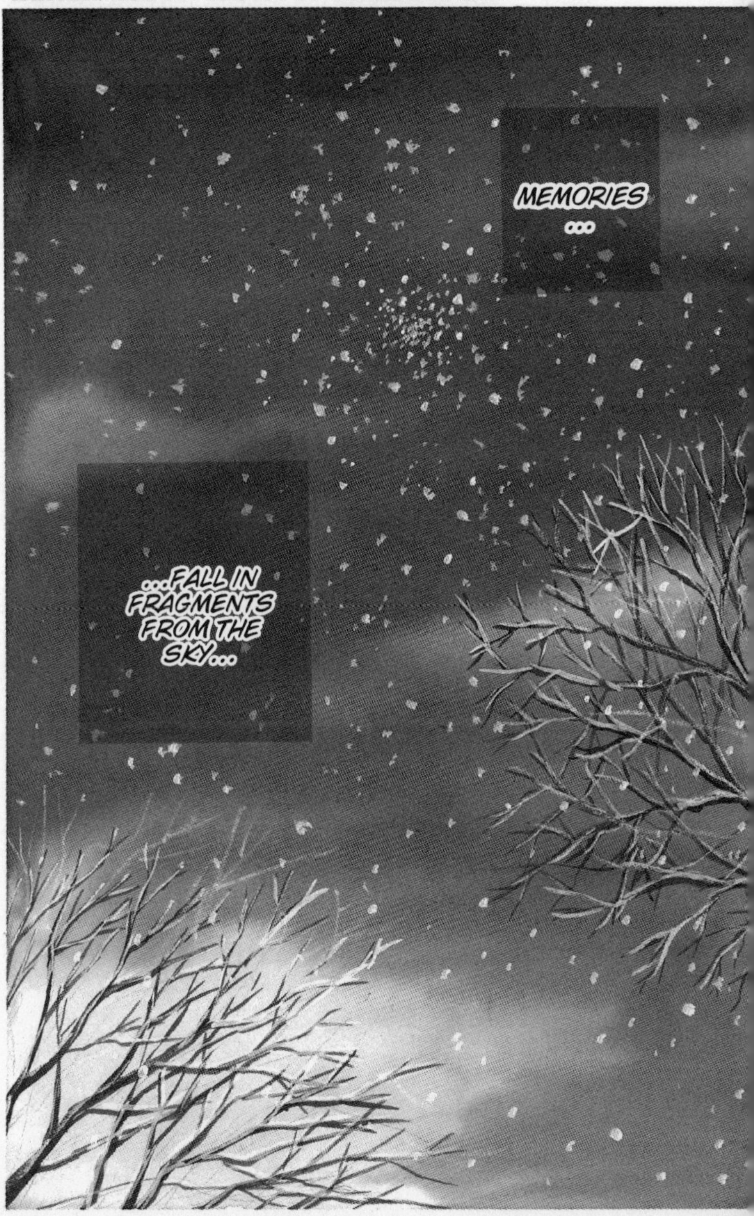
MEMORIES...
...FALL IN FRAGMENTS FROM THE SKY...

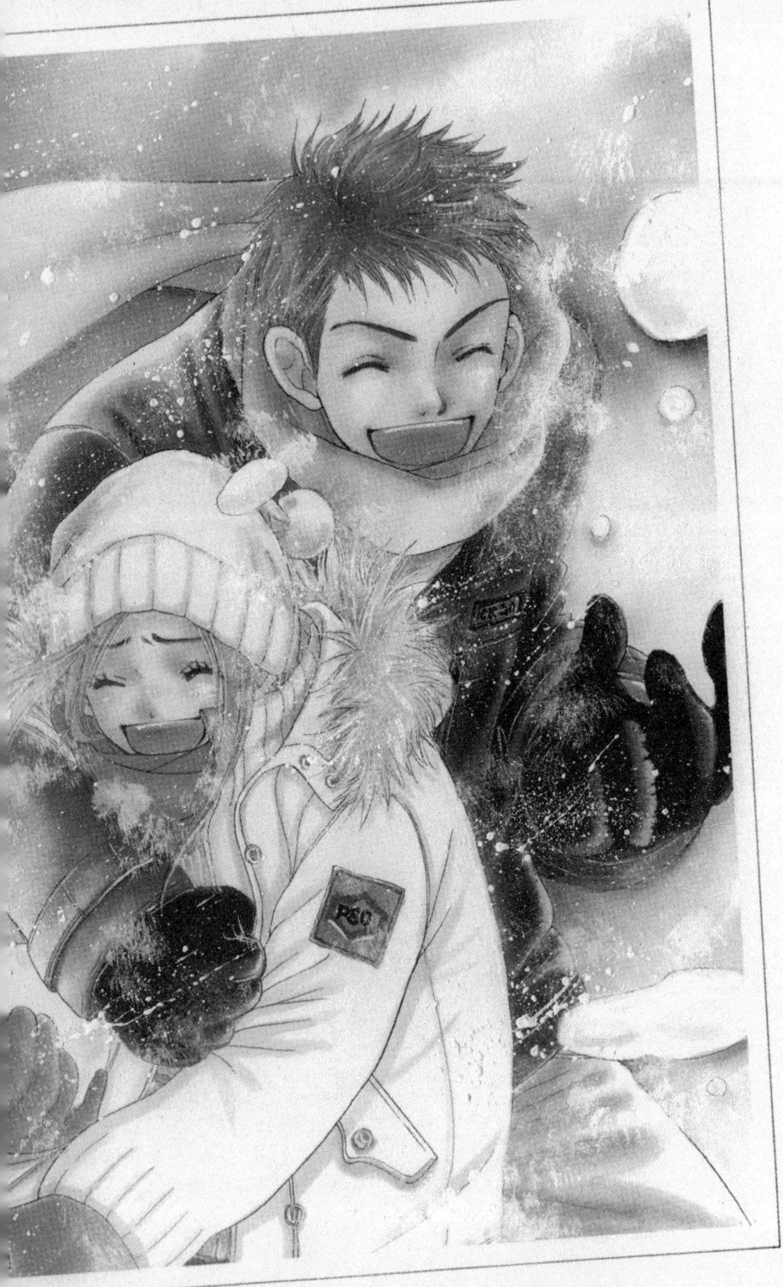

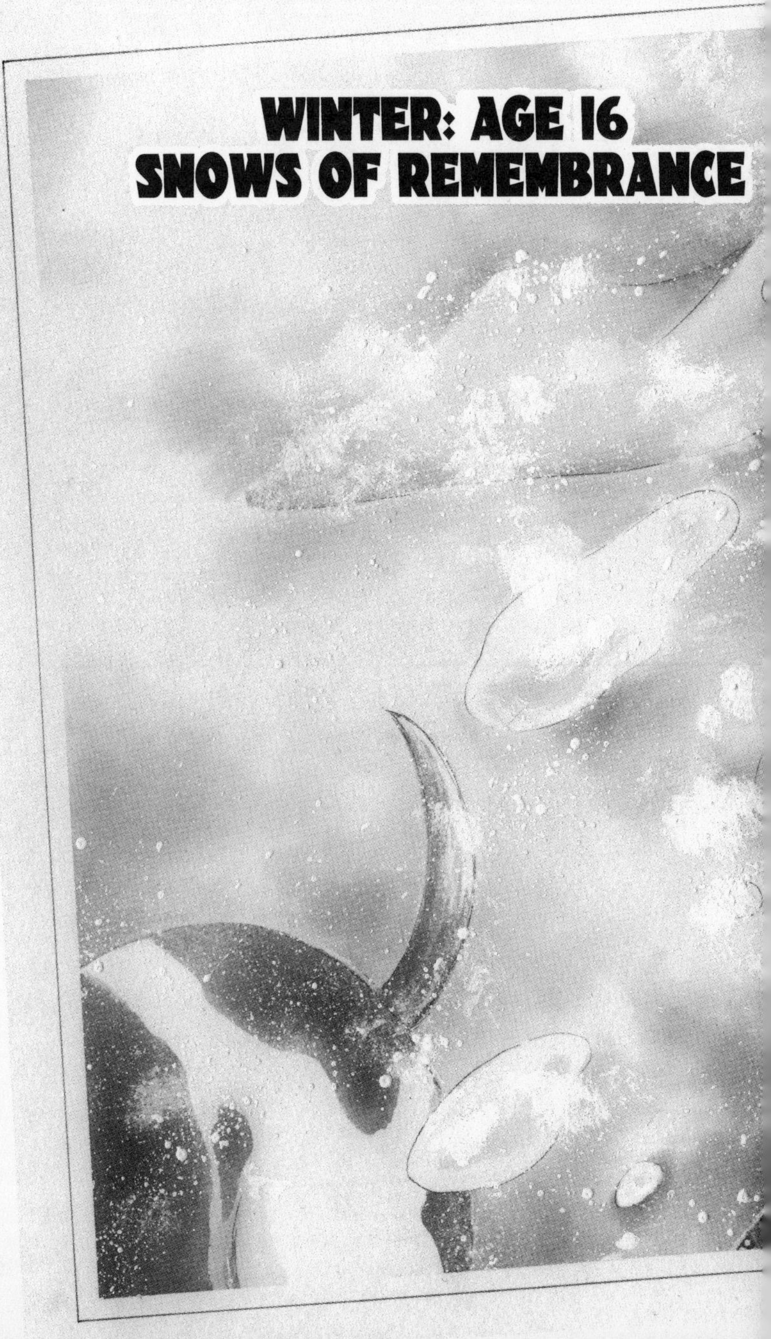
WINTER: AGE 16
SNOWS OF REMEMBRANCE

Sand Chronicles

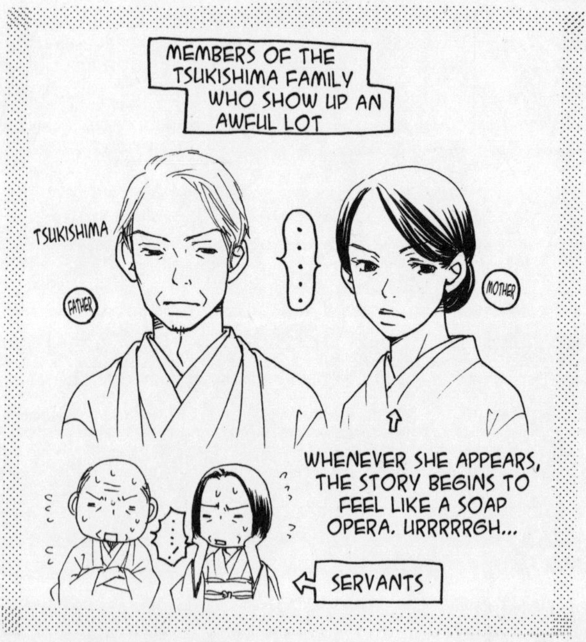
MEMBERS OF THE TSUKISHIMA FAMILY WHO SHOW UP AN AWFUL LOT
MOTHER
...
TSUKISHIMA
FATHER
WHENEVER SHE APPEARS, THE STORY BEGINS TO FEEL LIKE A SOAP OPERA. URRRRRGH...
SERVANTS
...

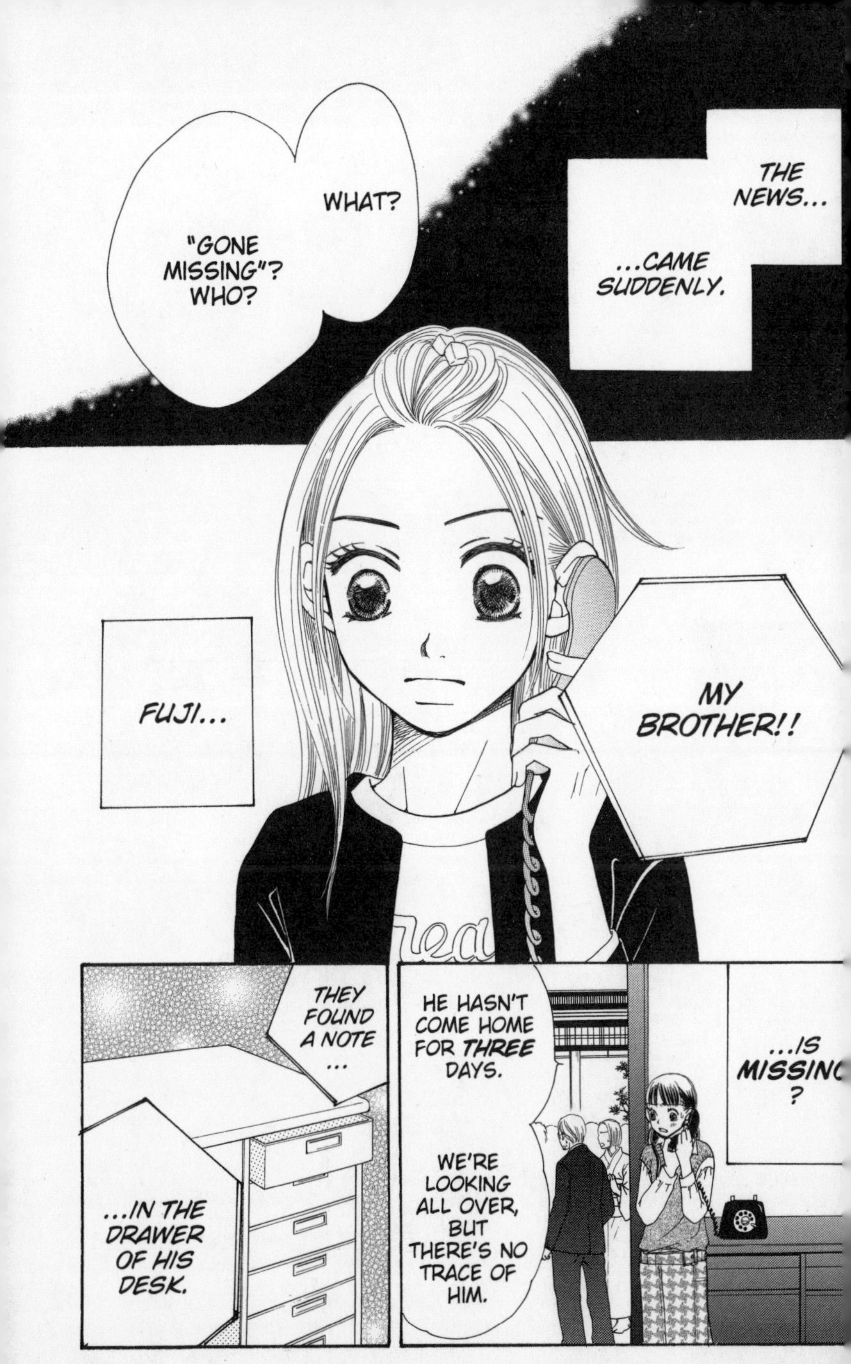
THE NEWS...
...CAME SUDDENLY.
WHAT?
"GONE MISSING"? WHO?
MY BROTHER!!
FUJI...
...IS MISSIN ?
HE HASN'T COME HOME FOR THREE DAYS.
WE'RE LOOKING ALL OVER, BUT THERE'S NO TRACE OF HIM.
THEY FOUND A NOTE ...
...IN THE DRAWER OF HIS DESK.

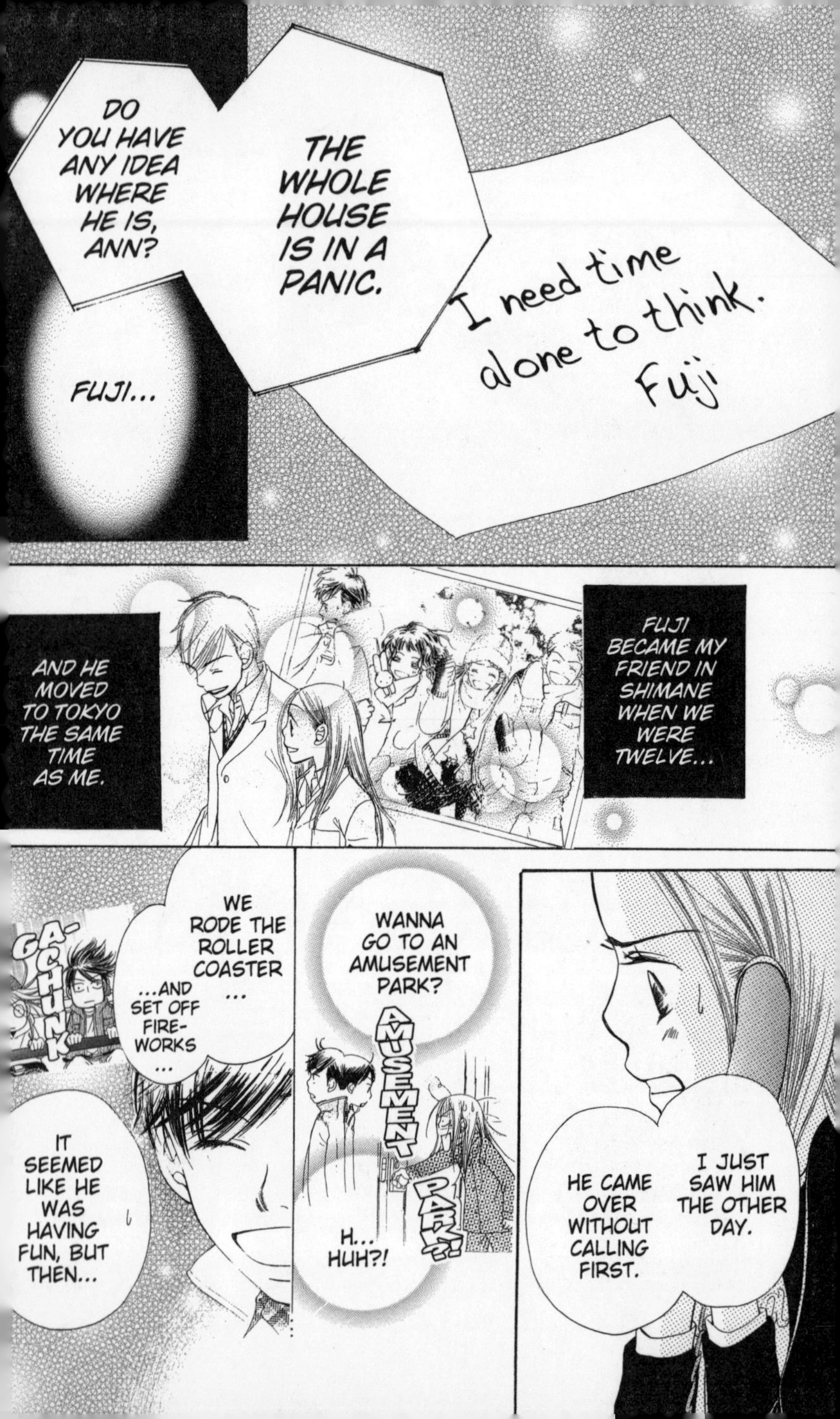
I need time alone to think. Fuji
THE WHOLE HOUSE IS IN A PANIC.
DO YOU HAVE ANY IDEA WHERE HE IS, ANN?
FUJI...
FUJI BECAME MY FRIEND IN SHIMANE WHEN WE WERE TWELVE...
AND HE MOVED TO TOKYO THE SAME TIME AS ME.
I JUST SAW HIM THE OTHER DAY.
HE CAME OVER WITHOUT CALLING FIRST.
WANNA GO TO AN AMUSEMENT PARK?
AMUSEMENT PARK?!
H... HUH?!
WE RODE THE ROLLER COASTER...
...AND SET OFF FIRE-WORKS...
GA-CHUNK
IT SEEMED LIKE HE WAS HAVING FUN, BUT THEN...

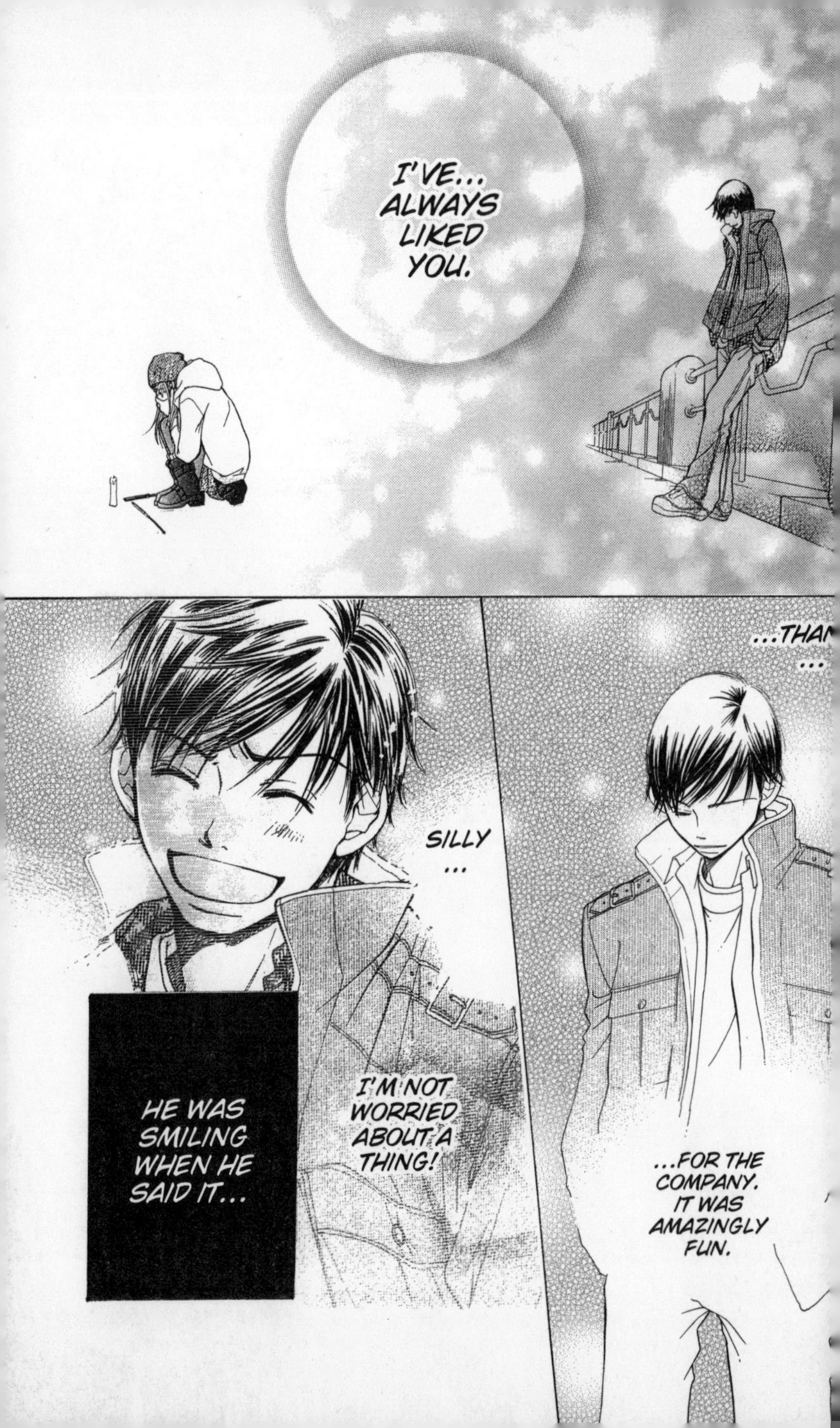
I'VE... ALWAYS LIKED YOU.
...THAN ...
...FOR THE COMPANY. IT WAS AMAZINGLY FUN.
SILLY ...
I'M NOT WORRIED ABOUT A THING!
HE WAS SMILING WHEN HE SAID IT...

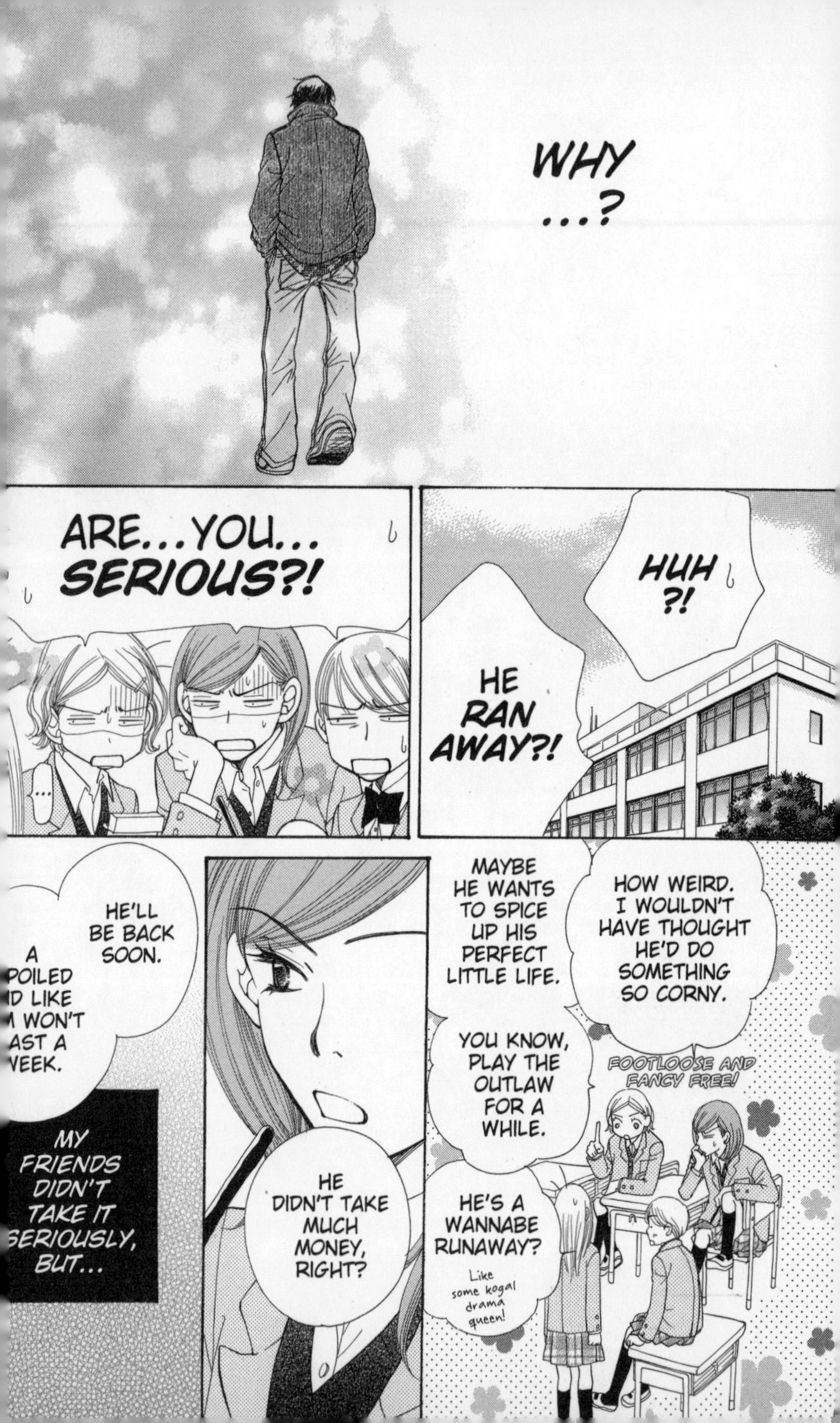
WHY ...?
HUH ?!
HE RAN AWAY?!
ARE...YOU... SERIOUS?!
...
HOW WEIRD. I WOULDN'T HAVE THOUGHT HE'D DO SOMETHING SO CORNY.
MAYBE HE WANTS TO SPICE UP HIS PERFECT LITTLE LIFE.
FOOTLOOSE AND FANCY FREE!
YOU KNOW, PLAY THE OUTLAW FOR A WHILE.
HE'S A WANNABE RUNAWAY?
Like some kogal drama queen!
HE DIDN'T TAKE MUCH MONEY, RIGHT?
HE'LL BE BACK SOON.
A POILED D LIKE M WON'T AST A VEEK.
MY FRIENDS DIDN'T TAKE IT SERIOUSLY, BUT...

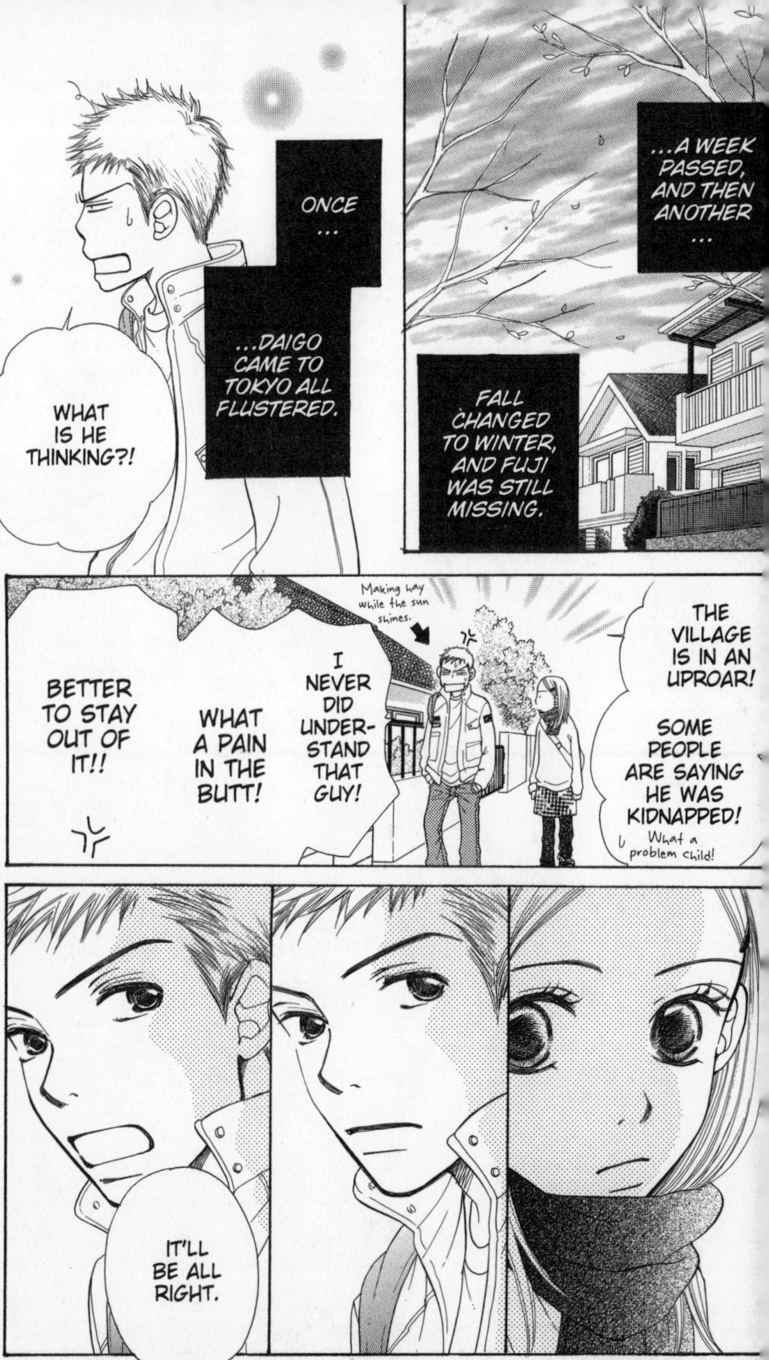
...A WEEK PASSED, AND THEN ANOTHER ...
FALL CHANGED TO WINTER, AND FUJI WAS STILL MISSING.
ONCE ...
...DAIGO CAME TO TOKYO ALL FLUSTERED.
WHAT IS HE THINKING?!
THE VILLAGE IS IN AN UPROAR!
SOME PEOPLE ARE SAYING HE WAS KIDNAPPED!
What a problem child!
Making hay while the sun shines.
I NEVER DID UNDERSTAND THAT GUY!
WHAT A PAIN IN THE BUTT!
BETTER TO STAY OUT OF IT!!
IT'LL BE ALL RIGHT.

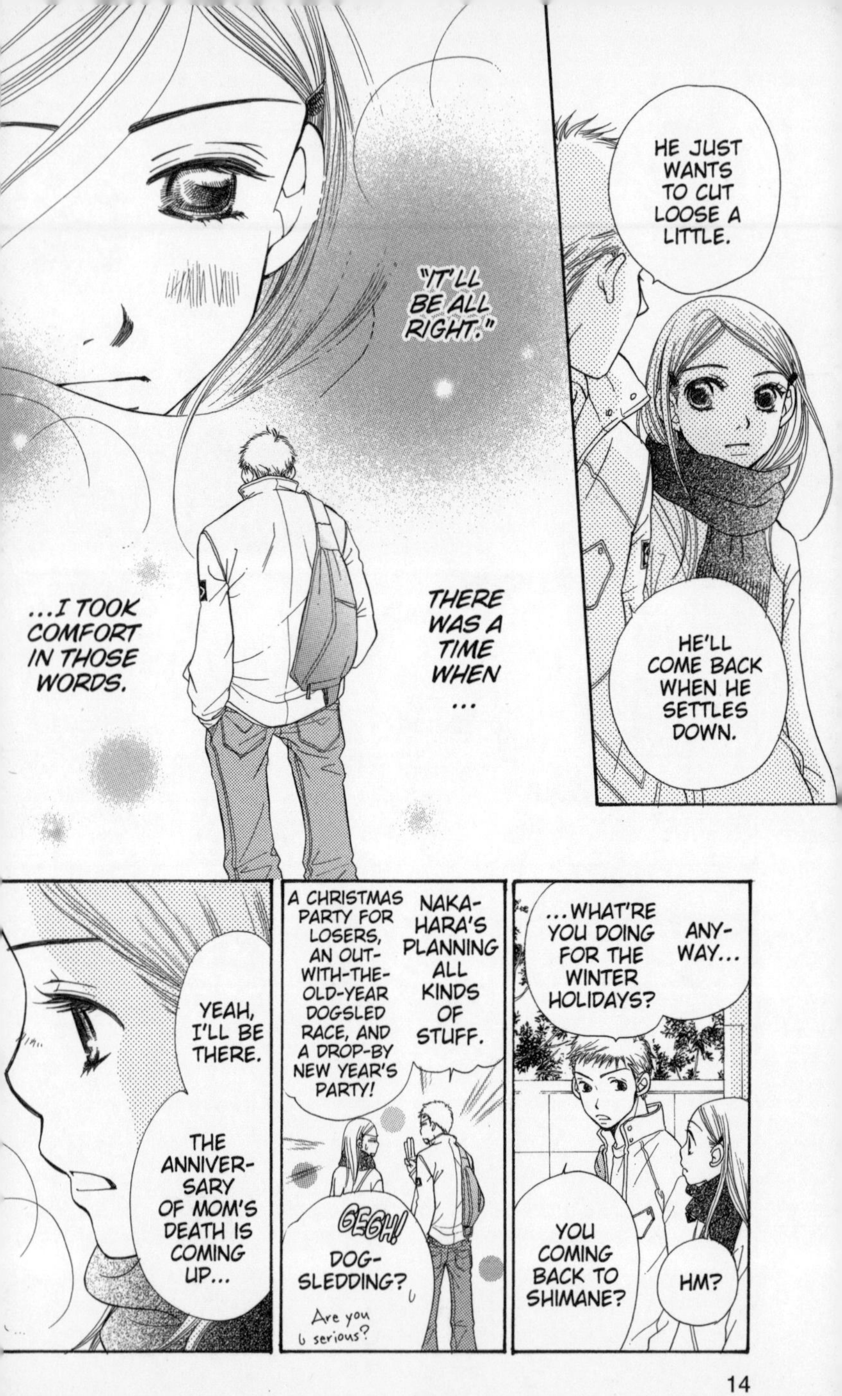
HE JUST WANTS TO CUT LOOSE A LITTLE.
HE'LL COME BACK WHEN HE SETTLES DOWN.
"IT'LL BE ALL RIGHT."
THERE WAS A TIME WHEN ...
...I TOOK COMFORT IN THOSE WORDS.
ANY-WAY...
...WHAT'RE YOU DOING FOR THE WINTER HOLIDAYS?
HM?
YOU COMING BACK TO SHIMANE?
NAKA-HARA'S PLANNING ALL KINDS OF STUFF.
A CHRISTMAS PARTY FOR LOSERS, AN OUT-WITH-THE-OLD-YEAR DOGSLED RACE, AND A DROP-BY NEW YEAR'S PARTY!
GEGH!
DOG-SLEDDING?
Are you serious?
YEAH, I'LL BE THERE.
THE ANNIVERSARY OF MOM'S DEATH IS COMING UP...

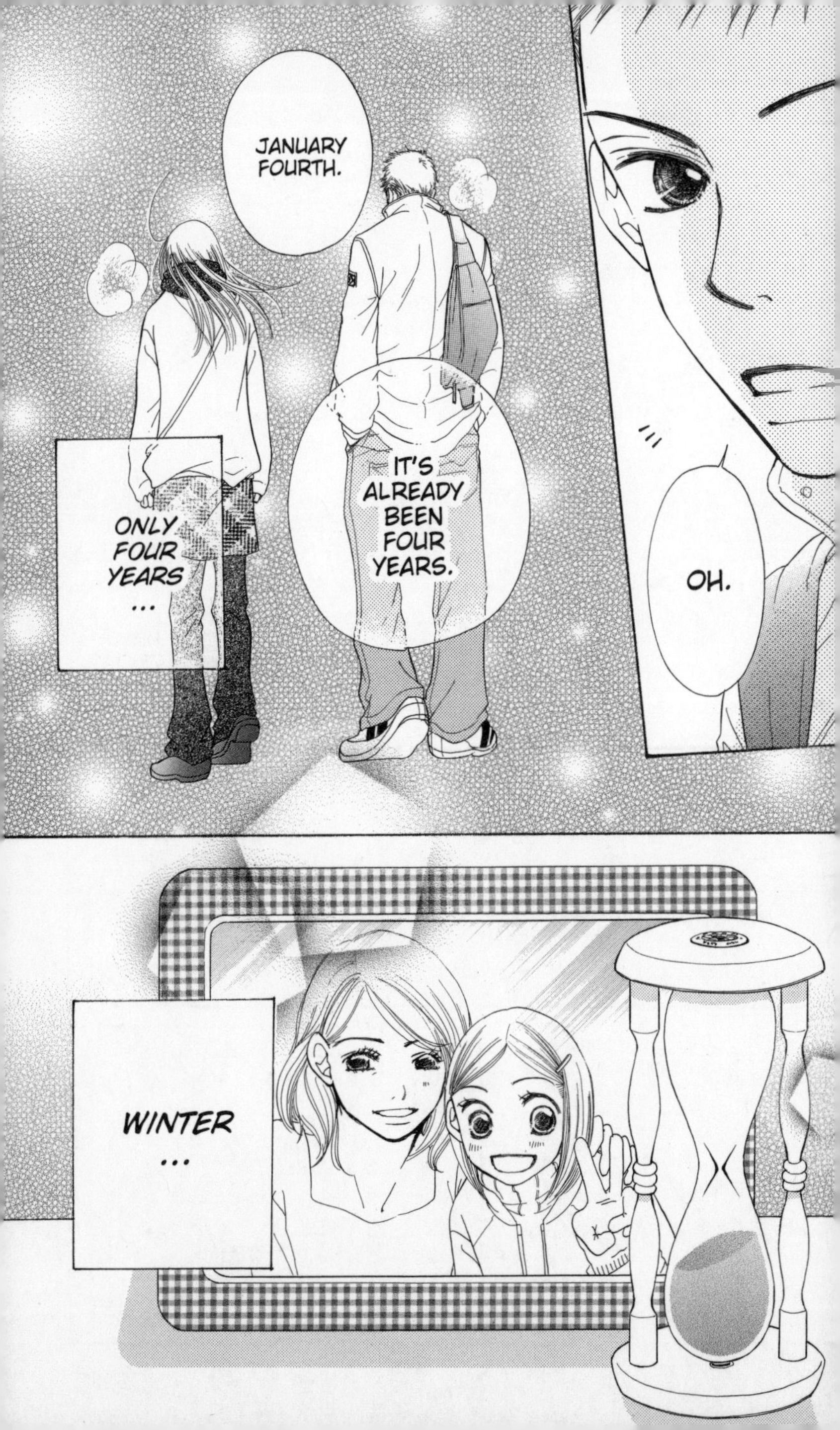
OH.
JANUARY FOURTH.
IT'S ALREADY BEEN FOUR YEARS.
ONLY FOUR YEARS ...
WINTER ...

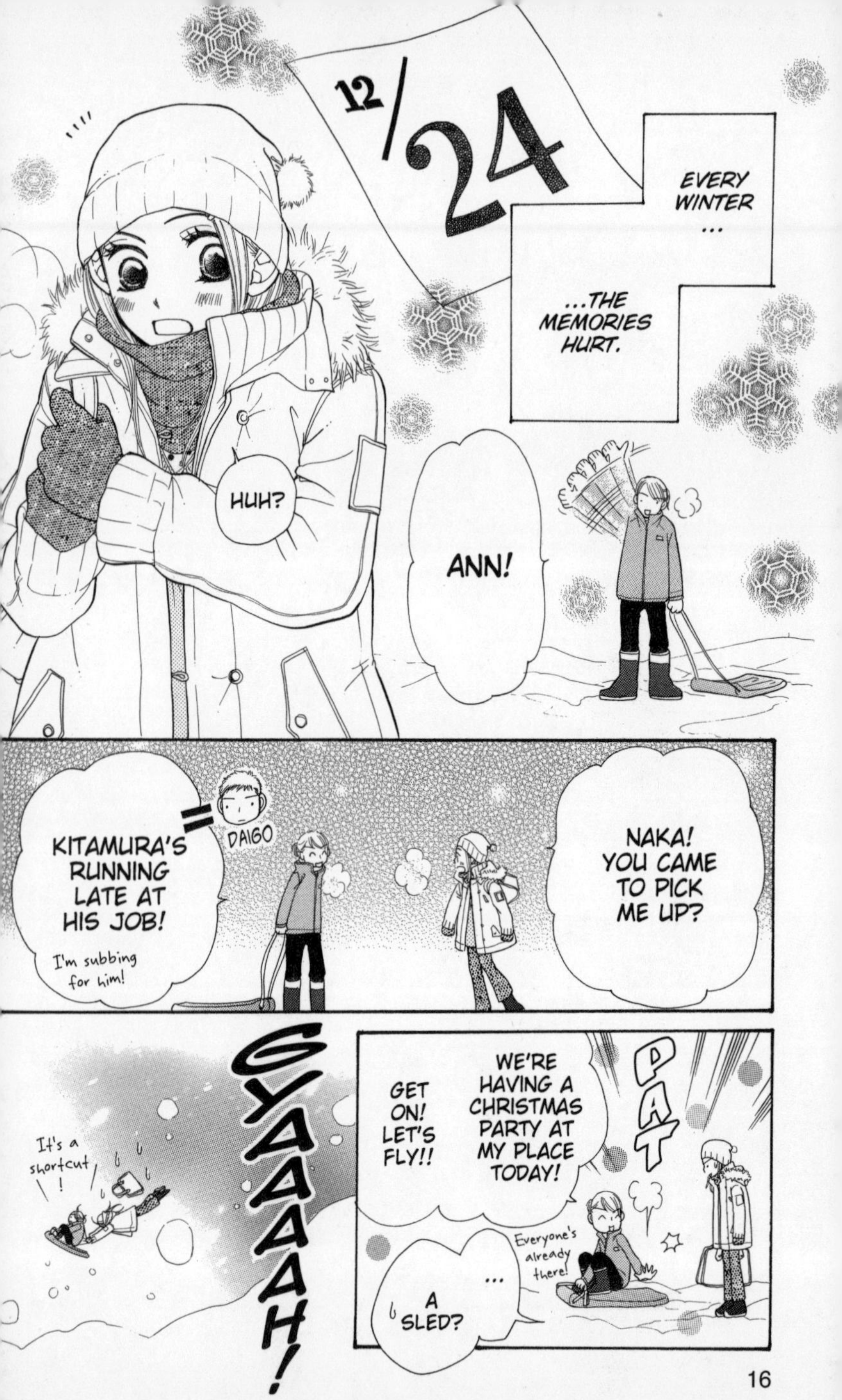
12/24
EVERY WINTER ...
...THE MEMORIES HURT.
ANN!
HUH?
NAKA! YOU CAME TO PICK ME UP?
KITAMURA'S RUNNING LATE AT HIS JOB!
I'm subbing for him!
DAIGO
PAT
WE'RE HAVING A CHRISTMAS PARTY AT MY PLACE TODAY!
GET ON! LET'S FLY!!
Everyone's already there!
...
A SLED?
GYAAAAH!
It's a shortcut!

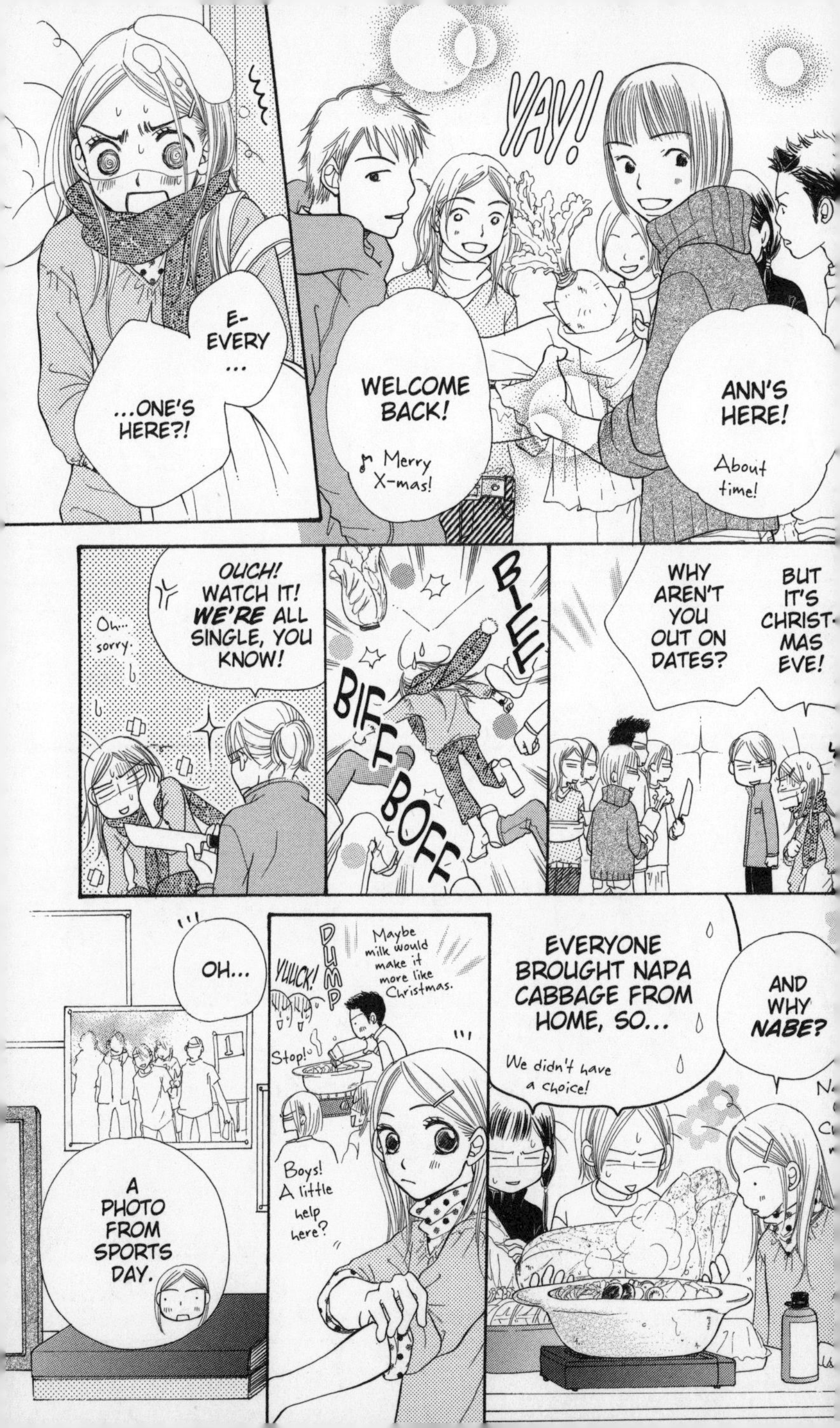
YAY!
ANN'S HERE!
About time!
WELCOME BACK!
Merry X-mas!
E-EVERY...
...ONE'S HERE?!
BUT IT'S CHRISTMAS EVE!
WHY AREN'T YOU OUT ON DATES?
BIFF
BIFF
BOFF
OUCH! WATCH IT! WE'RE ALL SINGLE, YOU KNOW!
Oh... sorry.
AND WHY NABE?
EVERYONE BROUGHT NAPA CABBAGE FROM HOME, SO...
We didn't have a choice!
Maybe milk would make it more like Christmas.
DUMP
YUUCK!
Stop!
Boys! A little help here?
OH...
A PHOTO FROM SPORTS DAY.

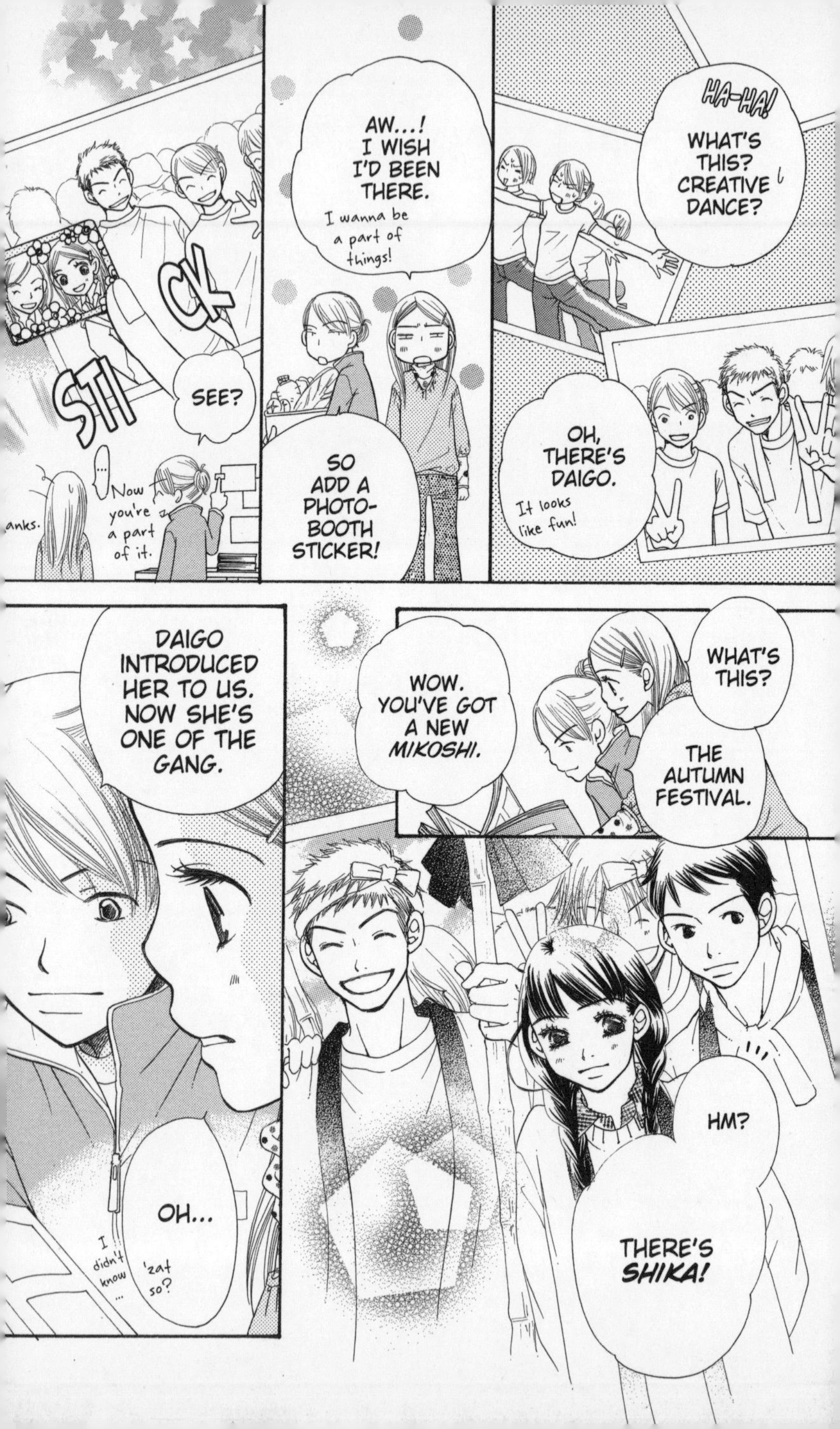
HA-HA!
WHAT'S THIS? CREATIVE DANCE?
OH, THERE'S DAIGO.
It looks like fun!
AW...! I WISH I'D BEEN THERE.
I wanna be a part of things!
SO ADD A PHOTO-BOOTH STICKER!
STICK
SEE?
...
Now you're a part of it.
anks.
WHAT'S THIS?
THE AUTUMN FESTIVAL.
WOW. YOU'VE GOT A NEW *MIKOSHI.*
HM?
THERE'S *SHIKA!*
DAIGO INTRODUCED HER TO US. NOW SHE'S ONE OF THE GANG.
OH...
'zat so?
I didn't know...

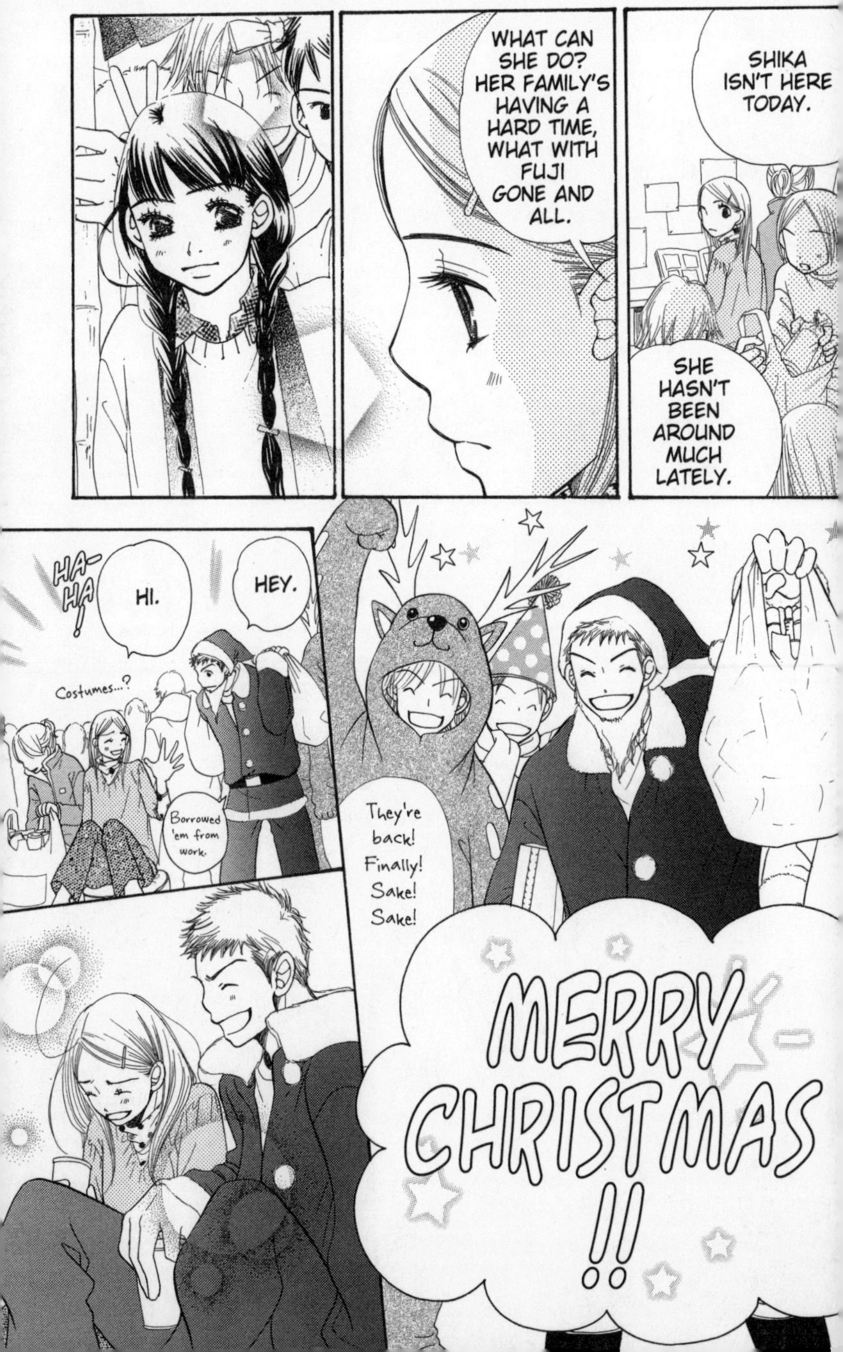
SHIKA ISN'T HERE TODAY.
SHE HASN'T BEEN AROUND MUCH LATELY.
WHAT CAN SHE DO? HER FAMILY'S HAVING A HARD TIME, WHAT WITH FUJI GONE AND ALL.
They're back! Finally! Sake! Sake!
MERRY CHRISTMAS!!
HEY.
HI.
HA-HA!
Costumes...?
Borrowed 'em from work.

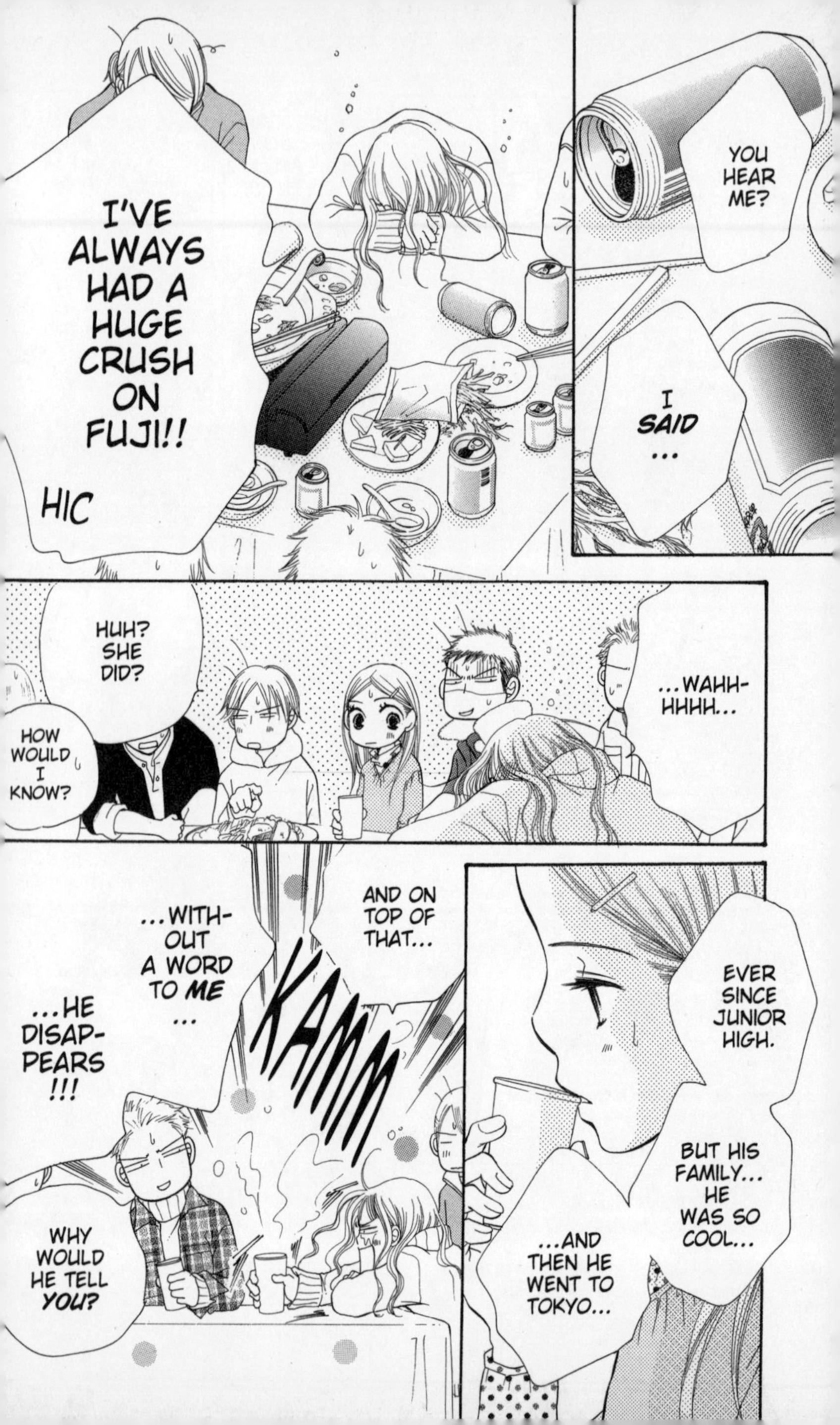
YOU HEAR ME?
I SAID ...
I'VE ALWAYS HAD A HUGE CRUSH ON FUJI!!
HIC
...WAHH-HHHH...
HUH? SHE DID?
HOW WOULD I KNOW?
EVER SINCE JUNIOR HIGH.
BUT HIS FAMILY... HE WAS SO COOL...
...AND THEN HE WENT TO TOKYO...
AND ON TOP OF THAT...
KAMM
...WITH-OUT A WORD TO ME ...
...HE DISAP-PEARS !!!
WHY WOULD HE TELL YOU?

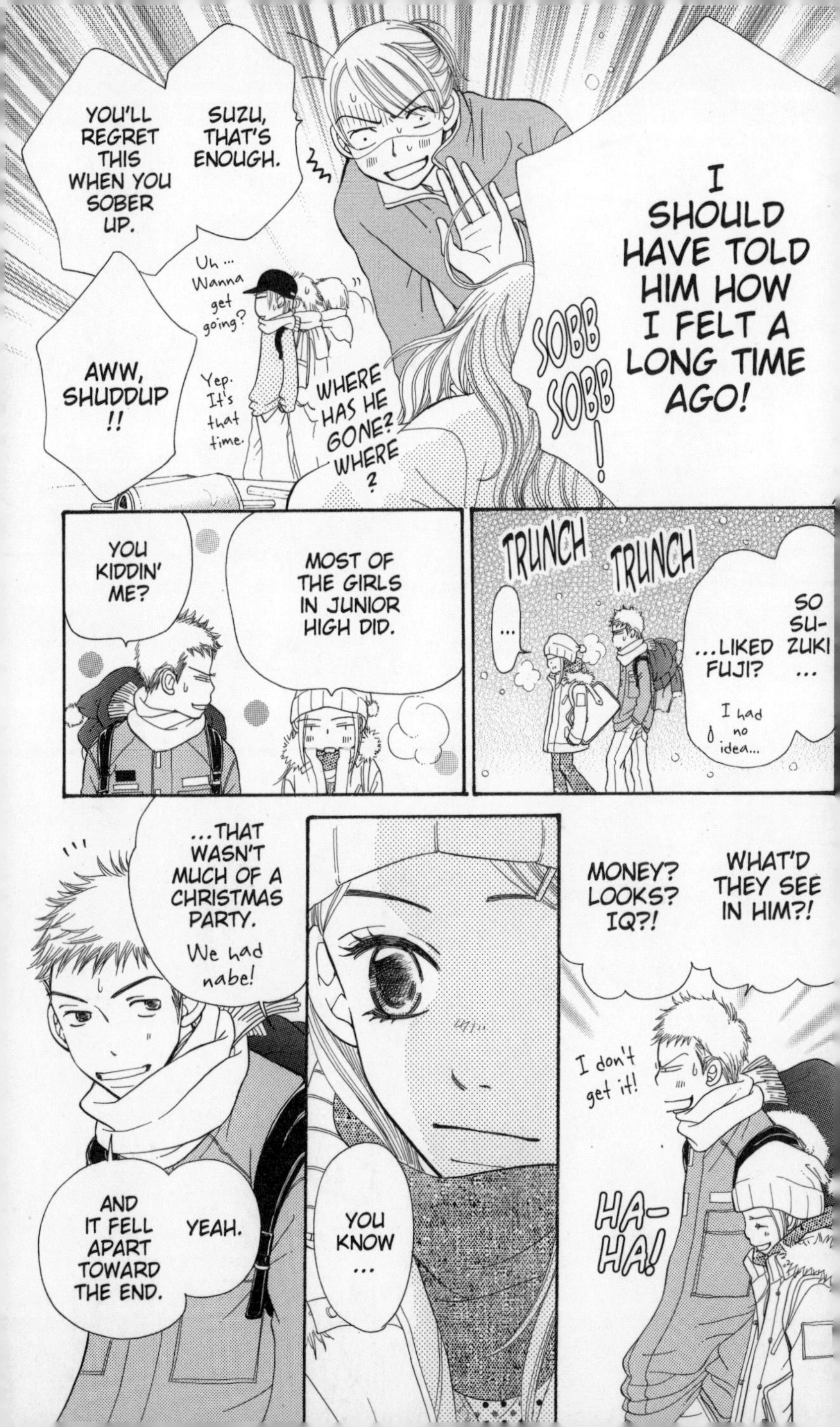
I SHOULD HAVE TOLD HIM HOW I FELT A LONG TIME AGO!
SOBB SOBB!
WHERE HAS HE GONE? WHERE?
SUZU, THAT'S ENOUGH.
YOU'LL REGRET THIS WHEN YOU SOBER UP.
Uh ... Wanna get going?
Yep. It's that time.
AWW, SHUDDUP!!
TRUNCH
TRUNCH
SO SU-ZUKI ...
...LIKED FUJI?
I had no idea...
...
MOST OF THE GIRLS IN JUNIOR HIGH DID.
YOU KIDDIN' ME?
WHAT'D THEY SEE IN HIM?!
MONEY? LOOKS? IQ?!
I don't get it!
HA-HA!
YOU KNOW ...
...THAT WASN'T MUCH OF A CHRISTMAS PARTY.
We had nabe!
YEAH.
AND IT FELL APART TOWARD THE END.

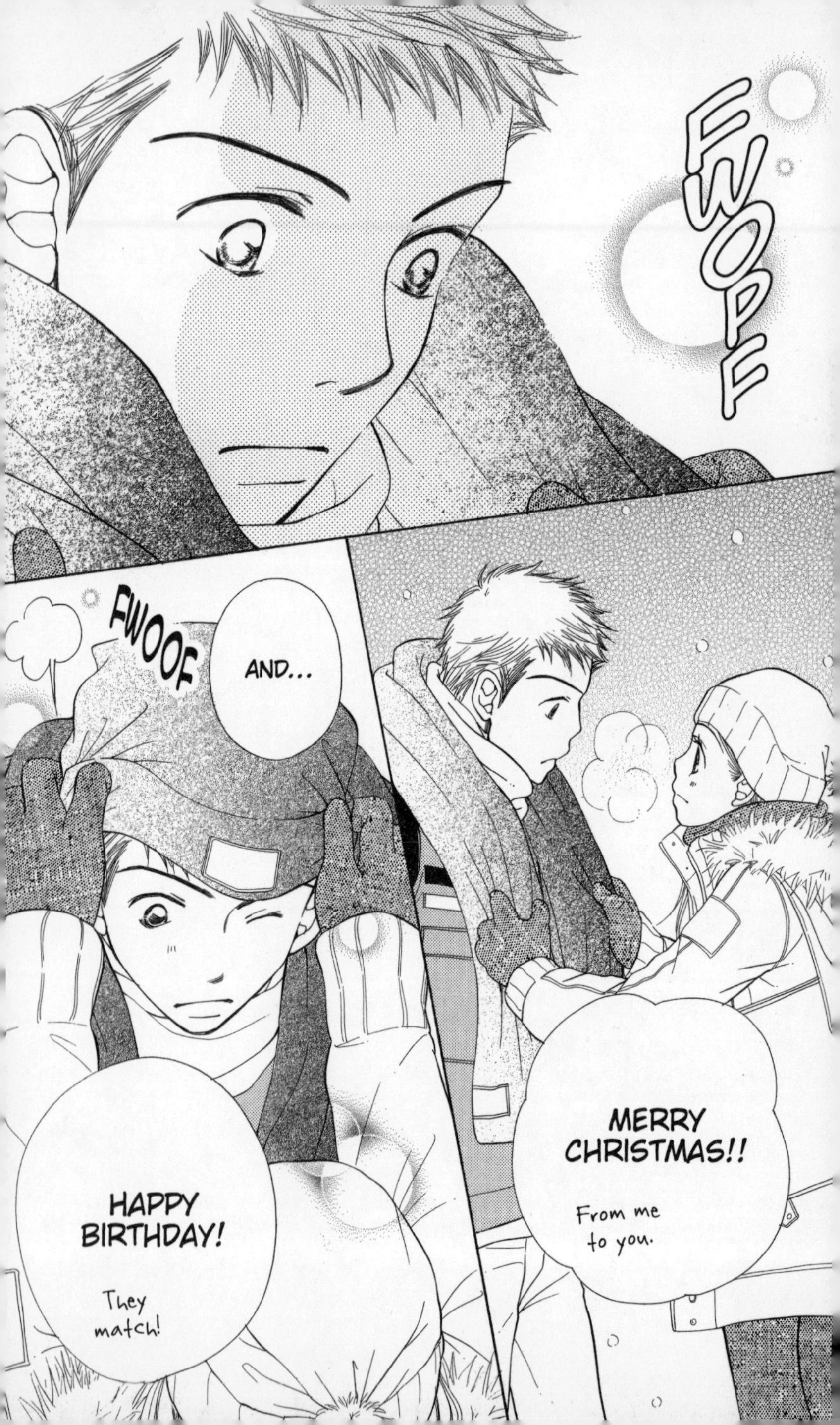
FWOPF
MERRY CHRISTMAS!!
From me to you.
FWOOF
AND...
HAPPY BIRTHDAY!
They match!

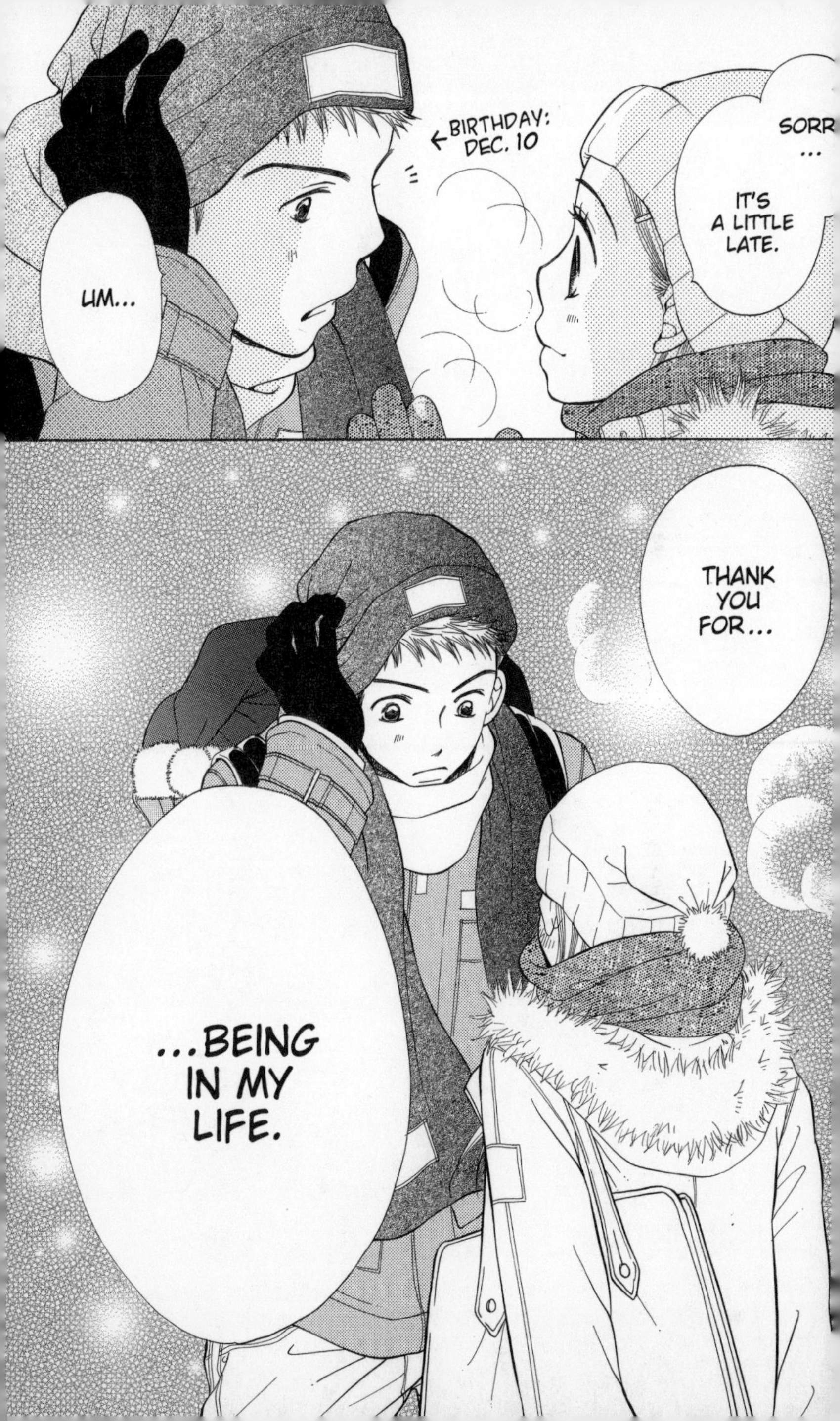
SORR
...
IT'S A LITTLE LATE.
← BIRTHDAY: DEC. 10
UM...
THANK YOU FOR...
...BEING IN MY LIFE.

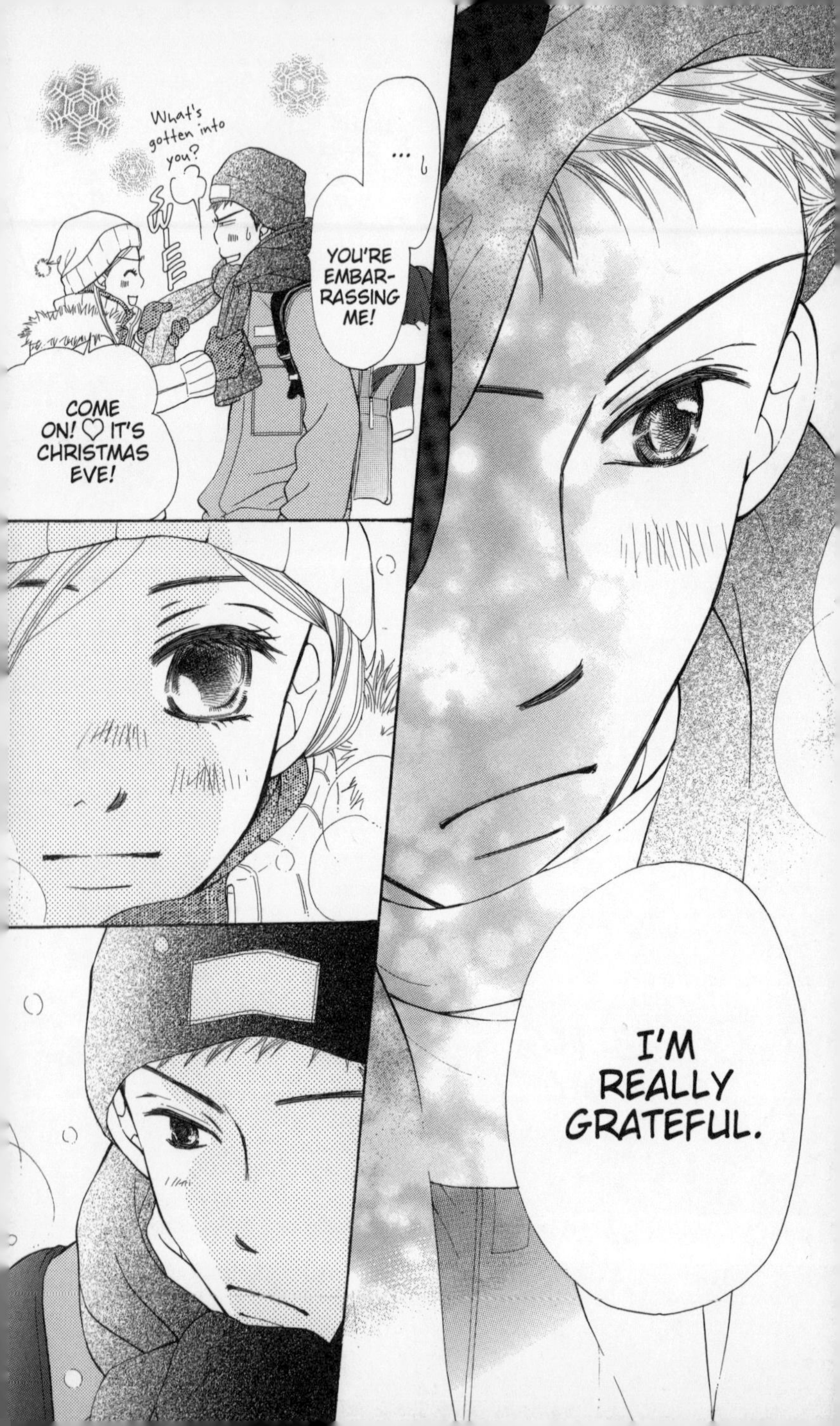
I'M REALLY GRATEFUL.
...
YOU'RE EMBARRASSING ME!
What's gotten into you?
COME ON! ♡ IT'S CHRISTMAS EVE!

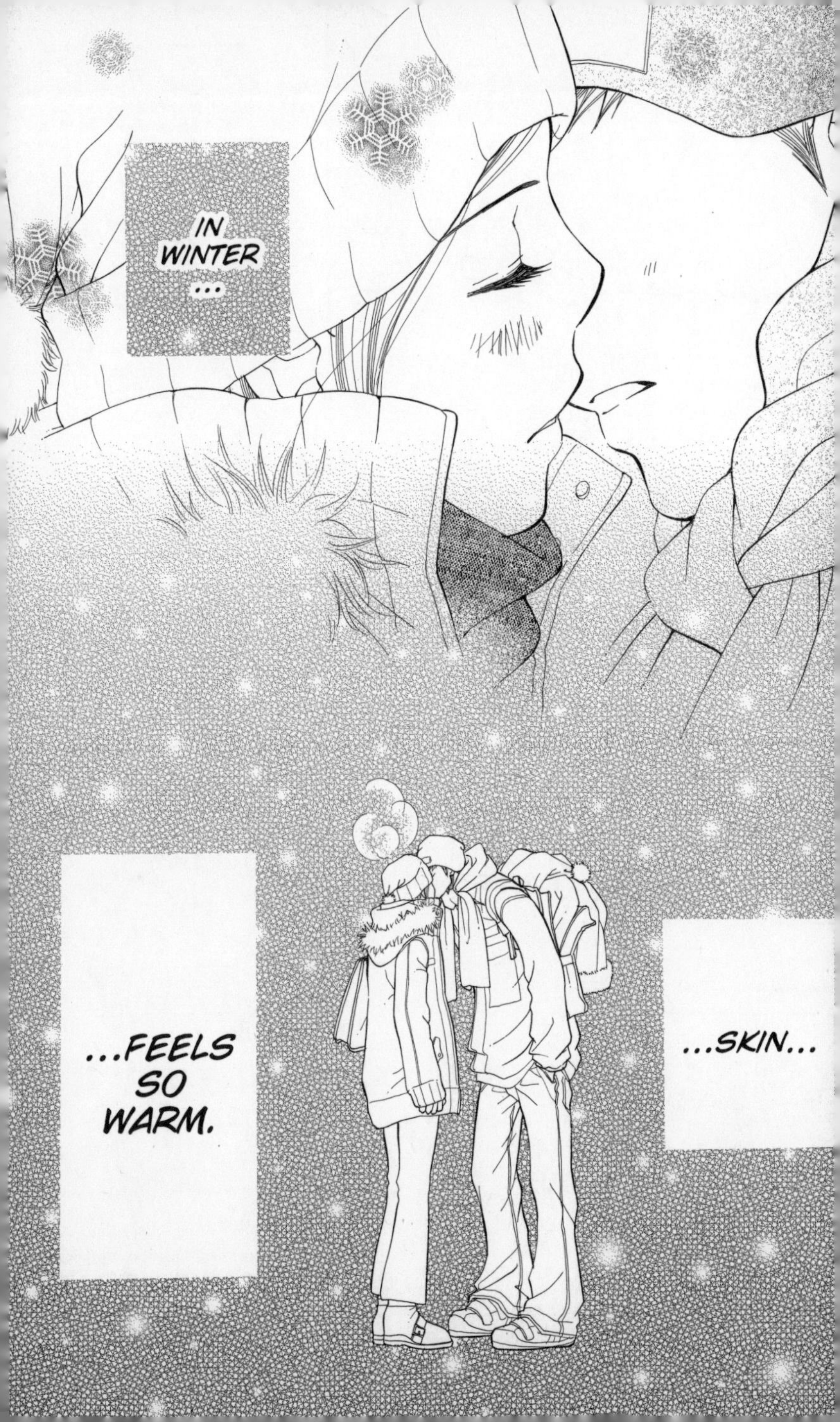
IN WINTER ...
...SKIN...
...FEELS SO WARM.

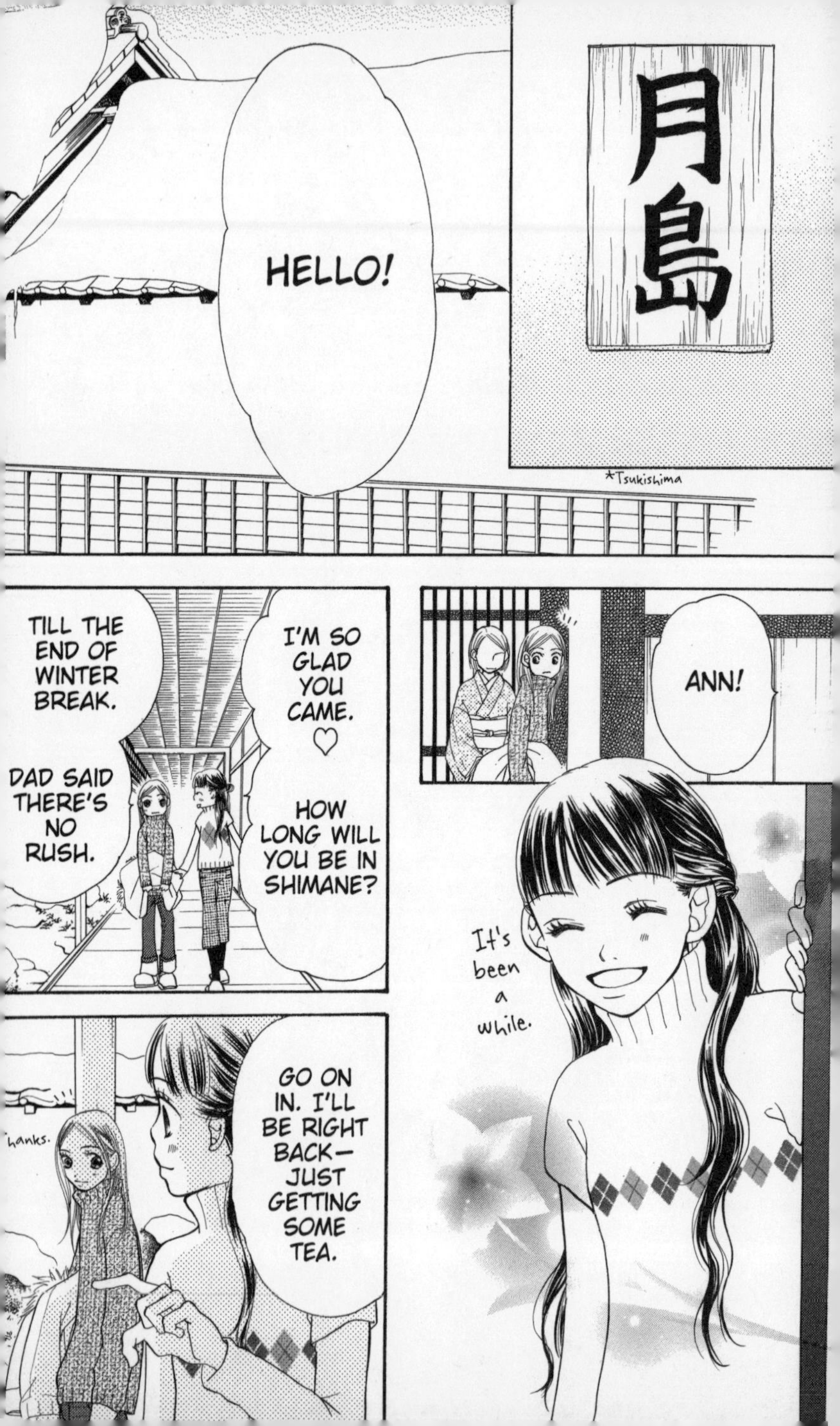
月島
*Tsukishima
HELLO!
ANN!
It's been a while.
I'M SO GLAD YOU CAME. ♡
HOW LONG WILL YOU BE IN SHIMANE?
TILL THE END OF WINTER BREAK.
DAD SAID THERE'S NO RUSH.
GO ON IN. I'LL BE RIGHT BACK—JUST GETTING SOME TEA.
hanks.

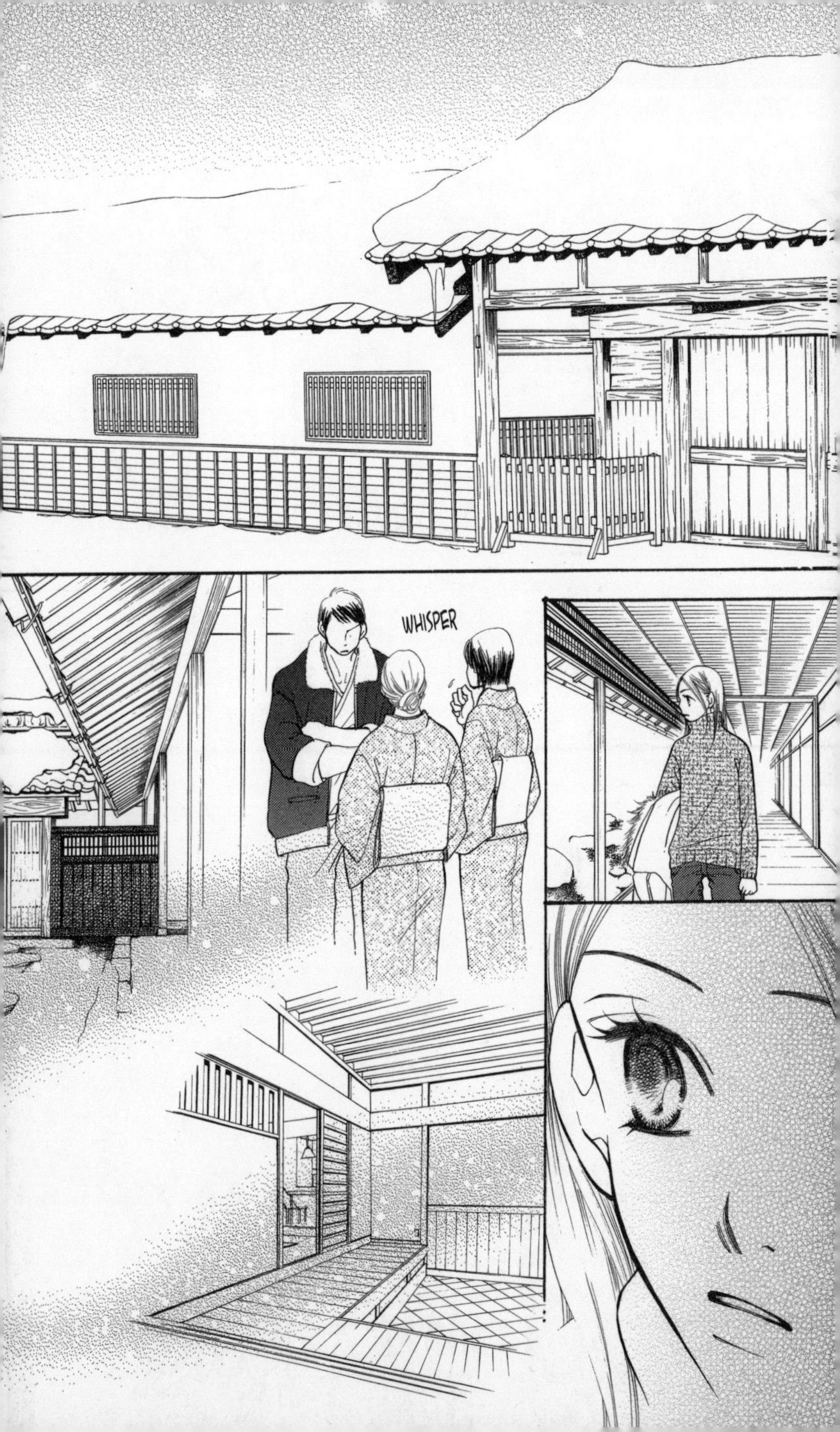
WHISPER

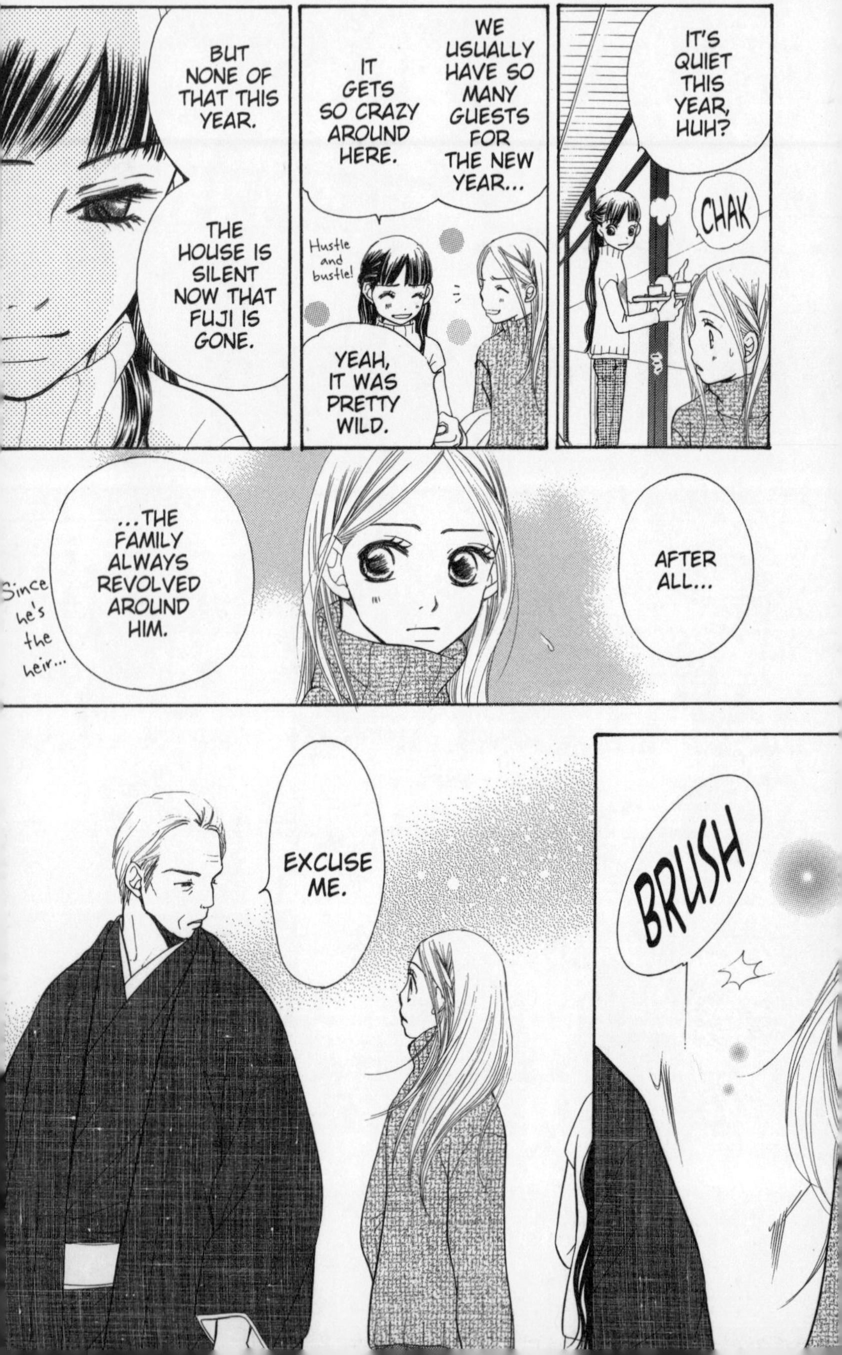
IT'S QUIET THIS YEAR, HUH?
CHAK
WE USUALLY HAVE SO MANY GUESTS FOR THE NEW YEAR...
IT GETS SO CRAZY AROUND HERE.
Hustle and bustle!
YEAH, IT WAS PRETTY WILD.
BUT NONE OF THAT THIS YEAR.
THE HOUSE IS SILENT NOW THAT FUJI IS GONE.
AFTER ALL...
...THE FAMILY ALWAYS REVOLVED AROUND HIM.
Since he's the heir...
BRUSH
EXCUSE ME.

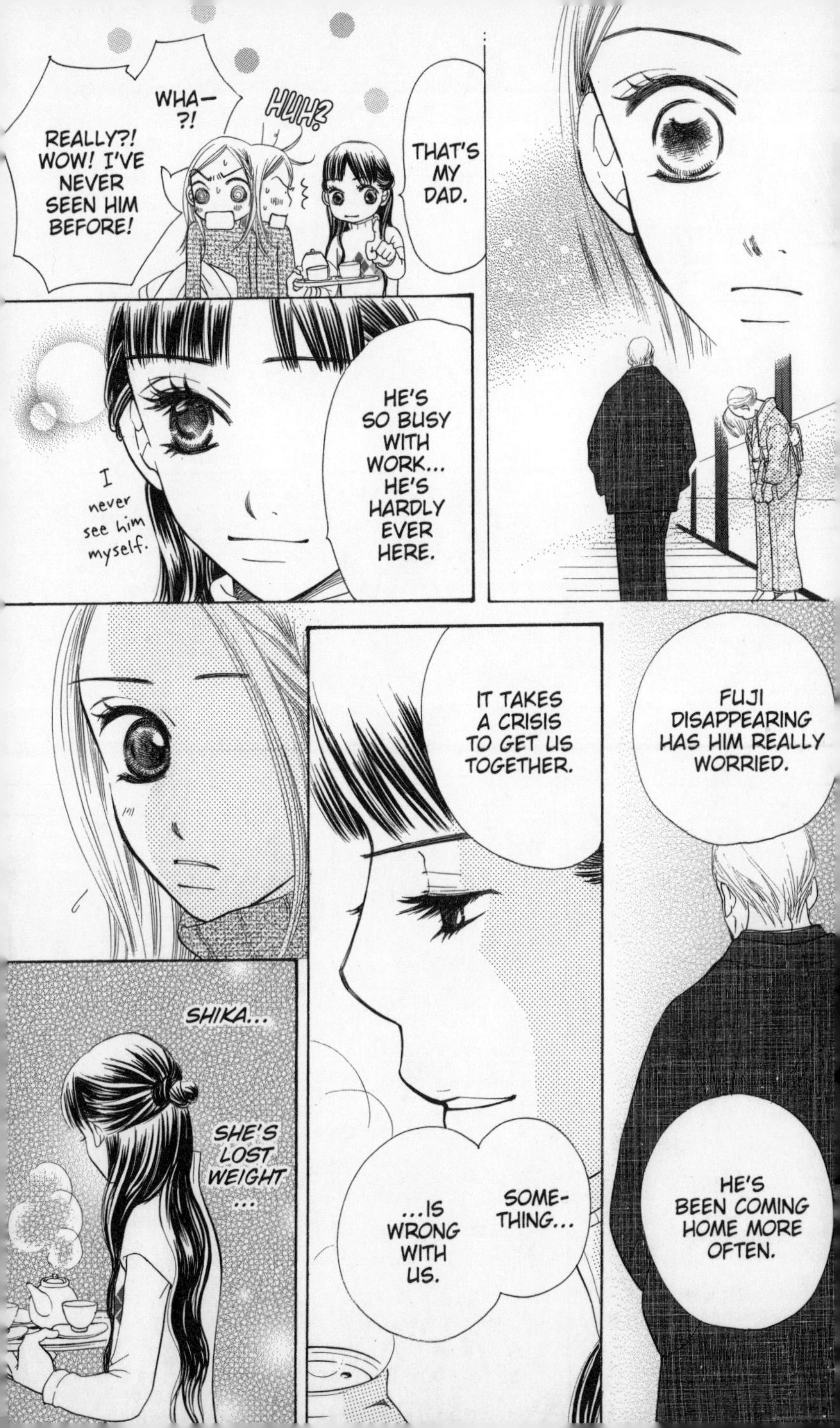
THAT'S MY DAD.
HUH?
WHA— ?!
REALLY?! WOW! I'VE NEVER SEEN HIM BEFORE!
HE'S SO BUSY WITH WORK... HE'S HARDLY EVER HERE.
I never see him myself.
FUJI DISAPPEARING HAS HIM REALLY WORRIED.
HE'S BEEN COMING HOME MORE OFTEN.
IT TAKES A CRISIS TO GET US TOGETHER.
SOME-THING...
...IS WRONG WITH US.
SHIKA...
SHE'S LOST WEIGHT...

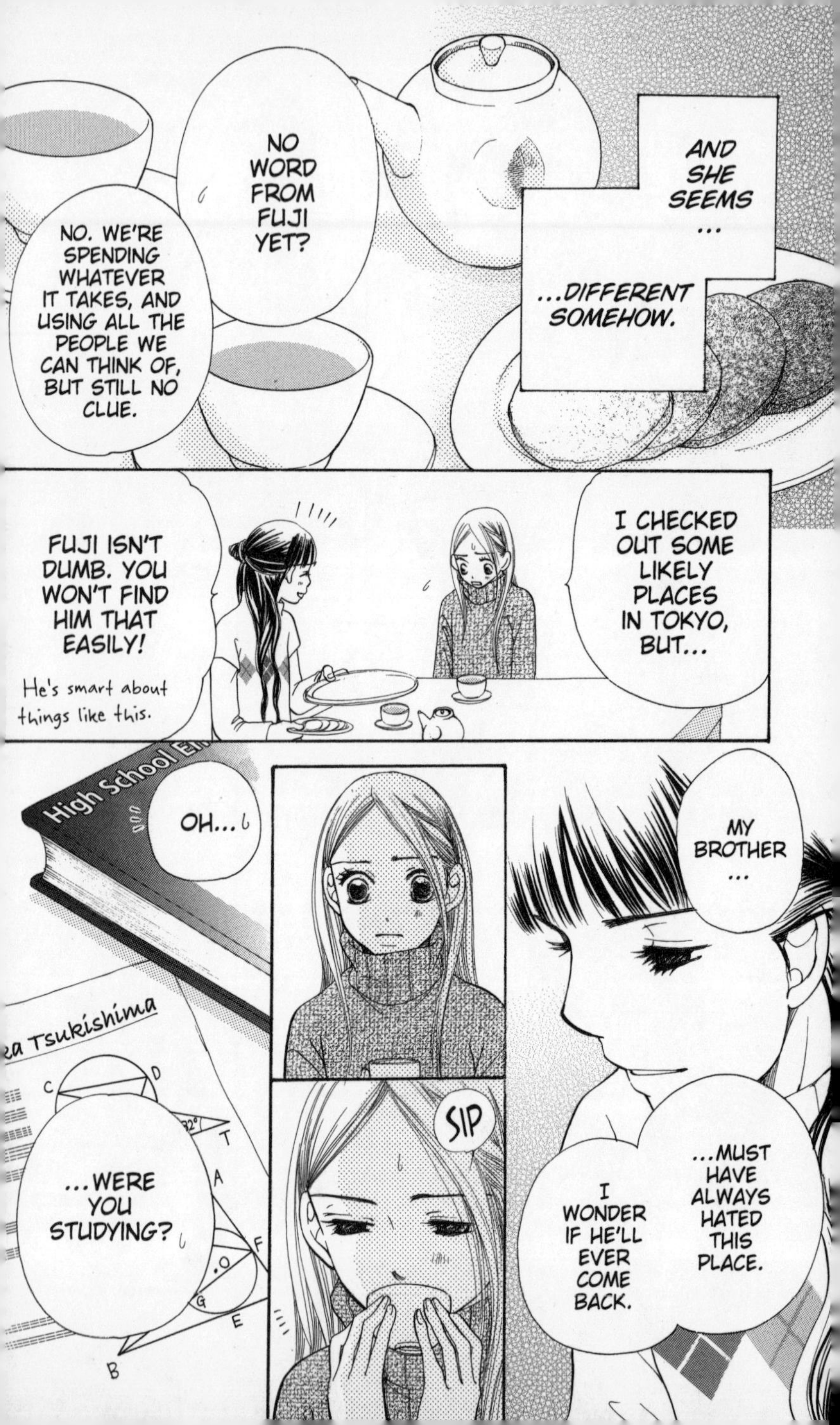
AND SHE SEEMS...
...DIFFERENT SOMEHOW.
NO WORD FROM FUJI YET?
NO. WE'RE SPENDING WHATEVER IT TAKES, AND USING ALL THE PEOPLE WE CAN THINK OF, BUT STILL NO CLUE.
I CHECKED OUT SOME LIKELY PLACES IN TOKYO, BUT...
FUJI ISN'T DUMB. YOU WON'T FIND HIM THAT EASILY!
He's smart about things like this.
MY BROTHER...
...MUST HAVE ALWAYS HATED THIS PLACE.
I WONDER IF HE'LL EVER COME BACK.
SIP
OH...
High School En
...WERE YOU STUDYING?
Tsukishima

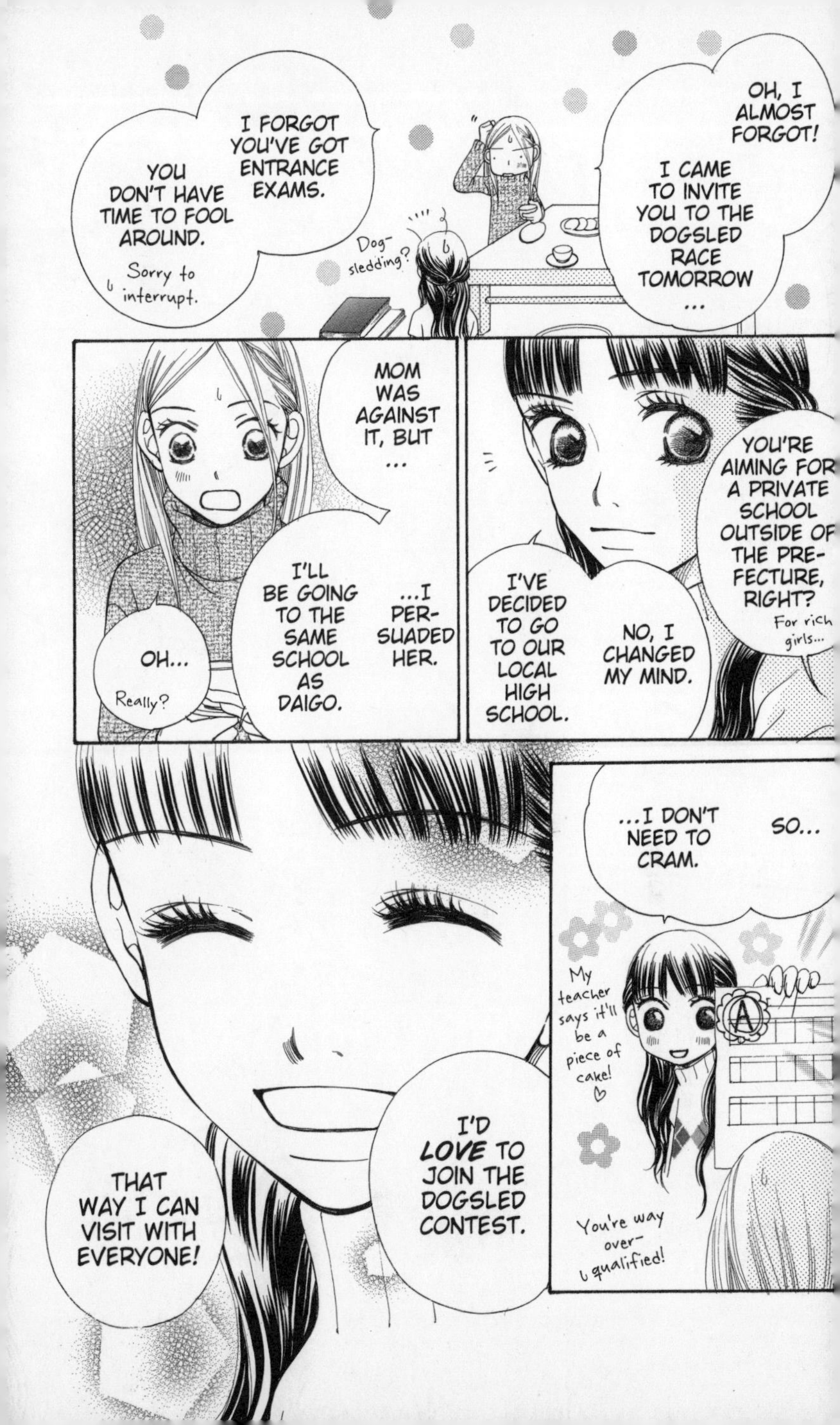
OH, I ALMOST FORGOT!
I CAME TO INVITE YOU TO THE DOGSLED RACE TOMORROW...
Dog-sledding?
I FORGOT YOU'VE GOT ENTRANCE EXAMS.
YOU DON'T HAVE TIME TO FOOL AROUND.
Sorry to interrupt.
YOU'RE AIMING FOR A PRIVATE SCHOOL OUTSIDE OF THE PREFECTURE, RIGHT?
For rich girls...
NO, I CHANGED MY MIND.
I'VE DECIDED TO GO TO OUR LOCAL HIGH SCHOOL.
MOM WAS AGAINST IT, BUT...
...I PERSUADED HER.
I'LL BE GOING TO THE SAME SCHOOL AS DAIGO.
OH...
Really?
SO...
...I DON'T NEED TO CRAM.
My teacher says it'll be a piece of cake! ♡
You're way over-qualified!
I'D *LOVE* TO JOIN THE DOGSLED CONTEST.
THAT WAY I CAN VISIT WITH EVERYONE!

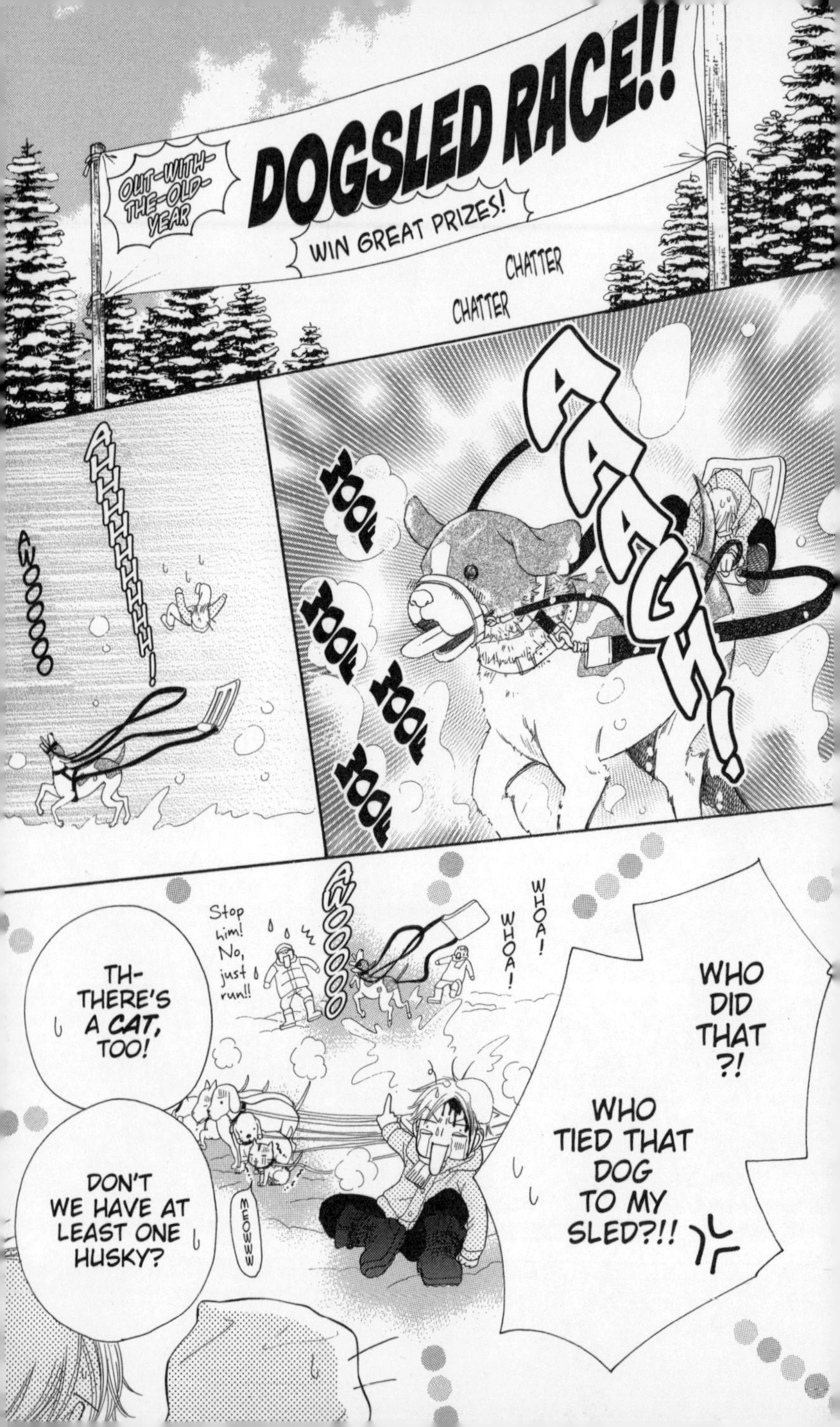
OUT-WITH-THE-OLD-YEAR
DOGSLED RACE!!
WIN GREAT PRIZES!
CHATTER
CHATTER
AAAGH!
WOOF
WOOF
WOOF
WOOF
AHHHHHHHHH!
AWOOOOOO
WHO DID THAT?!
WHO TIED THAT DOG TO MY SLED?!!
WHOA! WHOA!
AWOOOOO
Stop him! No, just run!!
TH-THERE'S A CAT, TOO!
MEOWWW
DON'T WE HAVE AT LEAST ONE HUSKY?

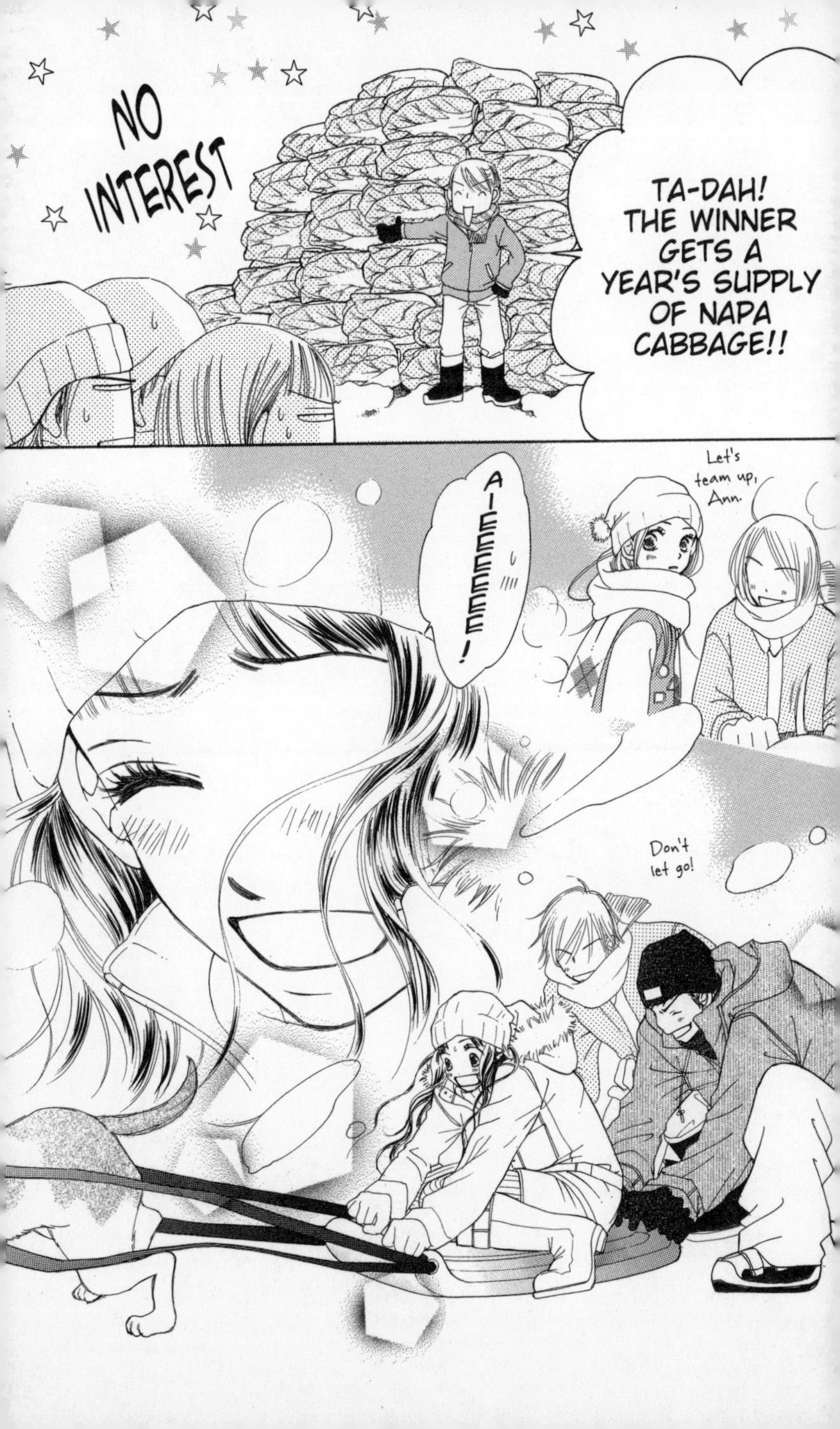
TA-DAH! THE WINNER GETS A YEAR'S SUPPLY OF NAPA CABBAGE!!
NO INTEREST
Let's team up, Ann.
AIEEEEEEE!
Don't let go!

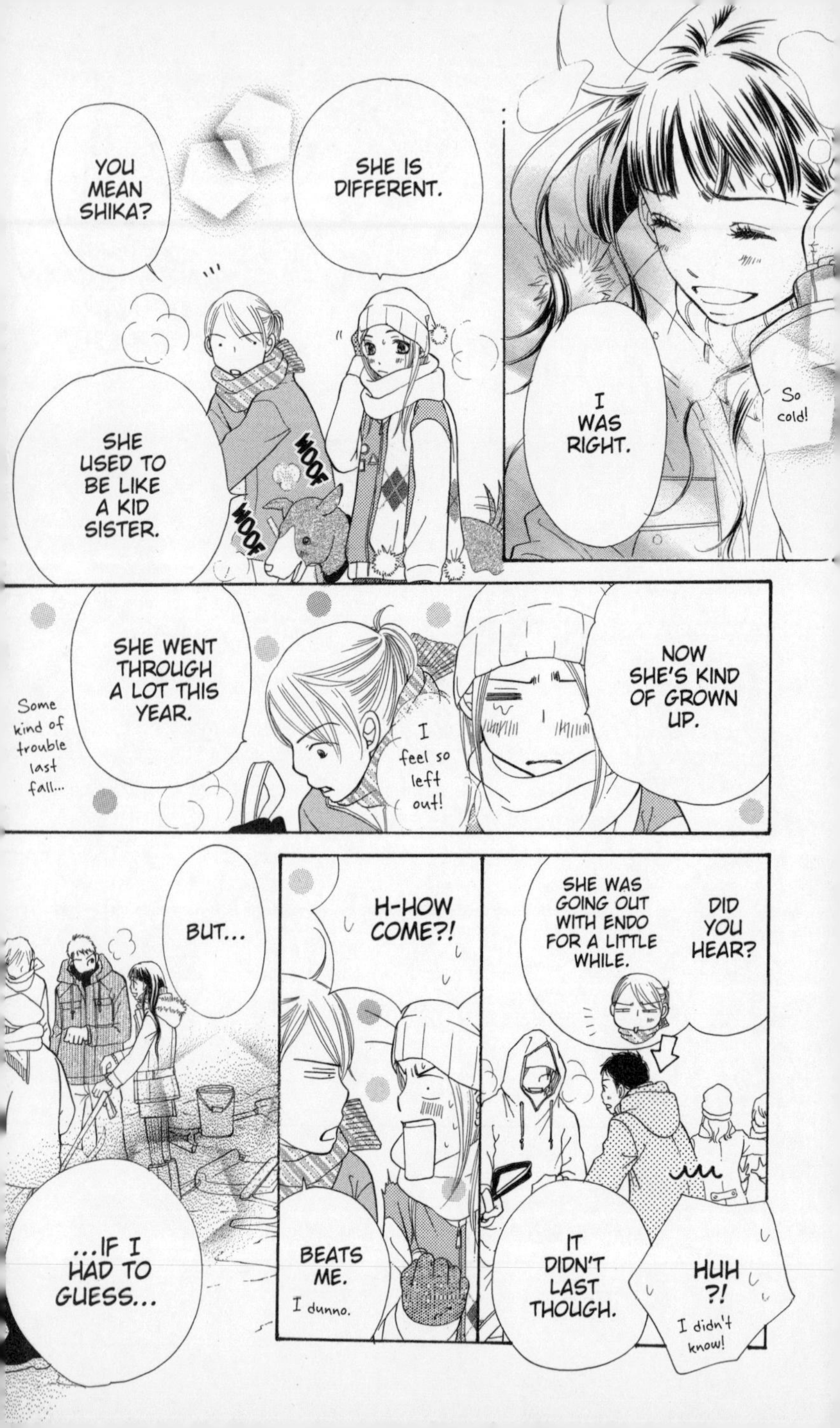

I WAS RIGHT.
So cold!
SHE IS DIFFERENT.
YOU MEAN SHIKA?
SHE USED TO BE LIKE A KID SISTER.
WOOF
WOOF
NOW SHE'S KIND OF GROWN UP.
I feel so left out!
SHE WENT THROUGH A LOT THIS YEAR.
Some kind of trouble last fall...
DID YOU HEAR?
SHE WAS GOING OUT WITH ENDO FOR A LITTLE WHILE.
HUH ?!
I didn't know!
IT DIDN'T LAST THOUGH.
H-HOW COME?!
BEATS ME.
I dunno.
BUT...
...IF I HAD TO GUESS...

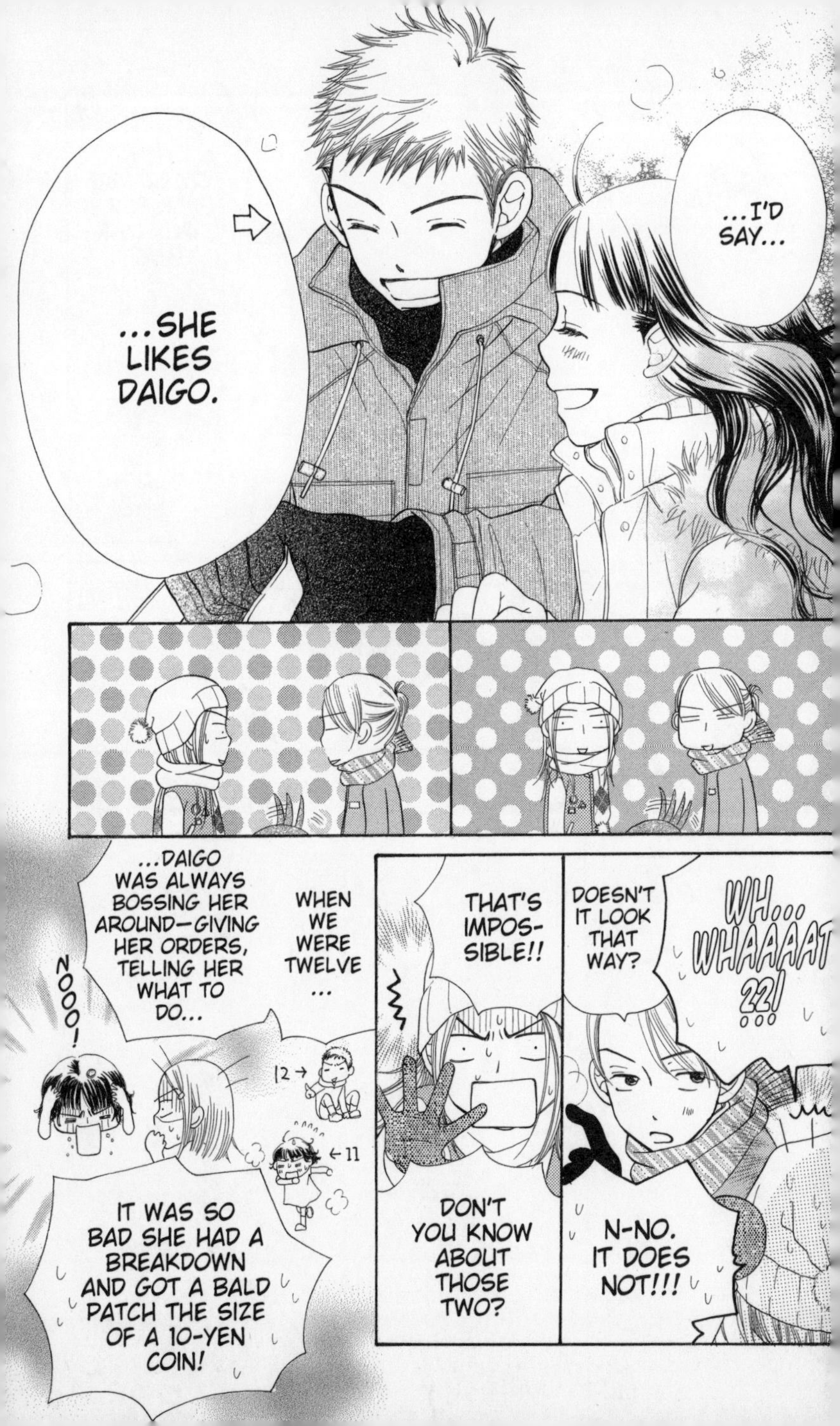
...I'D SAY...
...SHE LIKES DAIGO.
WH... WHAAAAT ??!
DOESN'T IT LOOK THAT WAY?
N-NO. IT DOES NOT!!!
THAT'S IMPOS-SIBLE!!
DON'T YOU KNOW ABOUT THOSE TWO?
WHEN WE WERE TWELVE...
...DAIGO WAS ALWAYS BOSSING HER AROUND—GIVING HER ORDERS, TELLING HER WHAT TO DO...
NOOOO!
12 →
← 11
IT WAS SO BAD SHE HAD A BREAKDOWN AND GOT A BALD PATCH THE SIZE OF A 10-YEN COIN!

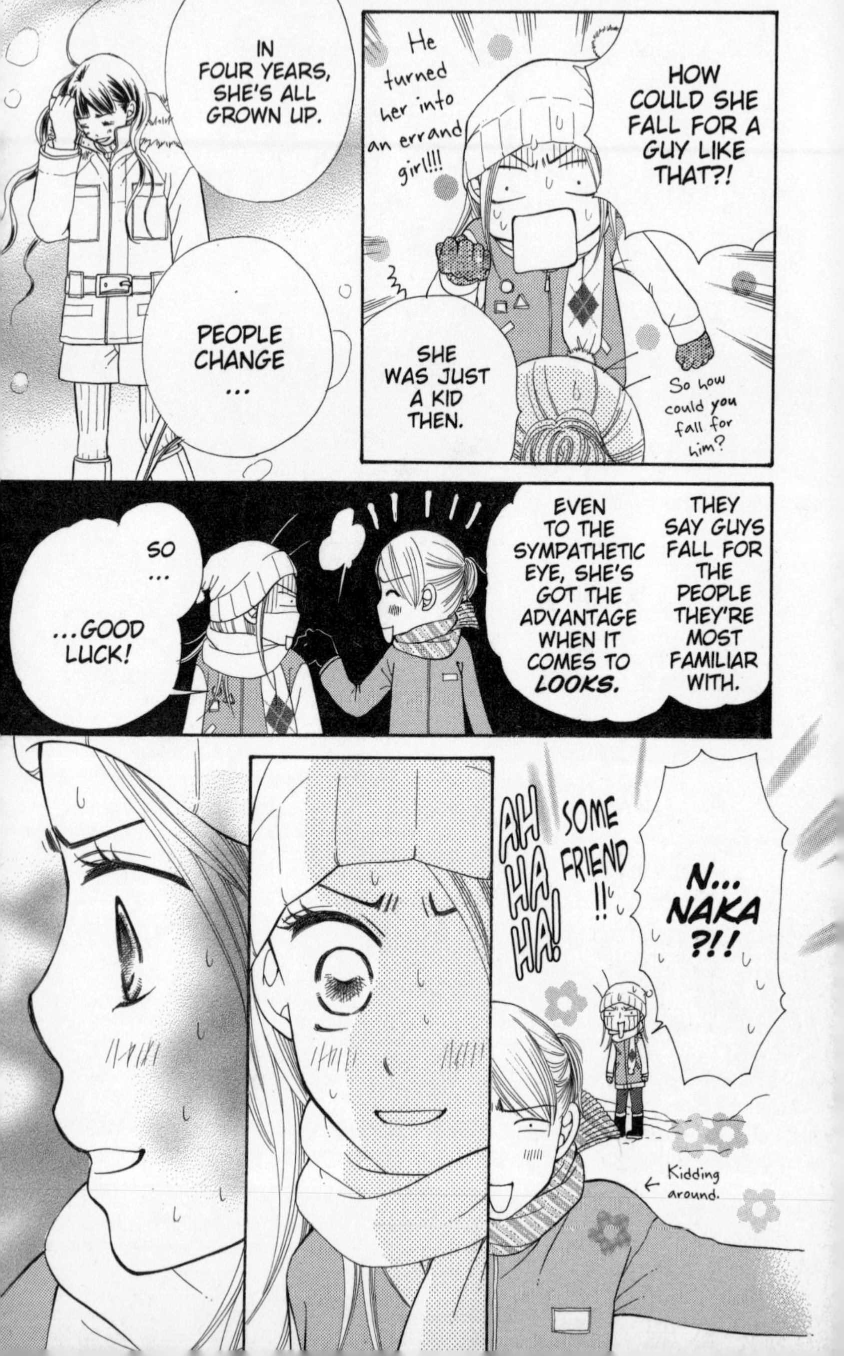
HOW COULD SHE FALL FOR A GUY LIKE THAT?!
He turned her into an errand girl!!!
So how could you fall for him?
SHE WAS JUST A KID THEN.
IN FOUR YEARS, SHE'S ALL GROWN UP.
PEOPLE CHANGE ...
THEY SAY GUYS FALL FOR THE PEOPLE THEY'RE MOST FAMILIAR WITH.
EVEN TO THE SYMPATHETIC EYE, SHE'S GOT THE ADVANTAGE WHEN IT COMES TO *LOOKS.*
SO ...
...GOOD LUCK!
N... NAKA ?!!
SOME FRIEND !!
AH HA HA HA!
Kidding around.

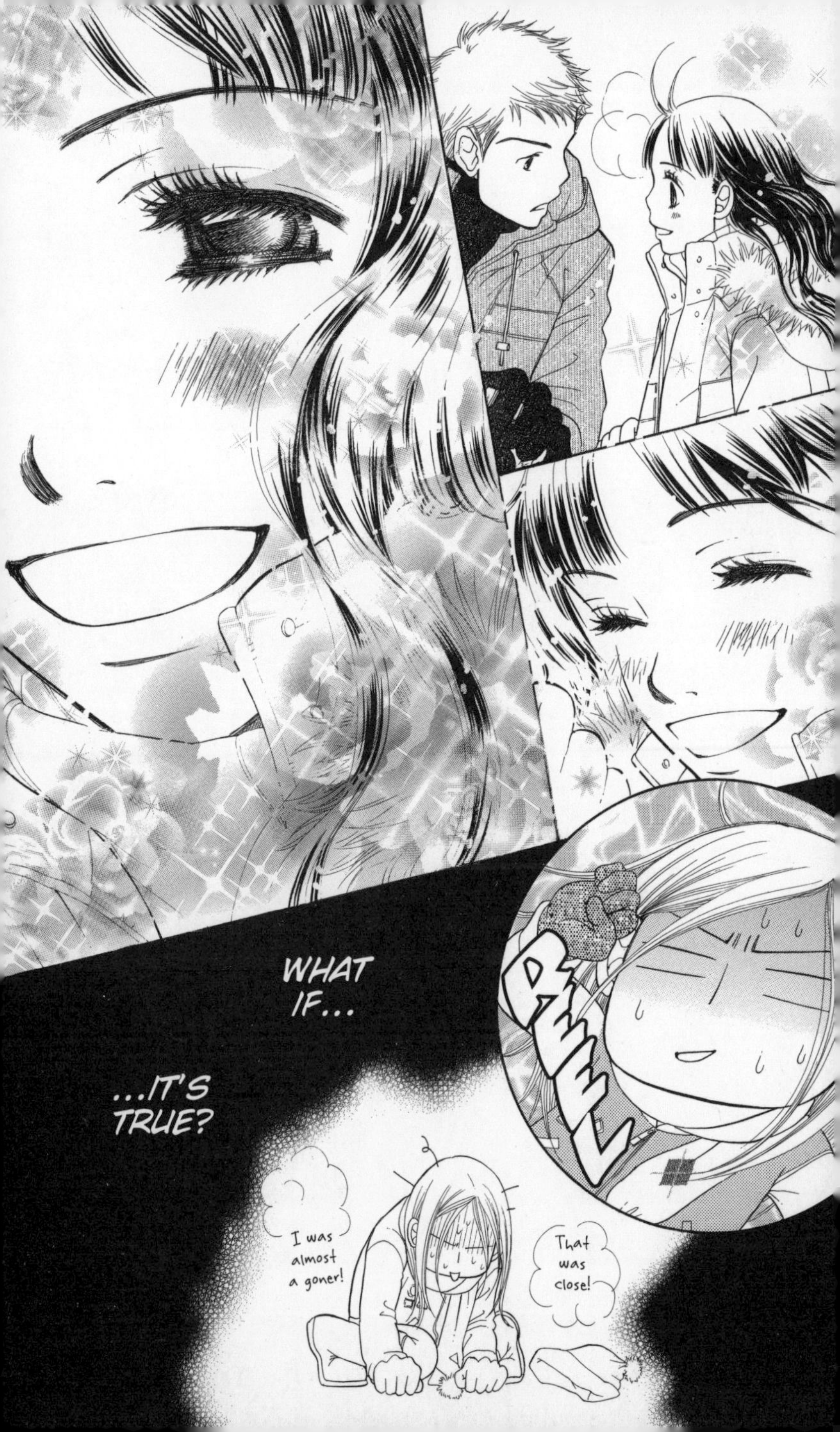
WHAT IF...
...IT'S TRUE?
I was almost a goner!
That was close!

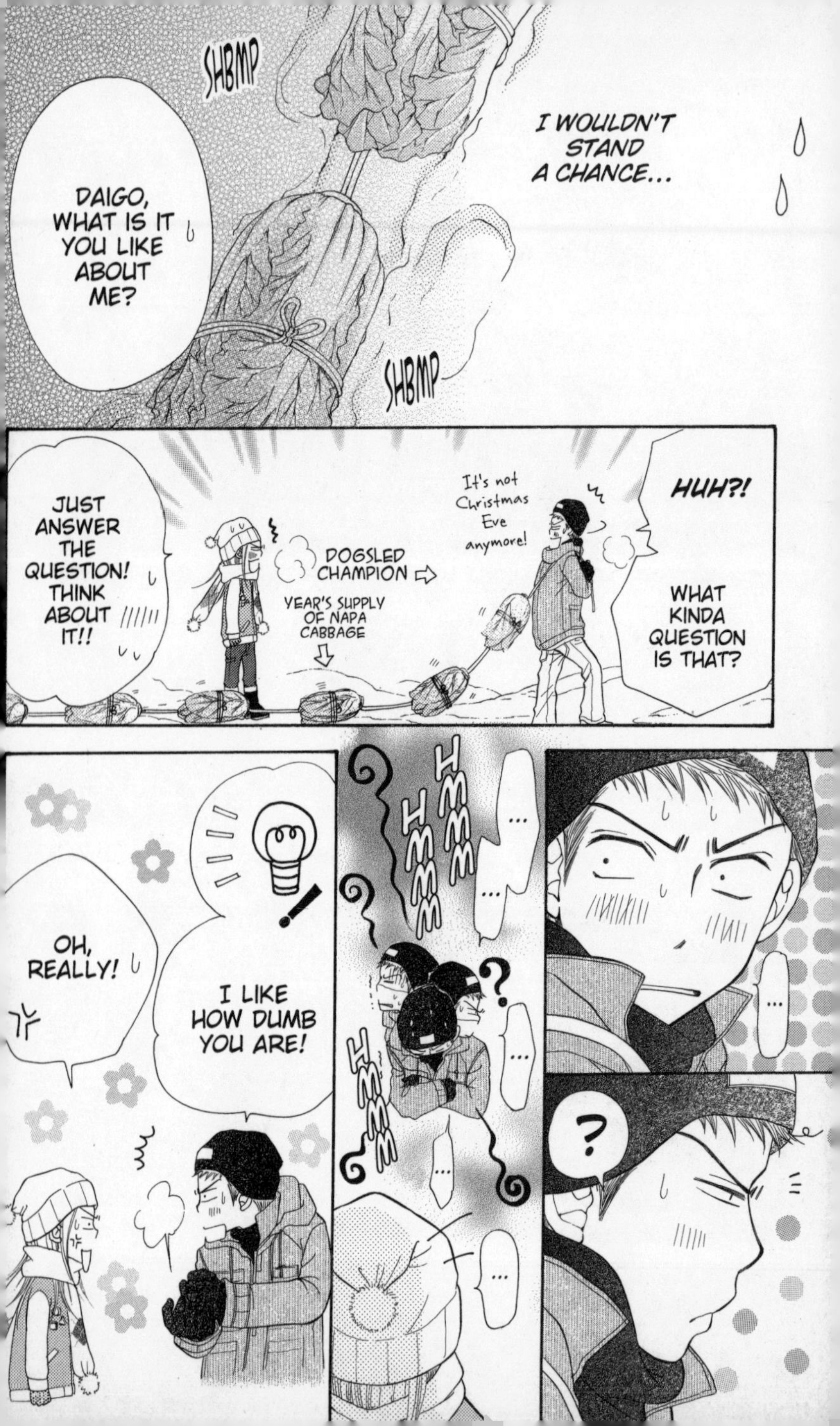
I WOULDN'T STAND A CHANCE...
SHBMP
DAIGO, WHAT IS IT YOU LIKE ABOUT ME?
SHBMP
HUH?!
WHAT KINDA QUESTION IS THAT?
It's not Christmas Eve anymore!
DOGSLED CHAMPION
YEAR'S SUPPLY OF NAPA CABBAGE
JUST ANSWER THE QUESTION! THINK ABOUT IT!!
...
?
HMMMM
HMMMM
...
...
...
...
HMMMM
I LIKE HOW DUMB YOU ARE!
OH, REALLY!

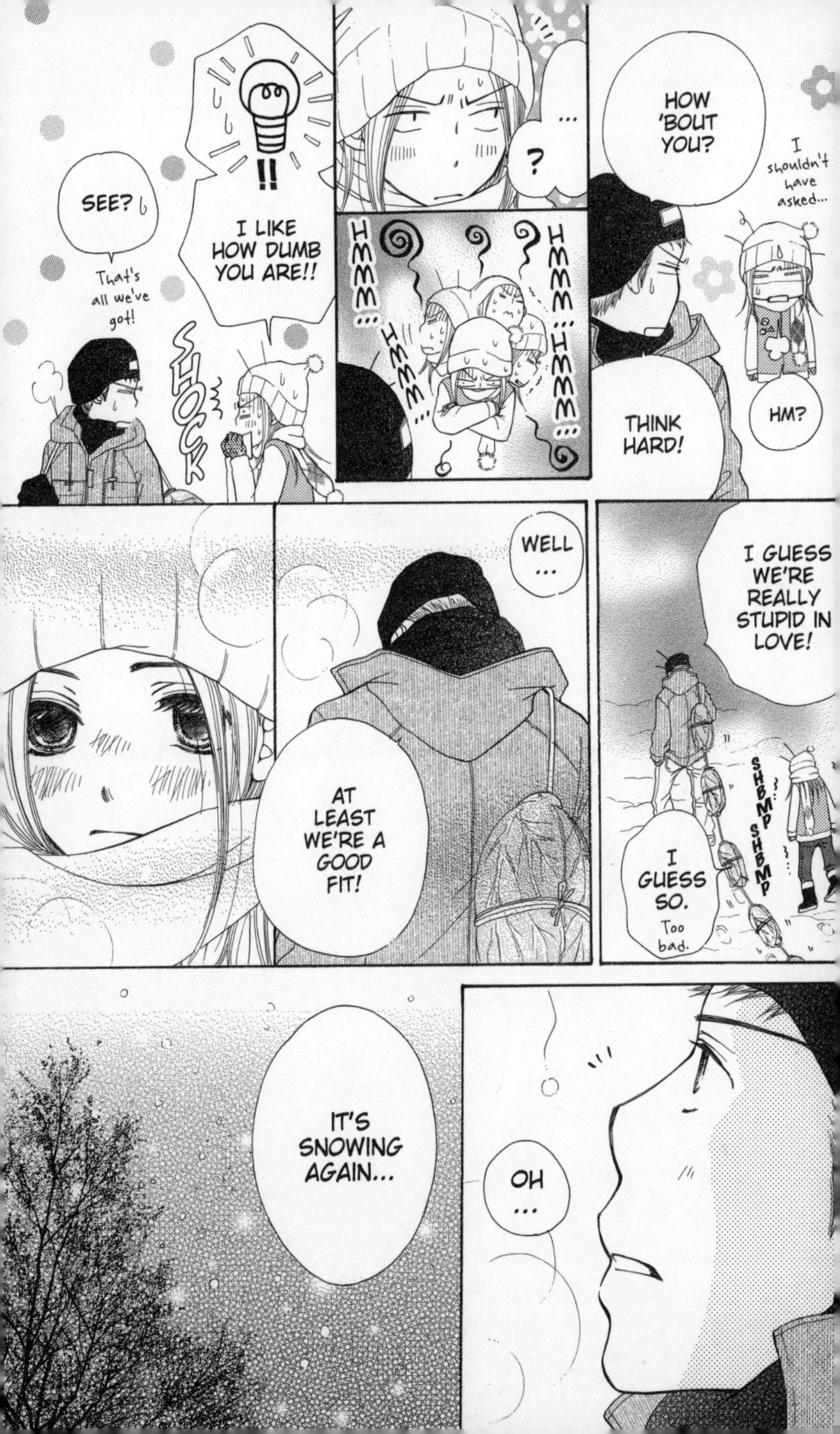
HOW 'BOUT YOU?
I shouldn't have asked...
HM?
THINK HARD!
...
?
HMMM...
HMMM...
HMMM...
HMMM...
I LIKE HOW DUMB YOU ARE!!
SHOCK
SEE?
That's all we've got!
I GUESS WE'RE REALLY STUPID IN LOVE!
SHBMP SHBMP
I GUESS SO.
Too bad.
WELL ...
AT LEAST WE'RE A GOOD FIT!
OH ...
IT'S SNOWING AGAIN...

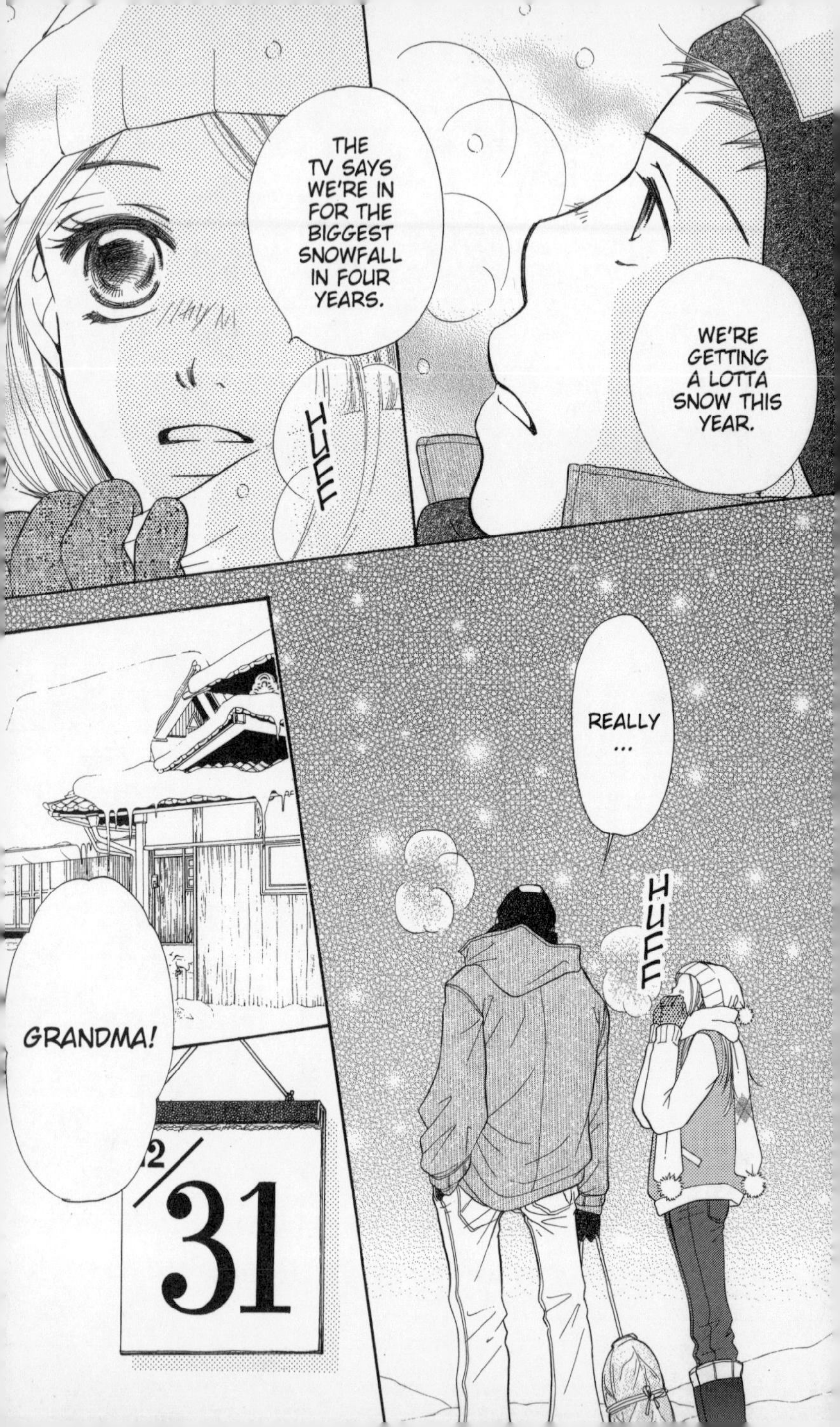
WE'RE GETTING A LOTTA SNOW THIS YEAR.
THE TV SAYS WE'RE IN FOR THE BIGGEST SNOWFALL IN FOUR YEARS.
HUFF
REALLY ...
HUFF
GRANDMA!
2/31

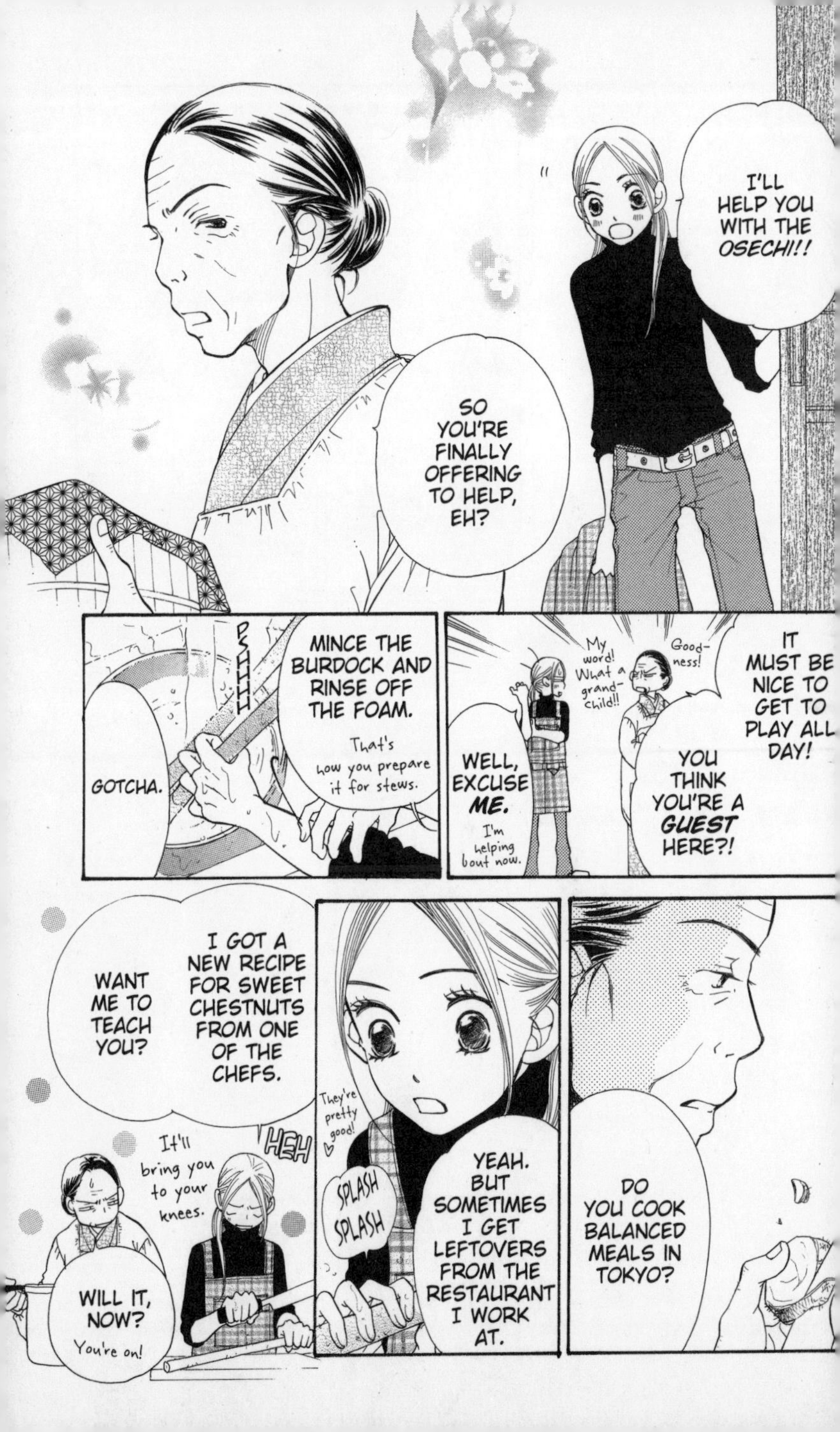
I'LL HELP YOU WITH THE *OSECHI!!*
SO YOU'RE FINALLY OFFERING TO HELP, EH?
IT MUST BE NICE TO GET TO PLAY ALL DAY!
Good-ness!
My word! What a grand-child!!
YOU THINK YOU'RE A **GUEST** HERE?!
WELL, EXCUSE **ME.**
I'm helping out now.
MINCE THE BURDOCK AND RINSE OFF THE FOAM.
That's how you prepare it for stews.
PSHHH
GOTCHA.
DO YOU COOK BALANCED MEALS IN TOKYO?
YEAH. BUT SOMETIMES I GET LEFTOVERS FROM THE RESTAURANT I WORK AT.
They're pretty good!
SPLASH SPLASH
I GOT A NEW RECIPE FOR SWEET CHESTNUTS FROM ONE OF THE CHEFS.
WANT ME TO TEACH YOU?
HEH
It'll bring you to your knees.
WILL IT, NOW?
You're on!

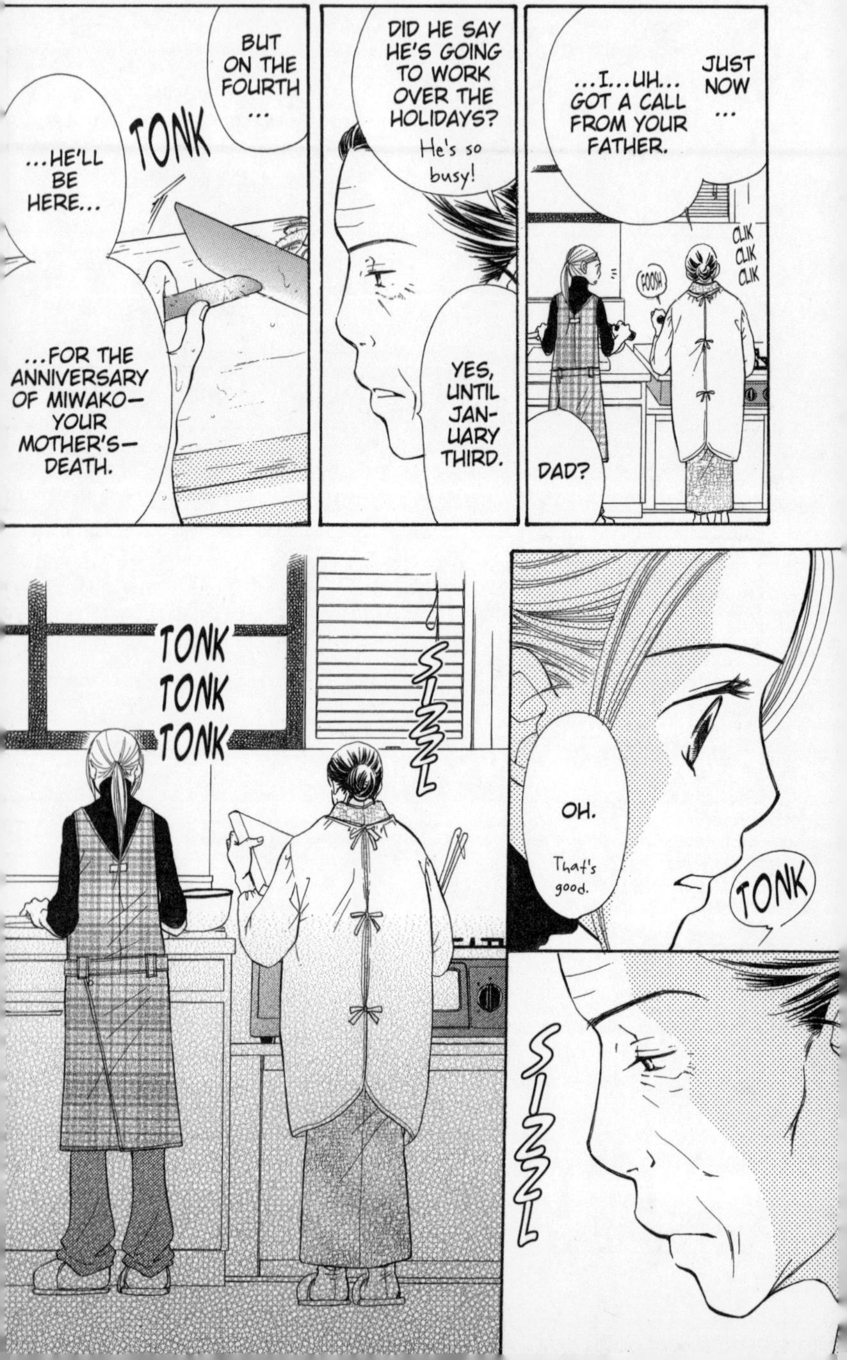
JUST NOW ...
...I...UH... GOT A CALL FROM YOUR FATHER.
FOOSH
CLIK CLIK CLIK
DAD?
DID HE SAY HE'S GOING TO WORK OVER THE HOLIDAYS?
He's so busy!
YES, UNTIL JANUARY THIRD.
BUT ON THE FOURTH ...
TONK
...HE'LL BE HERE...
...FOR THE ANNIVERSARY OF MIWAKO—YOUR MOTHER'S—DEATH.
OH.
That's good.
TONK
SIZZL
TONK TONK TONK
SIZZL

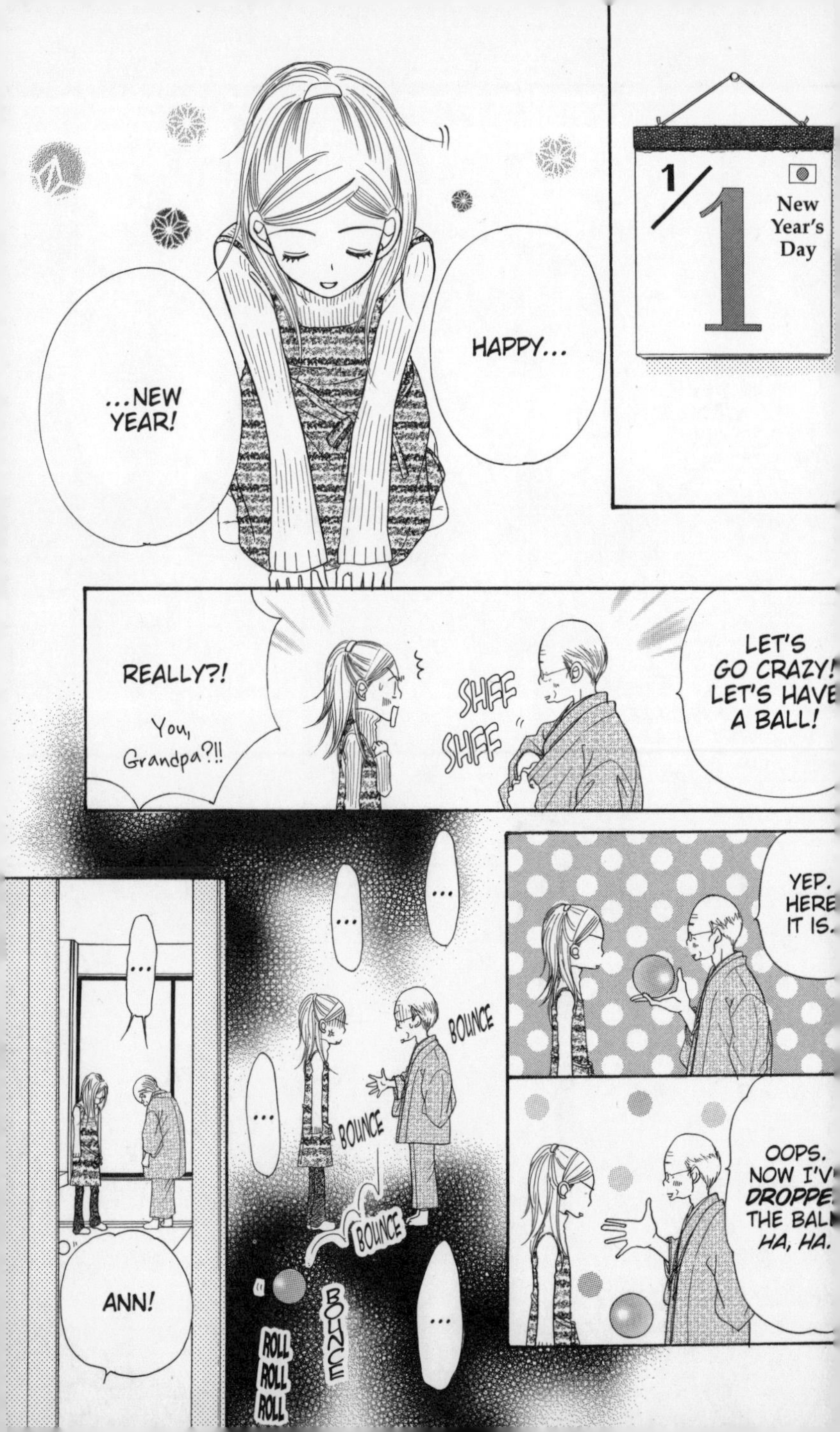
1/1
New Year's Day
HAPPY...
...NEW YEAR!
LET'S GO CRAZY! LET'S HAVE A BALL!
SHFF SHFF
REALLY?!
You, Grandpa?!!
YEP. HERE IT IS.
OOPS. NOW I'V DROPPE THE BAL HA, HA.
...
...
BOUNCE
...
BOUNCE
BOUNCE
BOUNCE
...
ROLL ROLL ROLL
...
ANN!

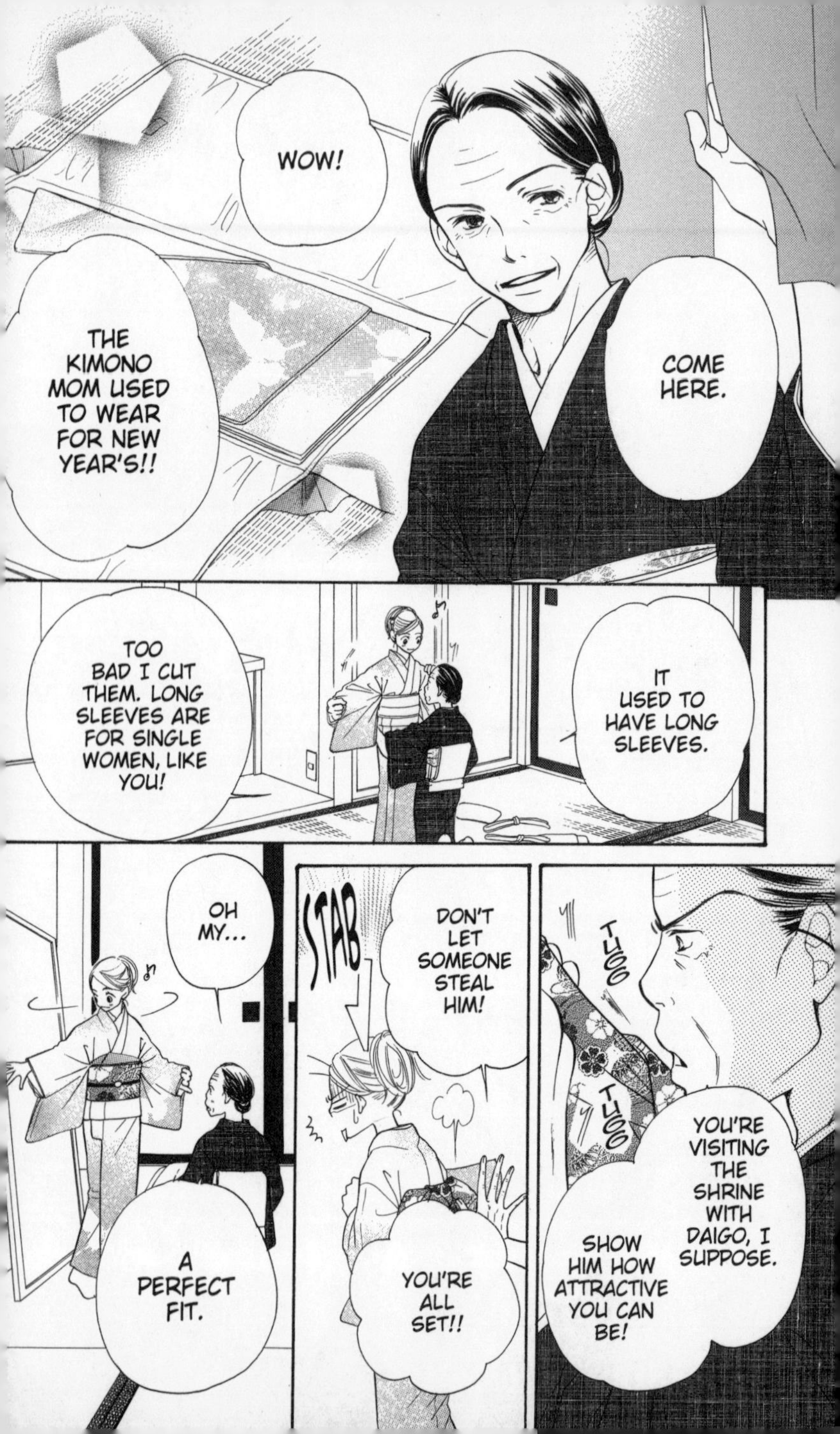
COME HERE.
WOW!
THE KIMONO MOM USED TO WEAR FOR NEW YEAR'S!!
IT USED TO HAVE LONG SLEEVES.
TOO BAD I CUT THEM. LONG SLEEVES ARE FOR SINGLE WOMEN, LIKE YOU!
TUGG
TUGG
YOU'RE VISITING THE SHRINE WITH DAIGO, I SUPPOSE.
SHOW HIM HOW ATTRACTIVE YOU CAN BE!
STAB
DON'T LET SOMEONE STEAL HIM!
YOU'RE ALL SET!!
OH MY...
A PERFECT FIT.

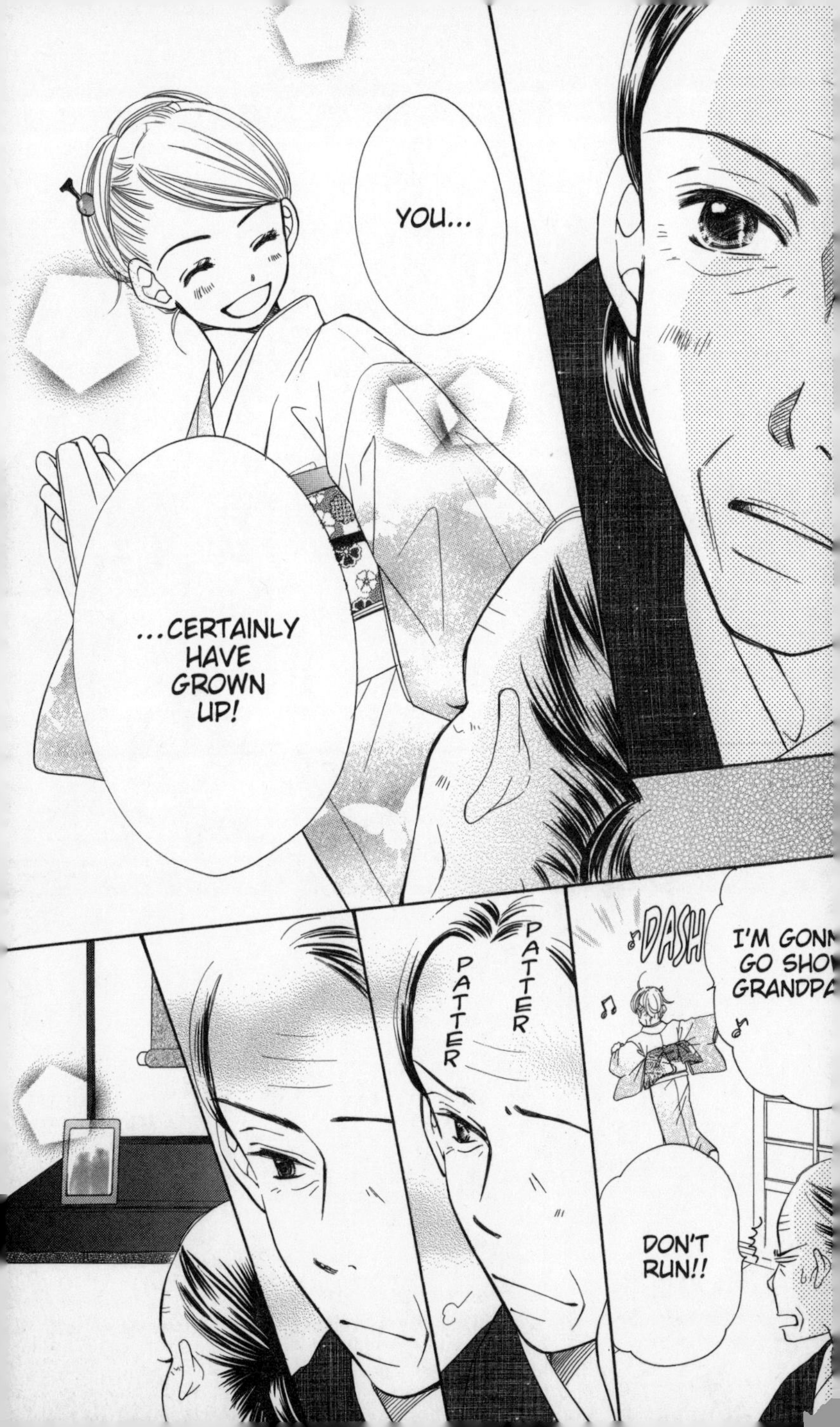
YOU...
...CERTAINLY HAVE GROWN UP!
DASH
I'M GONN GO SHO GRANDPA
DON'T RUN!!
PATTER PATTER

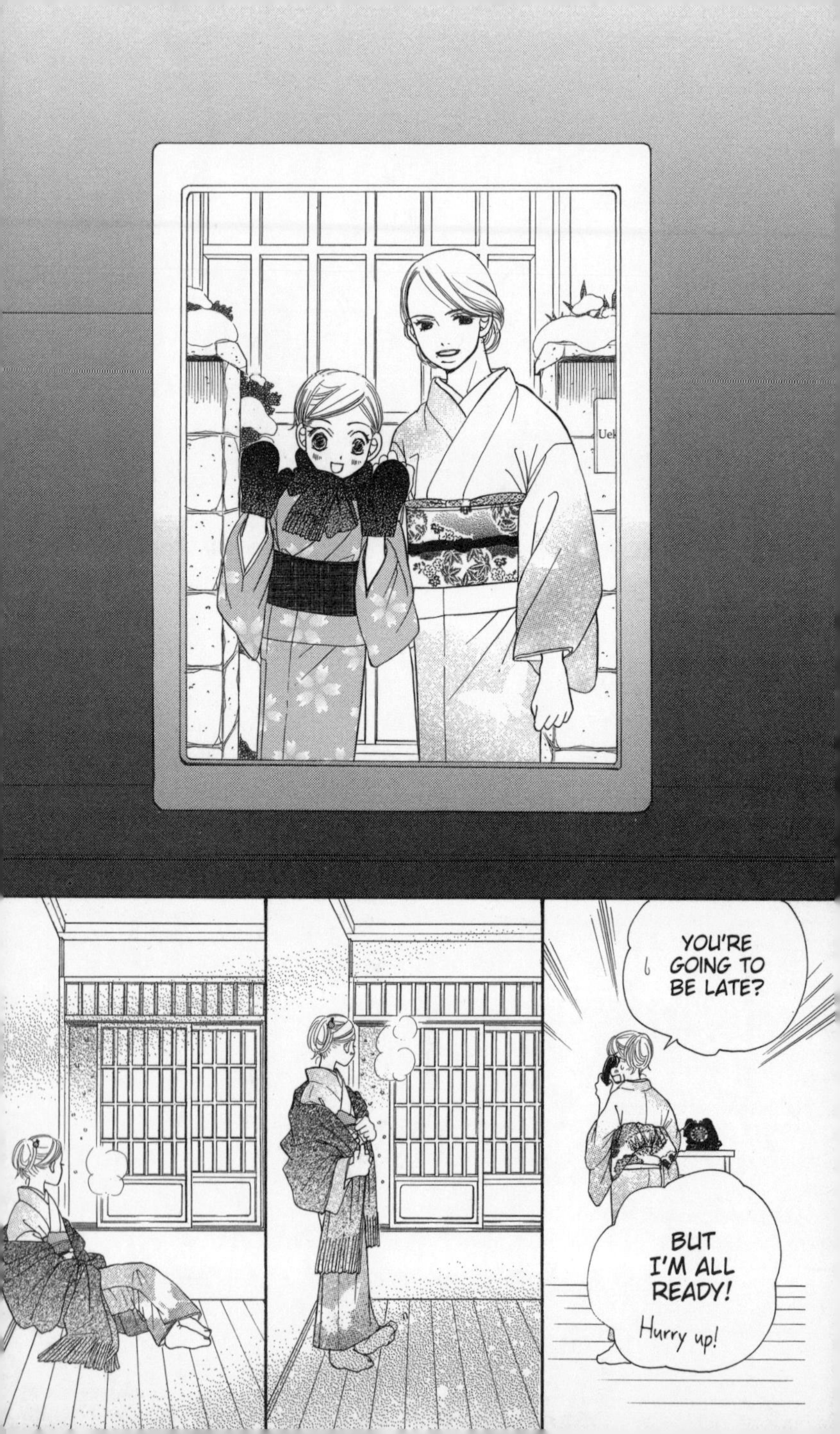
YOU'RE GOING TO BE LATE?
BUT I'M ALL READY!
Hurry up!

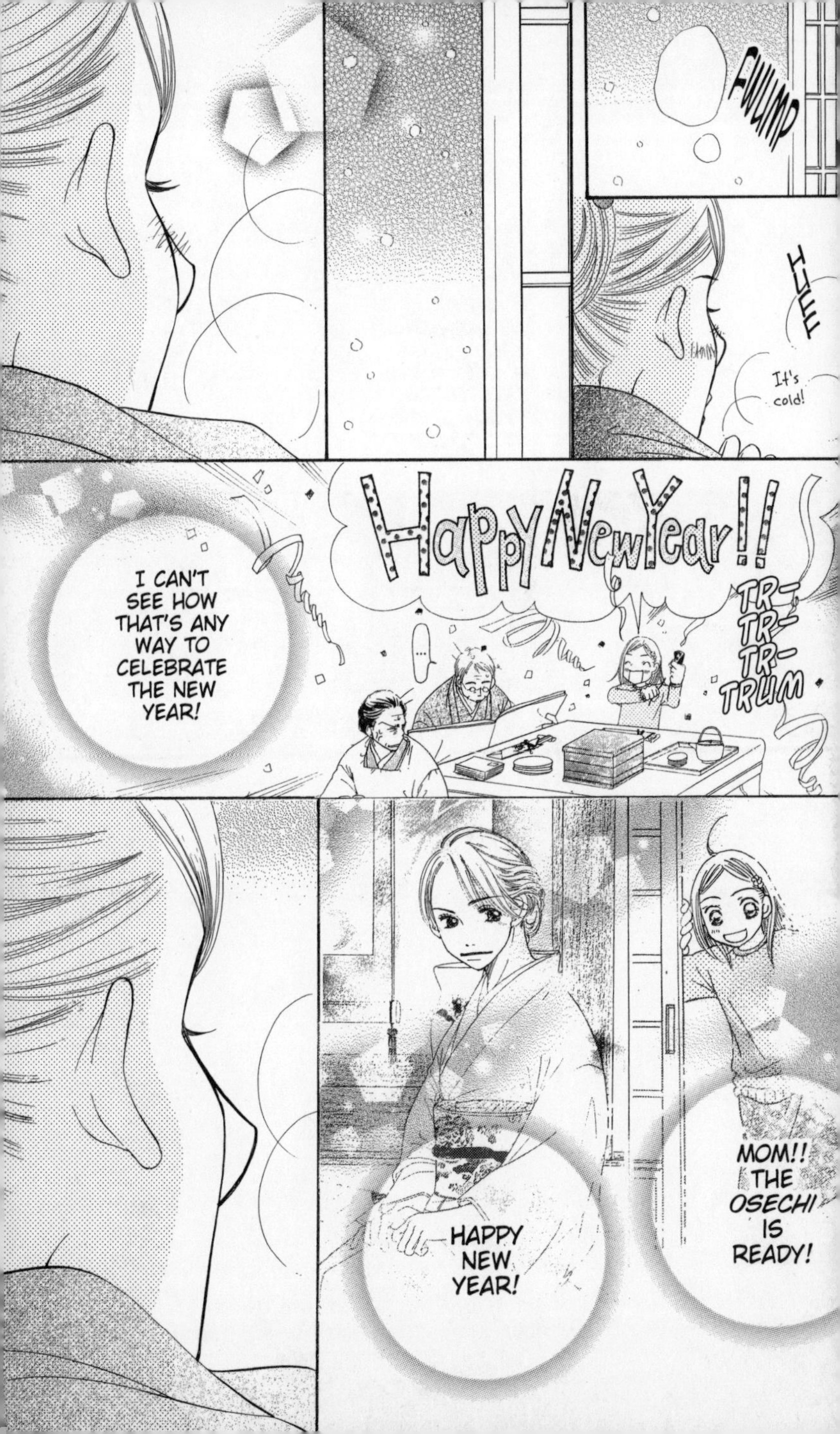
FWUMP
HUFF
It's cold!
Happy New Year!!
TR-
TR-
TR-
TRUM
...
I CAN'T SEE HOW THAT'S ANY WAY TO CELEBRATE THE NEW YEAR!
MOM!! THE OSECHI IS READY!
HAPPY NEW YEAR!

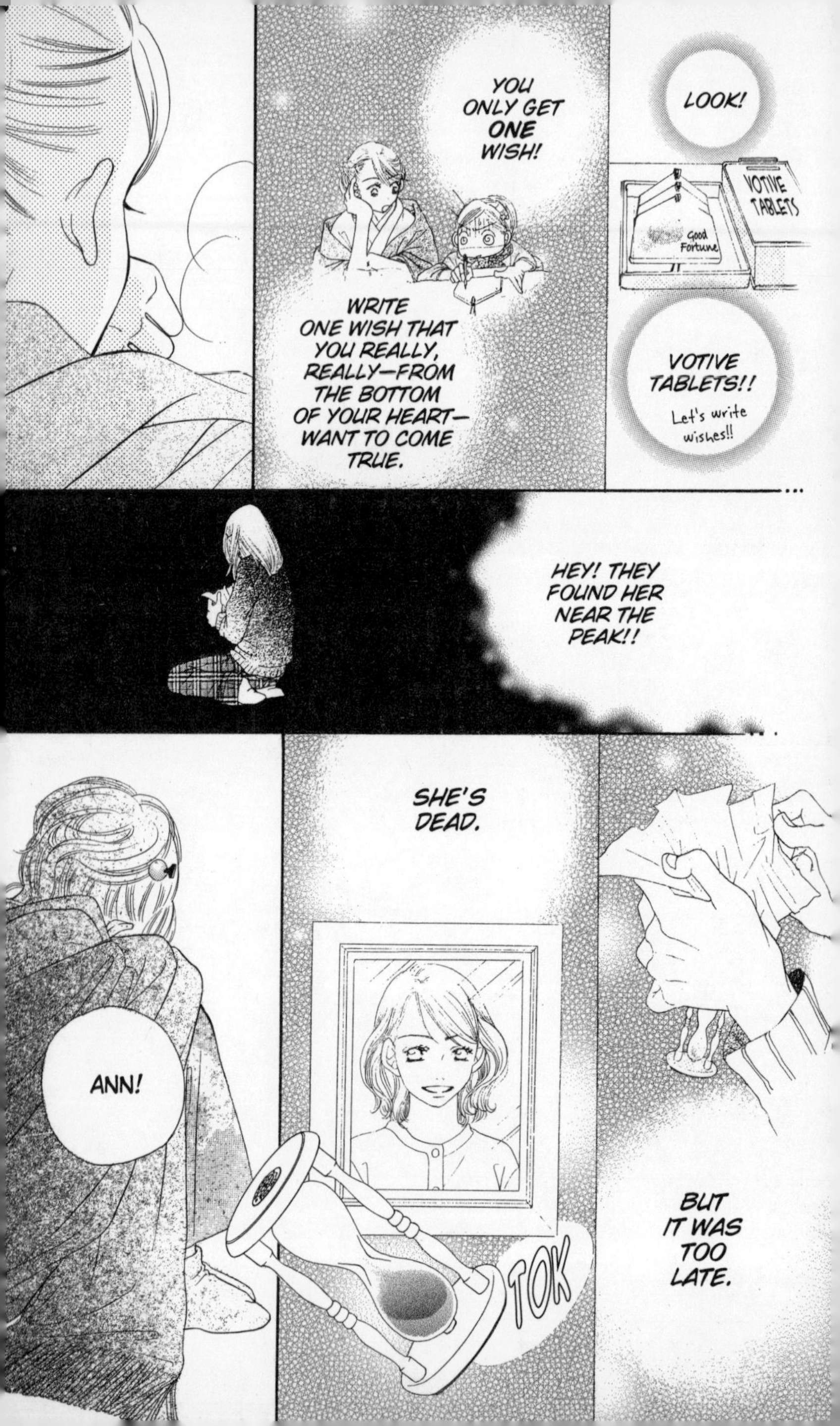
LOOK!
VOTIVE TABLETS
Good Fortune
VOTIVE TABLETS!!
Let's write wishes!!
YOU ONLY GET ONE WISH!
WRITE ONE WISH THAT YOU REALLY, REALLY—FROM THE BOTTOM OF YOUR HEART—WANT TO COME TRUE.
HEY! THEY FOUND HER NEAR THE PEAK!!
BUT IT WAS TOO LATE.
SHE'S DEAD.
TOK
ANN!

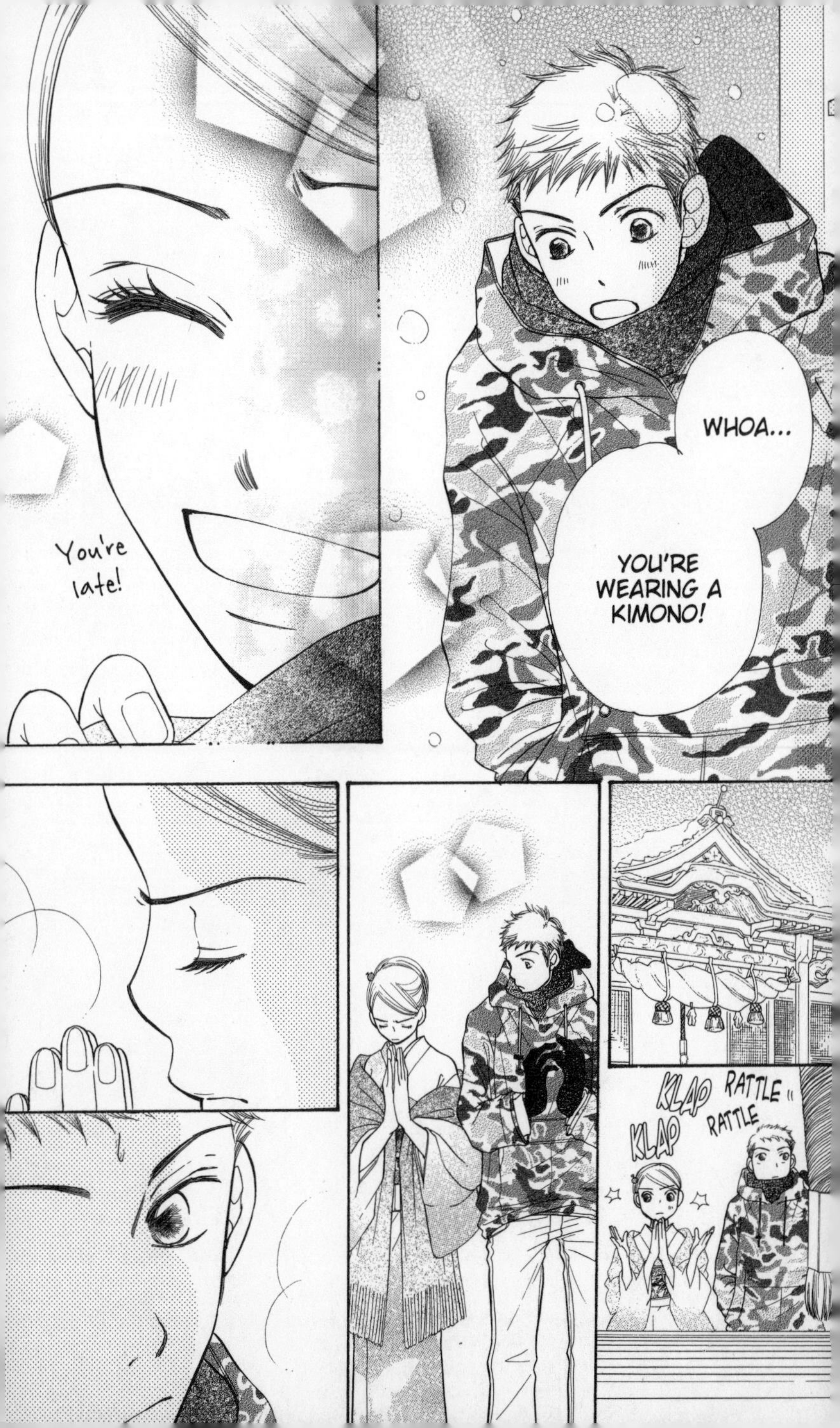
WHOA...
YOU'RE WEARING A KIMONO!
You're late!
KLAP
KLAP
RATTLE
RATTLE

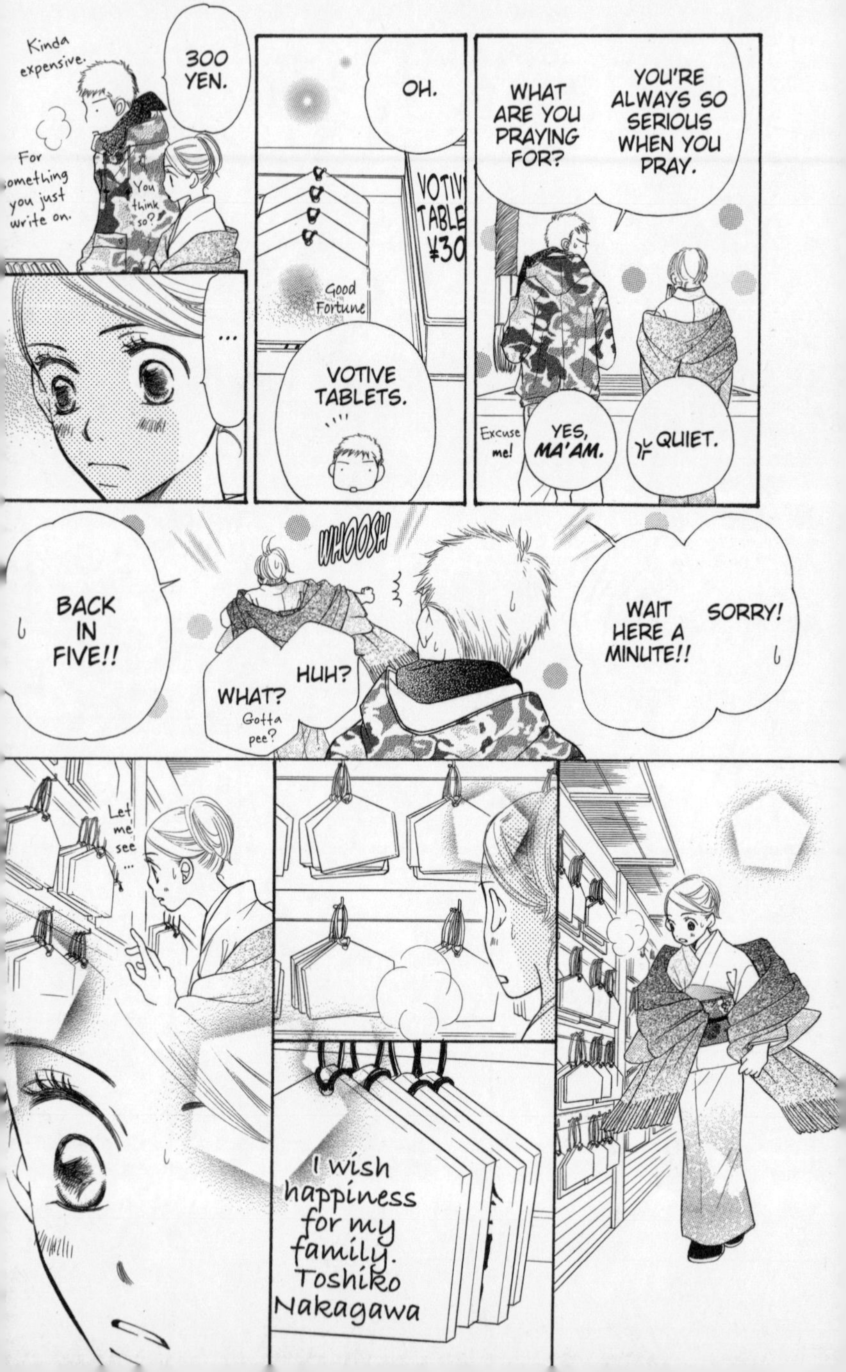

YOU'RE ALWAYS SO SERIOUS WHEN YOU PRAY.
WHAT ARE YOU PRAYING FOR?
QUIET.
YES, MA'AM.
Excuse me!
OH.
VOTIV TABLE ¥30
Good Fortune
VOTIVE TABLETS.
300 YEN.
Kinda expensive.
You think so?
For something you just write on.
...
SORRY!
WAIT HERE A MINUTE!!
WHOOSH
HUH?
WHAT?
Gotta pee?
BACK IN FIVE!!
I wish happiness for my family. Toshiko Nakagawa
Let me see...

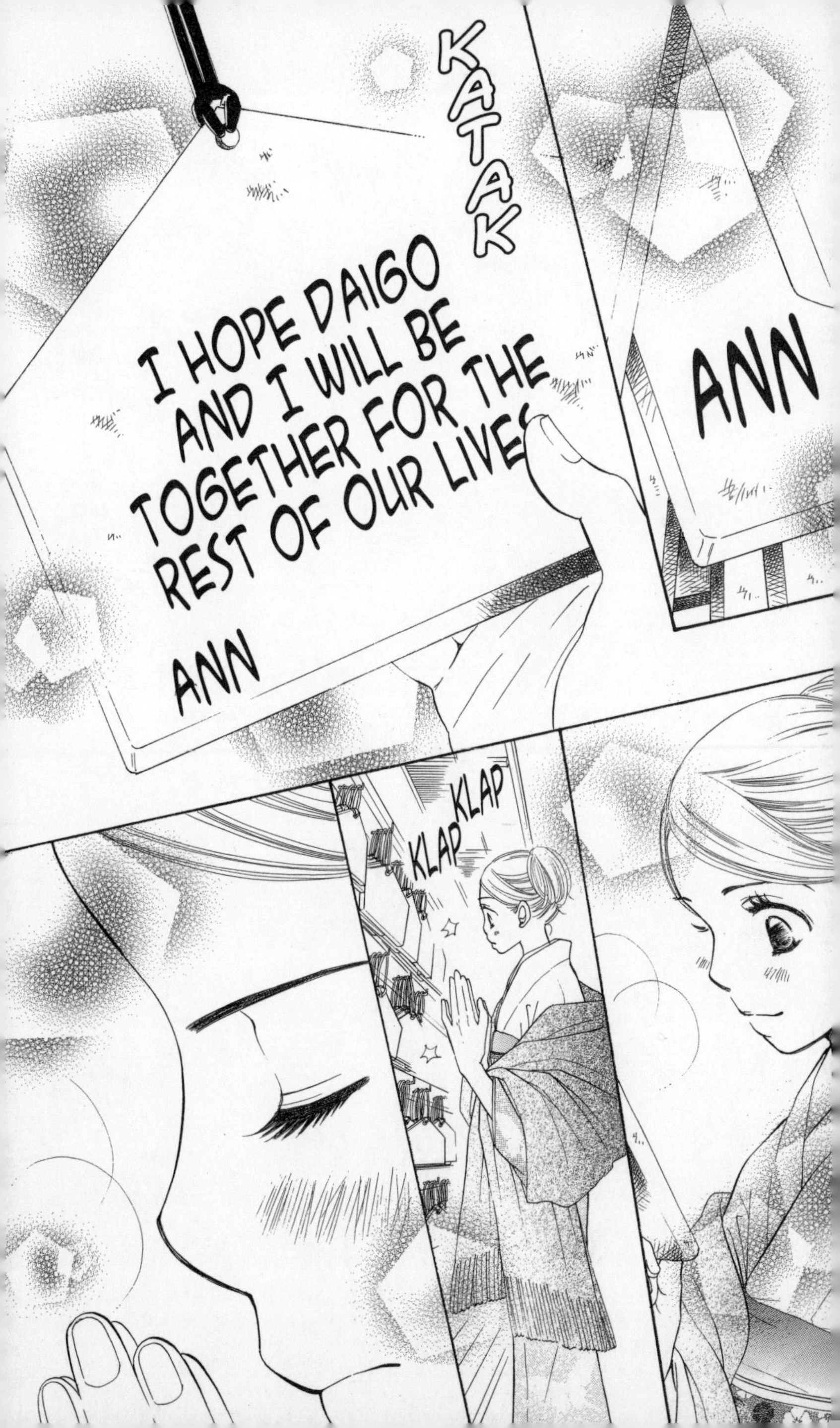
ANN
KATAK
I HOPE DAIGO AND I WILL BE TOGETHER FOR THE REST OF OUR LIVES
ANN
KLAP KLAP

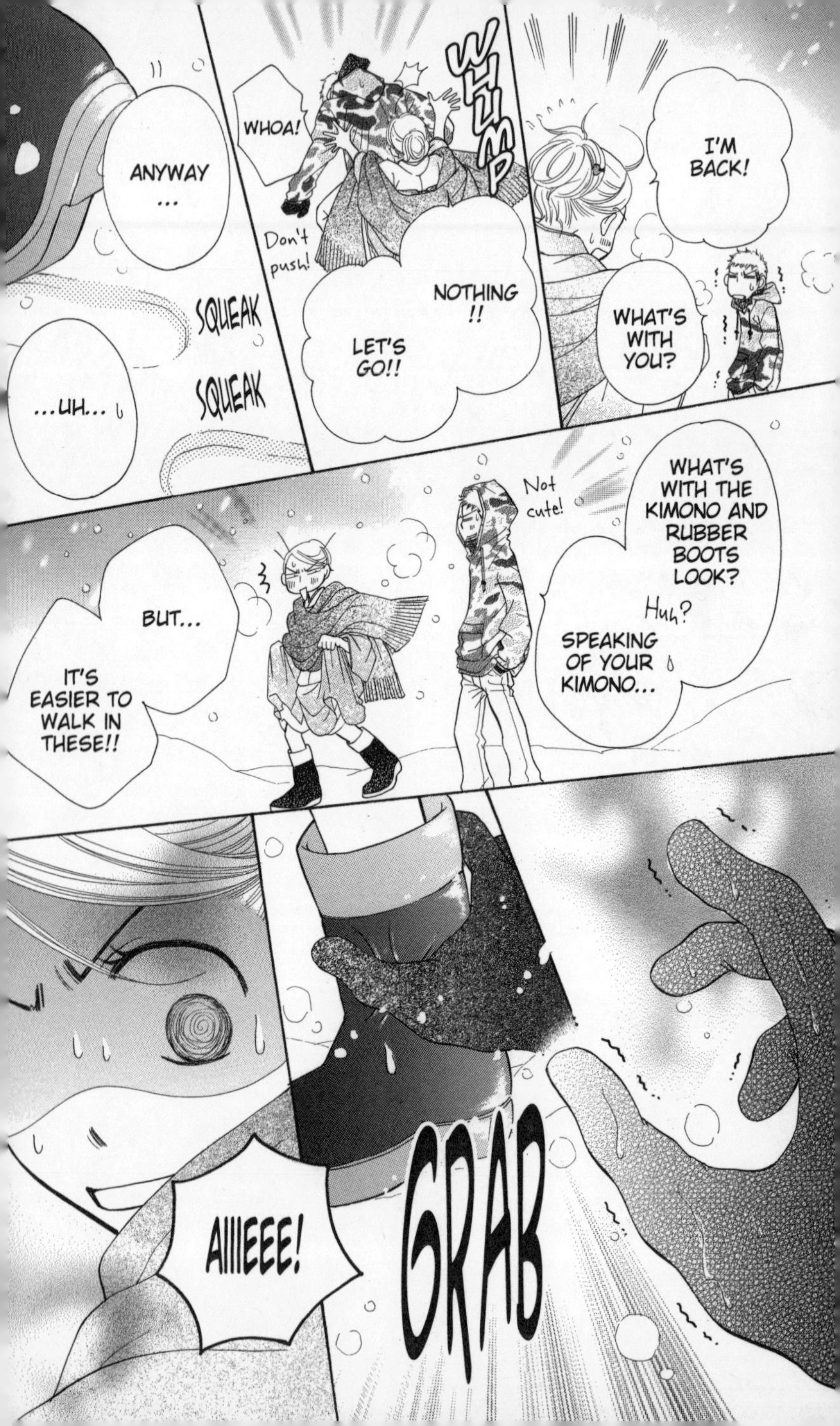
I'M BACK!
WHAT'S WITH YOU?
WHUMP
WHOA!
Don't push!
NOTHING!!
LET'S GO!!
ANYWAY...
SQUEAK
SQUEAK
...UH...
WHAT'S WITH THE KIMONO AND RUBBER BOOTS LOOK?
Huh?
SPEAKING OF YOUR KIMONO...
Not cute!
BUT...
IT'S EASIER TO WALK IN THESE!!
GRAB
AIIIEEE!

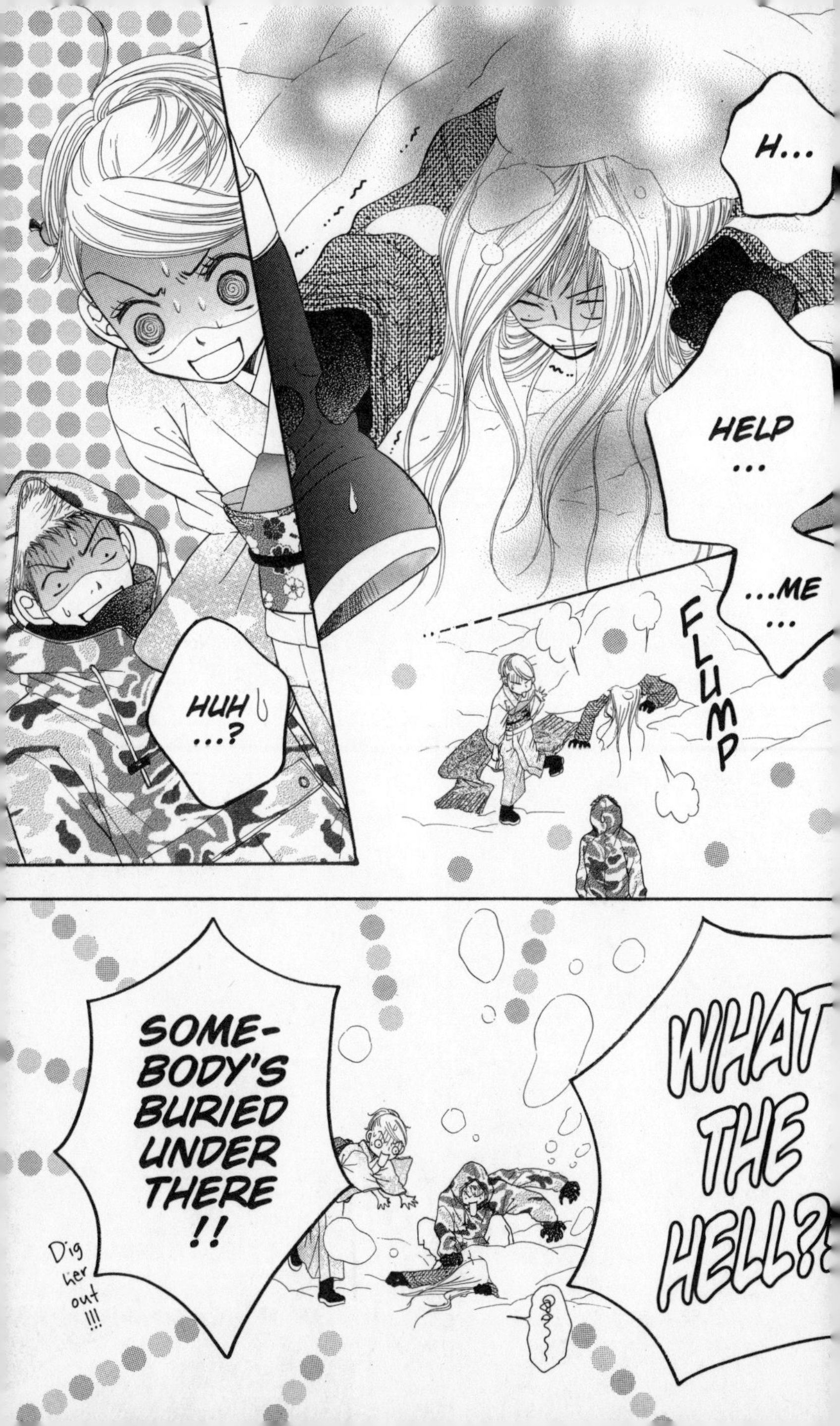
H...
HELP...
...ME...
FLUMP
HUH...?
WHAT THE HELL?!
SOMEBODY'S BURIED UNDER THERE!!
Dig her out!!!

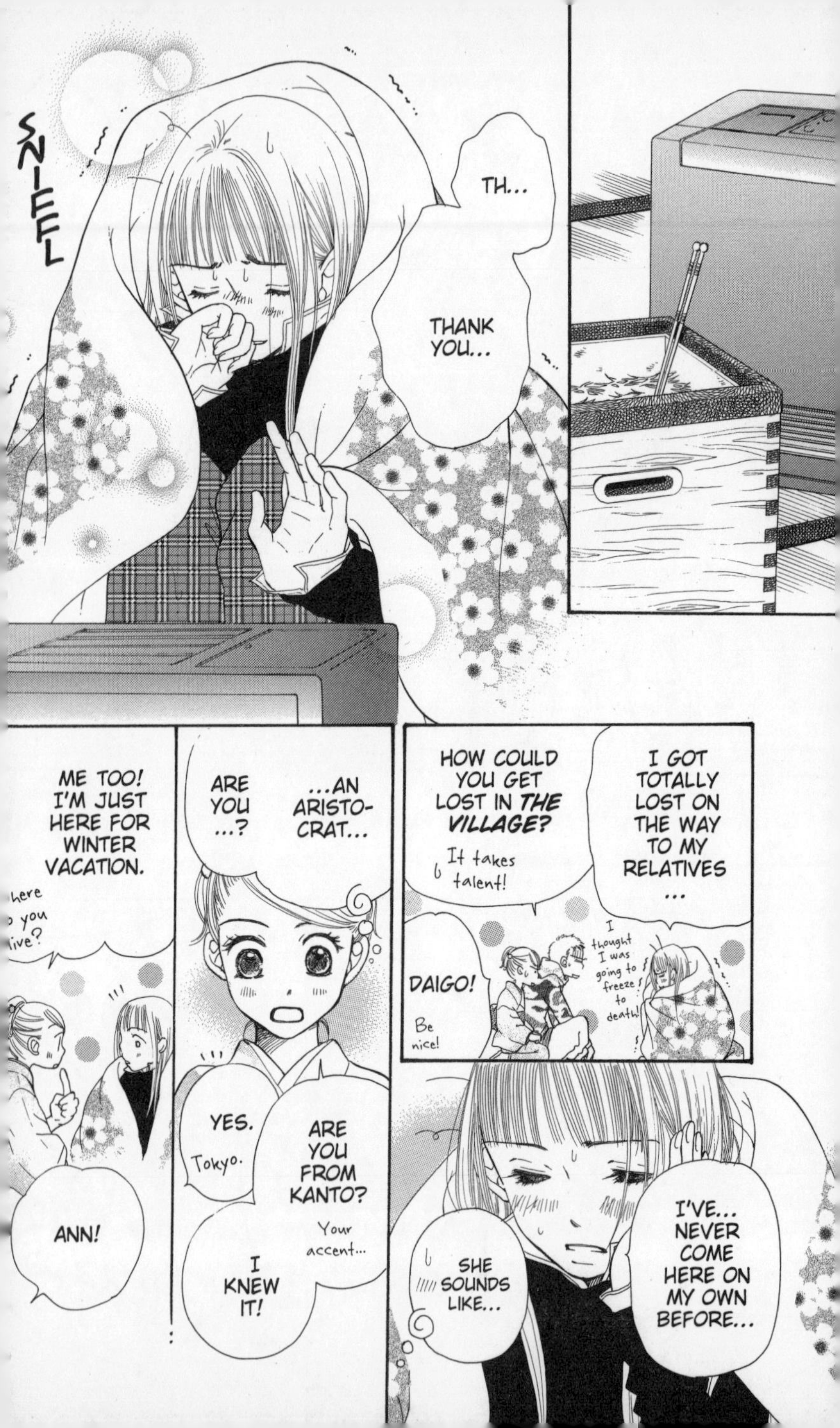
TH...
THANK YOU...
SNIFFL
I GOT TOTALLY LOST ON THE WAY TO MY RELATIVES...
HOW COULD YOU GET LOST IN *THE VILLAGE?*
It takes talent!
I thought I was going to freeze to death!
DAIGO!
Be nice!
I'VE... NEVER COME HERE ON MY OWN BEFORE...
SHE SOUNDS LIKE...
...AN ARISTOCRAT...
ARE YOU ...?
ARE YOU FROM KANTO?
Your accent...
YES.
Tokyo.
I KNEW IT!
ME TOO! I'M JUST HERE FOR WINTER VACATION.
here o you ive?
ANN!

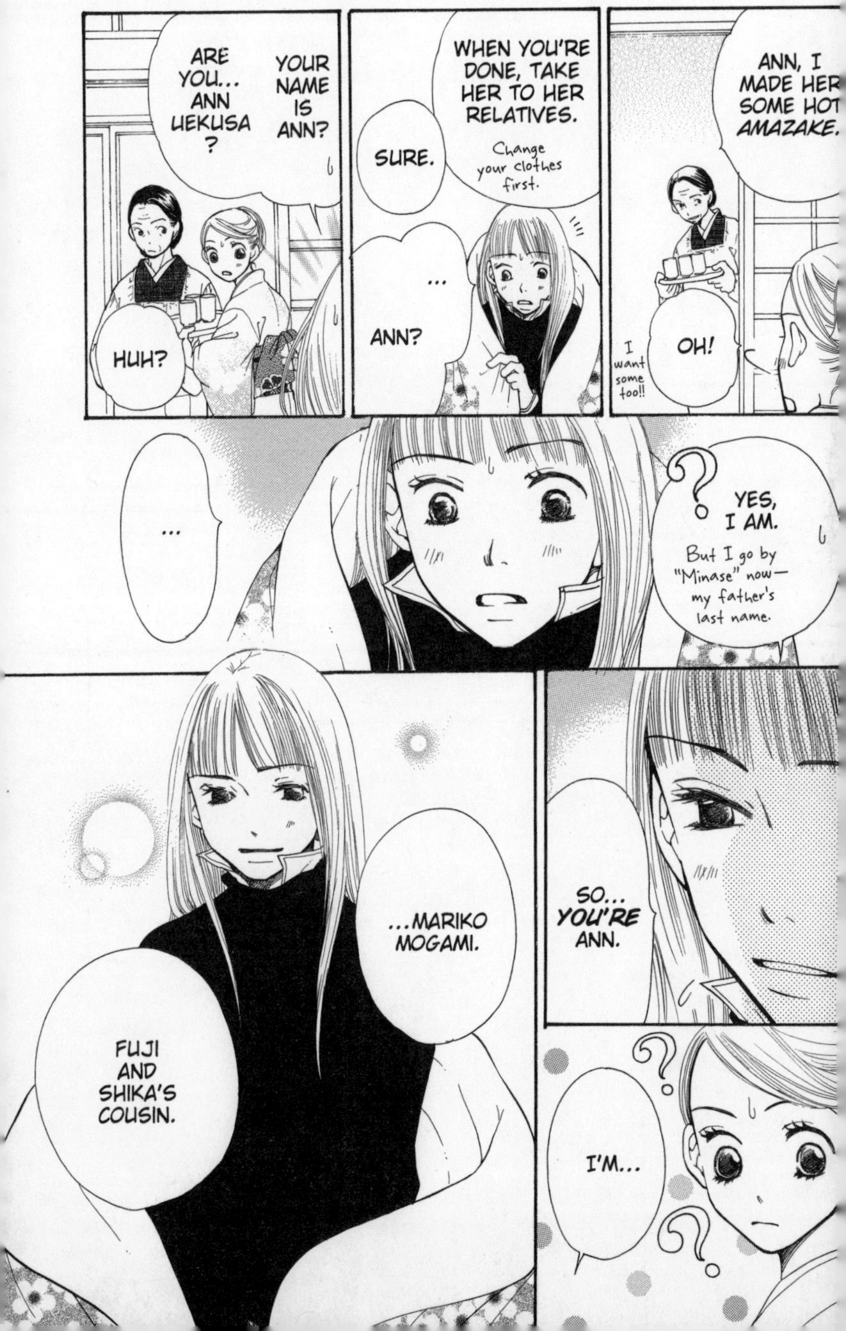
ANN, I MADE HER SOME HOT *AMAZAKE.*
OH!
I want some too!!
WHEN YOU'RE DONE, TAKE HER TO HER RELATIVES.
Change your clothes first.
SURE.
...
ANN?
YOUR NAME IS ANN?
ARE YOU... ANN UEKUSA?
HUH?
YES, I AM.
But I go by "Minase" now— my father's last name.
...
SO... *YOU'RE* ANN.
I'M...
...MARIKO MOGAMI.
FUJI AND SHIKA'S COUSIN.

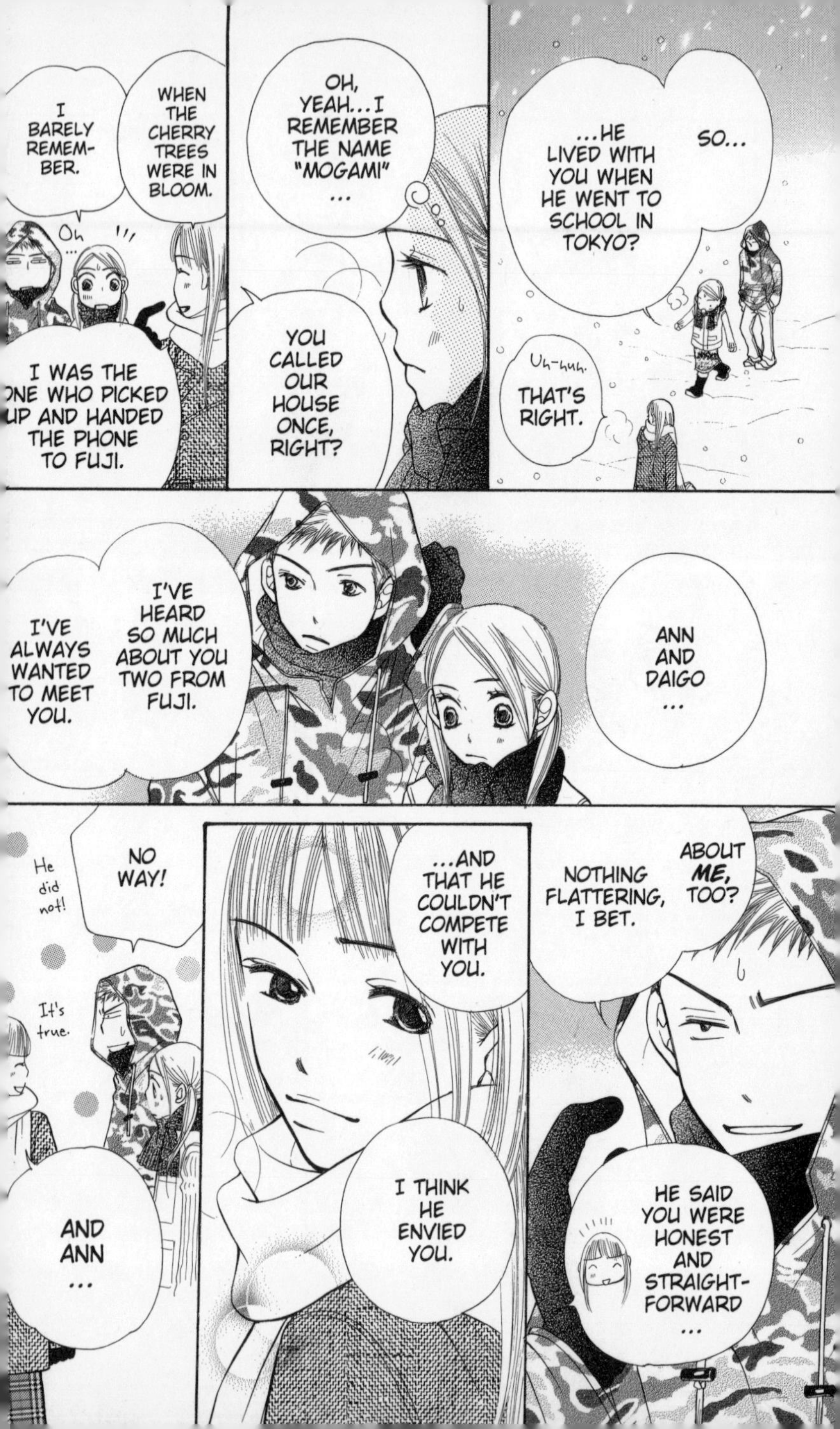
SO...
...HE LIVED WITH YOU WHEN HE WENT TO SCHOOL IN TOKYO?
Uh-huh.
THAT'S RIGHT.
OH, YEAH...I REMEMBER THE NAME "MOGAMI"...
YOU CALLED OUR HOUSE ONCE, RIGHT?
WHEN THE CHERRY TREES WERE IN BLOOM.
I BARELY REMEMBER.
Oh...
I WAS THE ONE WHO PICKED UP AND HANDED THE PHONE TO FUJI.
ANN AND DAIGO...
I'VE HEARD SO MUCH ABOUT YOU TWO FROM FUJI.
I'VE ALWAYS WANTED TO MEET YOU.
ABOUT *ME,* TOO?
NOTHING FLATTERING, I BET.
HE SAID YOU WERE HONEST AND STRAIGHT-FORWARD...
...AND THAT HE COULDN'T COMPETE WITH YOU.
I THINK HE ENVIED YOU.
NO WAY!
He did not!
It's true.
AND ANN...

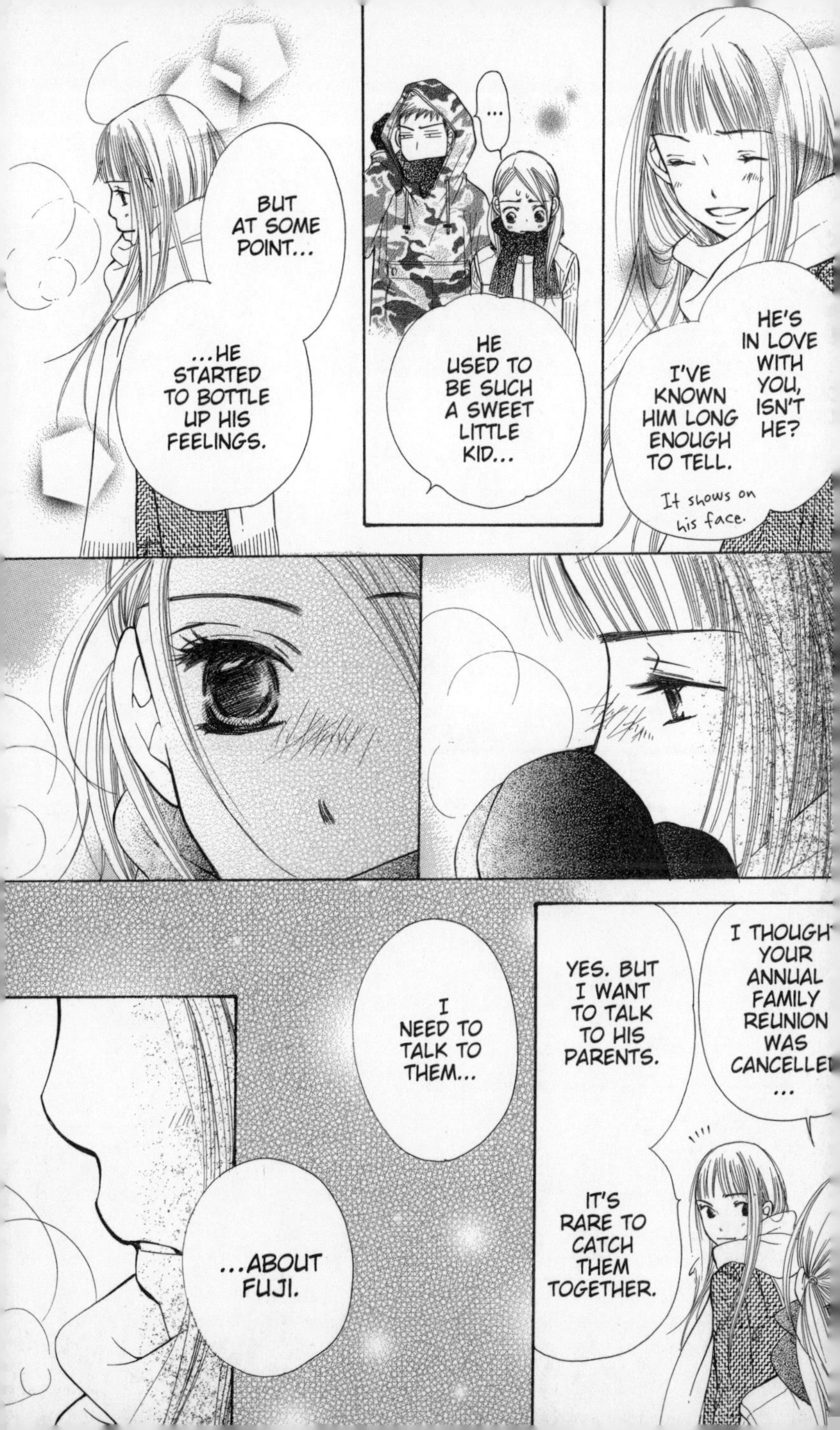
HE'S IN LOVE WITH YOU, ISN'T HE?
I'VE KNOWN HIM LONG ENOUGH TO TELL.
It shows on his face.
...
HE USED TO BE SUCH A SWEET LITTLE KID...
BUT AT SOME POINT...
...HE STARTED TO BOTTLE UP HIS FEELINGS.
I THOUGH YOUR ANNUAL FAMILY REUNION WAS CANCELLE ...
YES. BUT I WANT TO TALK TO HIS PARENTS.
IT'S RARE TO CATCH THEM TOGETHER.
I NEED TO TALK TO THEM...
...ABOUT FUJI.

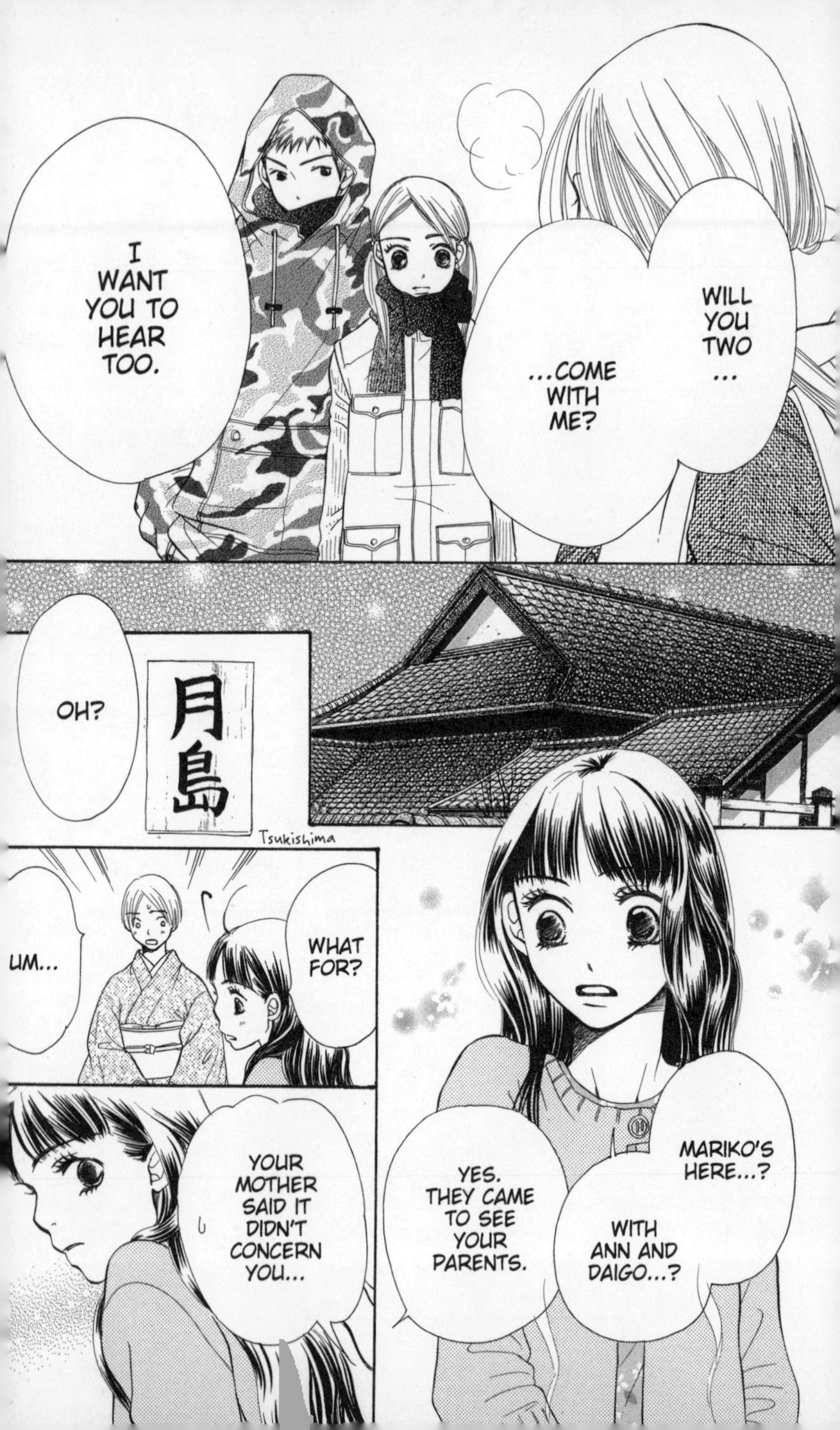
WILL YOU TWO ...
...COME WITH ME?
I WANT YOU TO HEAR TOO.
月島
Tsukishima
OH?
MARIKO'S HERE...?
WITH ANN AND DAIGO...?
YES. THEY CAME TO SEE YOUR PARENTS.
WHAT FOR?
UM...
YOUR MOTHER SAID IT DIDN'T CONCERN YOU...

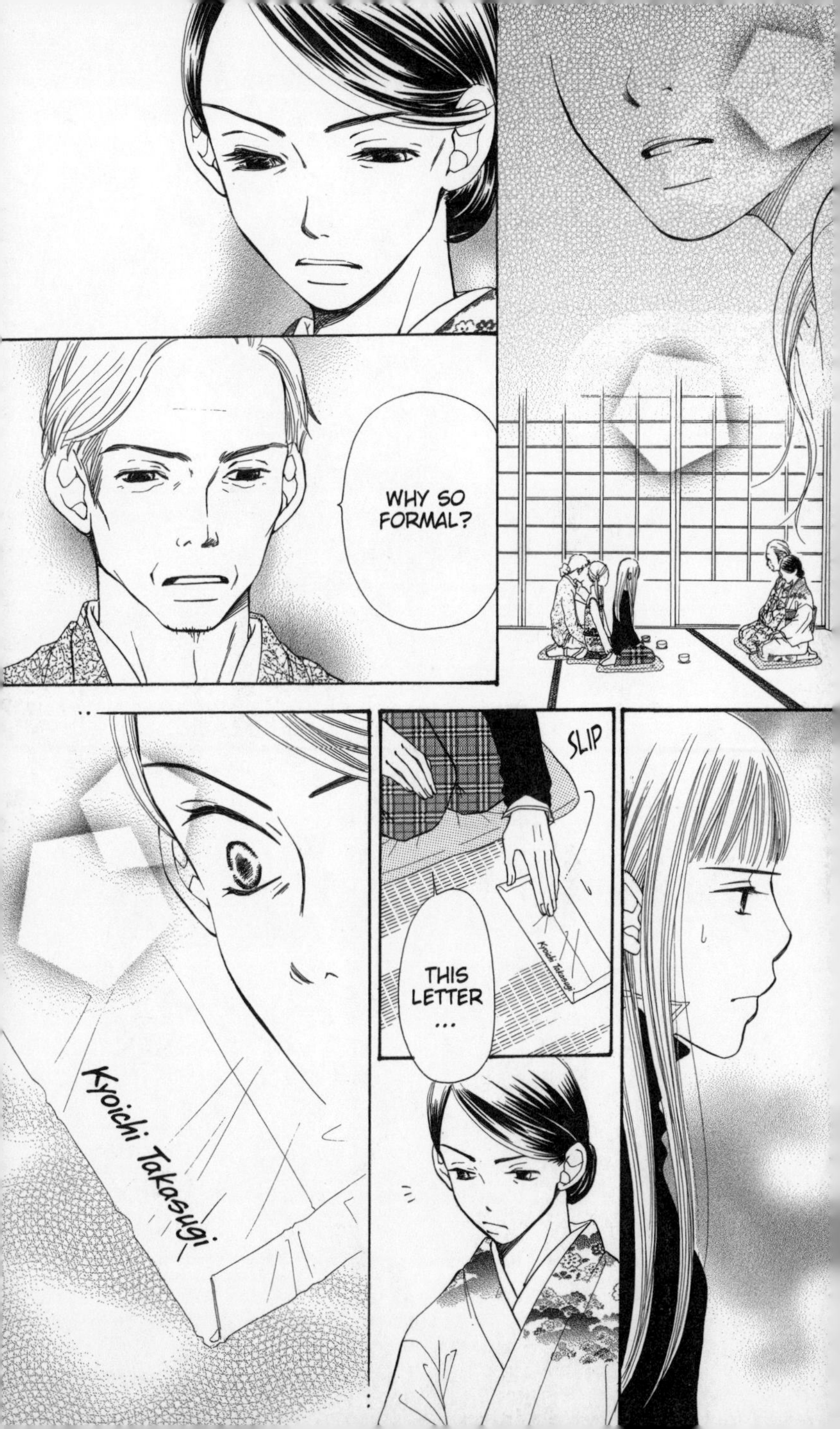
WHY SO FORMAL?
SLIP
Kyoichi Takasugi
THIS LETTER ...
Kyoichi Takasugi

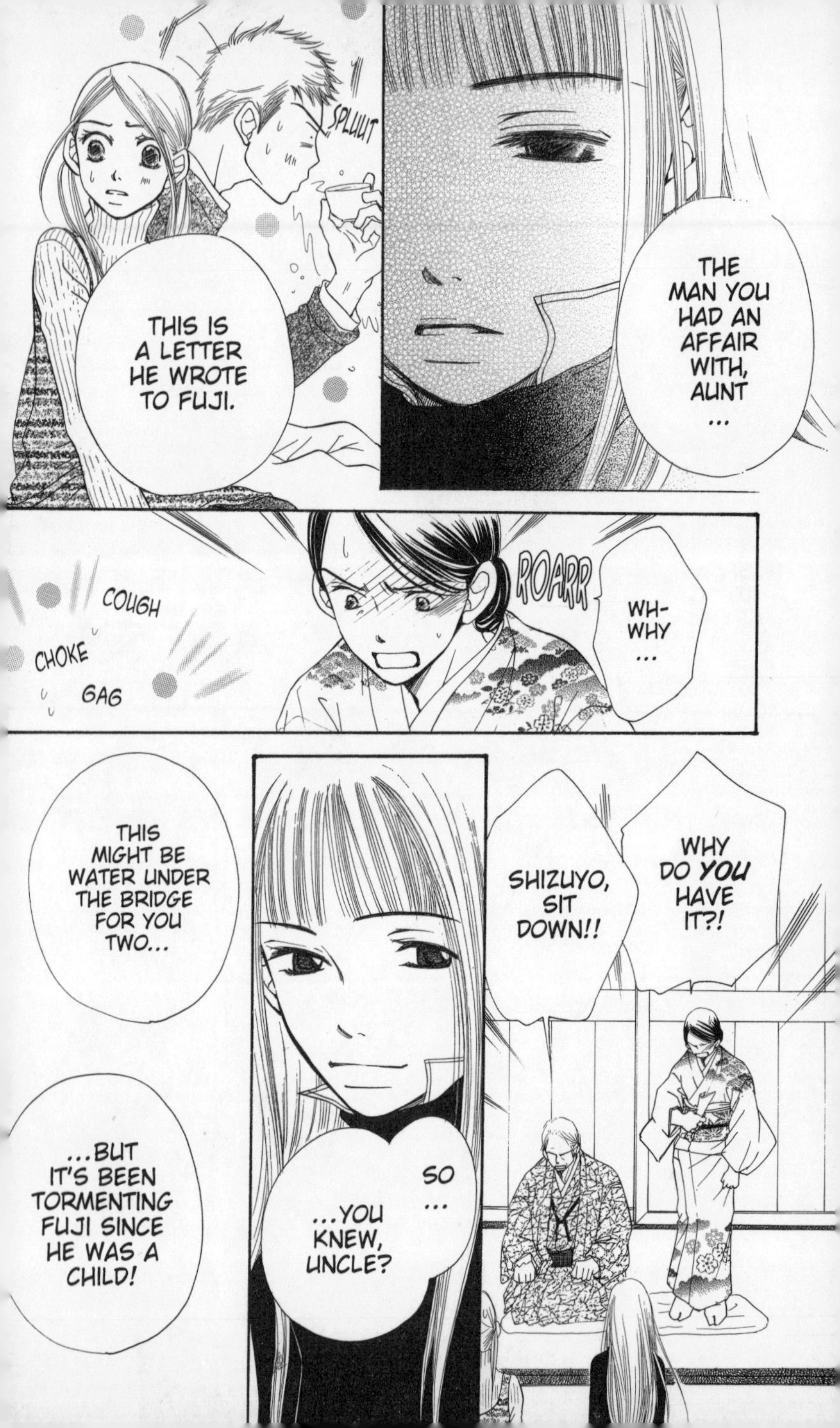
THE MAN YOU HAD AN AFFAIR WITH, AUNT ...
SPLUUT
THIS IS A LETTER HE WROTE TO FUJI.
WH- WHY ...
ROARR
COUGH
CHOKE
GAG
WHY DO YOU HAVE IT?!
SHIZUYO, SIT DOWN!!
SO ...
...YOU KNEW, UNCLE?
THIS MIGHT BE WATER UNDER THE BRIDGE FOR YOU TWO...
...BUT IT'S BEEN TORMENTING FUJI SINCE HE WAS A CHILD!

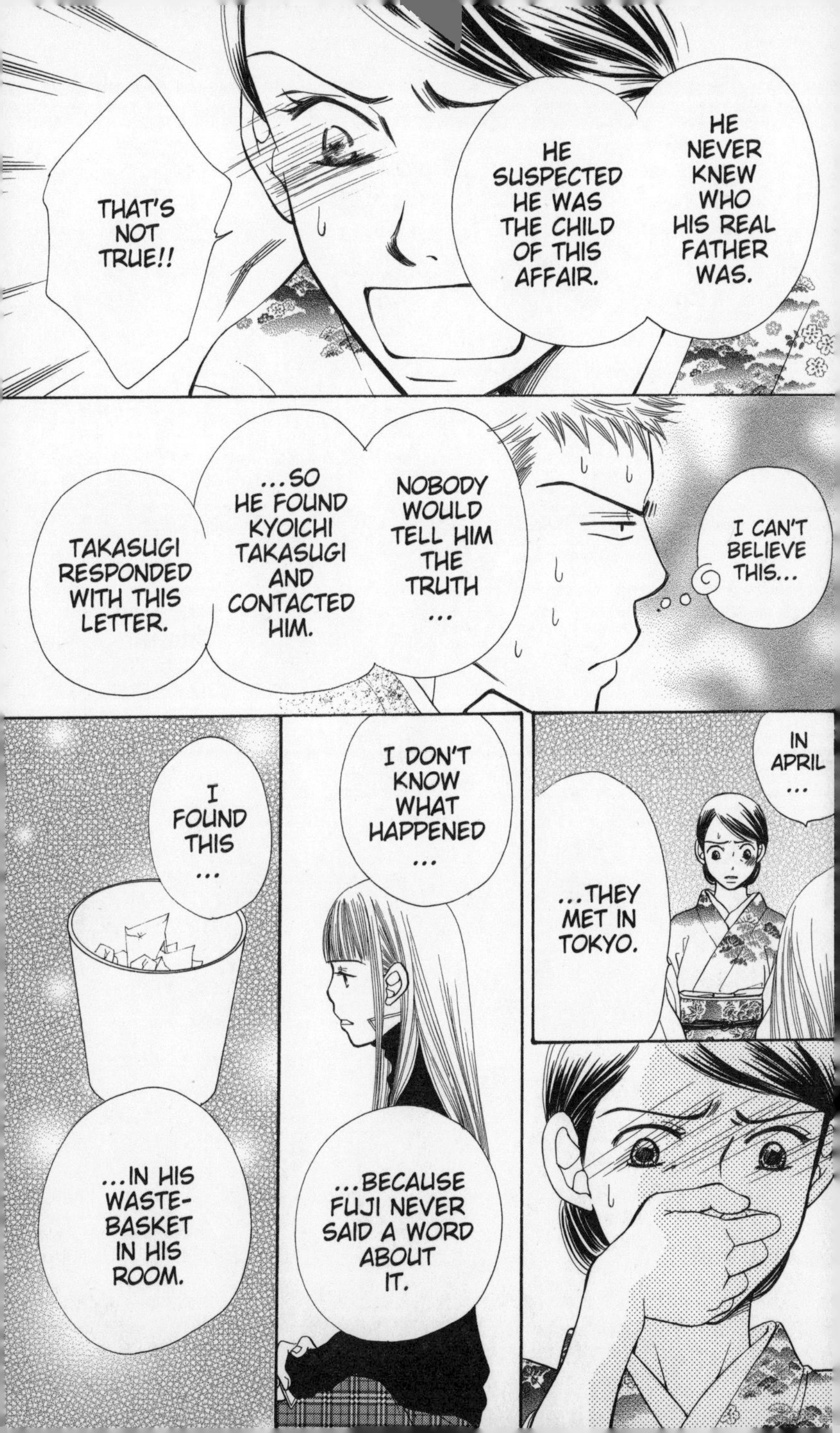
HE NEVER KNEW WHO HIS REAL FATHER WAS.
HE SUSPECTED HE WAS THE CHILD OF THIS AFFAIR.
THAT'S NOT TRUE!!
I CAN'T BELIEVE THIS...
NOBODY WOULD TELL HIM THE TRUTH...
...SO HE FOUND KYOICHI TAKASUGI AND CONTACTED HIM.
TAKASUGI RESPONDED WITH THIS LETTER.
IN APRIL...
...THEY MET IN TOKYO.
I DON'T KNOW WHAT HAPPENED...
...BECAUSE FUJI NEVER SAID A WORD ABOUT IT.
I FOUND THIS...
...IN HIS WASTE-BASKET IN HIS ROOM.

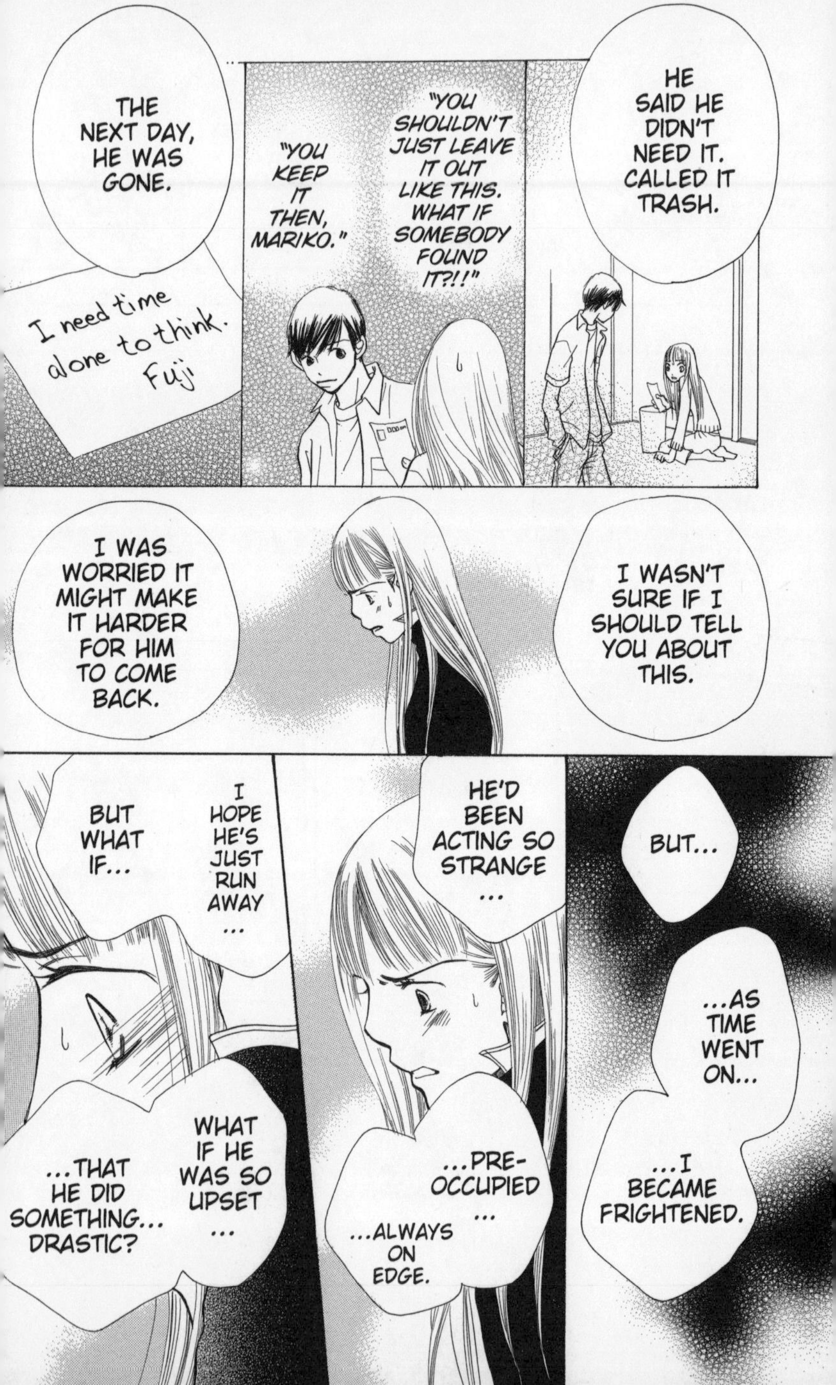
HE SAID HE DIDN'T NEED IT. CALLED IT TRASH.
"YOU SHOULDN'T JUST LEAVE IT OUT LIKE THIS. WHAT IF SOMEBODY FOUND IT?!!"
"YOU KEEP IT THEN, MARIKO."
THE NEXT DAY, HE WAS GONE.
I need time alone to think.
Fuji
I WASN'T SURE IF I SHOULD TELL YOU ABOUT THIS.
I WAS WORRIED IT MIGHT MAKE IT HARDER FOR HIM TO COME BACK.
BUT...
...AS TIME WENT ON...
...I BECAME FRIGHTENED.
HE'D BEEN ACTING SO STRANGE...
...PRE-OCCUPIED...
...ALWAYS ON EDGE.
I HOPE HE'S JUST RUN AWAY...
BUT WHAT IF...
WHAT IF HE WAS SO UPSET...
...THAT HE DID SOMETHING... DRASTIC?

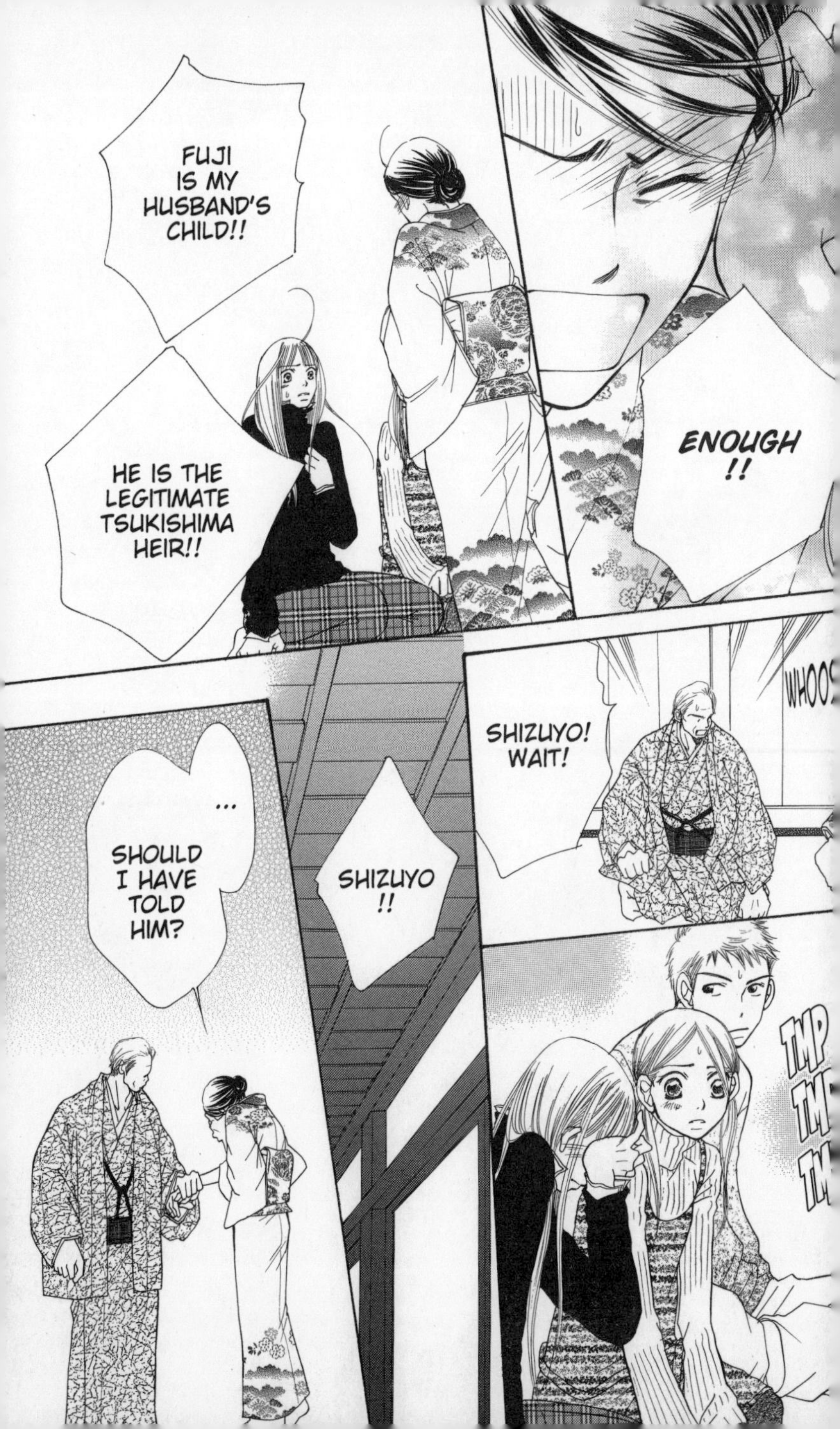
ENOUGH!!
FUJI IS MY HUSBAND'S CHILD!!
HE IS THE LEGITIMATE TSUKISHIMA HEIR!!
WHOOS
SHIZUYO! WAIT!
TMP
TM
TM
SHIZUYO!!
...
SHOULD I HAVE TOLD HIM?

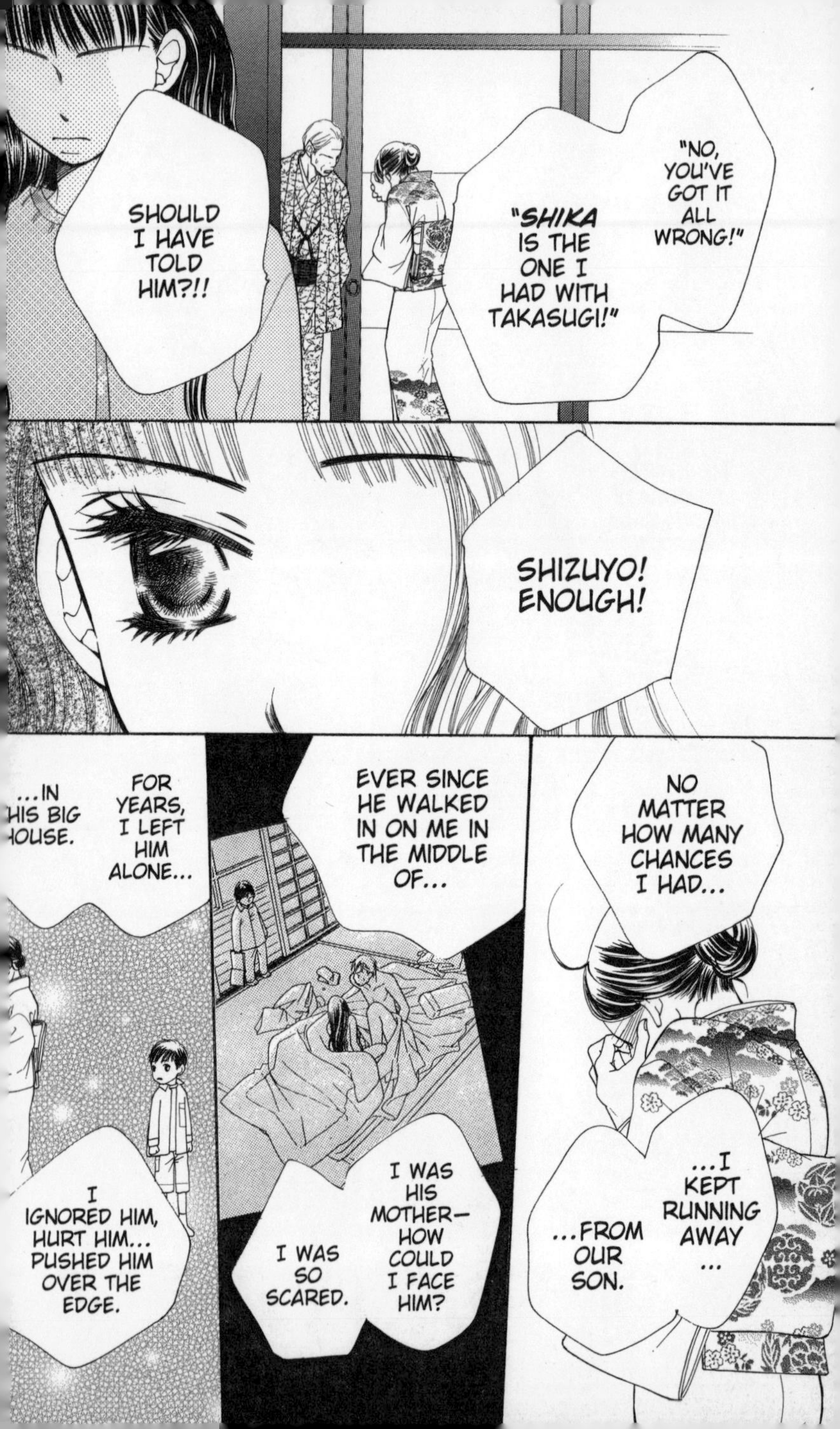
"NO, YOU'VE GOT IT ALL WRONG!"
"SHIKA IS THE ONE I HAD WITH TAKASUGI!"
SHOULD I HAVE TOLD HIM?!!
SHIZUYO! ENOUGH!
NO MATTER HOW MANY CHANCES I HAD...
...I KEPT RUNNING AWAY...
...FROM OUR SON.
EVER SINCE HE WALKED IN ON ME IN THE MIDDLE OF...
I WAS HIS MOTHER— HOW COULD I FACE HIM?
I WAS SO SCARED.
FOR YEARS, I LEFT HIM ALONE...
...IN HIS BIG HOUSE.
I IGNORED HIM, HURT HIM... PUSHED HIM OVER THE EDGE.

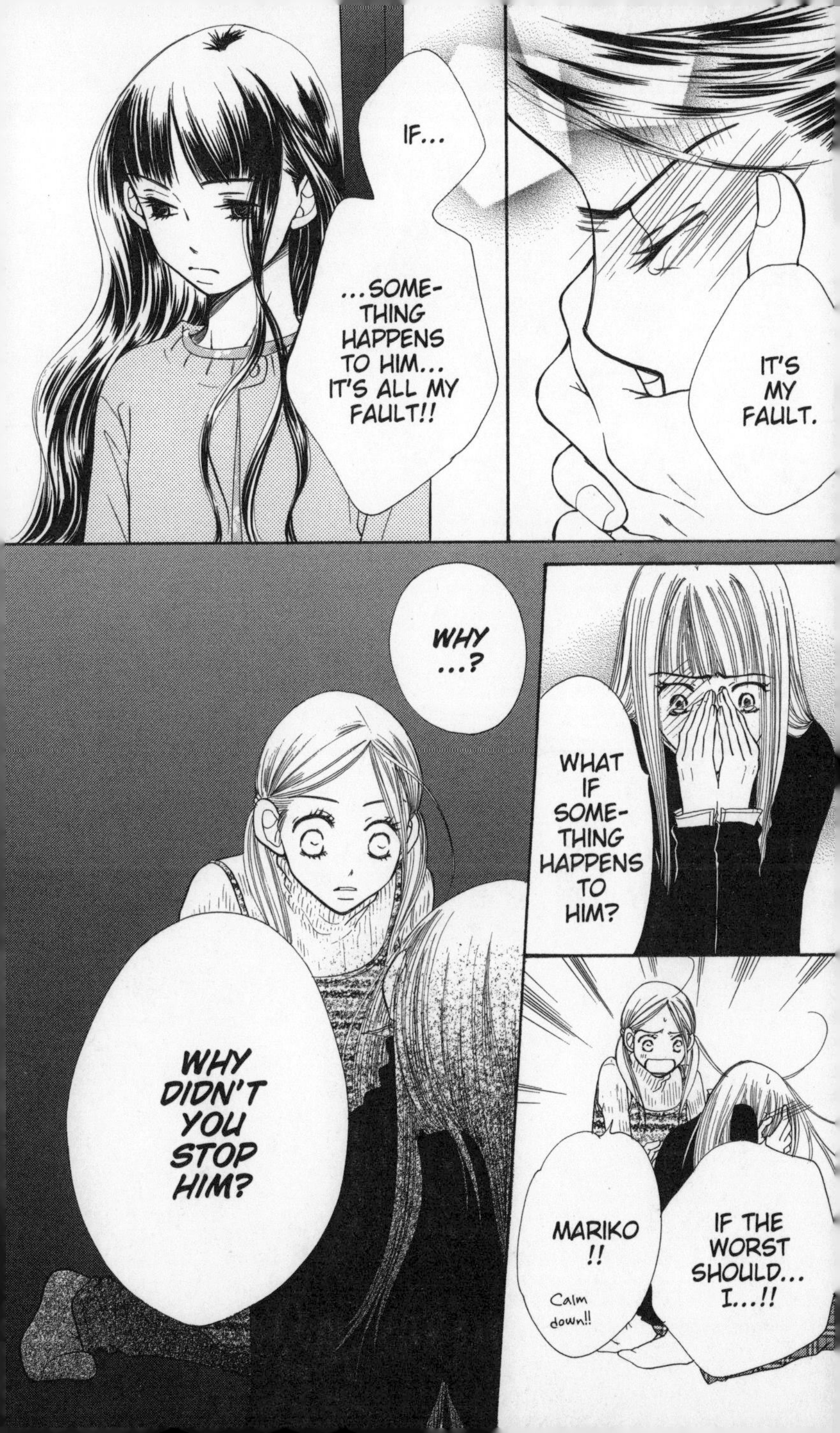
IT'S MY FAULT.
IF...
...SOMETHING HAPPENS TO HIM... IT'S ALL MY FAULT!!
WHAT IF SOMETHING HAPPENS TO HIM?
IF THE WORST SHOULD... I...!!
MARIKO!!
Calm down!!
WHY...?
WHY DIDN'T YOU STOP HIM?

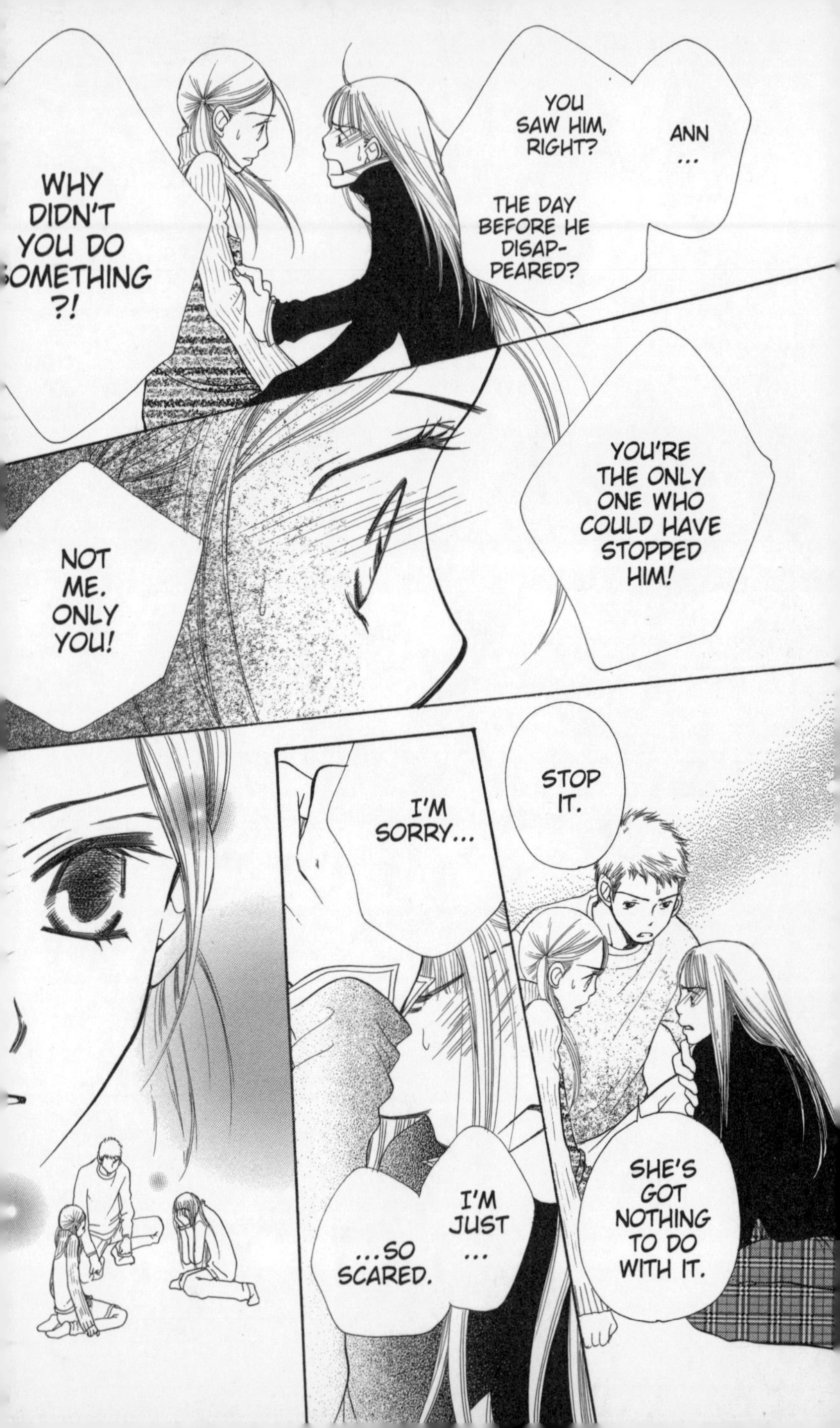
ANN ...
YOU SAW HIM, RIGHT?
THE DAY BEFORE HE DISAP-PEARED?
WHY DIDN'T YOU DO SOMETHING ?!
YOU'RE THE ONLY ONE WHO COULD HAVE STOPPED HIM!
NOT ME. ONLY YOU!
STOP IT.
SHE'S GOT NOTHING TO DO WITH IT.
I'M SORRY...
I'M JUST ...
...SO SCARED.

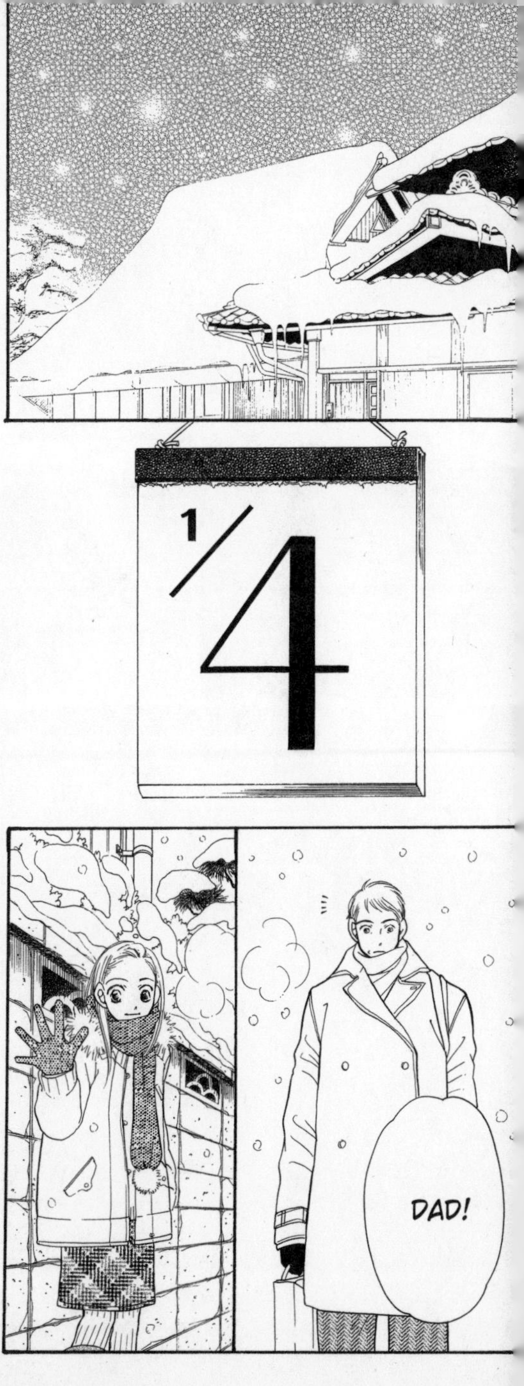
1/4
DAD!

Winter, Age 16: Snows of Remembrance

Volume 4! Now the characters are 16 and 17.

"Snows of Remembrance" comes from the Japanese word *wasure-yuki*, which technically refers to snow that falls in the spring. Here, I'm using it in a slightly different way. I'm referring back to the snows when Ann and the others were 12, since in this chapter a number of events and memories from that past winter return and finally come to a boiling point.

Sand Chronicles is developing at a leisurely pace...

Maybe I can only say this because I grew up in a relatively warm area and have never known the severity of colder climes, but...**I love snow!** ♡

I went to Canada once to see the aurora borealis. They had dog sledding in the daytime—and I was really looking forward to it—but there was an abnormal warm spell and the snow melted, so they called it off. I was **terribly disappointed!** I worked out my frustration in this volume's dogsled scene. (Not really!)

I'm definitely against global warming!

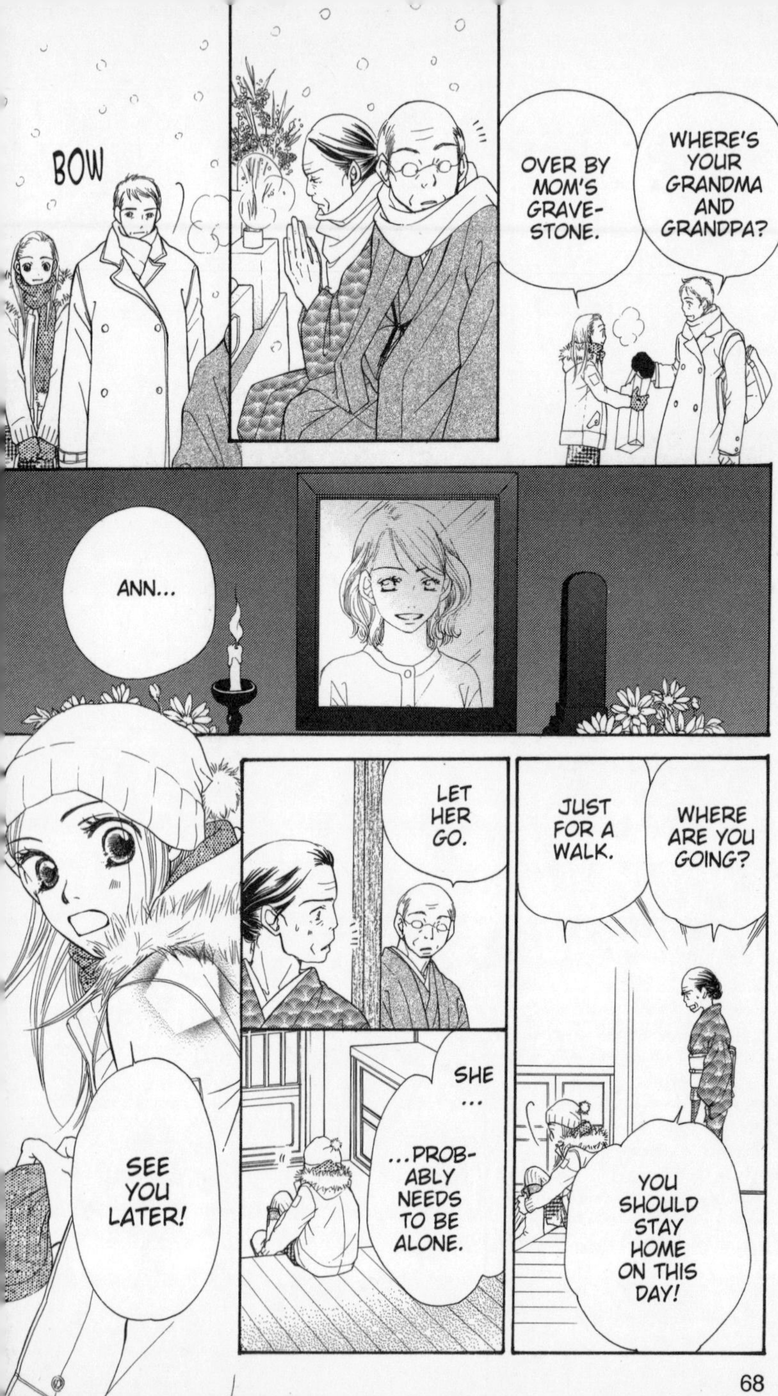
WHERE'S YOUR GRANDMA AND GRANDPA?
OVER BY MOM'S GRAVE-STONE.
BOW
ANN...
WHERE ARE YOU GOING?
JUST FOR A WALK.
YOU SHOULD STAY HOME ON THIS DAY!
LET HER GO.
SHE ...
...PROB-ABLY NEEDS TO BE ALONE.
SEE YOU LATER!

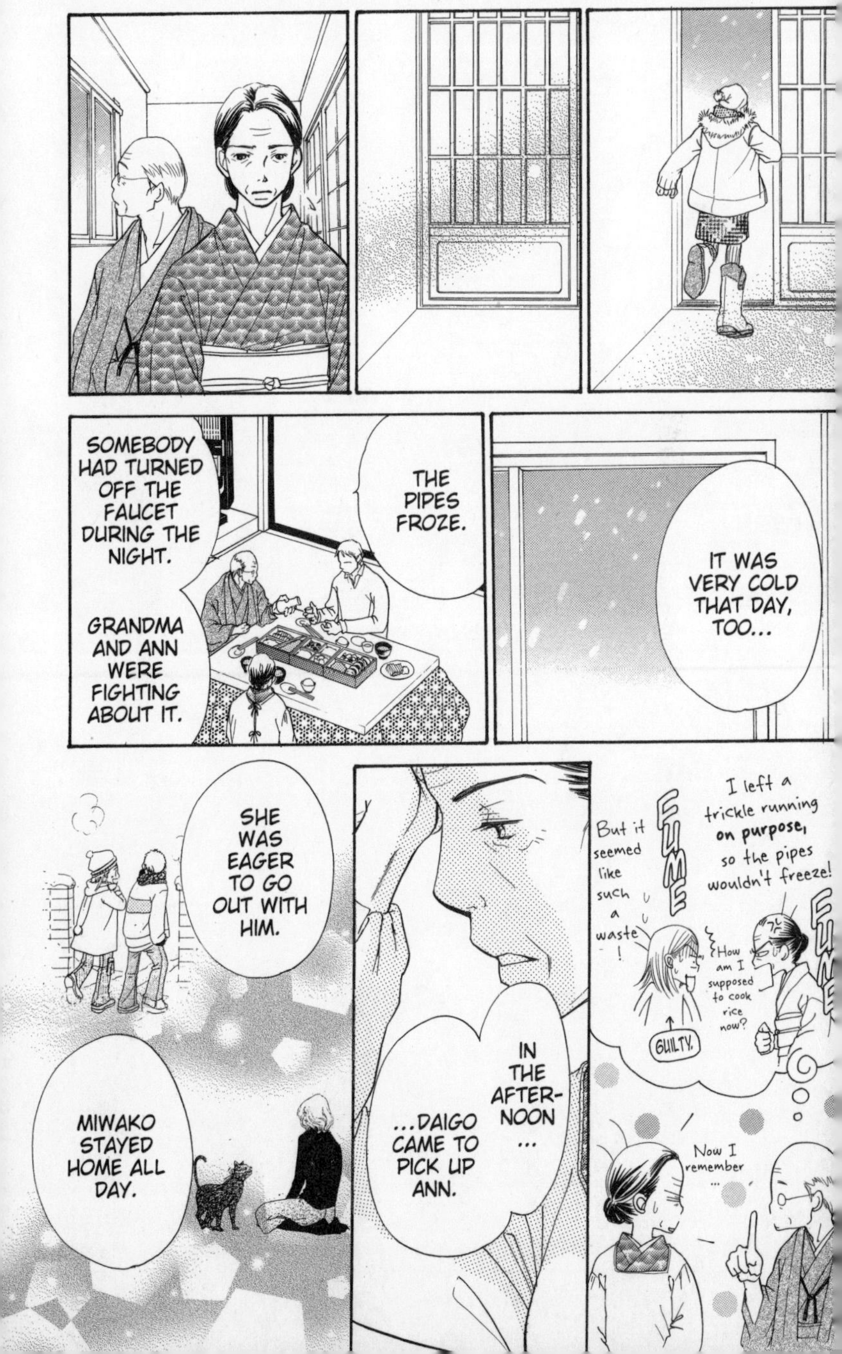
IT WAS VERY COLD THAT DAY, TOO...
THE PIPES FROZE.
SOMEBODY HAD TURNED OFF THE FAUCET DURING THE NIGHT.
GRANDMA AND ANN WERE FIGHTING ABOUT IT.
I left a trickle running on purpose, so the pipes wouldn't freeze!
FUME
How am I supposed to cook rice now?
FUME
But it seemed like such a waste-!
GUILTY.
Now I remember...
IN THE AFTERNOON...
...DAIGO CAME TO PICK UP ANN.
SHE WAS EAGER TO GO OUT WITH HIM.
MIWAKO STAYED HOME ALL DAY.

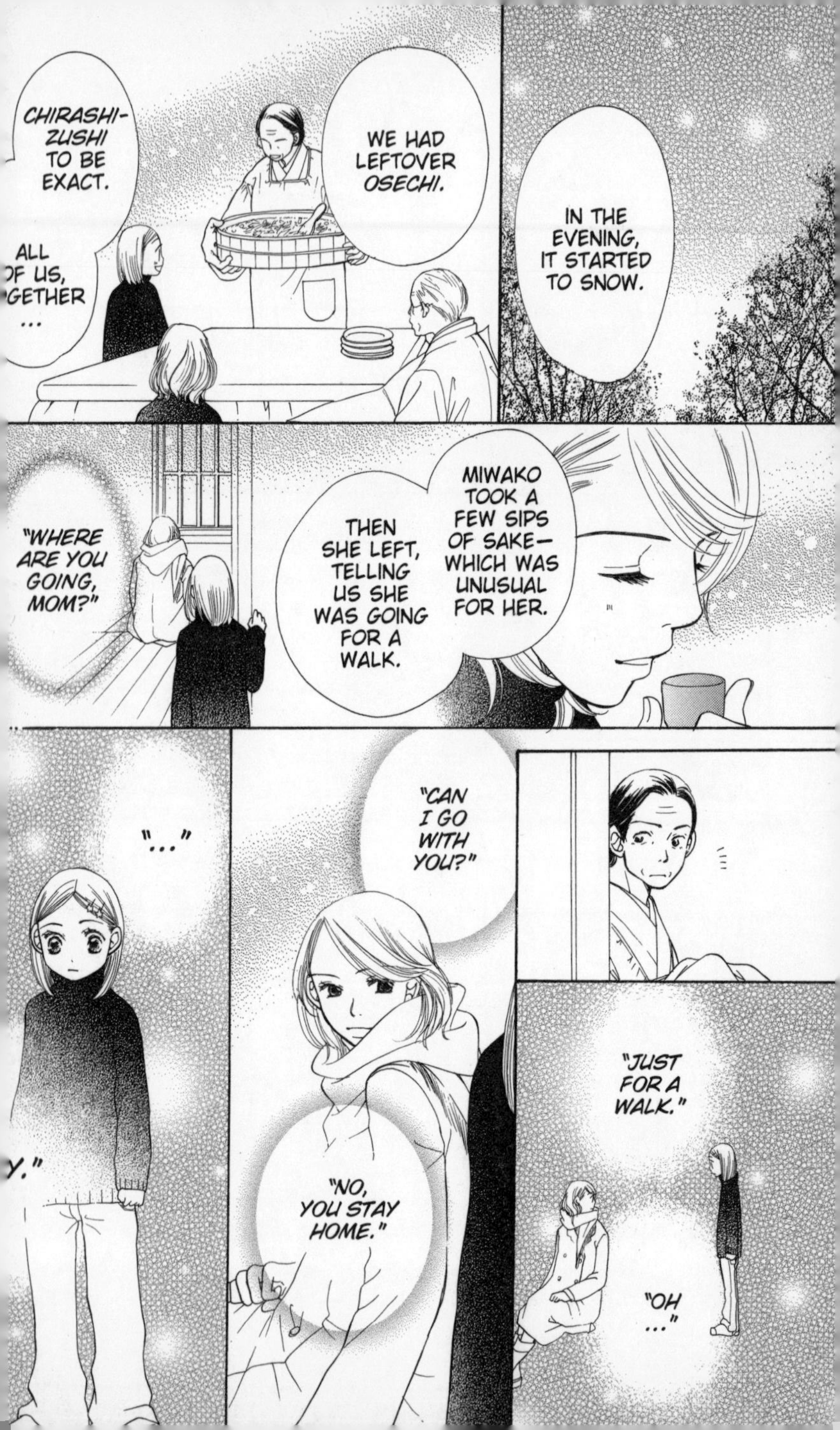
IN THE EVENING, IT STARTED TO SNOW.
WE HAD LEFTOVER OSECHI.
CHIRASHI-ZUSHI TO BE EXACT.
ALL
F US,
GETHER ...
MIWAKO TOOK A FEW SIPS OF SAKE— WHICH WAS UNUSUAL FOR HER.
THEN SHE LEFT, TELLING US SHE WAS GOING FOR A WALK.
"WHERE ARE YOU GOING, MOM?"
"JUST FOR A WALK."
"OH ..."
"CAN I GO WITH YOU?"
"NO, YOU STAY HOME."
"..."
Y."

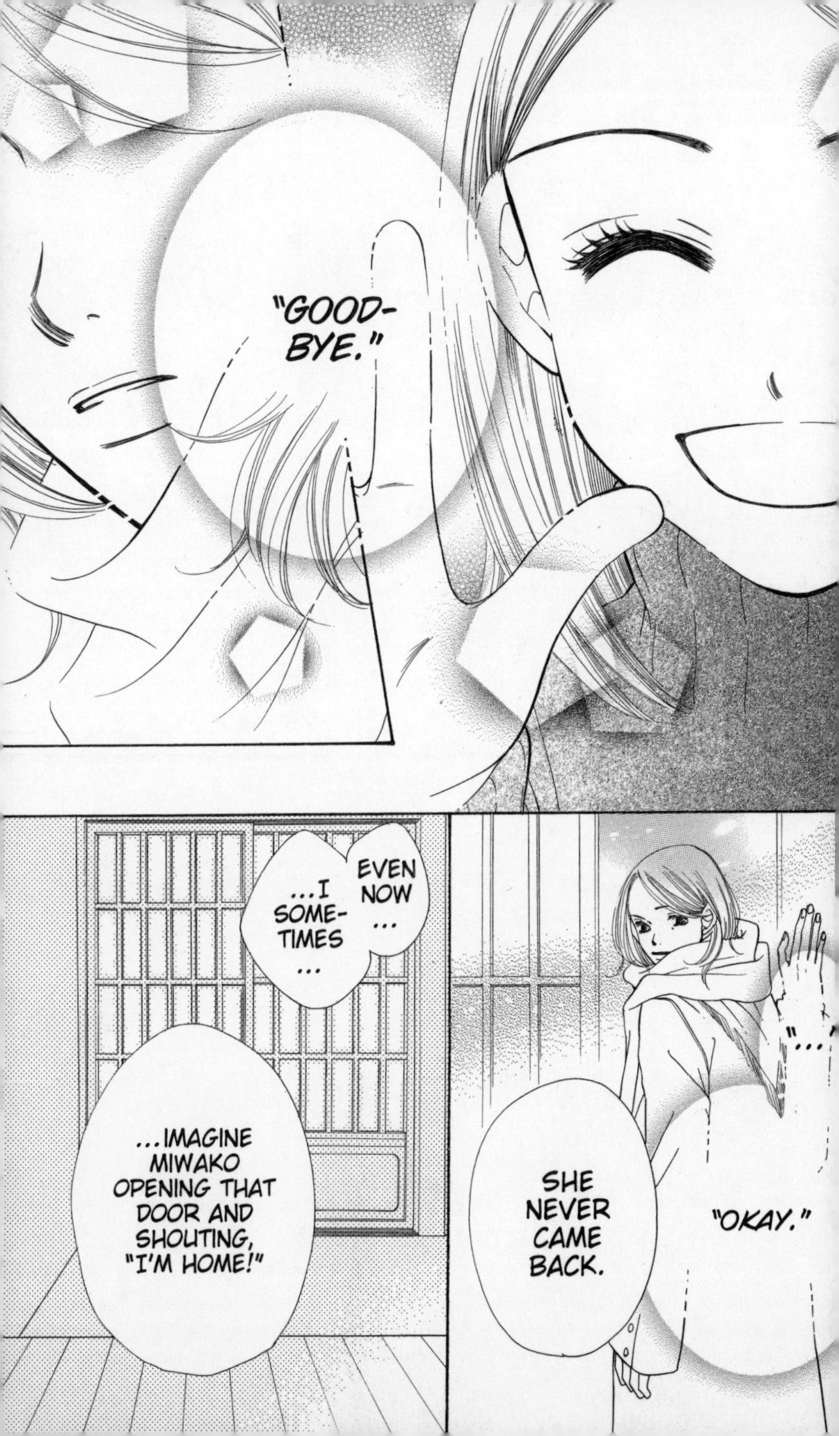
"GOOD-BYE."
"..."
"OKAY."
SHE NEVER CAME BACK.
EVEN NOW ...
...I SOMETIMES ...
...IMAGINE MIWAKO OPENING THAT DOOR AND SHOUTING, "I'M HOME!"

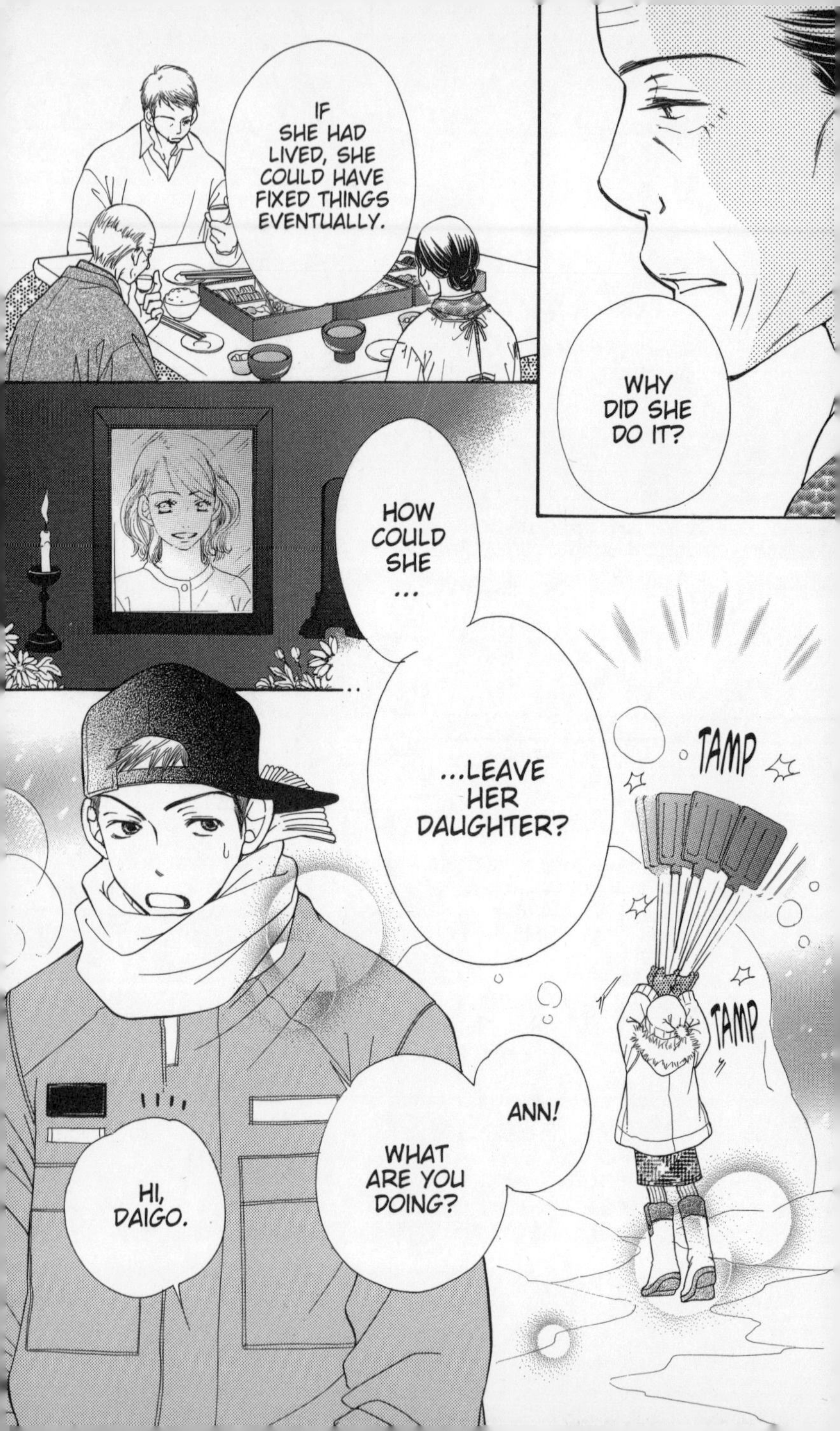
WHY DID SHE DO IT?
IF SHE HAD LIVED, SHE COULD HAVE FIXED THINGS EVENTUALLY.
HOW COULD SHE ...
...LEAVE HER DAUGHTER?
TAMP
TAMP
ANN!
WHAT ARE YOU DOING?
HI, DAIGO.

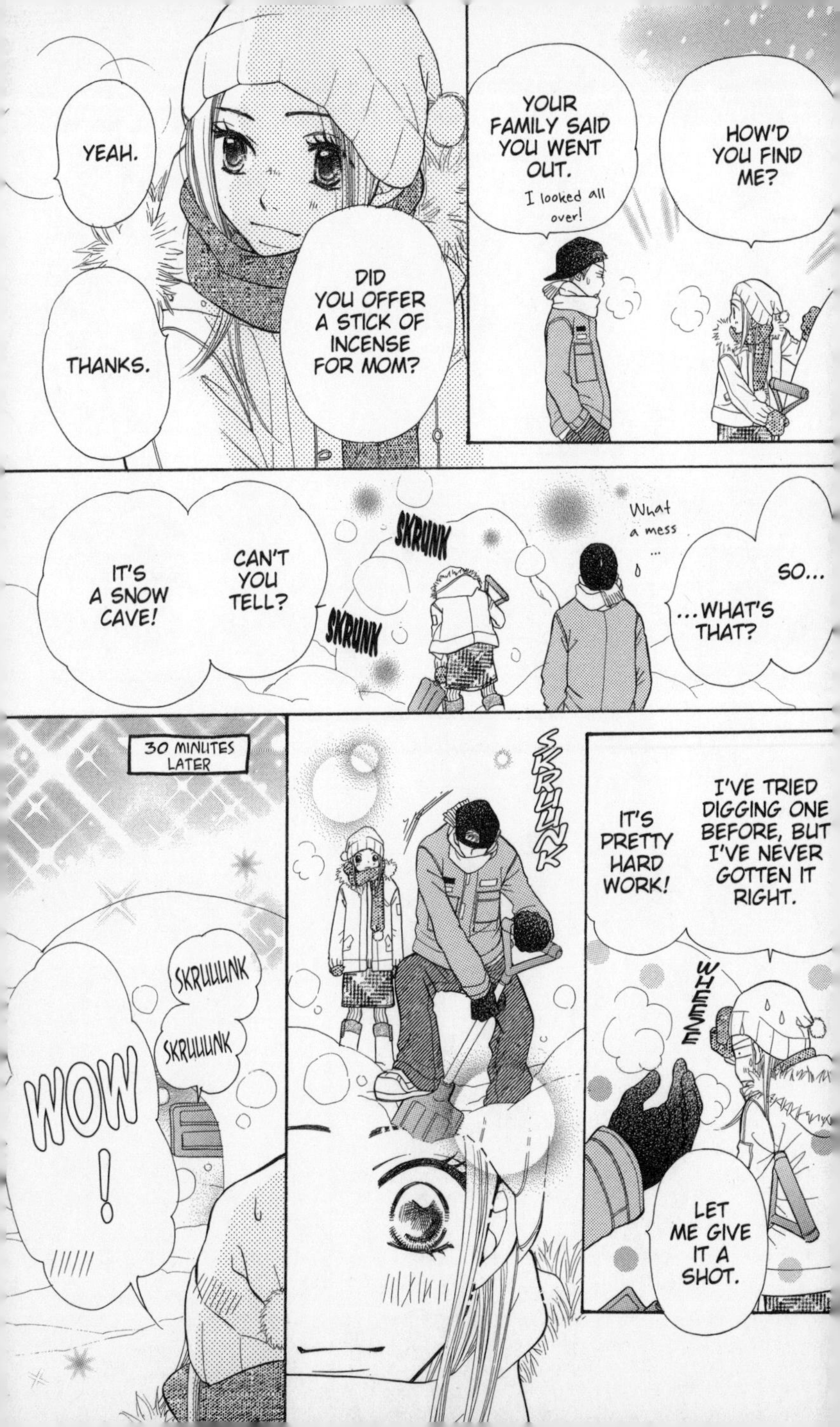
HOW'D YOU FIND ME?
YOUR FAMILY SAID YOU WENT OUT.
I looked all over!
DID YOU OFFER A STICK OF INCENSE FOR MOM?
YEAH.
THANKS.
SO...
...WHAT'S THAT?
What a mess ...
SKRUNK
SKRUNK
CAN'T YOU TELL?
IT'S A SNOW CAVE!
I'VE TRIED DIGGING ONE BEFORE, BUT I'VE NEVER GOTTEN IT RIGHT.
IT'S PRETTY HARD WORK!
WHEEZE
LET ME GIVE IT A SHOT.
SKRUNK
30 MINUTES LATER
SKRUUUNK
SKRUUUNK
WOW
!

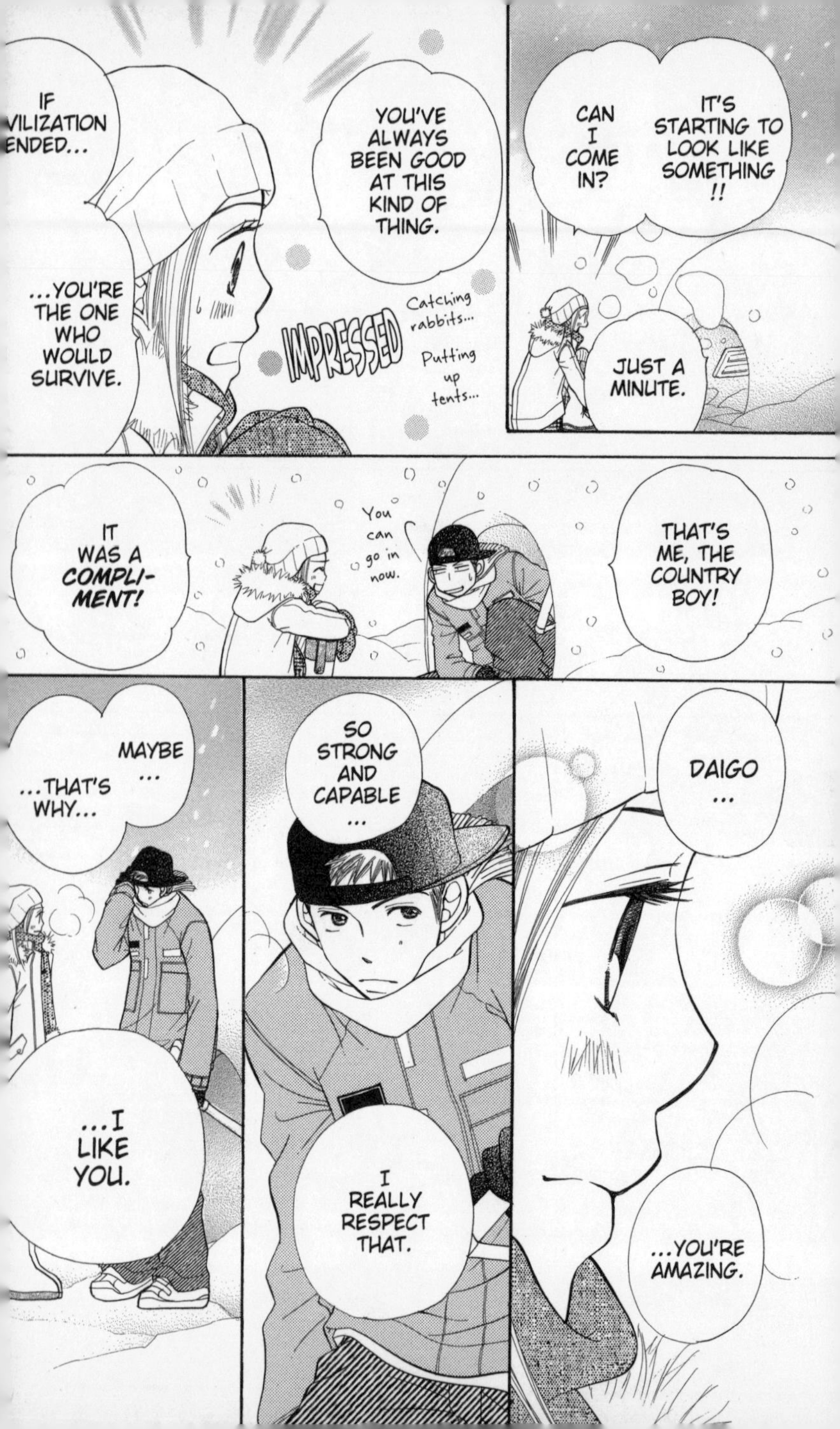
IT'S STARTING TO LOOK LIKE SOMETHING !!
CAN I COME IN?
JUST A MINUTE.
YOU'VE ALWAYS BEEN GOOD AT THIS KIND OF THING.
Catching rabbits... Putting up tents...
IMPRESSED
IF VILIZATION ENDED...
...YOU'RE THE ONE WHO WOULD SURVIVE.
THAT'S ME, THE COUNTRY BOY!
You can go in now.
IT WAS A COMPLIMENT!
DAIGO ...
...YOU'RE AMAZING.
SO STRONG AND CAPABLE ...
I REALLY RESPECT THAT.
MAYBE ...
...THAT'S WHY...
...I LIKE YOU.

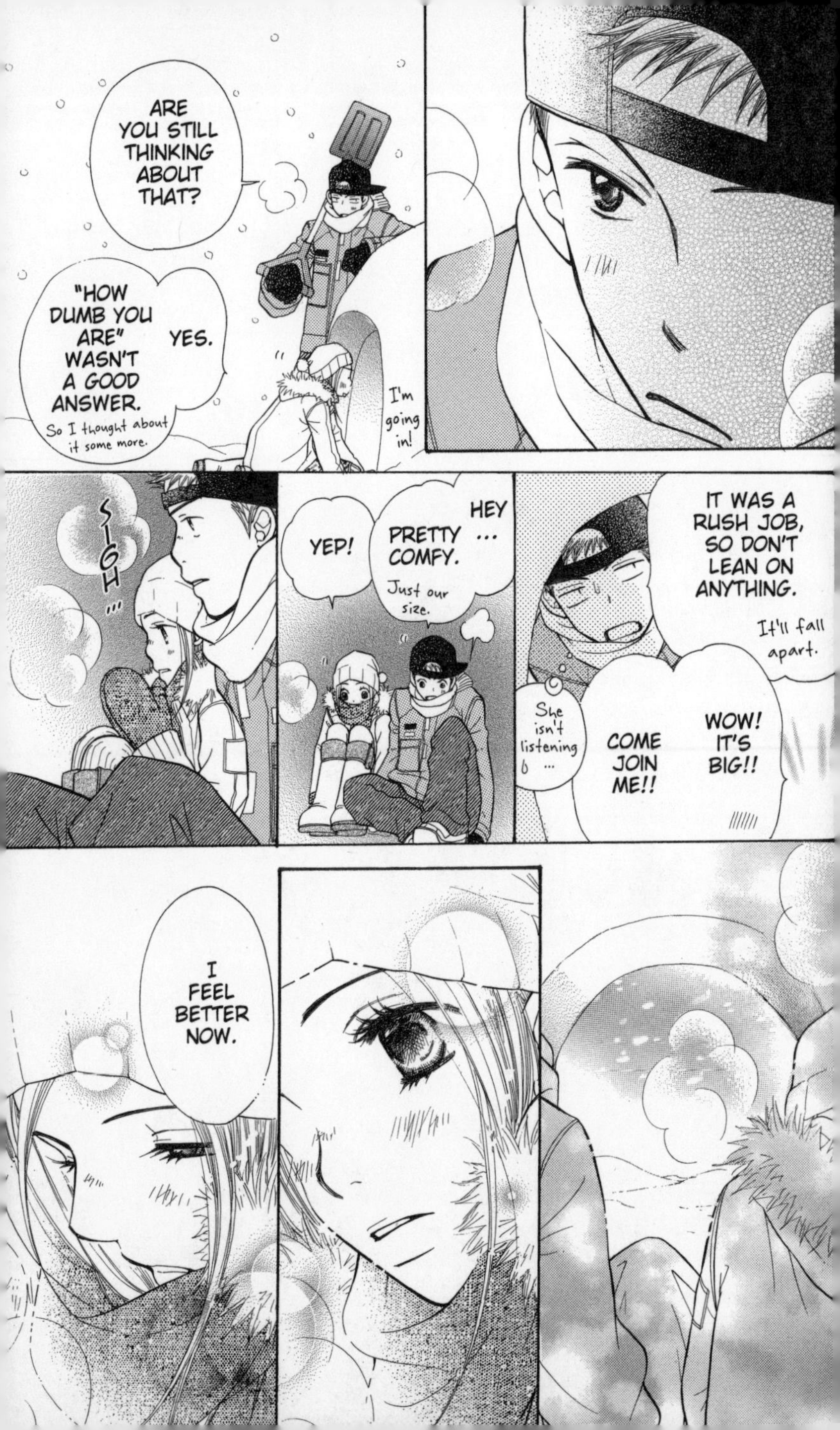
I'm going in!
ARE YOU STILL THINKING ABOUT THAT?
YES.
"HOW DUMB YOU ARE" WASN'T A GOOD ANSWER.
So I thought about it some more.
IT WAS A RUSH JOB, SO DON'T LEAN ON ANYTHING.
It'll fall apart.
WOW! IT'S BIG!!
COME JOIN ME!!
She isn't listening...
HEY...
PRETTY COMFY.
Just our size.
YEP!
SIGH...
I FEEL BETTER NOW.

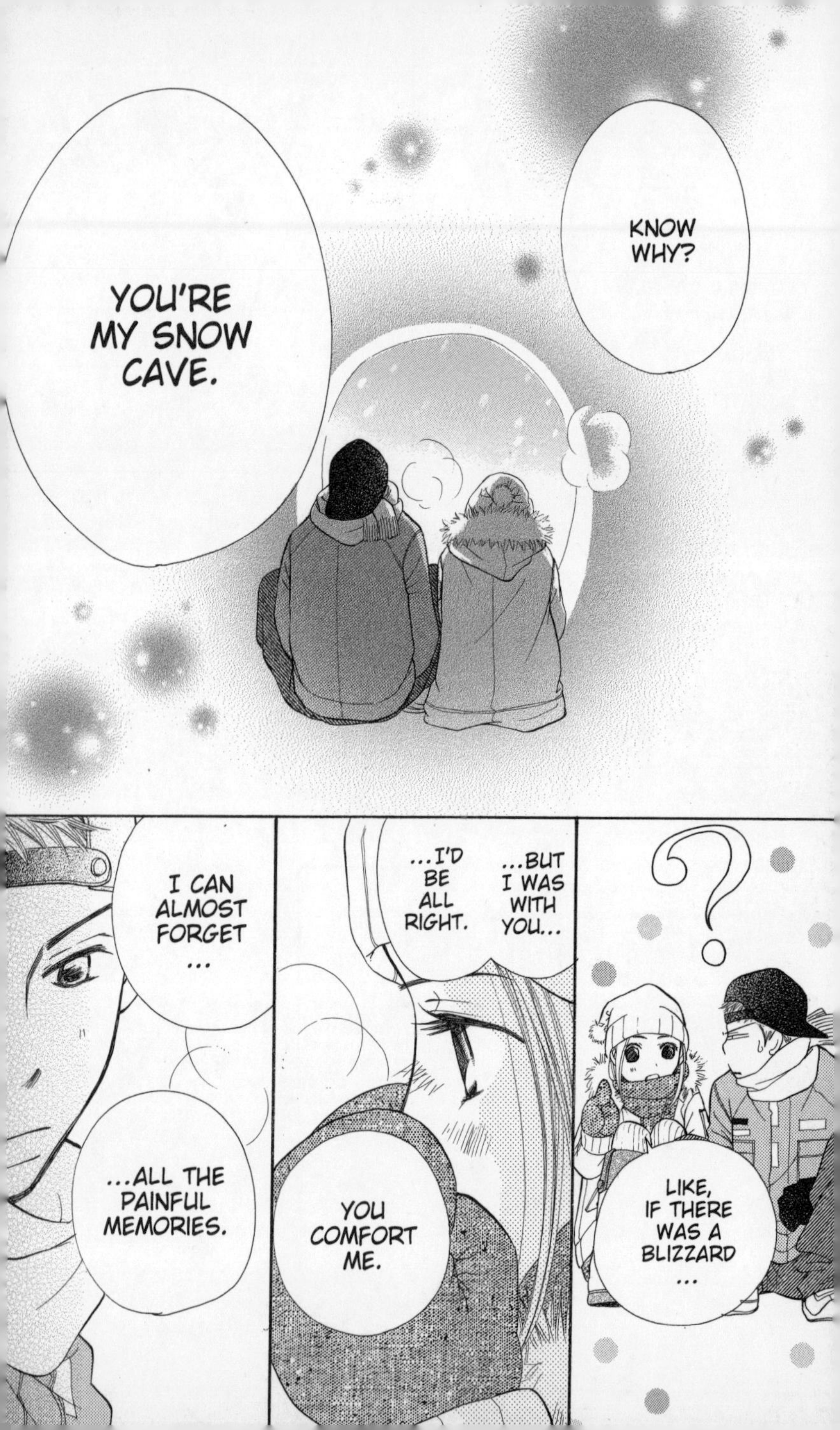
KNOW WHY?
YOU'RE MY SNOW CAVE.
LIKE, IF THERE WAS A BLIZZARD ...
...BUT I WAS WITH YOU...
...I'D BE ALL RIGHT.
YOU COMFORT ME.
I CAN ALMOST FORGET ...
...ALL THE PAINFUL MEMORIES.

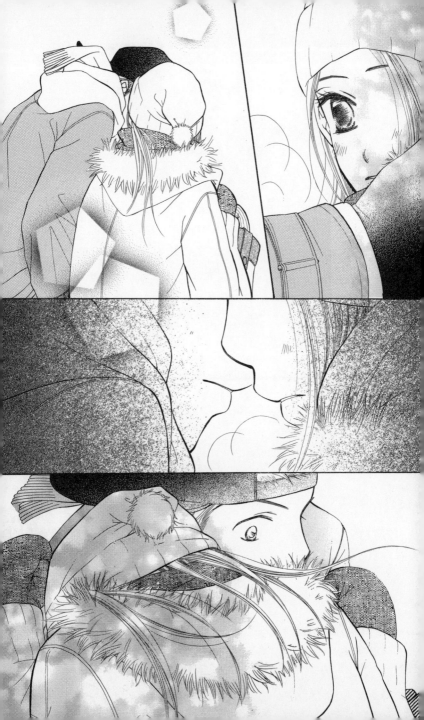

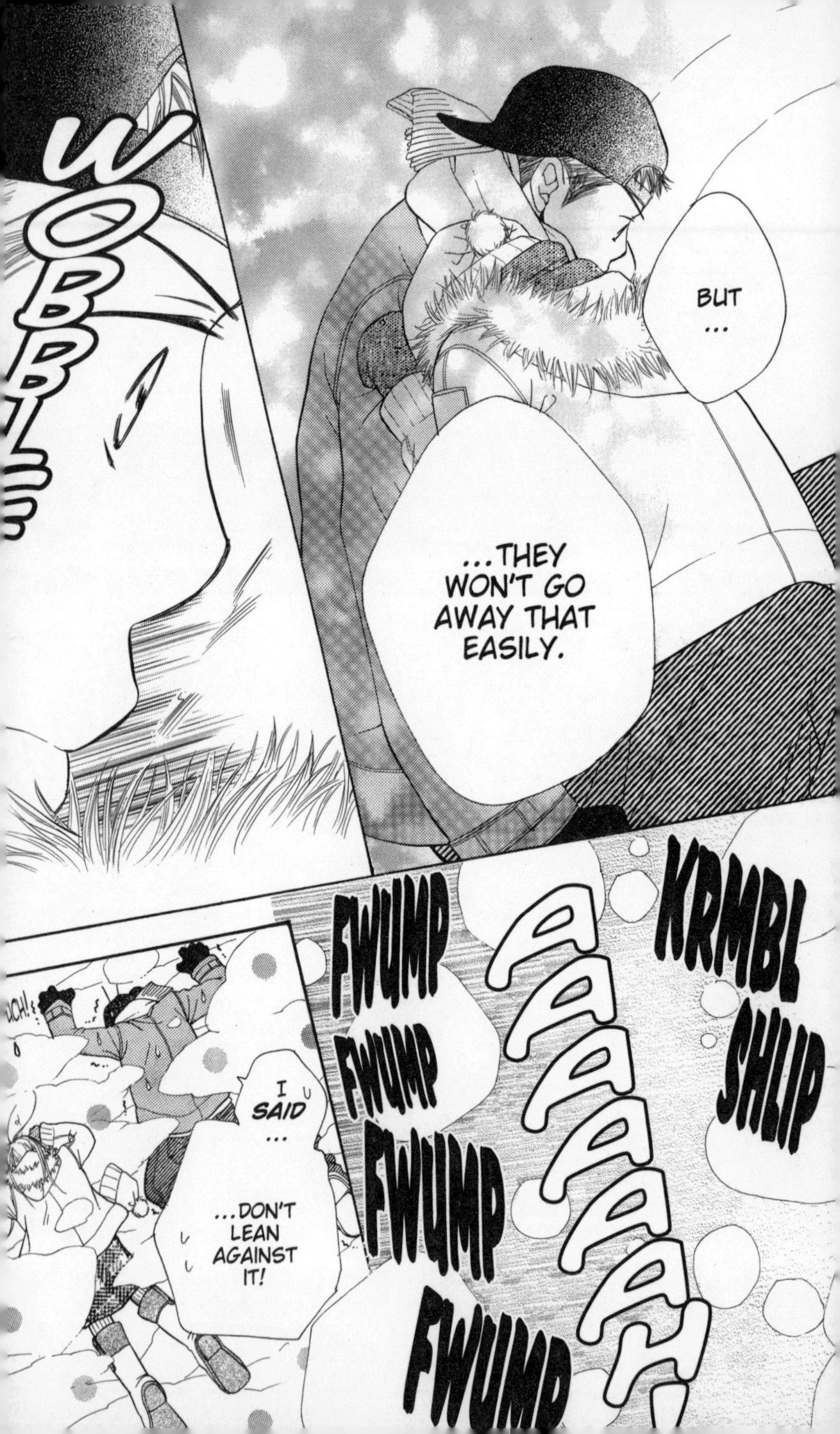

BUT ...
...THEY WON'T GO AWAY THAT EASILY.
WOBBL
KRMBL
SHLIP
AAAAAAAH
FWUMP
FWUMP
FWUMP
FWUMP
I SAID ...
...DON'T LEAN AGAINST IT!

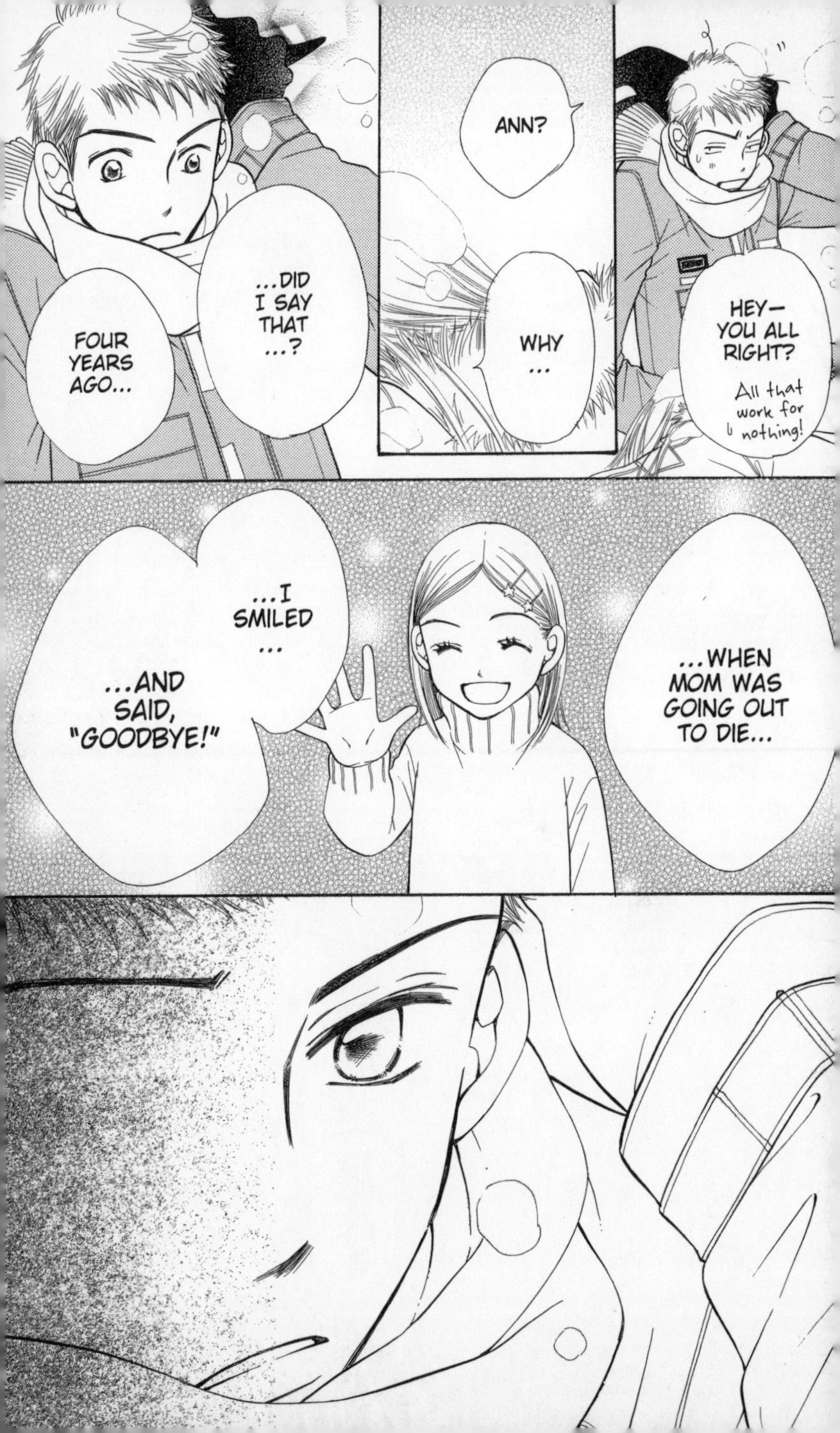
HEY— YOU ALL RIGHT?
All that work for nothing!
ANN?
WHY ...
...DID I SAY THAT ...?
FOUR YEARS AGO...
...WHEN MOM WAS GOING OUT TO DIE...
...I SMILED ...
...AND SAID, "GOODBYE!"

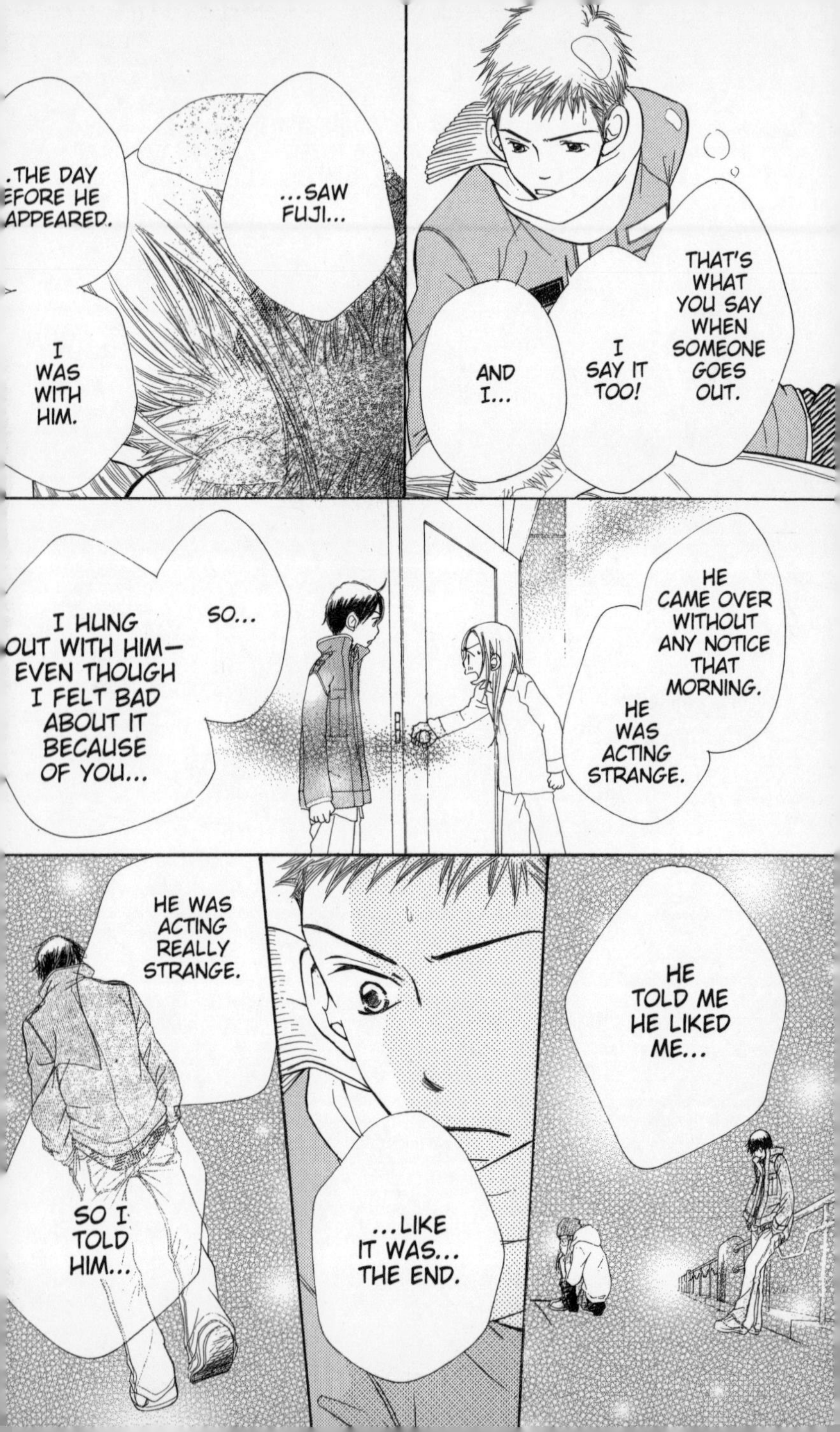
THAT'S WHAT YOU SAY WHEN SOMEONE GOES OUT.
I SAY IT TOO!
AND I...
...SAW FUJI...
.THE DAY EFORE HE APPEARED.
I WAS WITH HIM.
HE CAME OVER WITHOUT ANY NOTICE THAT MORNING.
HE WAS ACTING STRANGE.
SO...
I HUNG OUT WITH HIM—EVEN THOUGH I FELT BAD ABOUT IT BECAUSE OF YOU...
HE TOLD ME HE LIKED ME...
...LIKE IT WAS... THE END.
HE WAS ACTING REALLY STRANGE.
SO I TOLD HIM...

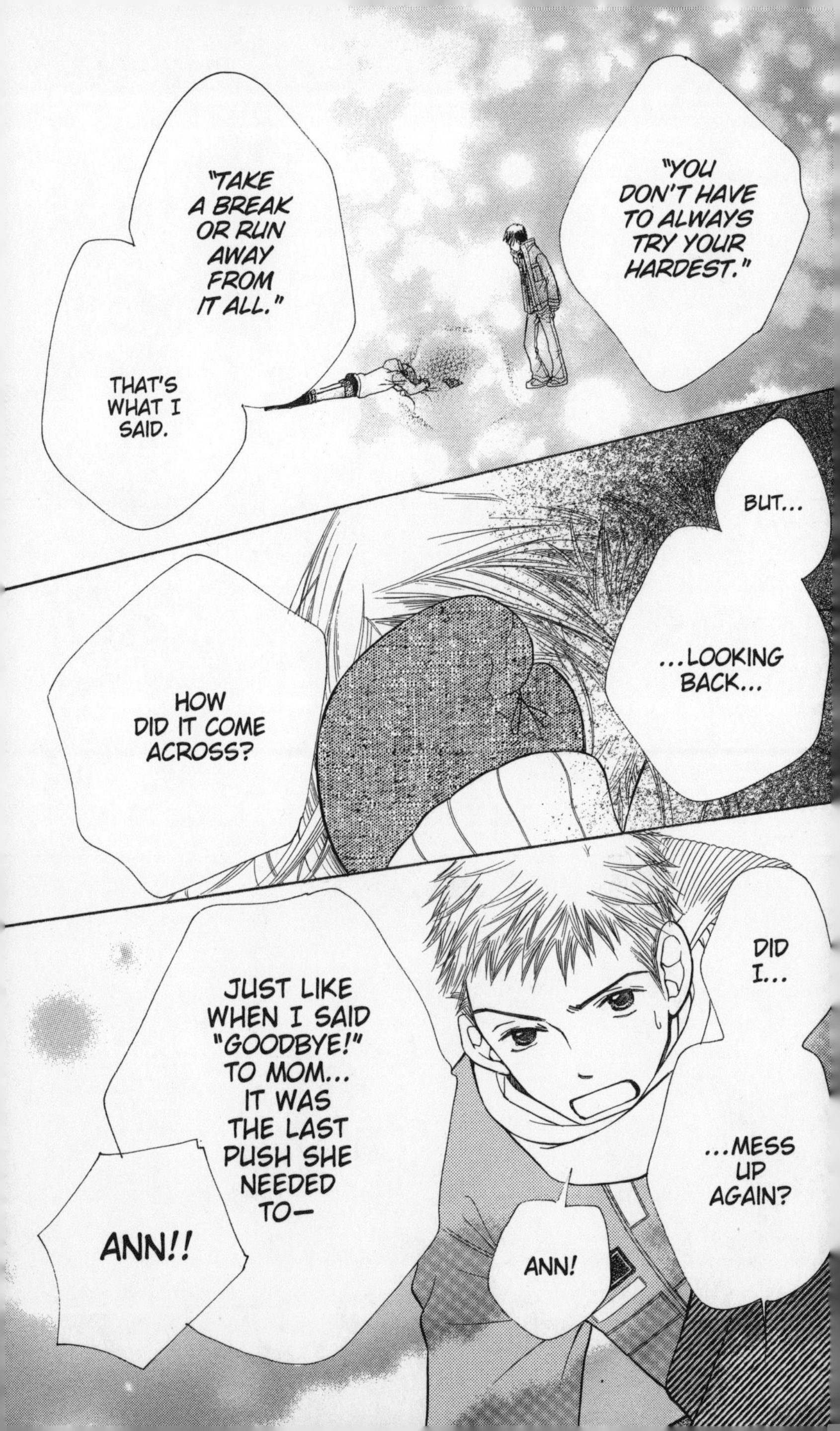
"YOU DON'T HAVE TO ALWAYS TRY YOUR HARDEST."
"TAKE A BREAK OR RUN AWAY FROM IT ALL."
THAT'S WHAT I SAID.
BUT...
...LOOKING BACK...
HOW DID IT COME ACROSS?
DID I...
...MESS UP AGAIN?
JUST LIKE WHEN I SAID "GOODBYE!" TO MOM... IT WAS THE LAST PUSH SHE NEEDED TO–
ANN!
ANN!!

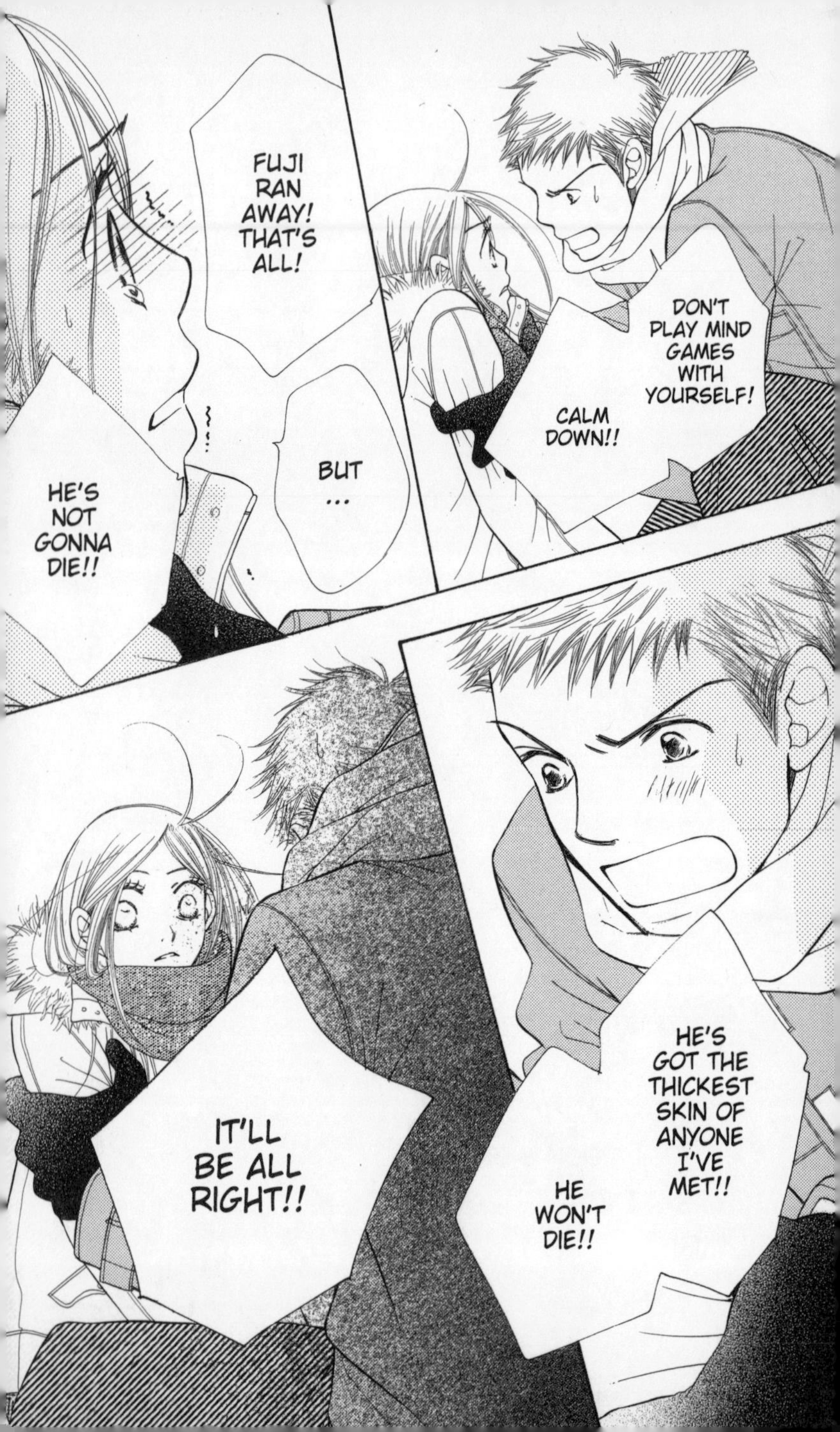
DON'T PLAY MIND GAMES WITH YOURSELF!
CALM DOWN!!
FUJI RAN AWAY! THAT'S ALL!
BUT ...
HE'S NOT GONNA DIE!!
HE'S GOT THE THICKEST SKIN OF ANYONE I'VE MET!!
HE WON'T DIE!!
IT'LL BE ALL RIGHT!!

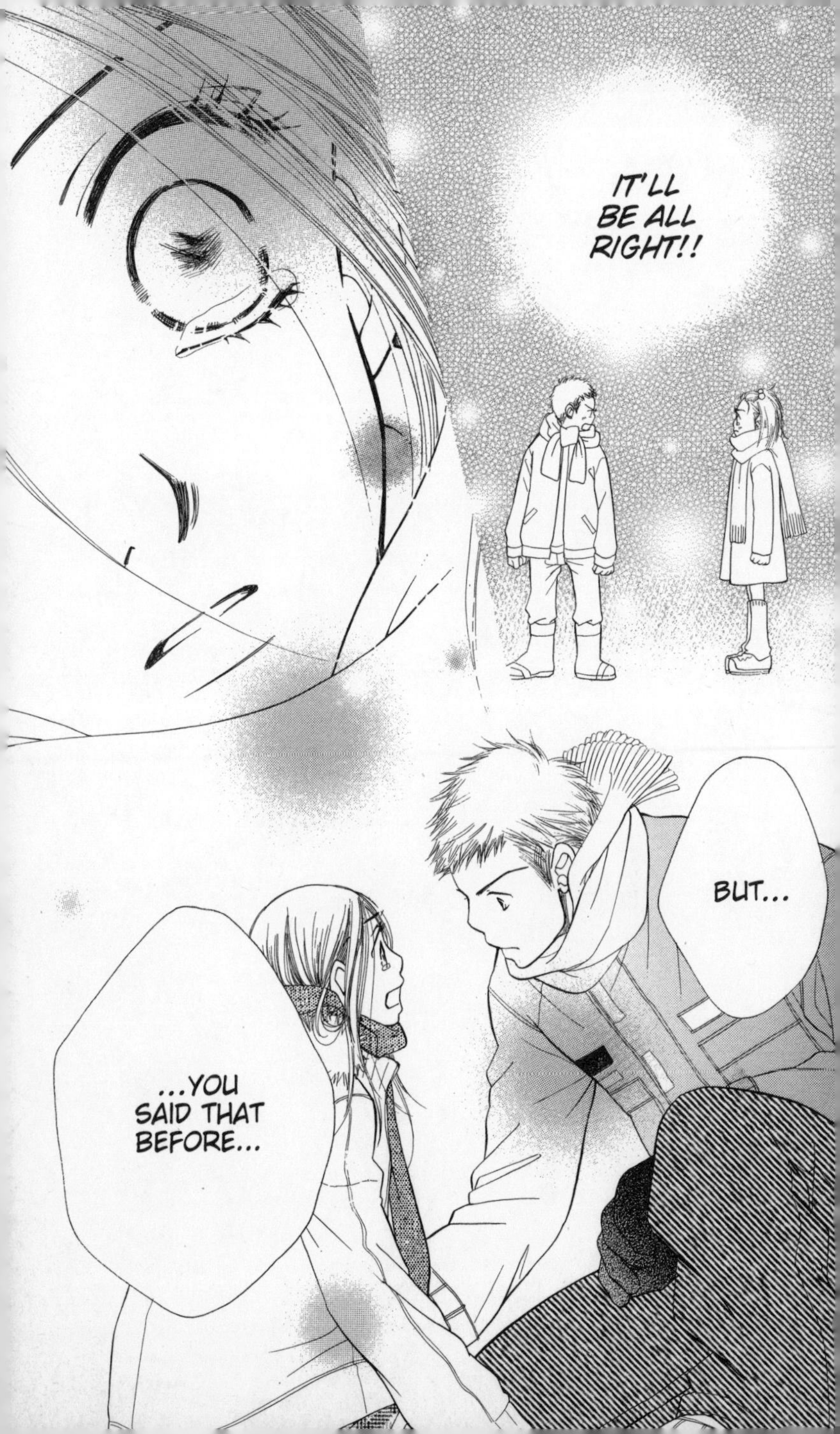
IT'LL BE ALL RIGHT!!
BUT...
...YOU SAID THAT BEFORE...

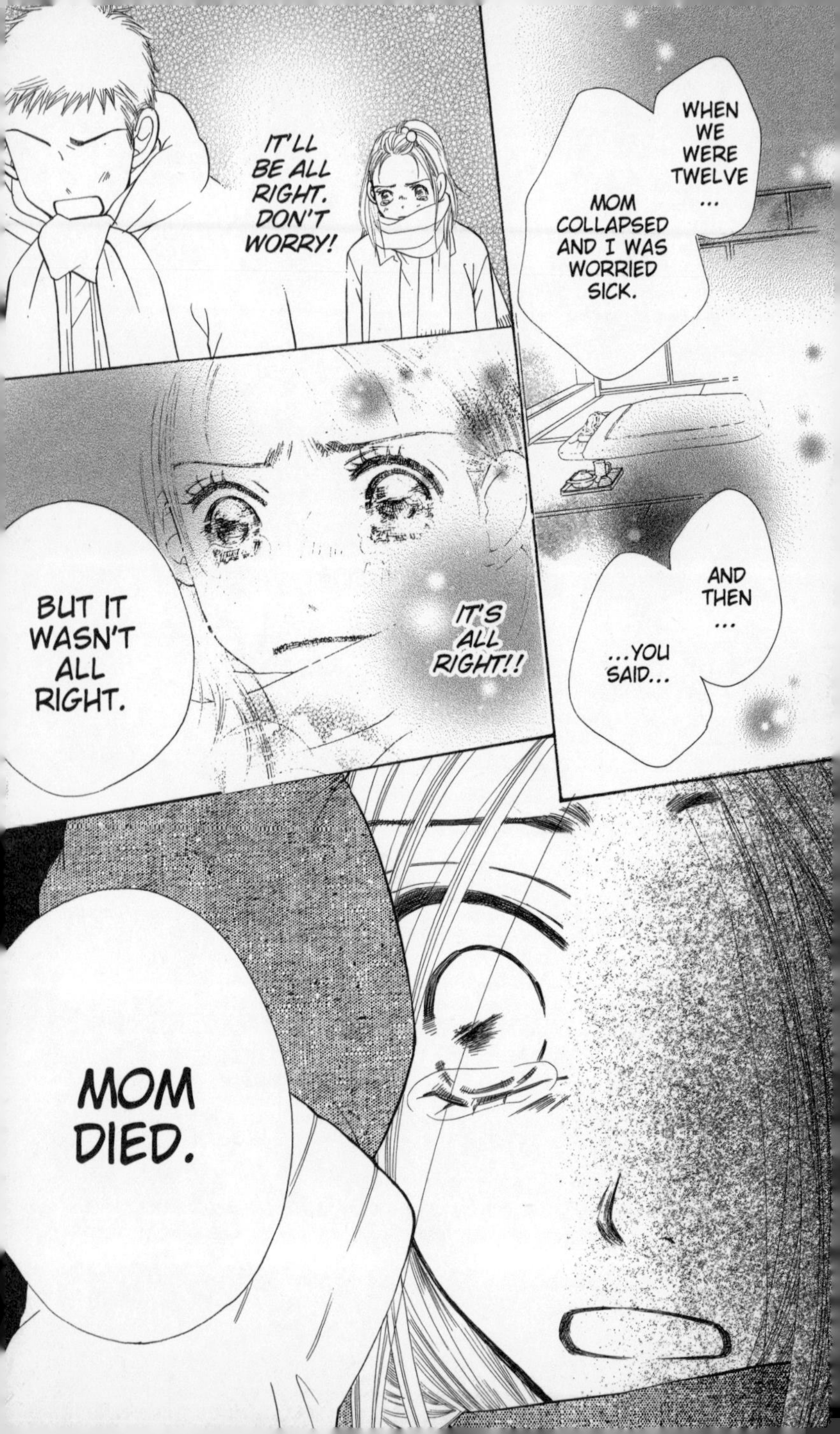
WHEN WE WERE TWELVE...
MOM COLLAPSED AND I WAS WORRIED SICK.
AND THEN...
...YOU SAID...
IT'LL BE ALL RIGHT. DON'T WORRY!
IT'S ALL RIGHT!!
BUT IT WASN'T ALL RIGHT.
MOM DIED.

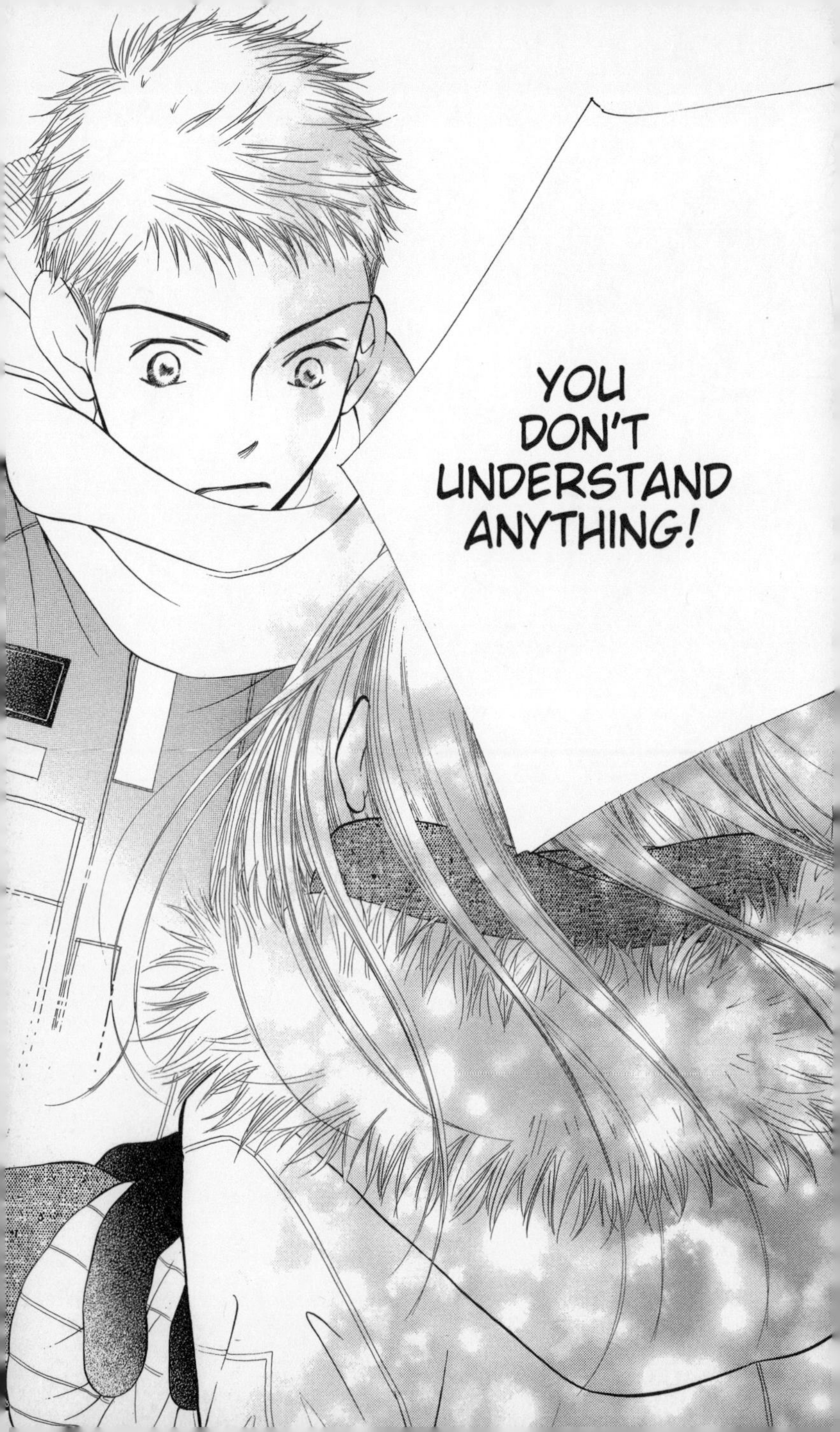
YOU DON'T UNDERSTAND ANYTHING!

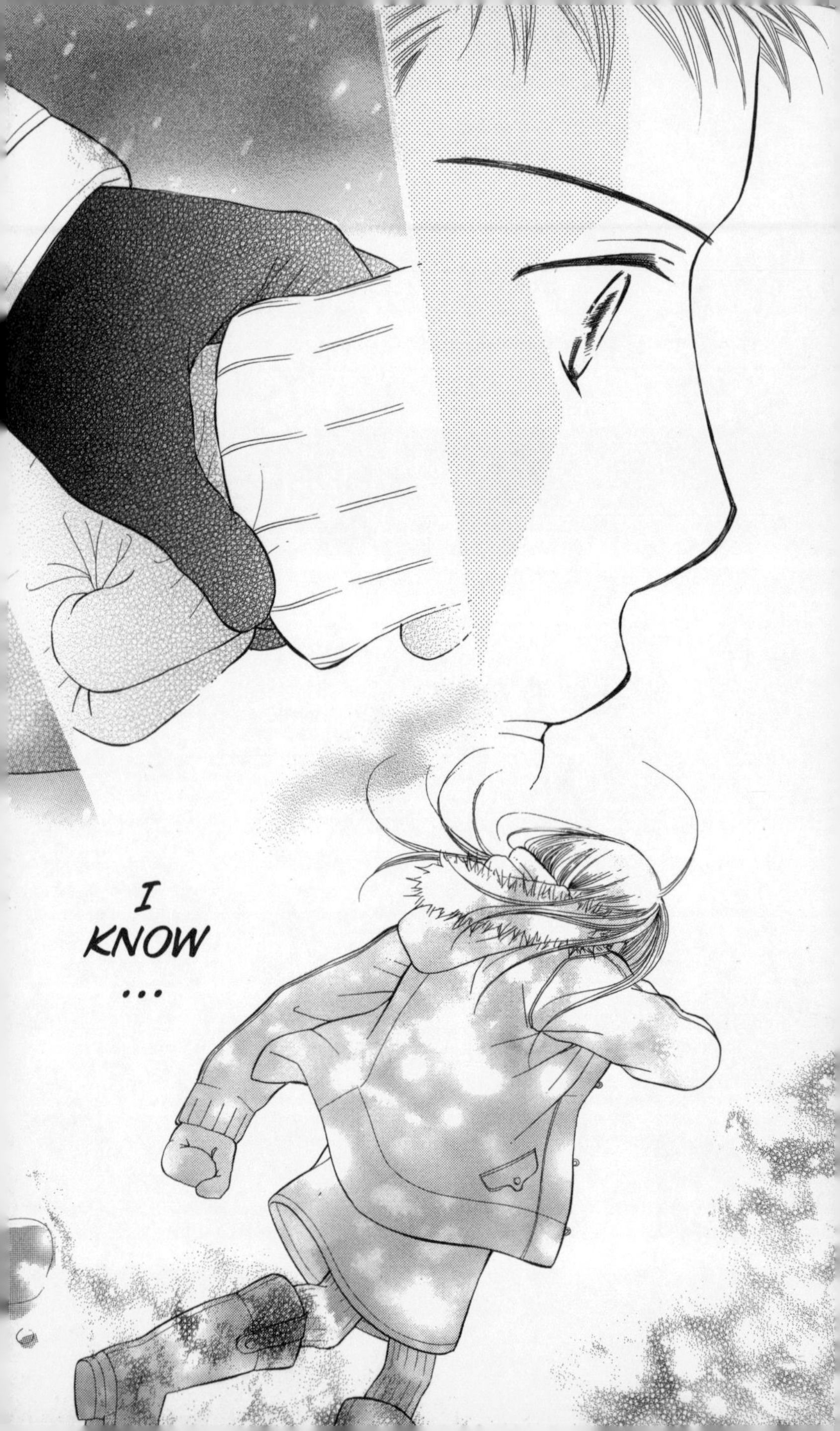
I KNOW ...

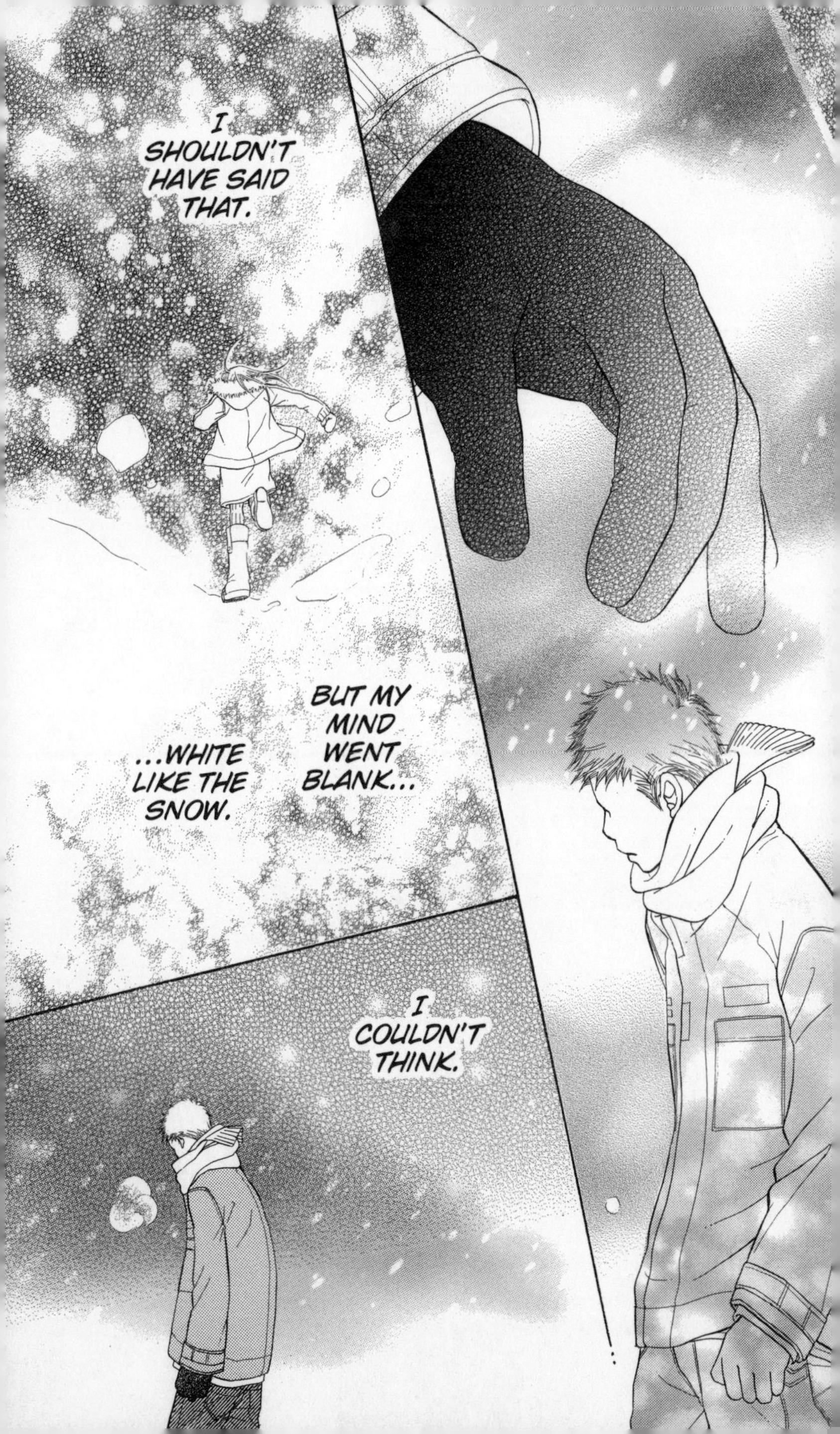
I SHOULDN'T HAVE SAID THAT.
BUT MY MIND WENT BLANK...
...WHITE LIKE THE SNOW.
I COULDN'T THINK.

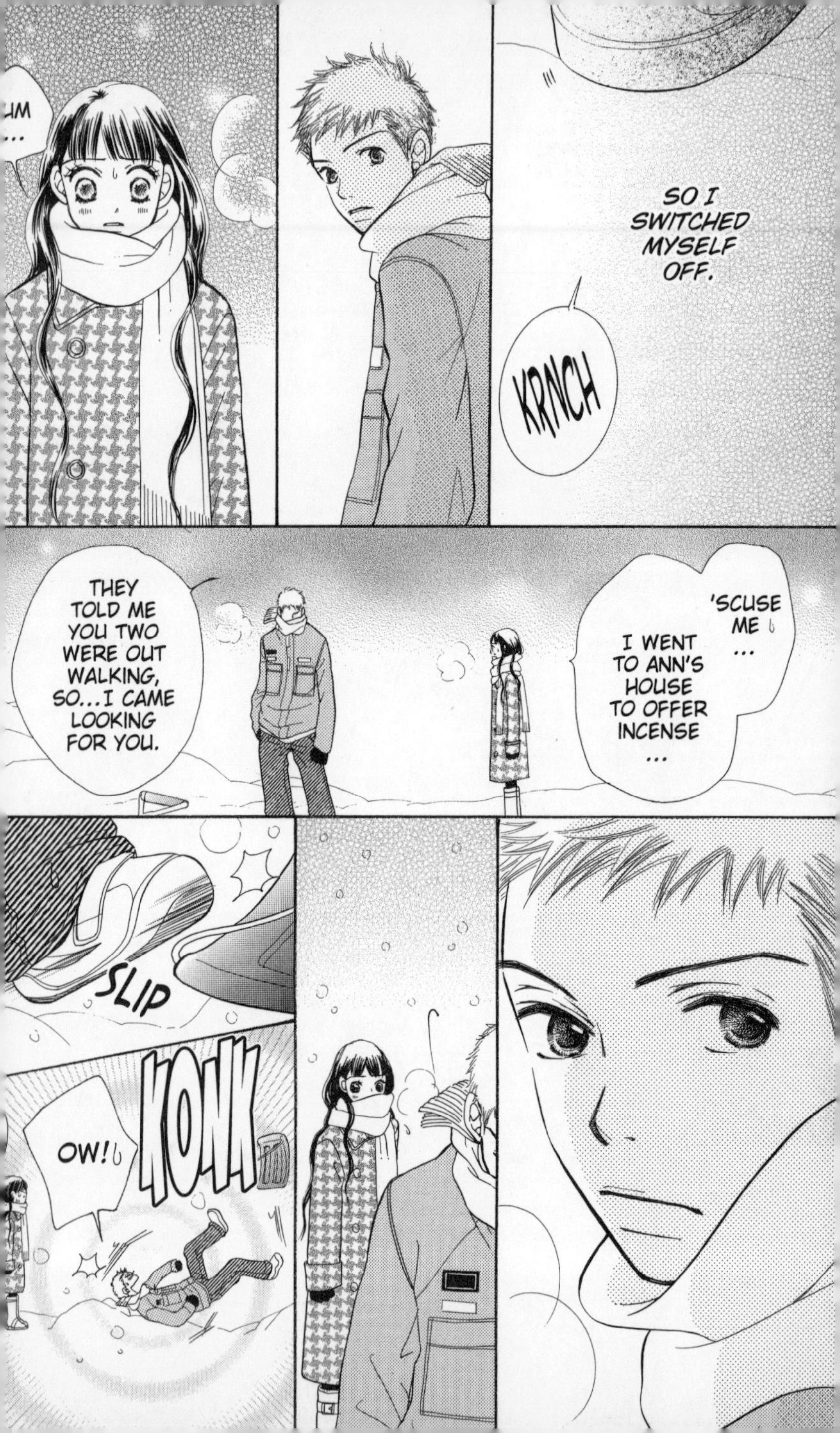
SO I SWITCHED MYSELF OFF.
KRNCH
HM ...
'SCUSE ME ...
I WENT TO ANN'S HOUSE TO OFFER INCENSE ...
THEY TOLD ME YOU TWO WERE OUT WALKING, SO...I CAME LOOKING FOR YOU.
SLIP
KONK
OW!

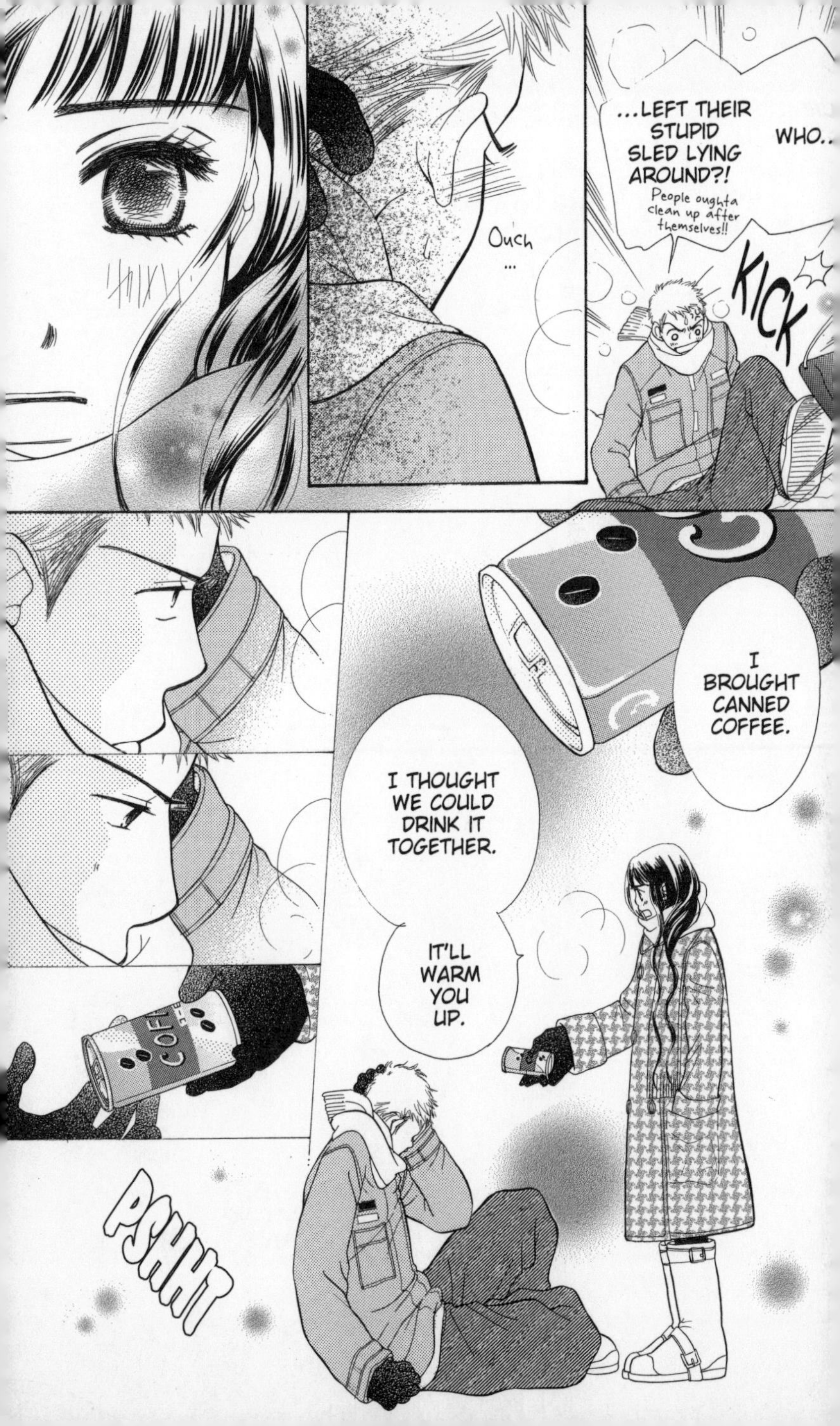
WHO...
...LEFT THEIR STUPID SLED LYING AROUND?!
People oughta clean up after themselves!!
KICK
Ouch ...
I BROUGHT CANNED COFFEE.
I THOUGHT WE COULD DRINK IT TOGETHER.
IT'LL WARM YOU UP.
PSHHT

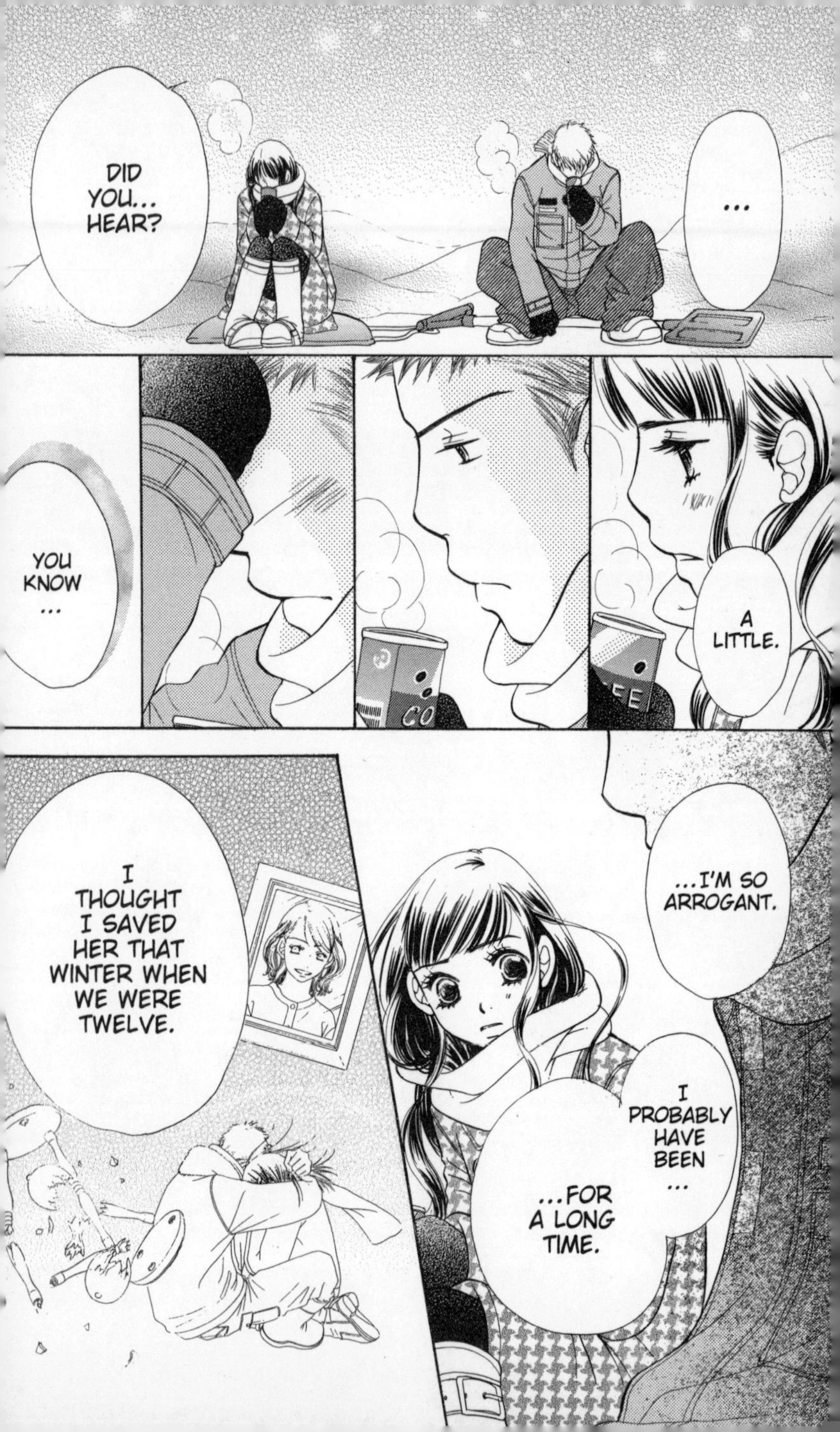
...
DID YOU... HEAR?
A LITTLE.
YOU KNOW ...
...I'M SO ARROGANT.
I PROBABLY HAVE BEEN ...
...FOR A LONG TIME.
I THOUGHT I SAVED HER THAT WINTER WHEN WE WERE TWELVE.

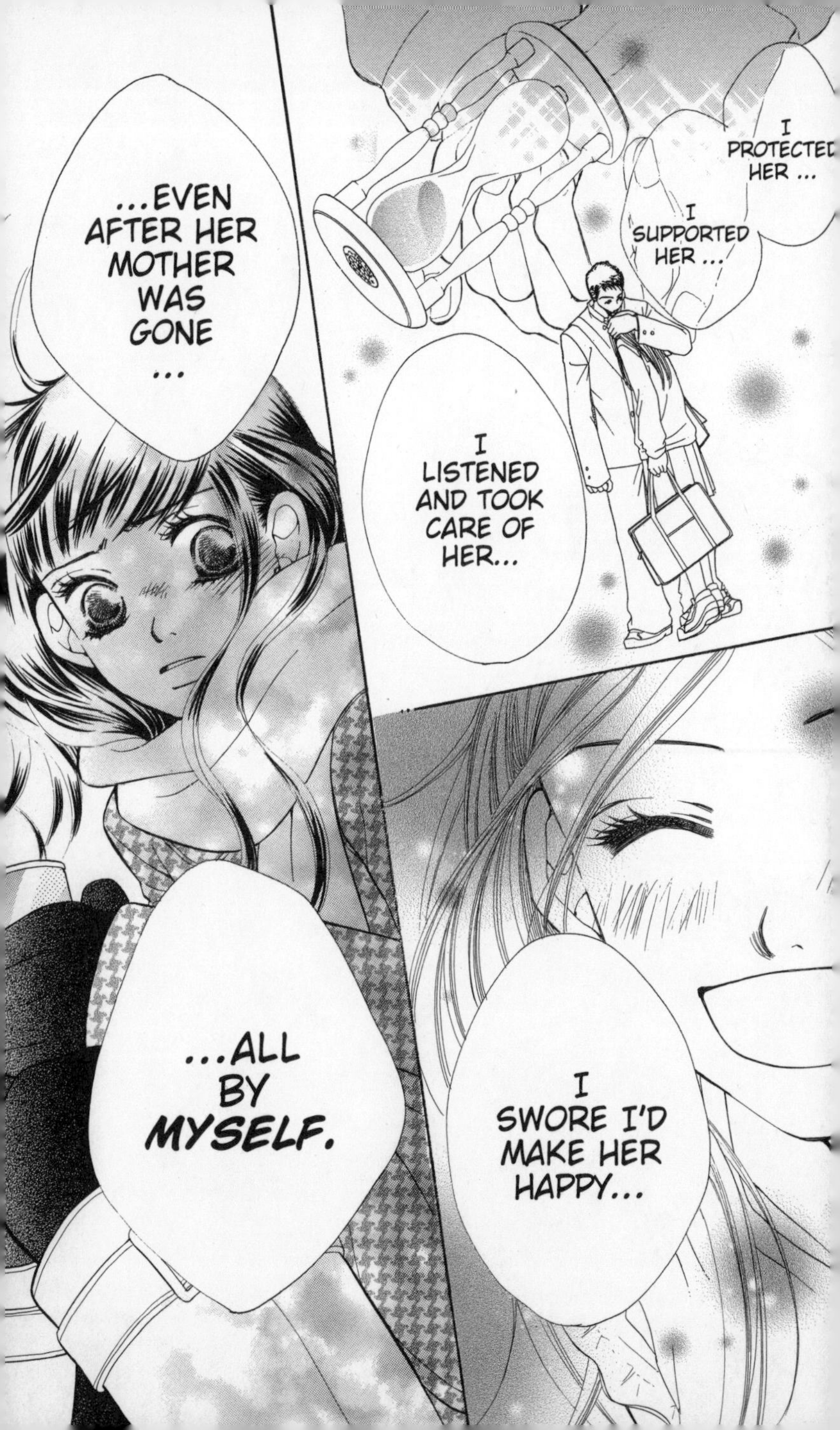
I PROTECTED HER ...
I SUPPORTED HER ...
I LISTENED AND TOOK CARE OF HER...
I SWORE I'D MAKE HER HAPPY...
...EVEN AFTER HER MOTHER WAS GONE ...
...ALL BY ***MYSELF.***

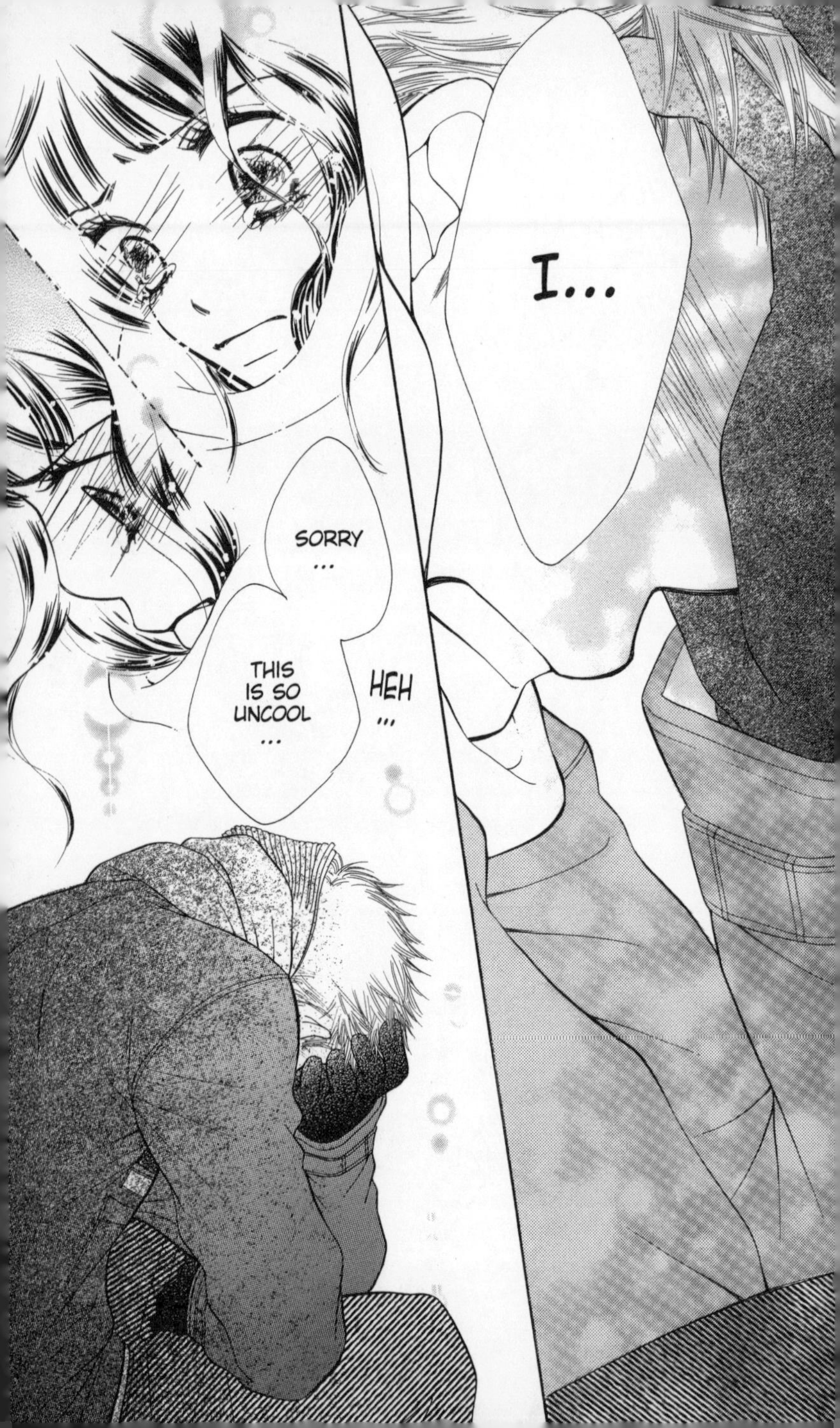
I...
SORRY ...
HEH ...
THIS IS SO UNCOOL ...

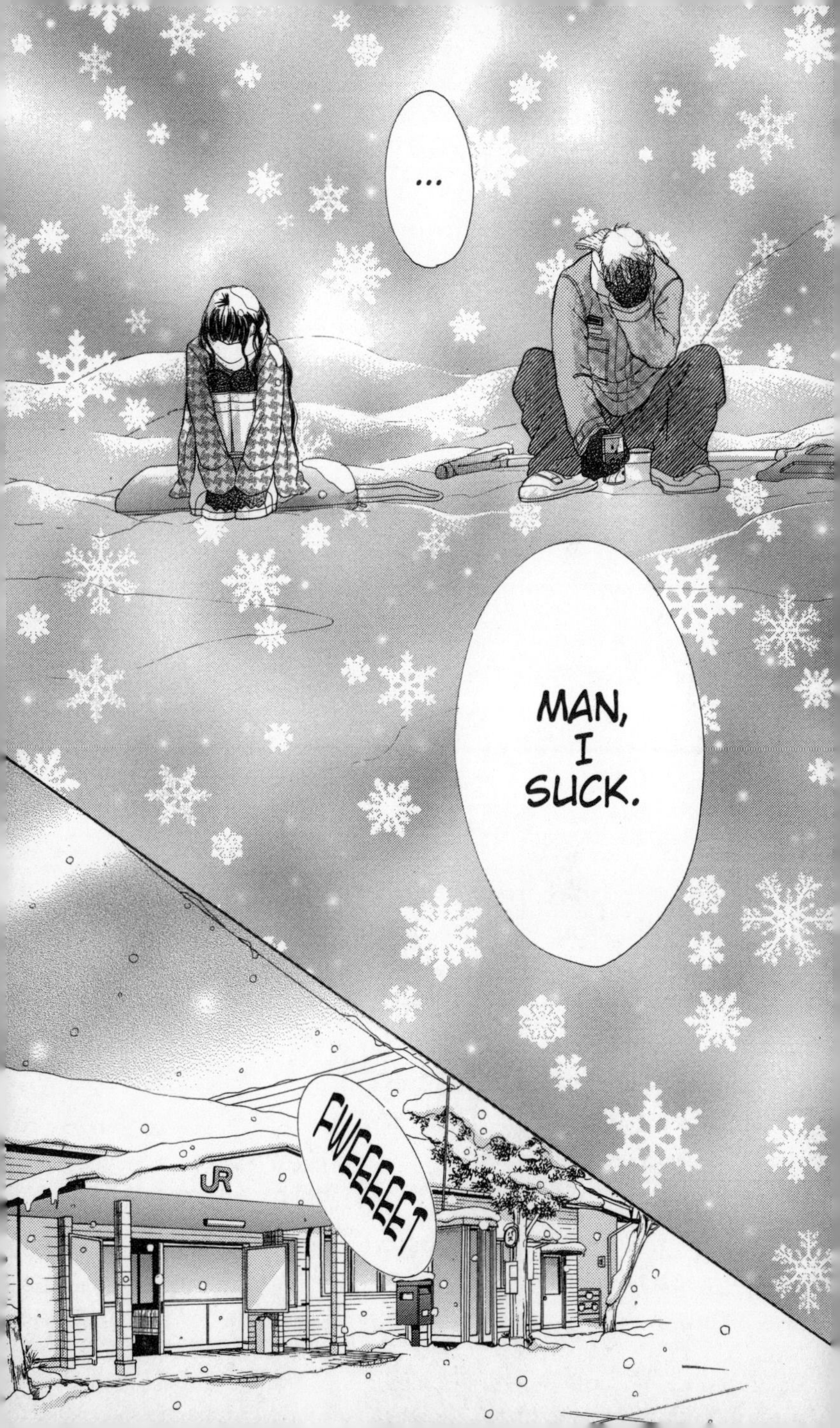
...
MAN, I SUCK.
FWEEEEET

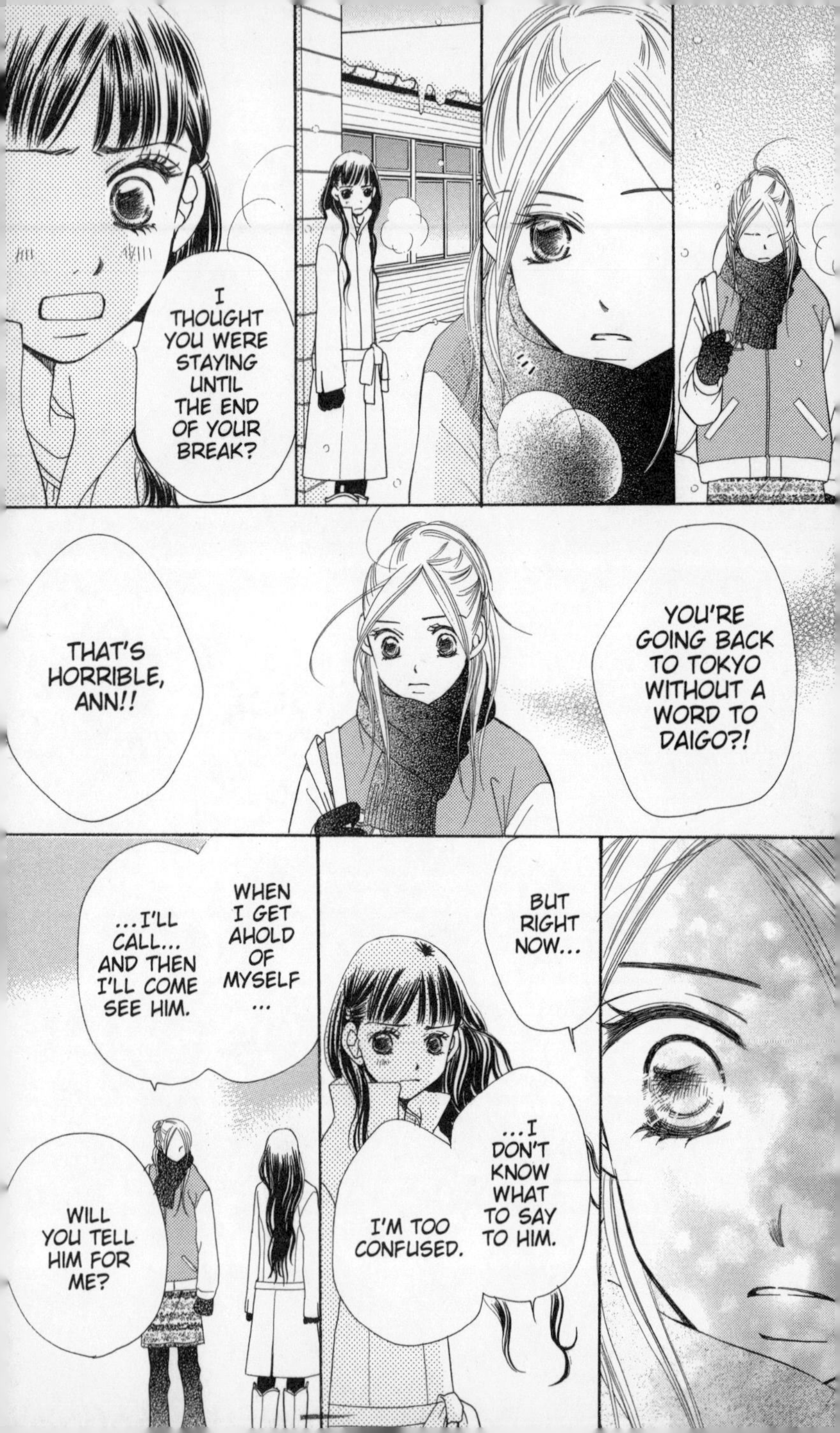
I THOUGHT YOU WERE STAYING UNTIL THE END OF YOUR BREAK?
YOU'RE GOING BACK TO TOKYO WITHOUT A WORD TO DAIGO?!
THAT'S HORRIBLE, ANN!!
BUT RIGHT NOW...
...I DON'T KNOW WHAT TO SAY TO HIM.
I'M TOO CONFUSED.
WHEN I GET AHOLD OF MYSELF ...
...I'LL CALL... AND THEN I'LL COME SEE HIM.
WILL YOU TELL HIM FOR ME?

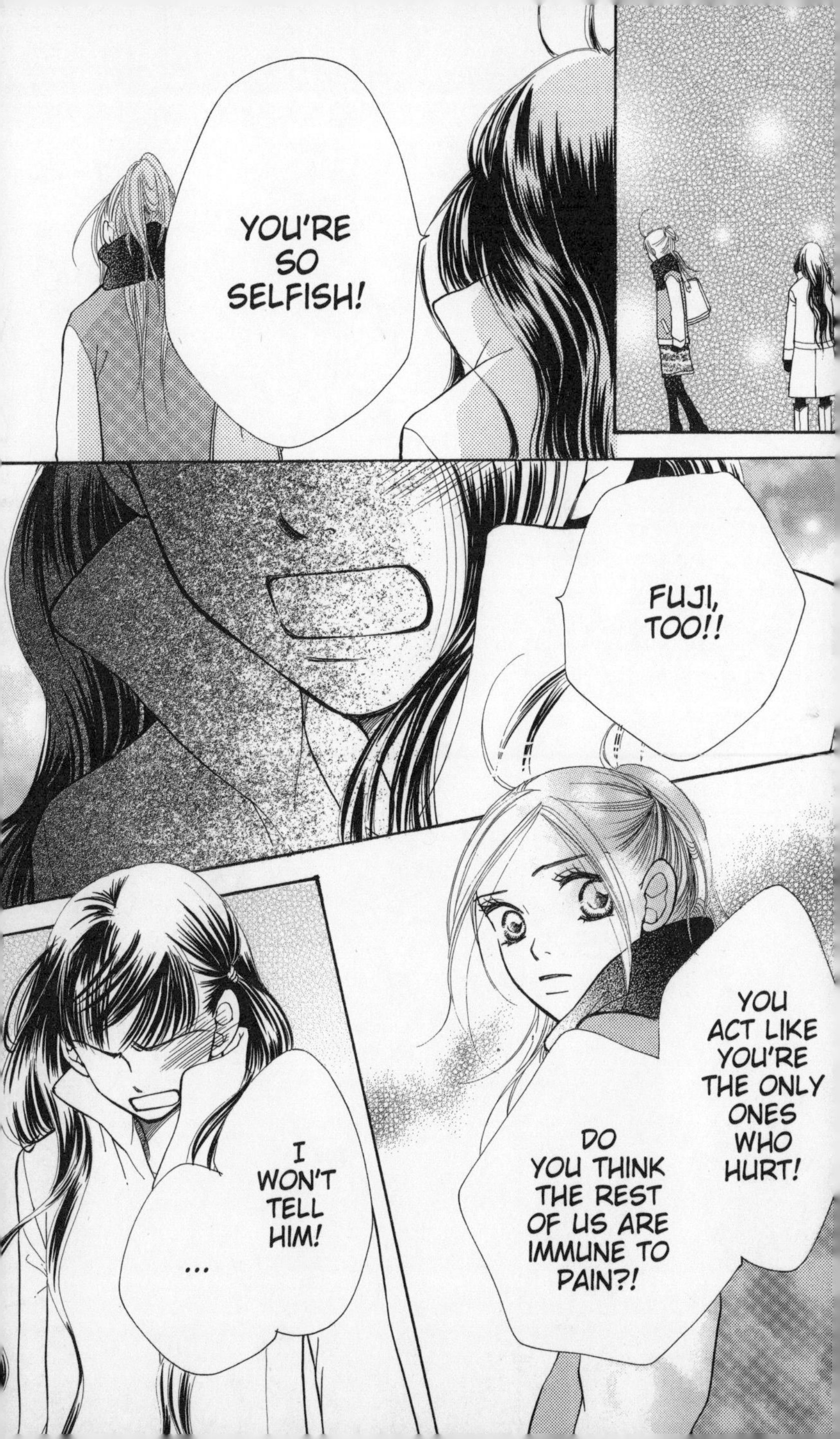
YOU'RE SO SELFISH!
FUJI, TOO!!
YOU ACT LIKE YOU'RE THE ONLY ONES WHO HURT!
DO YOU THINK THE REST OF US ARE IMMUNE TO PAIN?!
I WON'T TELL HIM!
...

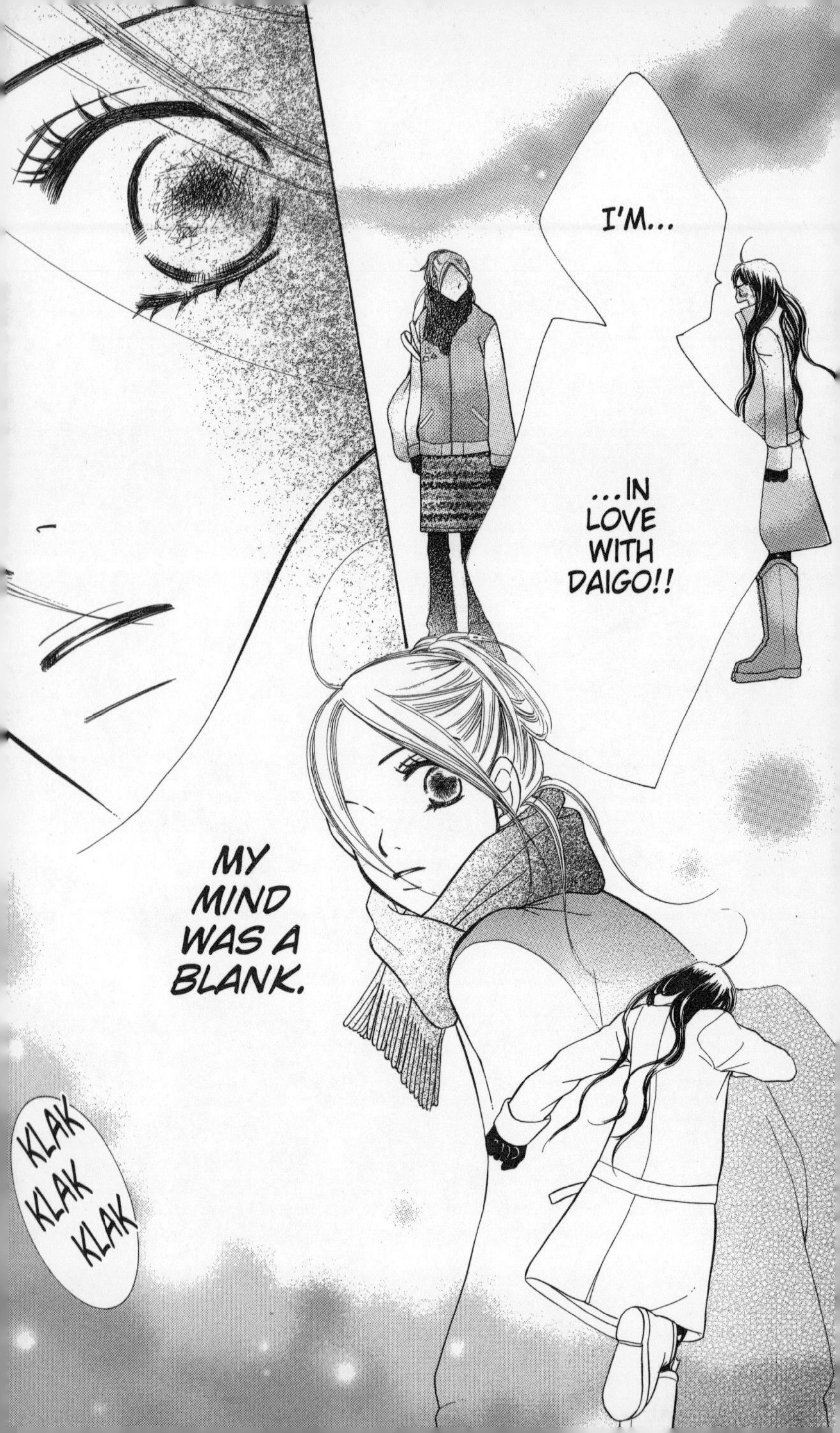
I'M...
...IN LOVE WITH DAIGO!!
MY MIND WAS A BLANK.
KLAK KLAK KLAK

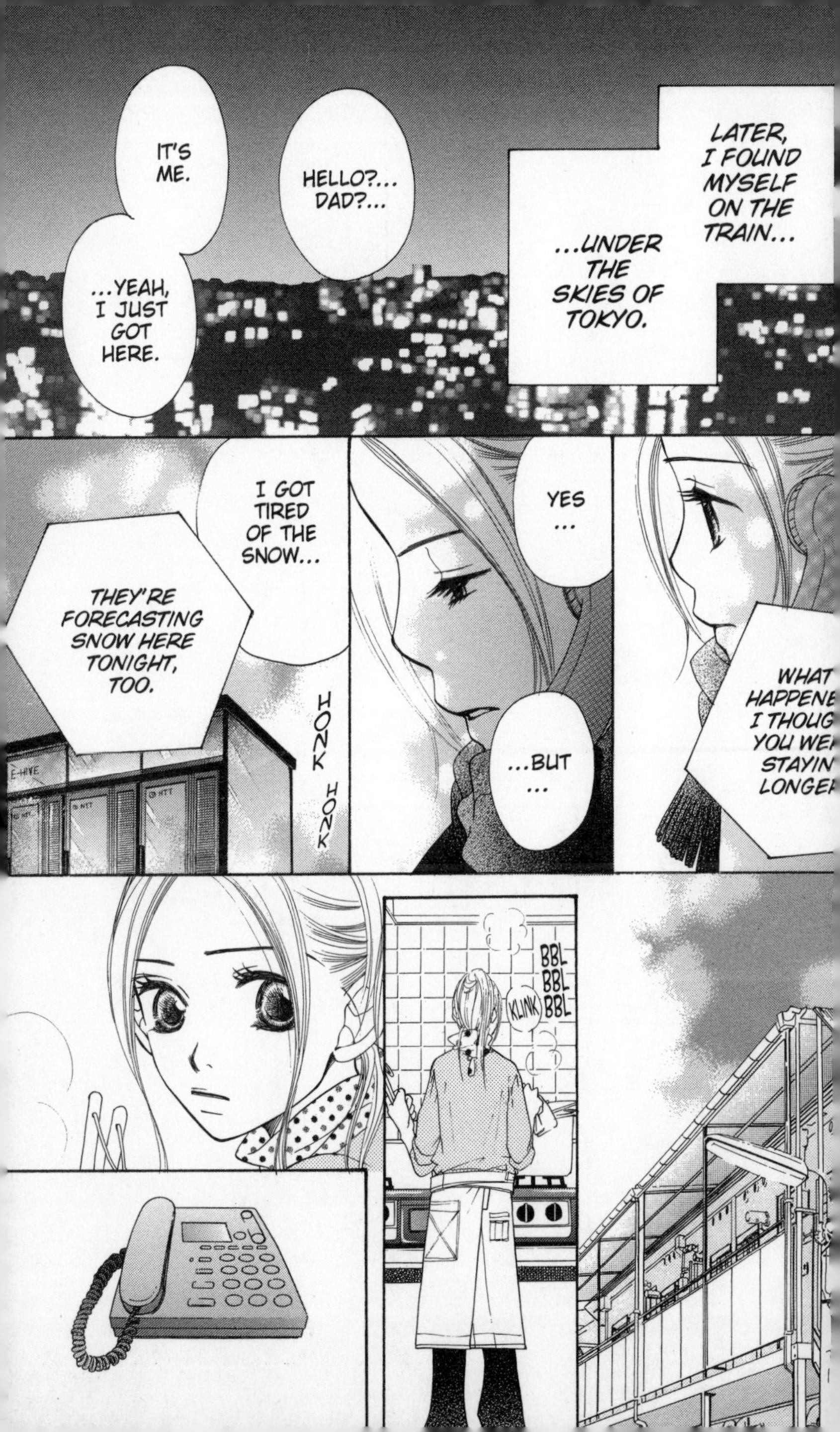
LATER, I FOUND MYSELF ON THE TRAIN...
...UNDER THE SKIES OF TOKYO.
HELLO?... DAD?...
IT'S ME.
...YEAH, I JUST GOT HERE.
WHAT HAPPENE I THOUG YOU WEI STAYIN LONGEI
YES ...
...BUT ...
I GOT TIRED OF THE SNOW...
THEY'RE FORECASTING SNOW HERE TONIGHT, TOO.
HONK HONK
BBL BBL BBL
KLINK

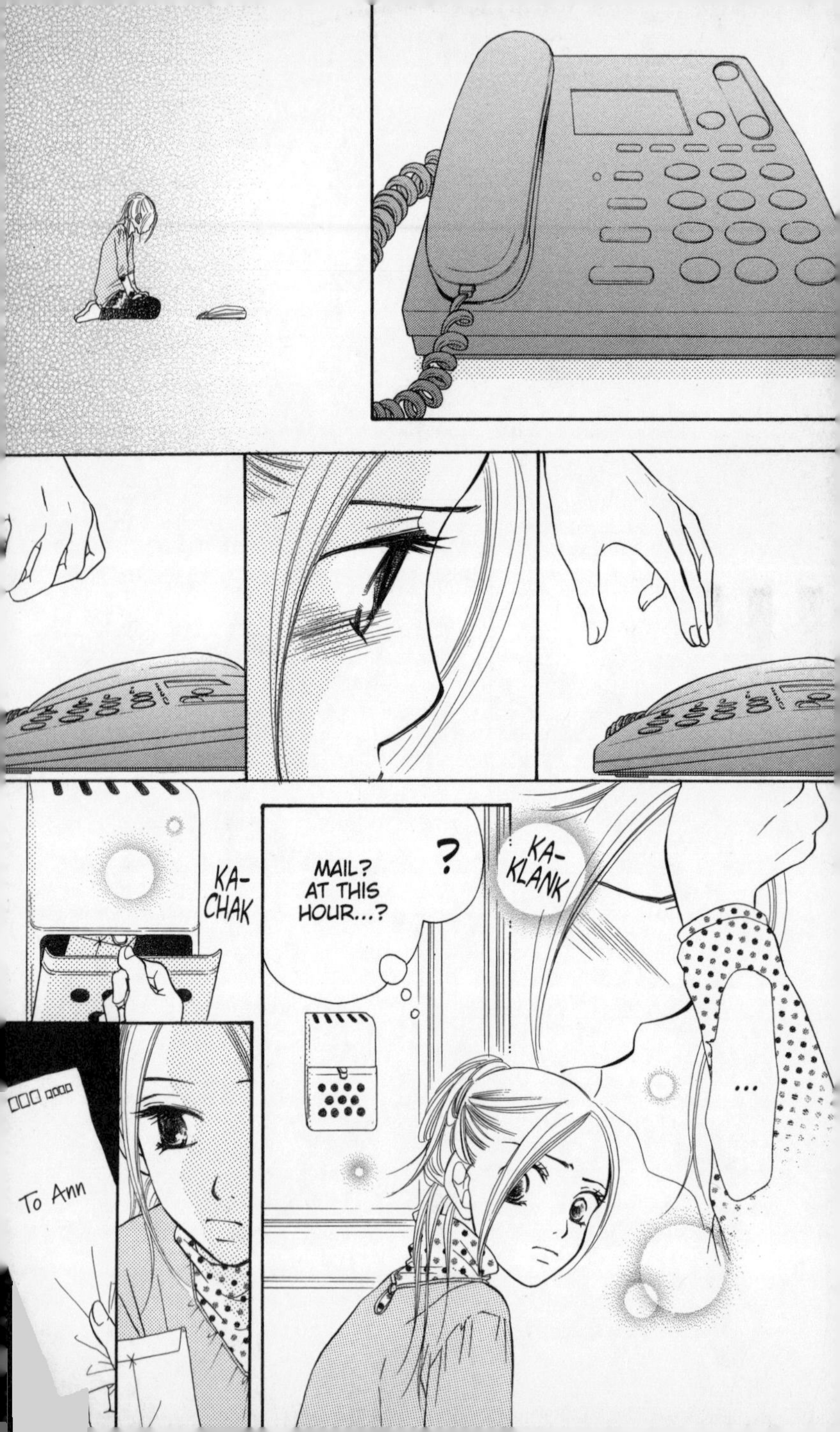
KA-KLANK
?
MAIL? AT THIS HOUR...?
...
KA-CHAK
To Ann

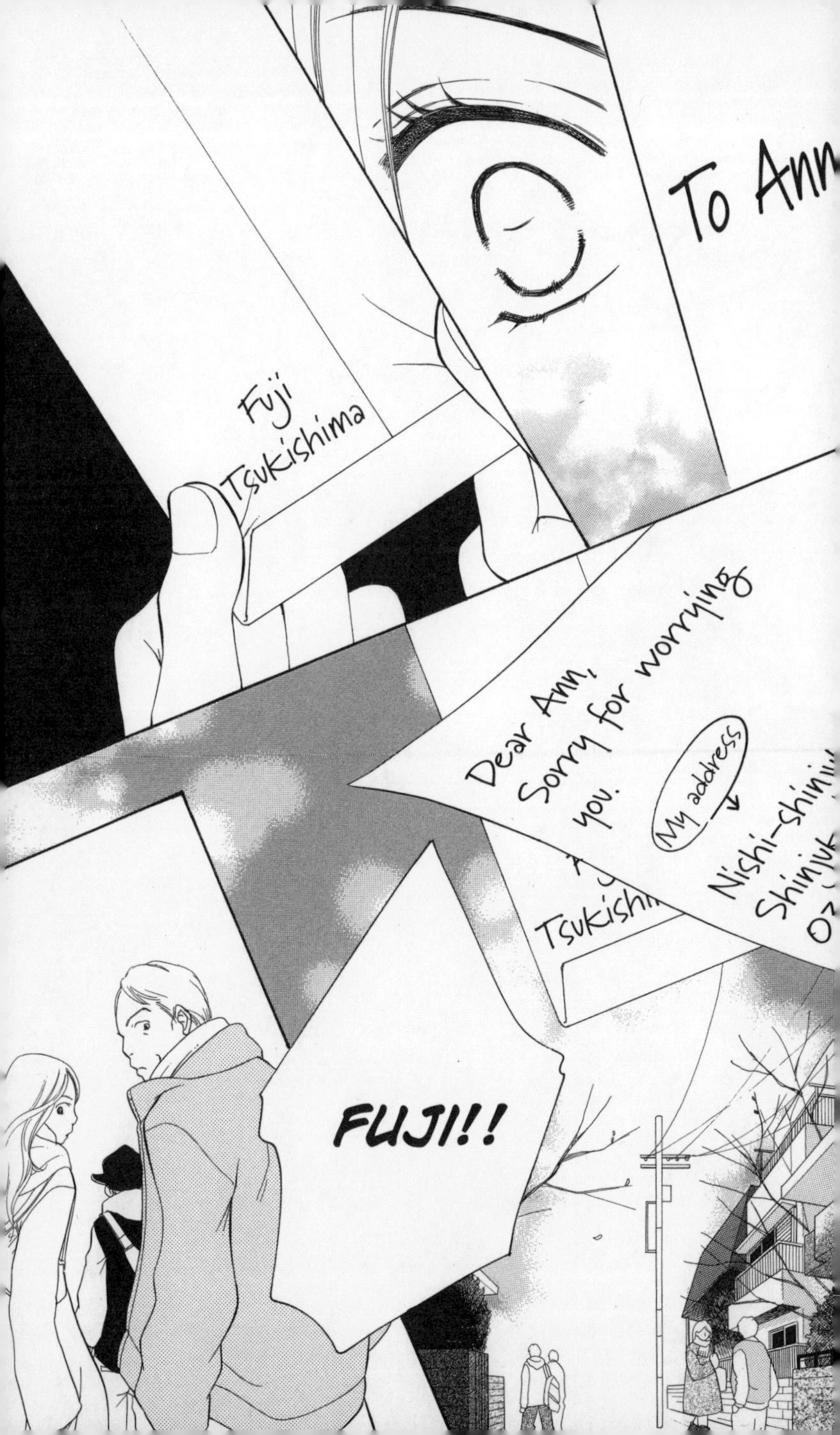

To Ann
Fuji Tsukishima
Dear Ann,
Sorry for worrying you.
My address
FUJI!!

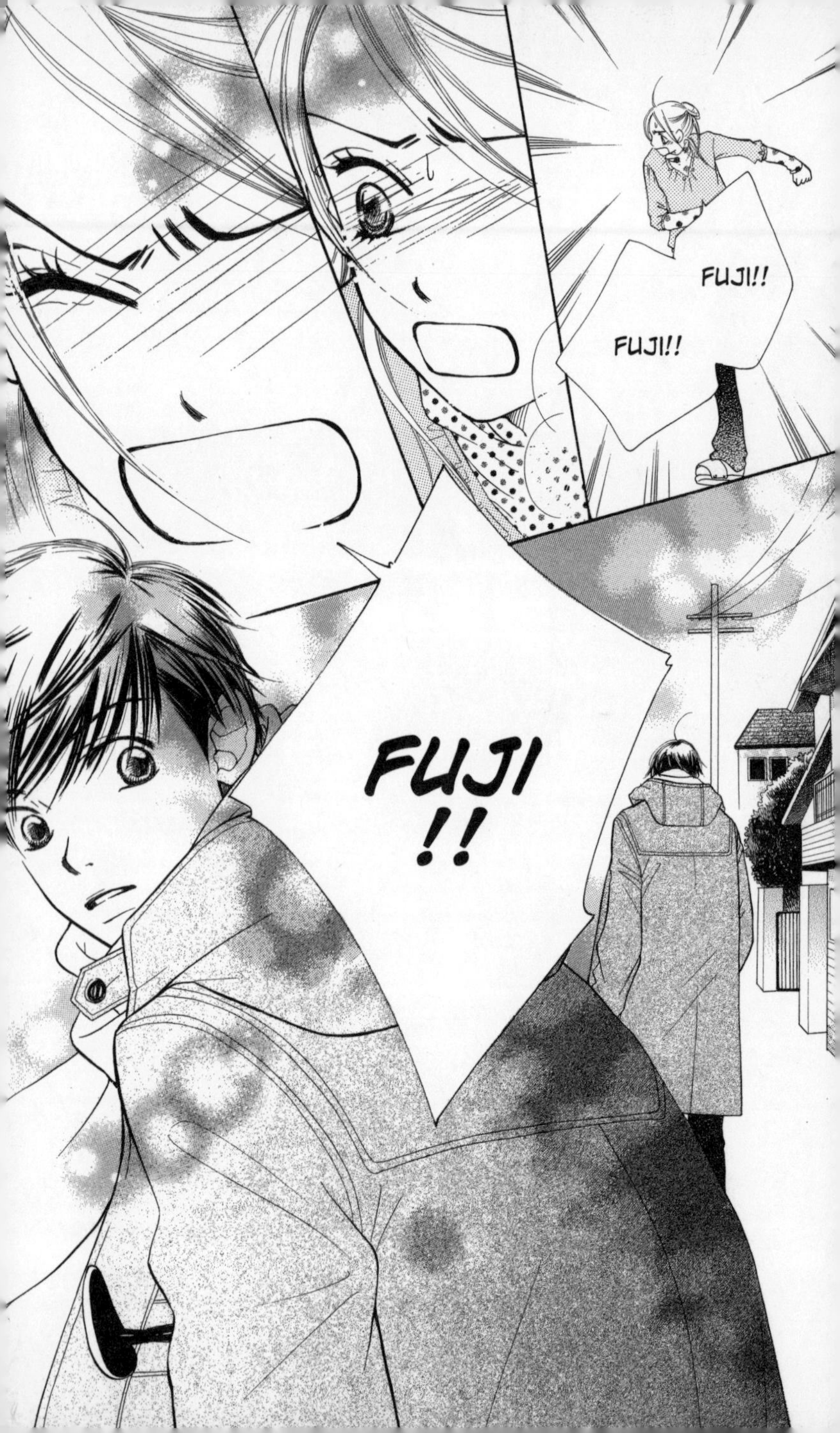
FUJI!!
FUJI!!
FUJI
!!

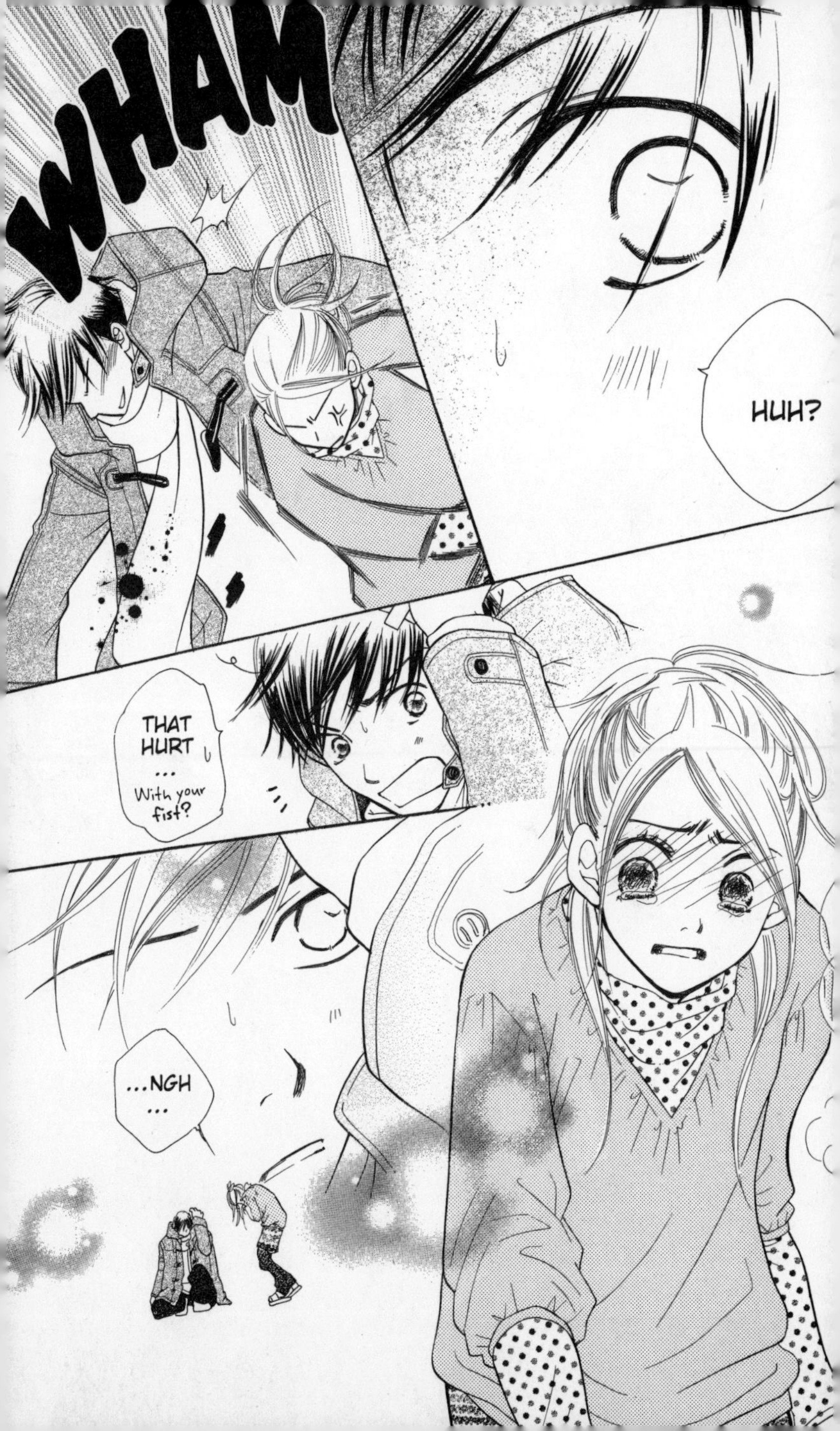
HUH?
WHAM
THAT HURT ... With your fist?
...NGH ...

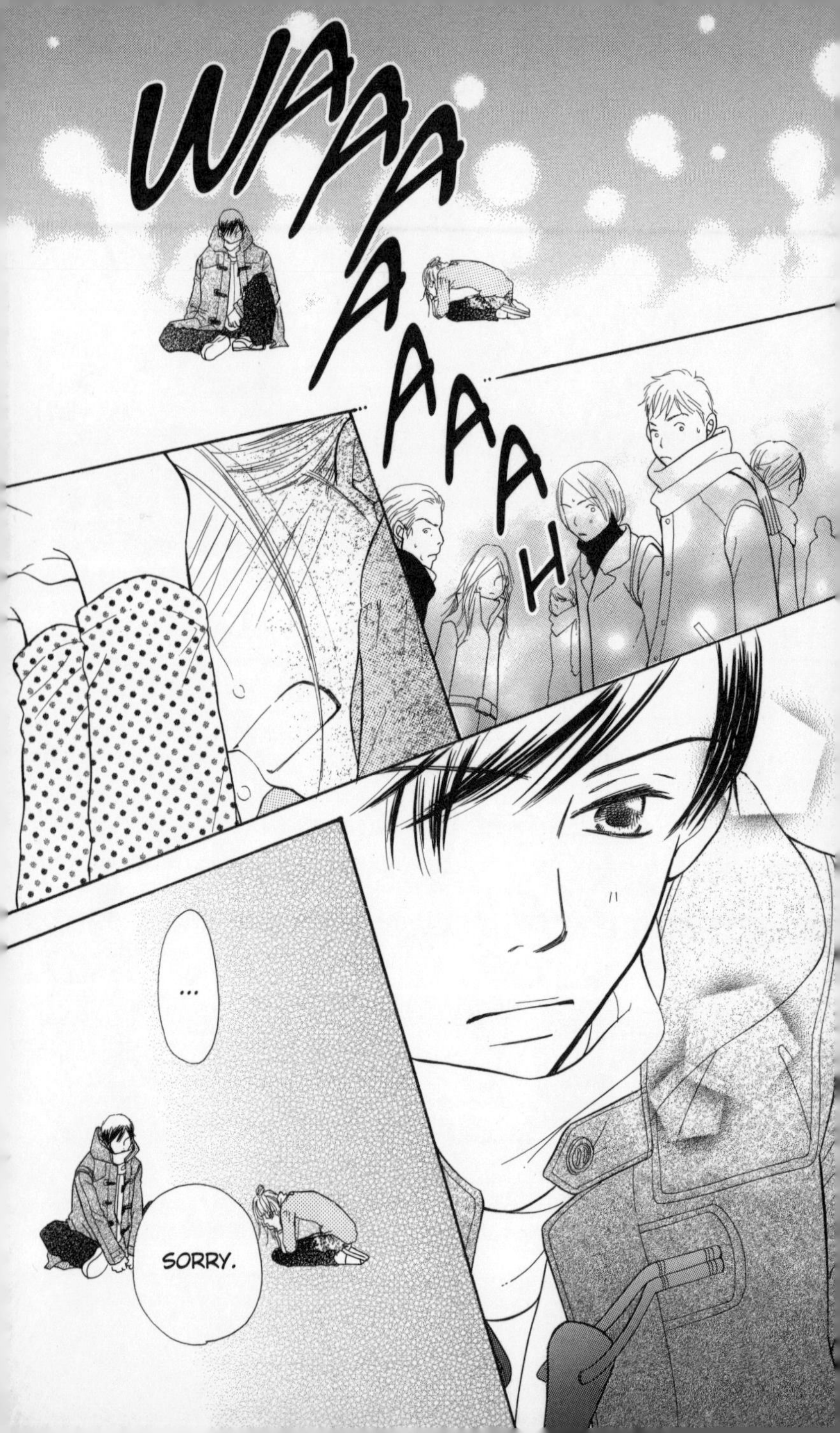
WAAAAAAAH
...
SORRY.

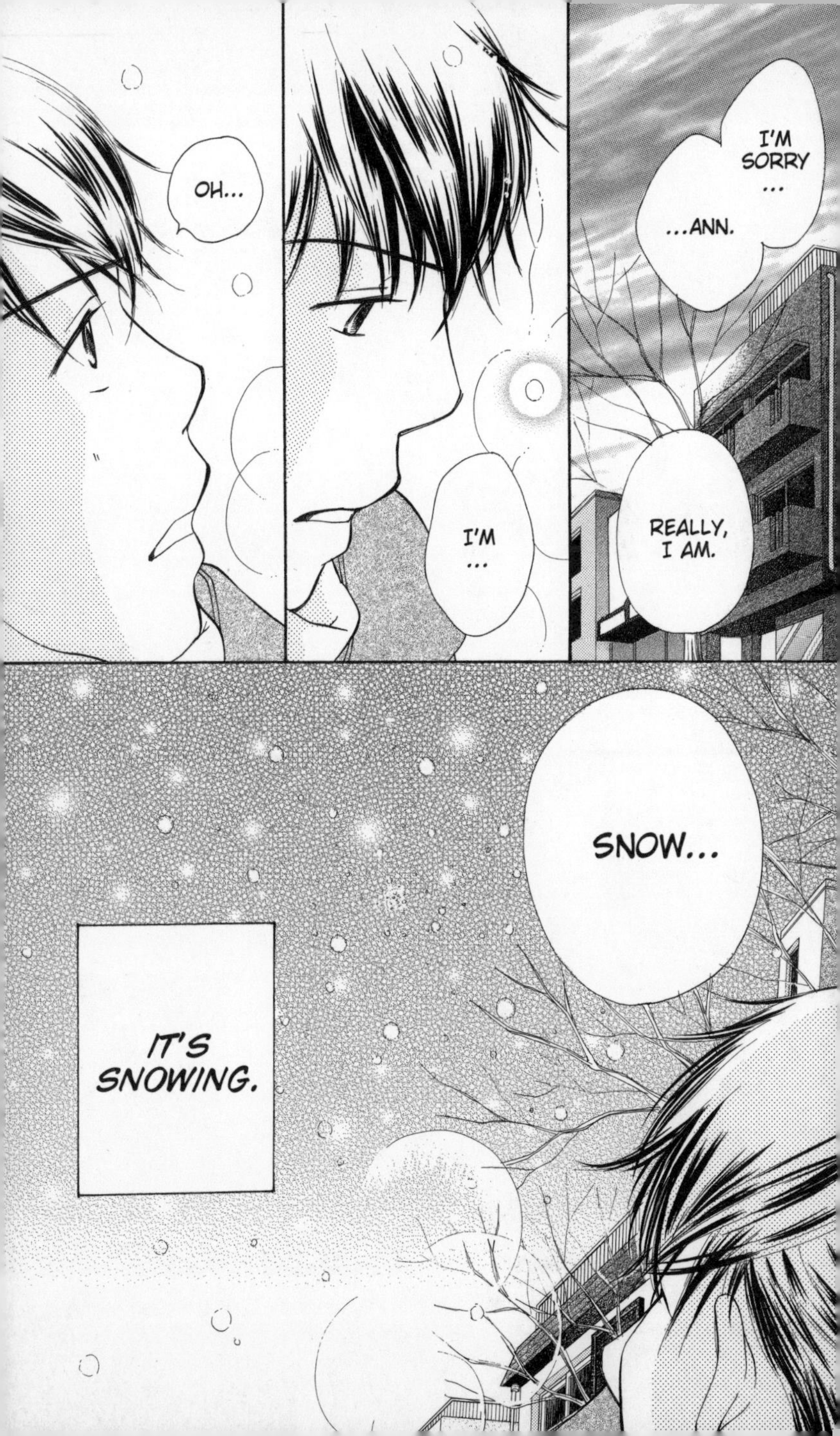
I'M SORRY ...
...ANN.
REALLY, I AM.
I'M ...
OH...
SNOW...
IT'S SNOWING.

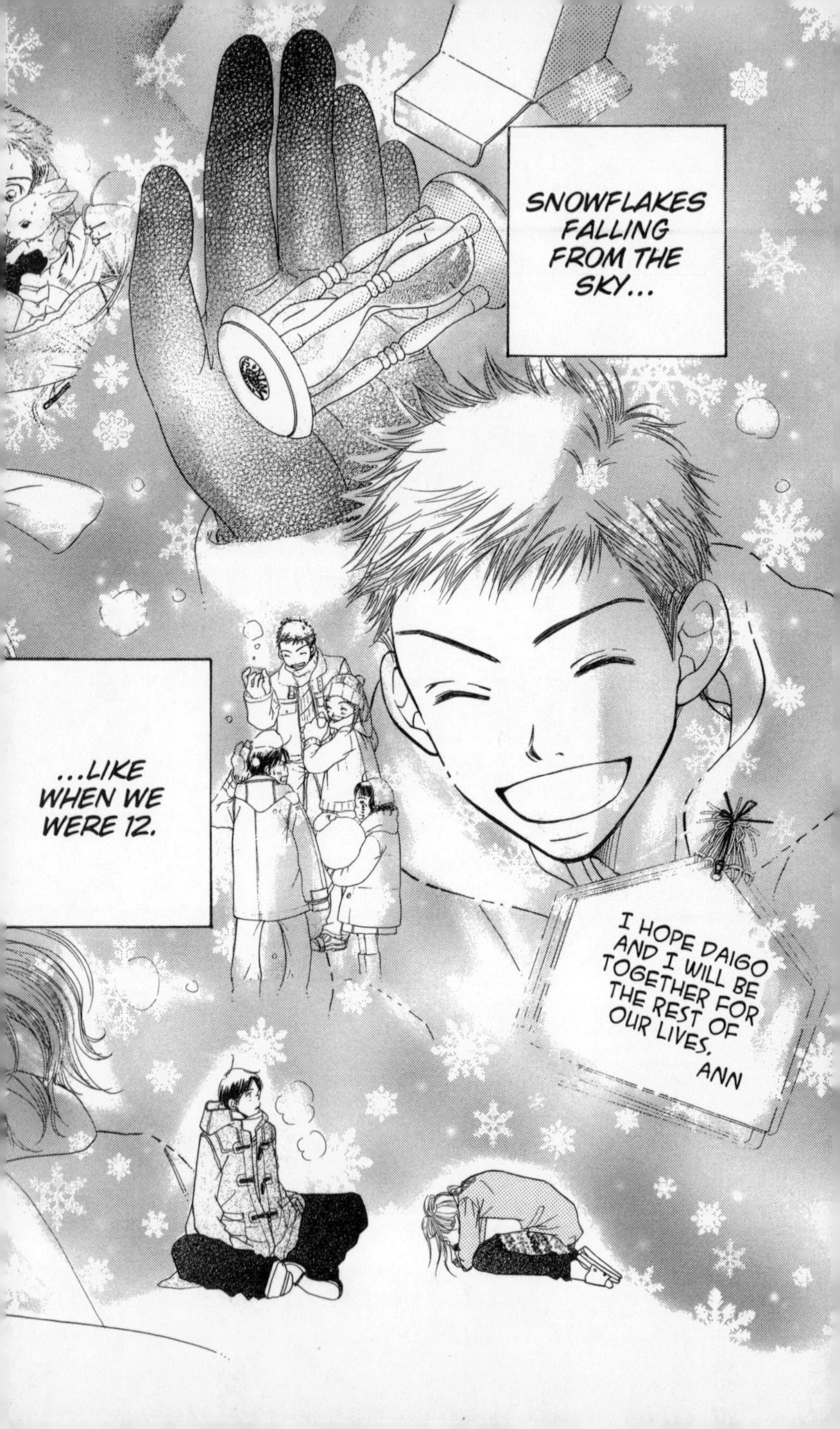
SNOWFLAKES FALLING FROM THE SKY...
...LIKE WHEN WE WERE 12.
I HOPE DAIGO AND I WILL BE TOGETHER FOR THE REST OF OUR LIVES.
ANN

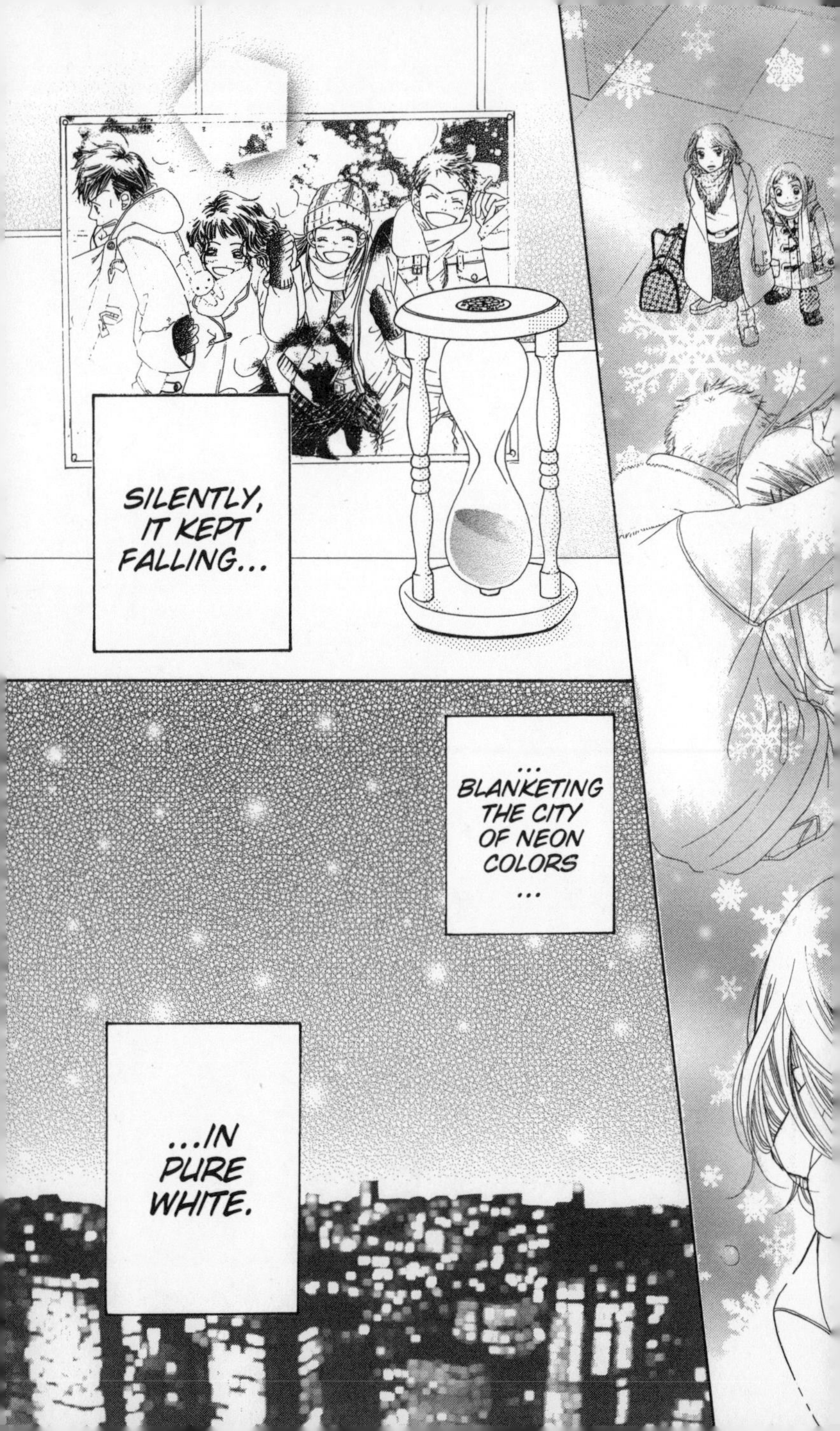
SILENTLY, IT KEPT FALLING...
...BLANKETING THE CITY OF NEON COLORS...
...IN PURE WHITE.

Sand Chronicles

AWOOOOO

YAMADA'S DUMB DOG

HE'S BACK!

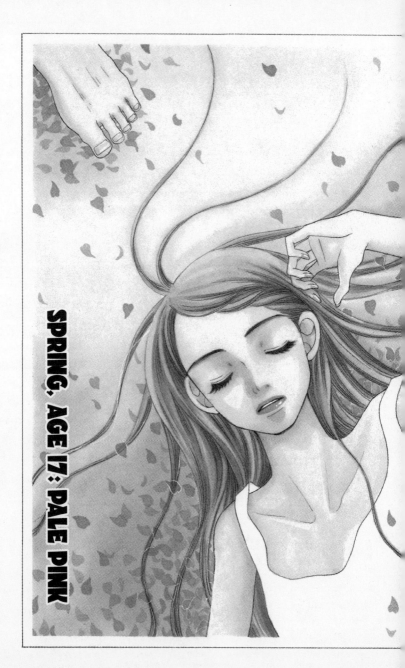

SPRING, AGE 17: PALE PINK

Sand Chronicles

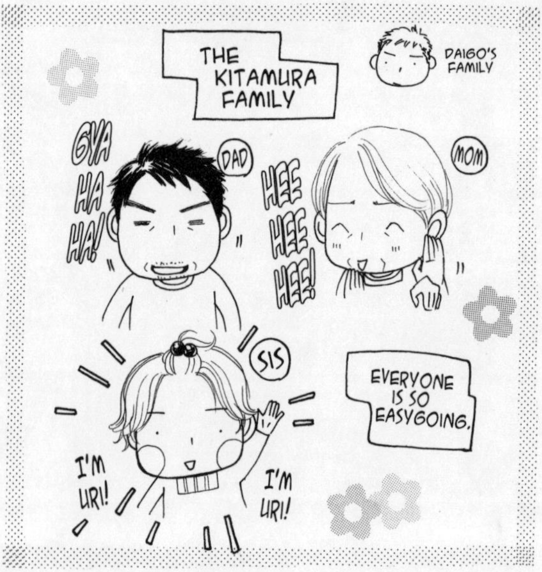
DAIGO'S FAMILY
THE KITAMURA FAMILY
MOM
HEE HEE HEE!
DAD
GYA HA HA!
EVERYONE IS SO EASYGOING.
SIS
I'M URI!
I'M URI!

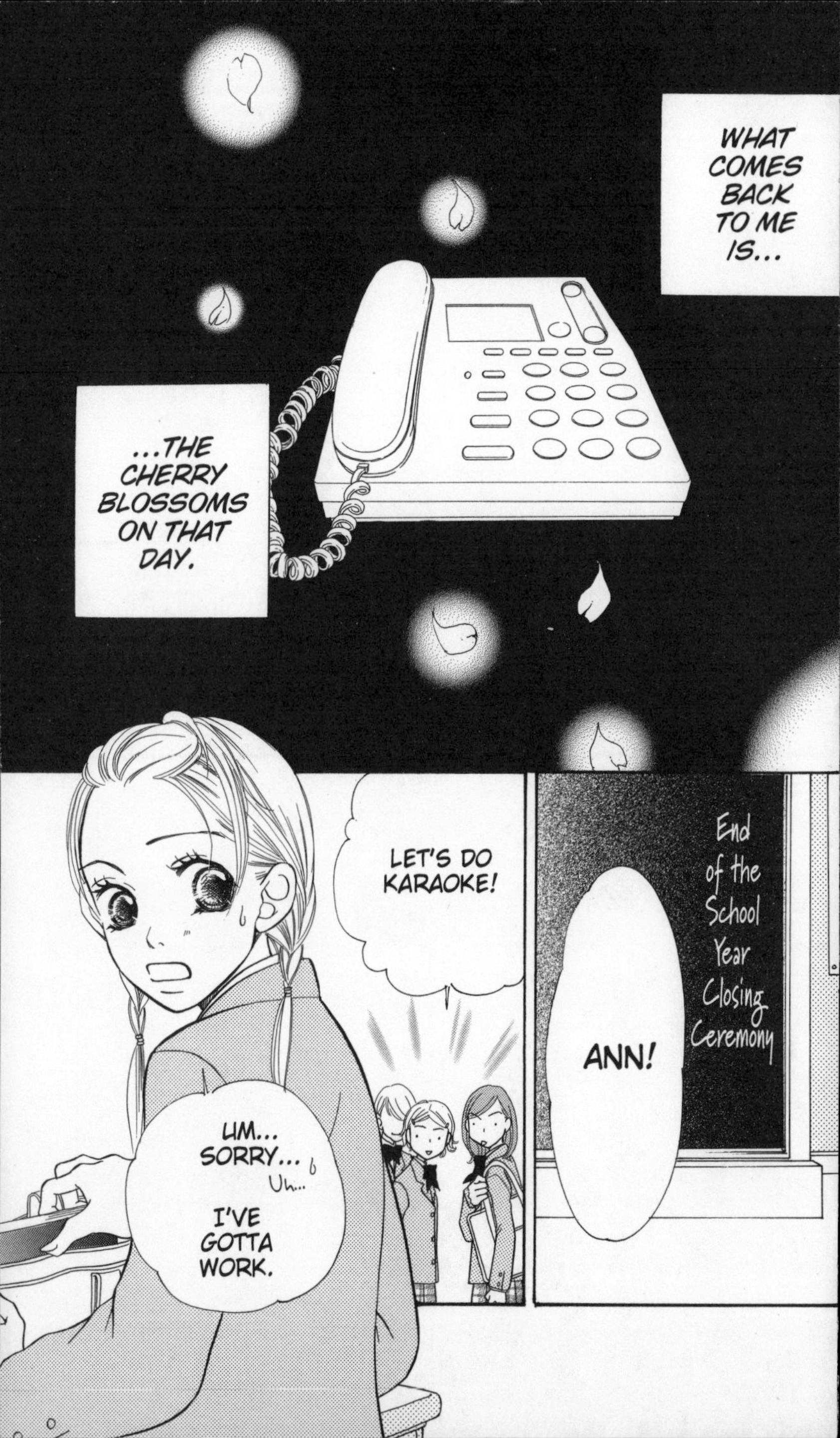
WHAT COMES BACK TO ME IS...
...THE CHERRY BLOSSOMS ON THAT DAY.
End of the School Year Closing Ceremony
ANN!
LET'S DO KARAOKE!
UM... SORRY...
Uh...
I'VE GOTTA WORK.

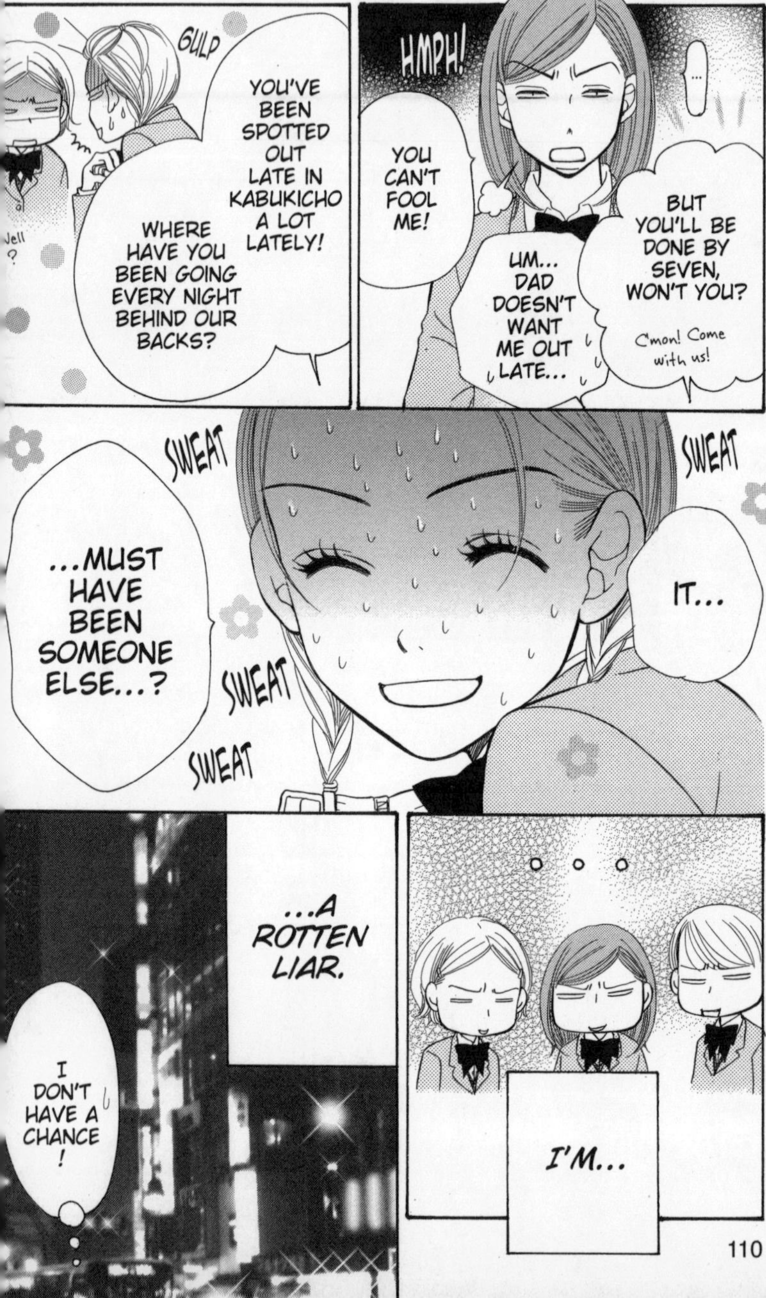
...
BUT YOU'LL BE DONE BY SEVEN, WON'T YOU?
C'mon! Come with us!
UM... DAD DOESN'T WANT ME OUT LATE...
HMPH!
YOU CAN'T FOOL ME!
GULP
YOU'VE BEEN SPOTTED OUT LATE IN KABUKICHO A LOT LATELY!
WHERE HAVE YOU BEEN GOING EVERY NIGHT BEHIND OUR BACKS?
Well ?
SWEAT
SWEAT
IT...
...MUST HAVE BEEN SOMEONE ELSE...?
SWEAT
SWEAT
○ ○ ○
I'M...
...A ROTTEN LIAR.
I DON'T HAVE A CHANCE !

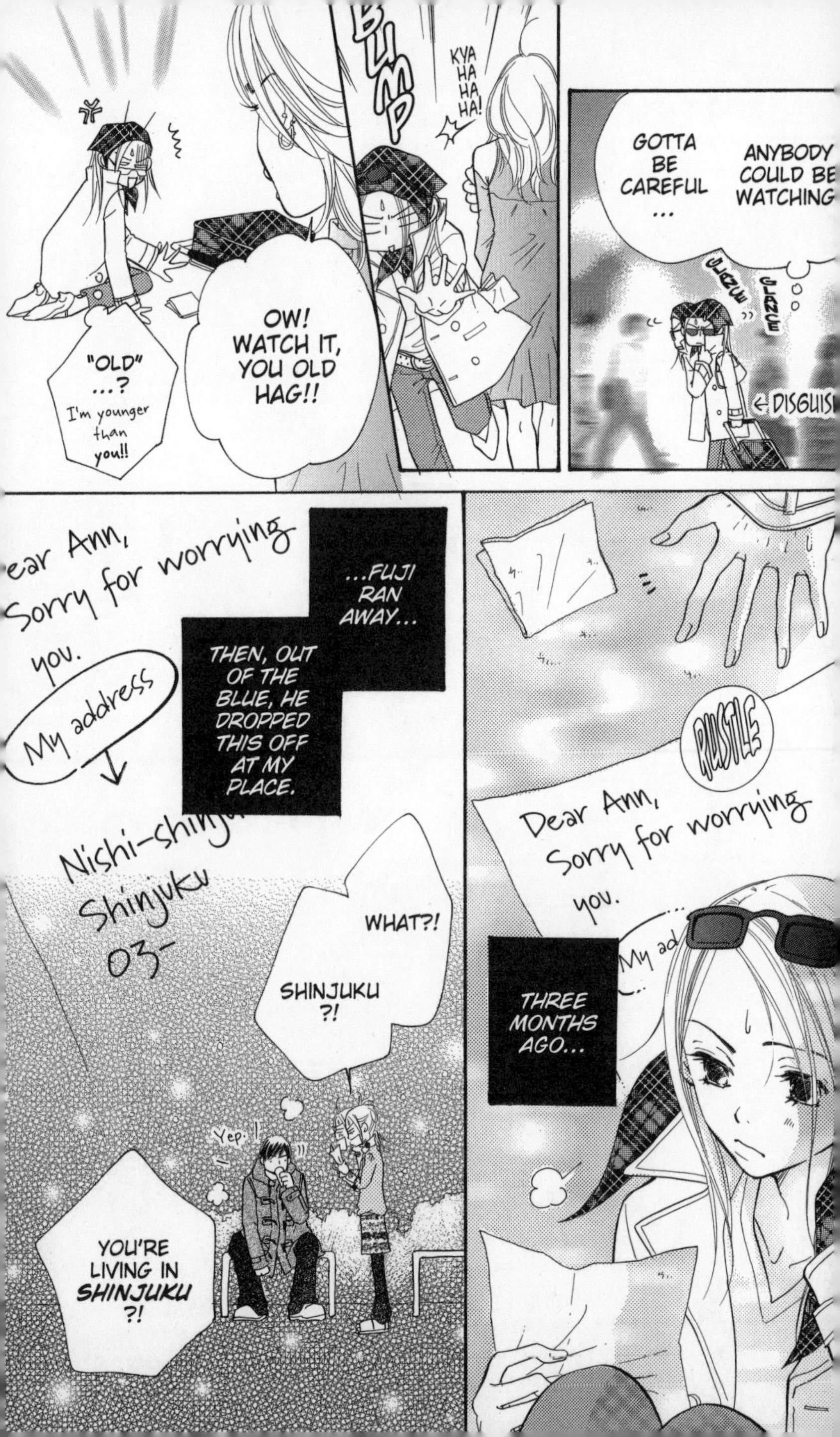
GOTTA BE CAREFUL...
ANYBODY COULD BE WATCHING
GLANCE
GLANCE
← DISGUIS
KYA HA HA HA!
BUMP
OW! WATCH IT, YOU OLD HAG!!
"OLD" ...? I'm younger than you!!
RUSTLE
Dear Ann, Sorry for worrying you.
...My ad...
THREE MONTHS AGO...
...FUJI RAN AWAY...
THEN, OUT OF THE BLUE, HE DROPPED THIS OFF AT MY PLACE.
ear Ann, Sorry for worrying you.
My address
Nishi-shinju
Shinjuku
03-
WHAT?!
SHINJUKU ?!
Yep.
YOU'RE LIVING IN SHINJUKU ?!

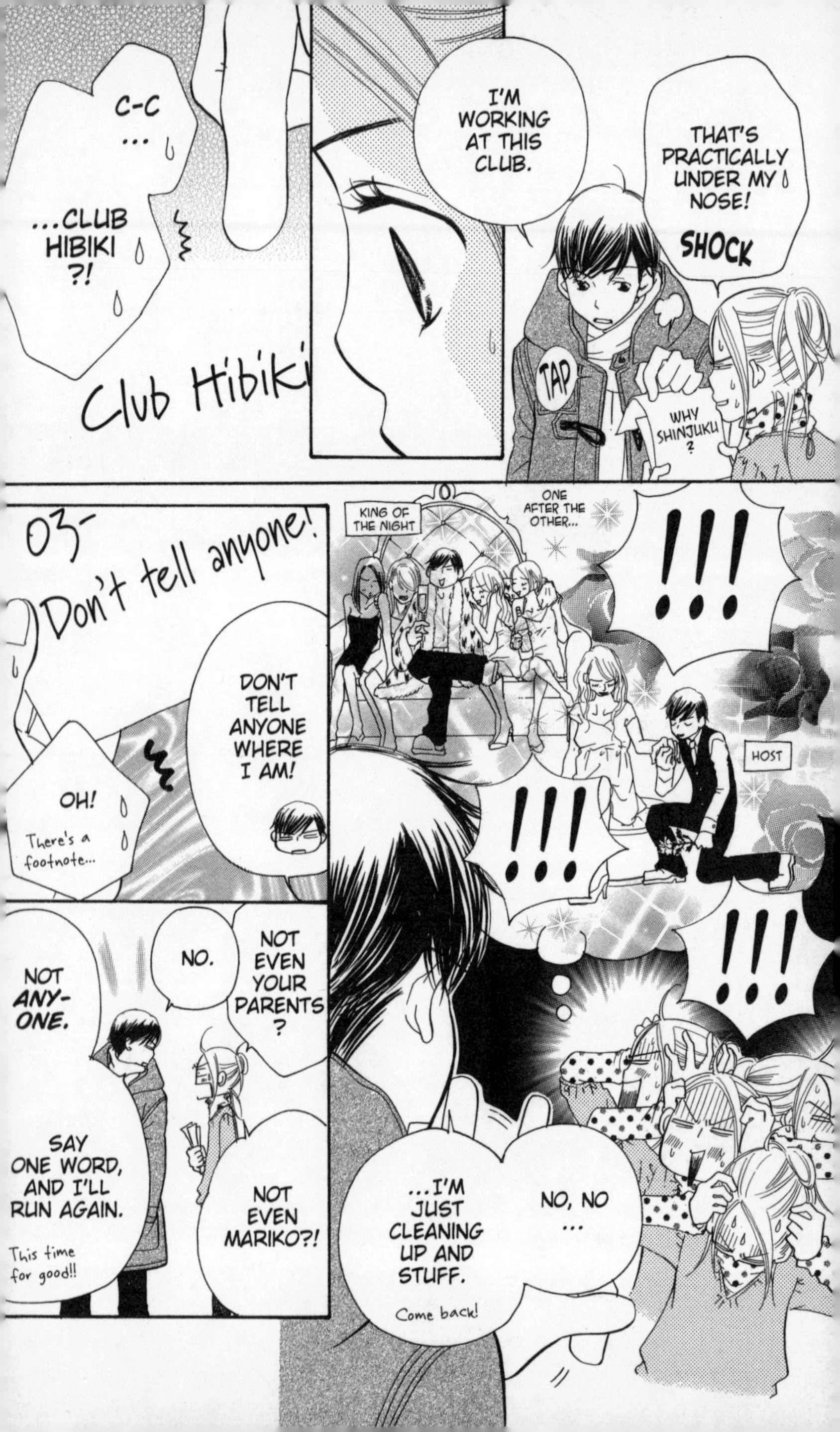
I'M WORKING AT THIS CLUB.
TAP
THAT'S PRACTICALLY UNDER MY NOSE!
SHOCK
WHY SHINJUKU?
Club Hibiki
C-C ...
...CLUB HIBIKI?!
KING OF THE NIGHT
ONE AFTER THE OTHER...
!!!
HOST
!!!
!!!
NO, NO ...
...I'M JUST CLEANING UP AND STUFF.
Come back!
03- Don't tell anyone!
DON'T TELL ANYONE WHERE I AM!
OH!
There's a footnote...
NOT EVEN YOUR PARENTS?
NO.
NOT ANY-ONE.
NOT EVEN MARIKO?!
SAY ONE WORD, AND I'LL RUN AGAIN.
This time for good!!

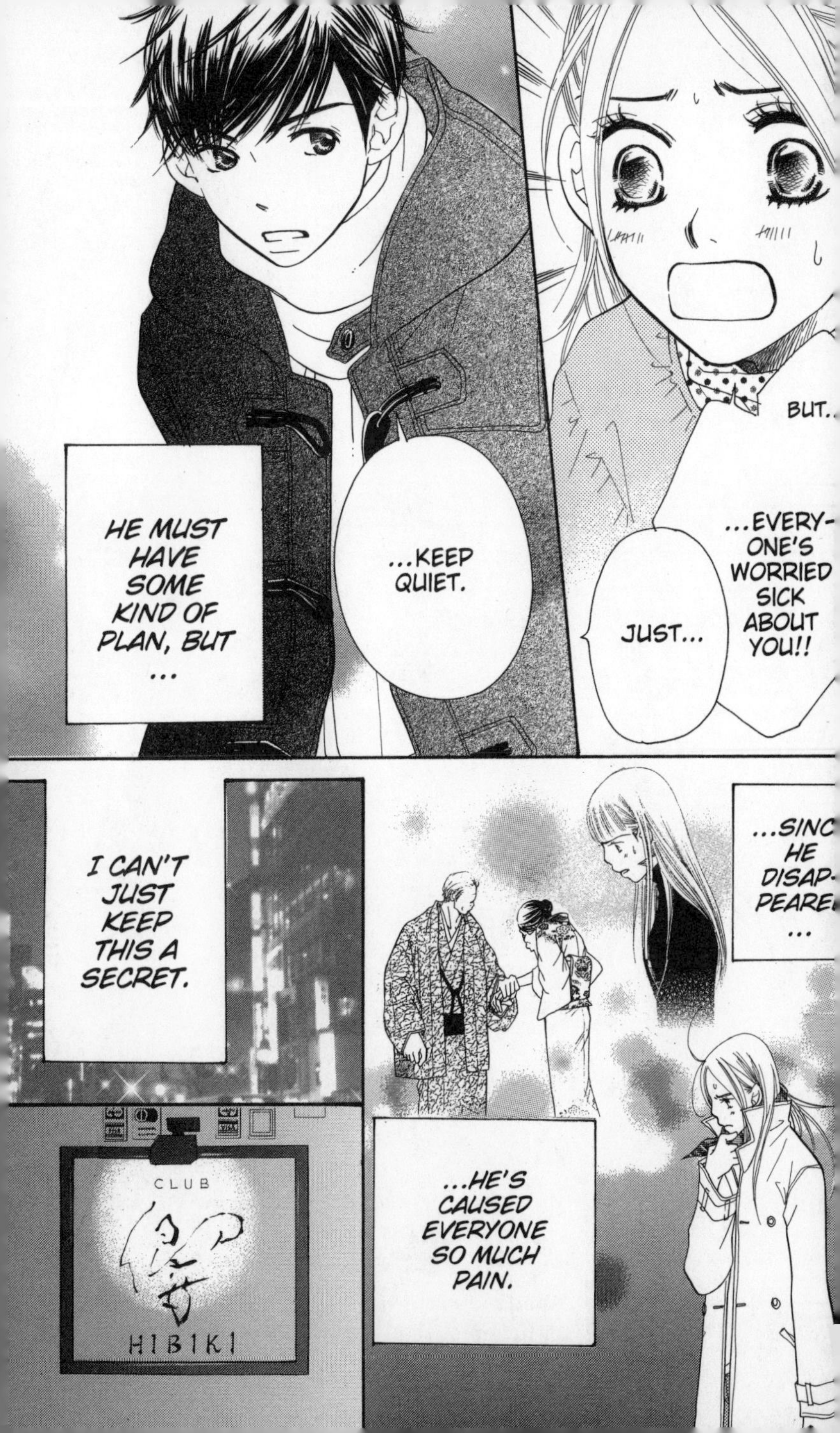
BUT...
...EVERYONE'S WORRIED SICK ABOUT YOU!!
JUST...
...KEEP QUIET.
HE MUST HAVE SOME KIND OF PLAN, BUT ...
...SINC HE DISAP-PEARE ...
...HE'S CAUSED EVERYONE SO MUCH PAIN.
I CAN'T JUST KEEP THIS A SECRET.
CLUB
HIBIKI

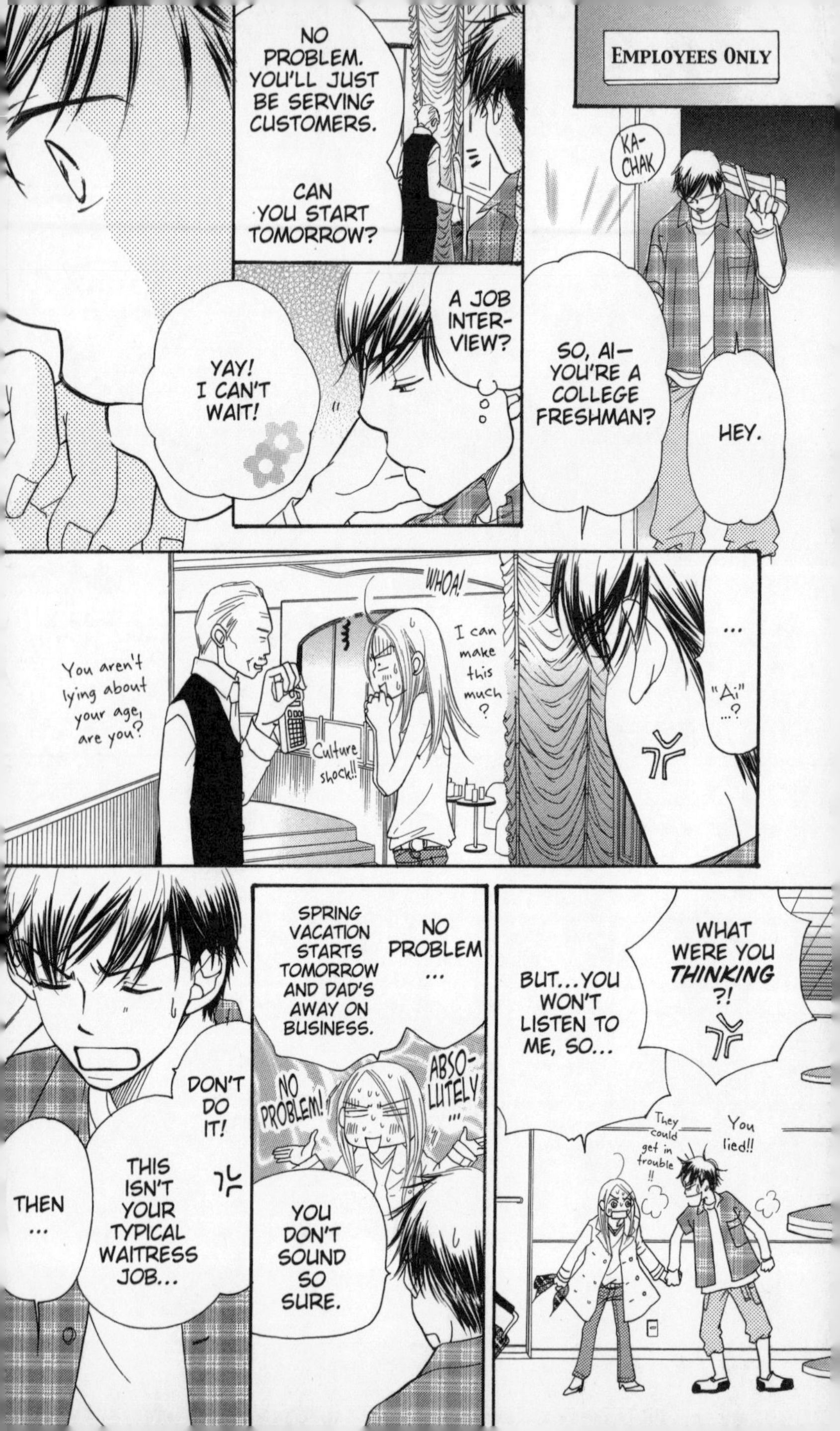
EMPLOYEES ONLY
KA-CHAK
HEY.
SO, AI— YOU'RE A COLLEGE FRESHMAN?
NO PROBLEM. YOU'LL JUST BE SERVING CUSTOMERS.
CAN YOU START TOMORROW?
A JOB INTER-VIEW?
YAY! I CAN'T WAIT!
...
"Ai" ...?
WHOA!
I can make this much?
Culture shock!!
You aren't lying about your age, are you?
WHAT WERE YOU THINKING?!
BUT...YOU WON'T LISTEN TO ME, SO...
You lied!!
They could get in trouble!!
NO PROBLEM...
SPRING VACATION STARTS TOMORROW AND DAD'S AWAY ON BUSINESS.
ABSO-LUTELY...
NO PROBLEM!
YOU DON'T SOUND SO SURE.
DON'T DO IT!
THIS ISN'T YOUR TYPICAL WAITRESS JOB...
THEN...

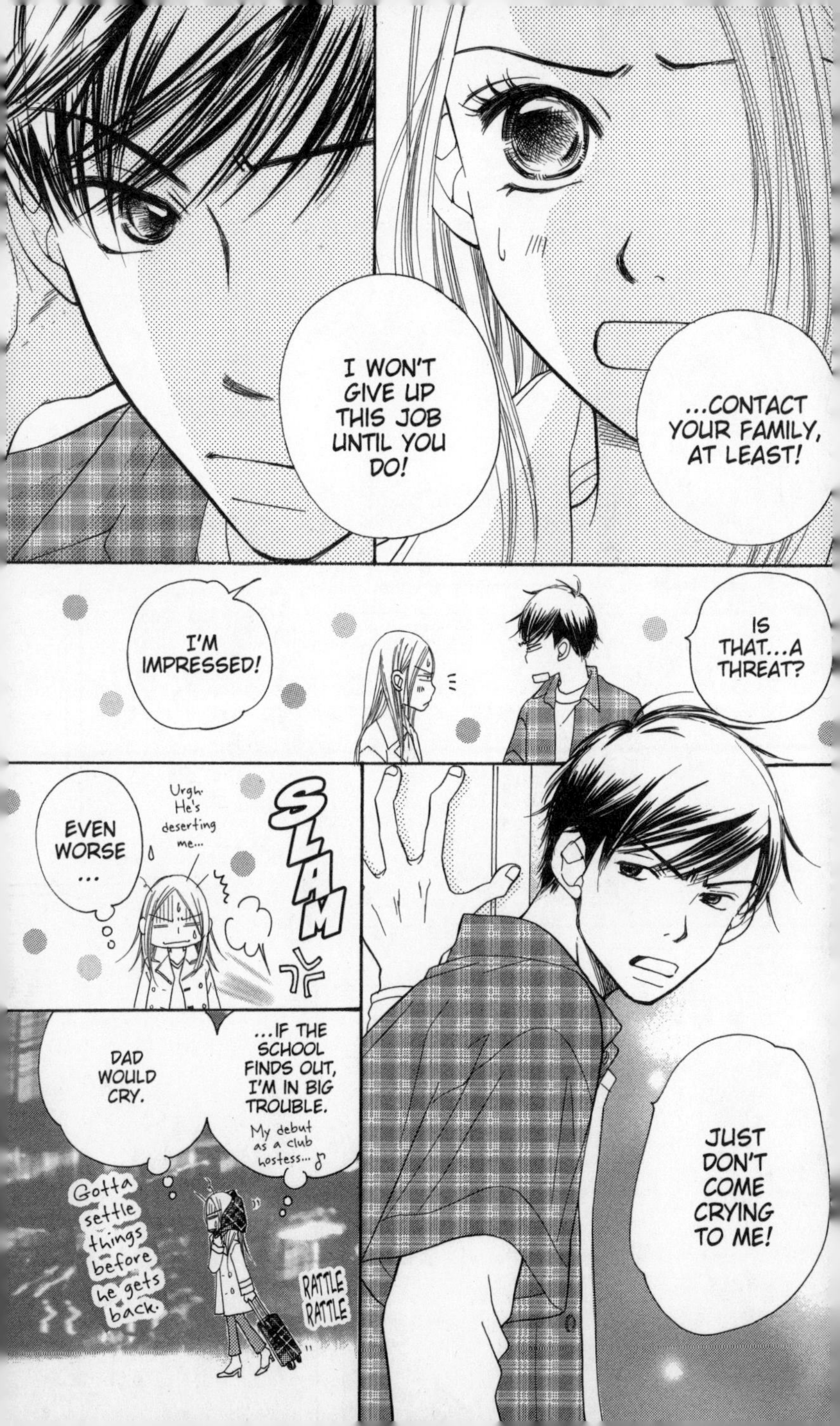
...CONTACT YOUR FAMILY, AT LEAST!
I WON'T GIVE UP THIS JOB UNTIL YOU DO!
IS THAT...A THREAT?
I'M IMPRESSED!
JUST DON'T COME CRYING TO ME!
SLAM
Urgh. He's deserting me...
EVEN WORSE ...
...IF THE SCHOOL FINDS OUT, I'M IN BIG TROUBLE.
My debut as a club hostess...♪
DAD WOULD CRY.
RATTLE RATTLE
Gotta settle things before he gets back.

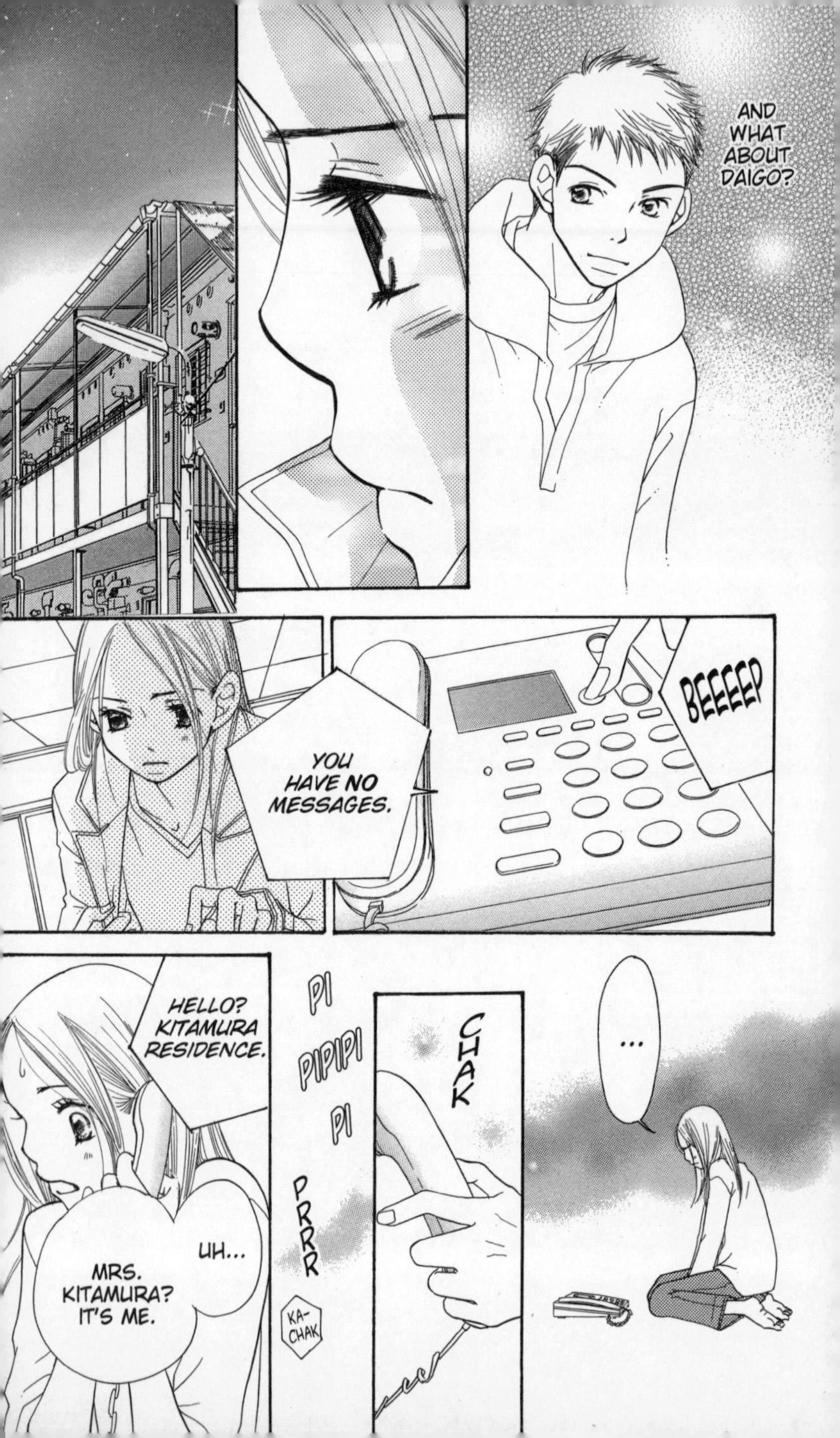
AND WHAT ABOUT DAIGO?
BEEEEP
YOU HAVE NO MESSAGES.
...
CHAK
PI
PIPIPI
PI
PRRR
KA-CHAK
HELLO? KITAMURA RESIDENCE.
UH...
MRS. KITAMURA? IT'S ME.

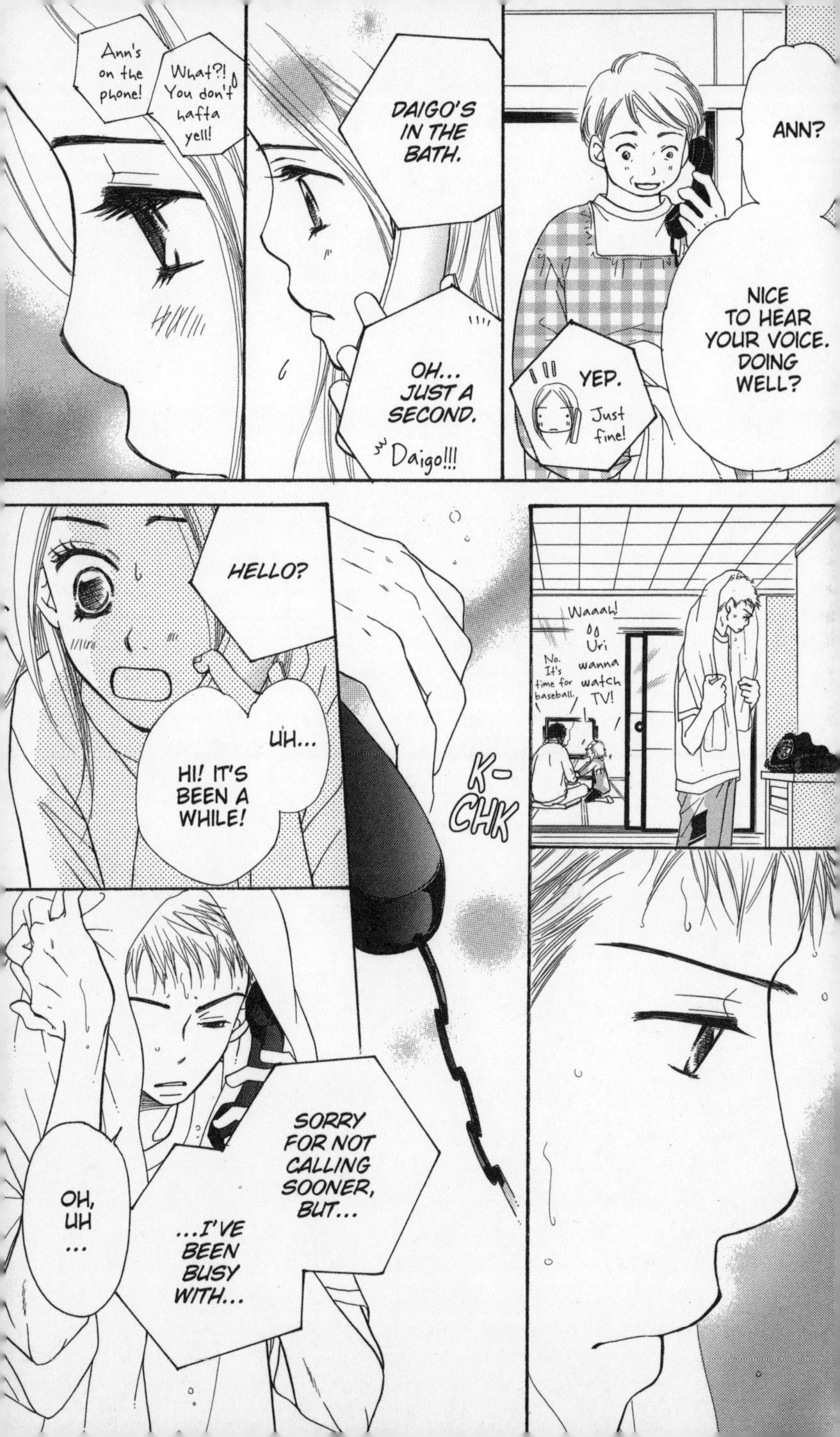
ANN?
NICE TO HEAR YOUR VOICE. DOING WELL?
YEP.
Just fine!
DAIGO'S IN THE BATH.
OH... JUST A SECOND.
Daigo!!!
Ann's on the phone!
What?! You don't hafta yell!
Waaah!
Uri wanna watch TV!
No. It's time for baseball.
K-CHK
HELLO?
UH...
HI! IT'S BEEN A WHILE!
SORRY FOR NOT CALLING SOONER, BUT...
...I'VE BEEN BUSY WITH...
OH, UH...

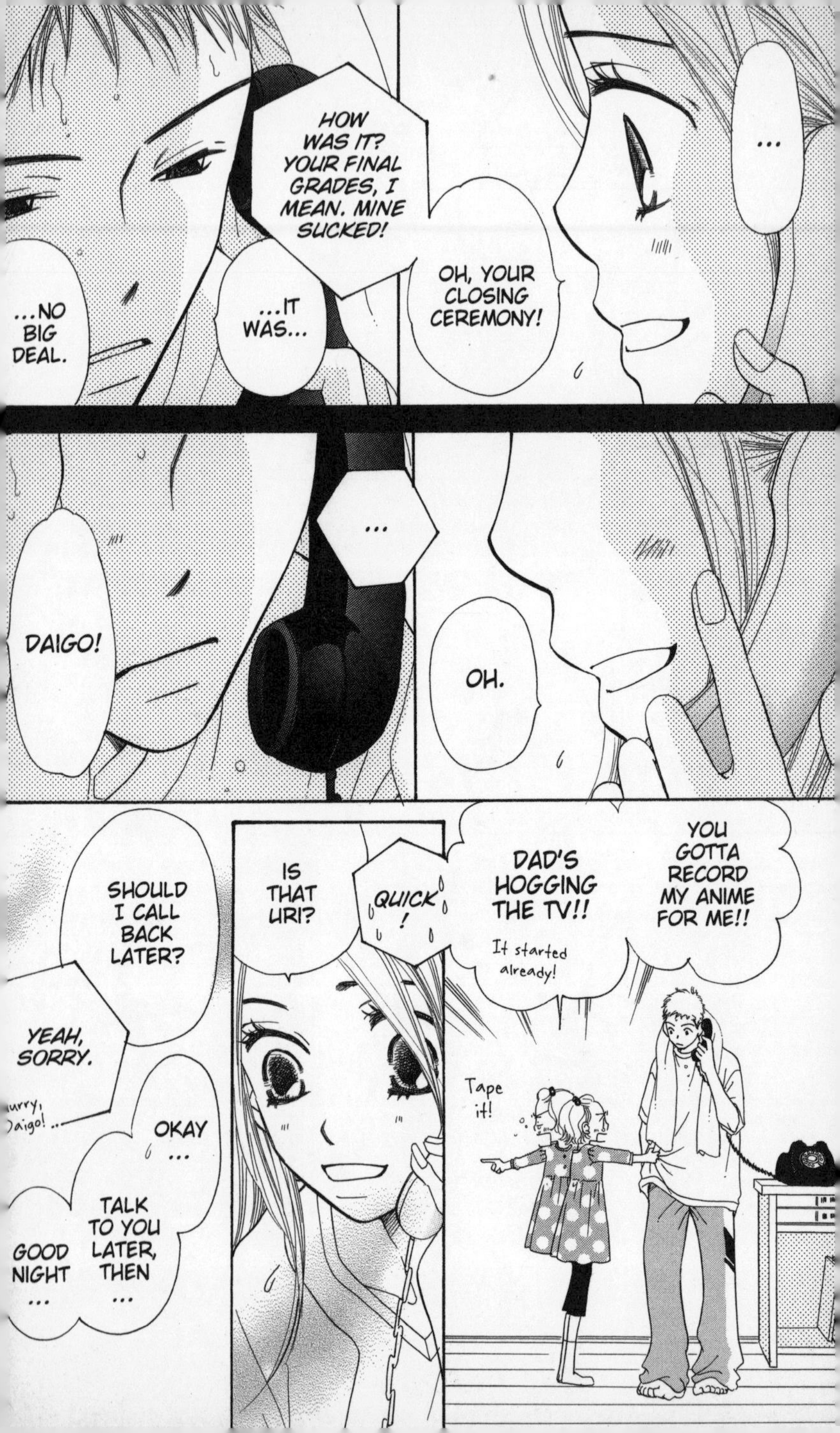
...
OH, YOUR CLOSING CEREMONY!
HOW WAS IT? YOUR FINAL GRADES, I MEAN. MINE SUCKED!
...IT WAS...
...NO BIG DEAL.
OH.
...
DAIGO!
YOU GOTTA RECORD MY ANIME FOR ME!!
DAD'S HOGGING THE TV!!
It started already!
Tape it!
QUICK!
IS THAT URI?
SHOULD I CALL BACK LATER?
YEAH, SORRY.
urry, Daigo! ...
OKAY...
TALK TO YOU LATER, THEN...
GOOD NIGHT...

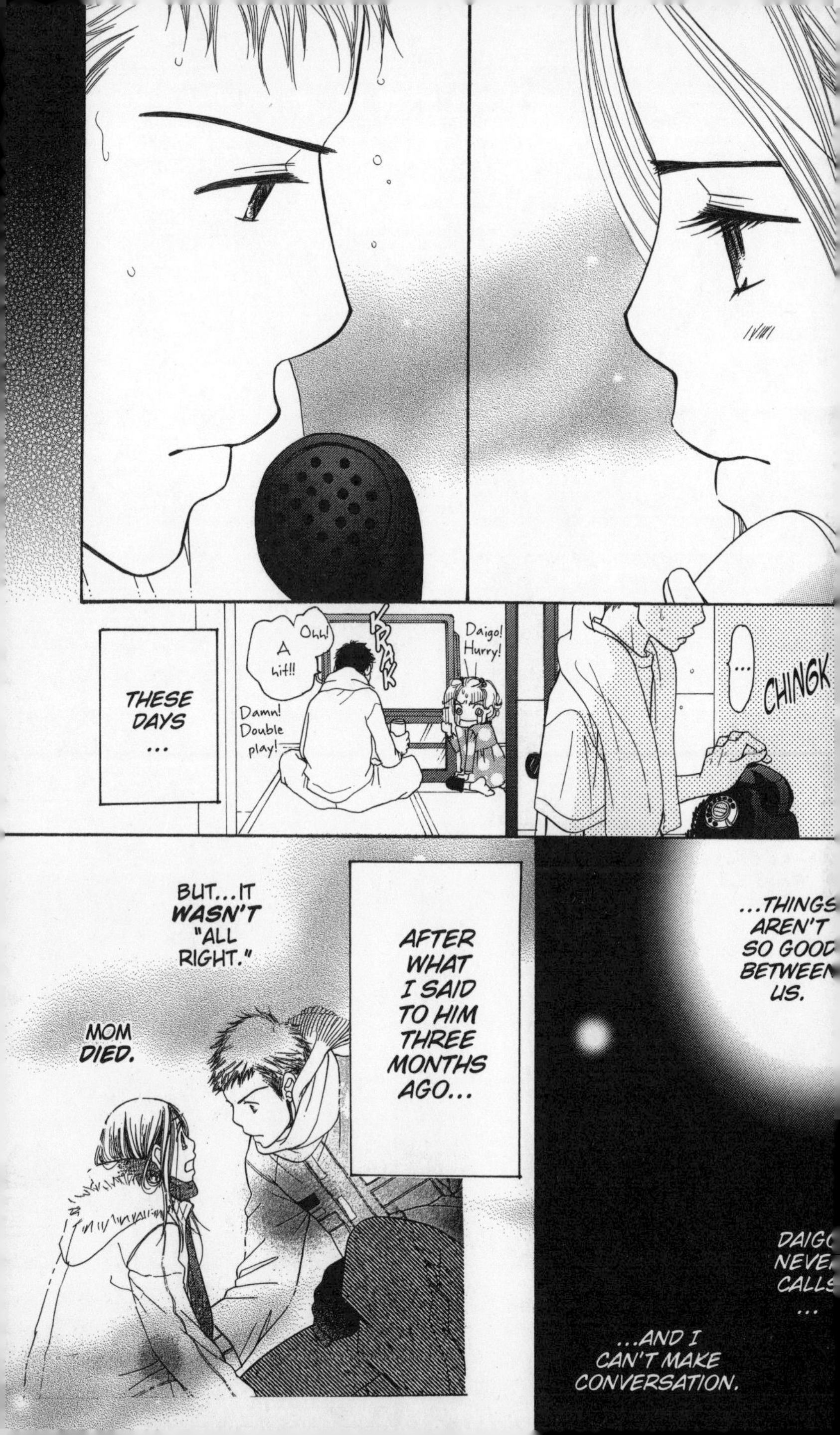

...
CHINGK
KRAK
Daigo! Hurry!
Ohh! A hit!!
Damn! Double play!
THESE DAYS ...
...THINGS AREN'T SO GOOD BETWEEN US.
DAIG NEVE CALLS ...
...AND I CAN'T MAKE CONVERSATION.
AFTER WHAT I SAID TO HIM THREE MONTHS AGO...
BUT...IT WASN'T "ALL RIGHT."
MOM DIED.

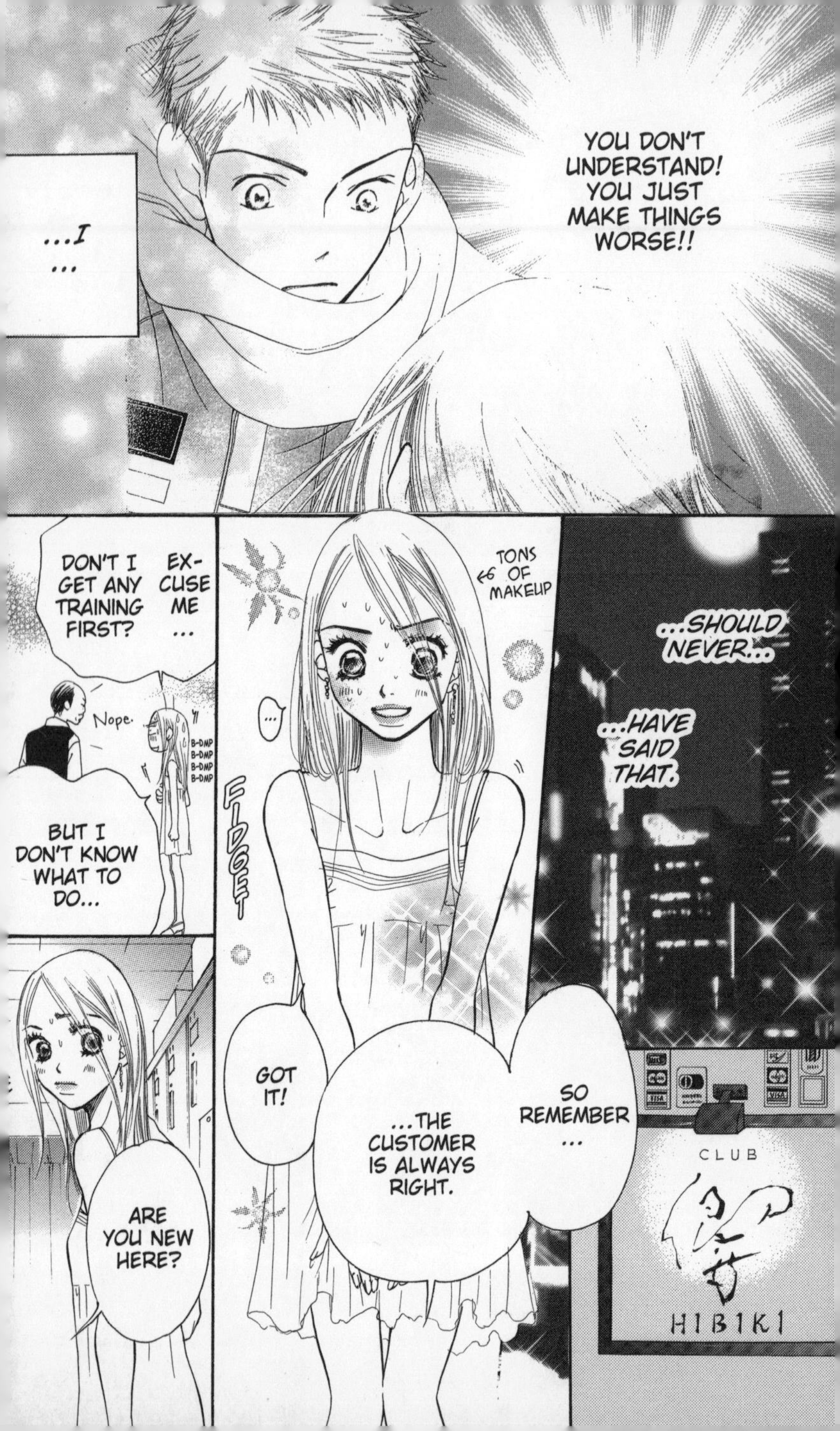

YOU DON'T UNDERSTAND! YOU JUST MAKE THINGS WORSE!!
...I ...
...SHOULD NEVER...
...HAVE SAID THAT.
CLUB
HIBIKI
SO REMEMBER ...
...THE CUSTOMER IS ALWAYS RIGHT.
GOT IT!
TONS OF MAKEUP
...
FIDGET
EX-CUSE ME ...
DON'T I GET ANY TRAINING FIRST?
Nope.
B-DMP B-DMP B-DMP B-DMP
BUT I DON'T KNOW WHAT TO DO...
ARE YOU NEW HERE?

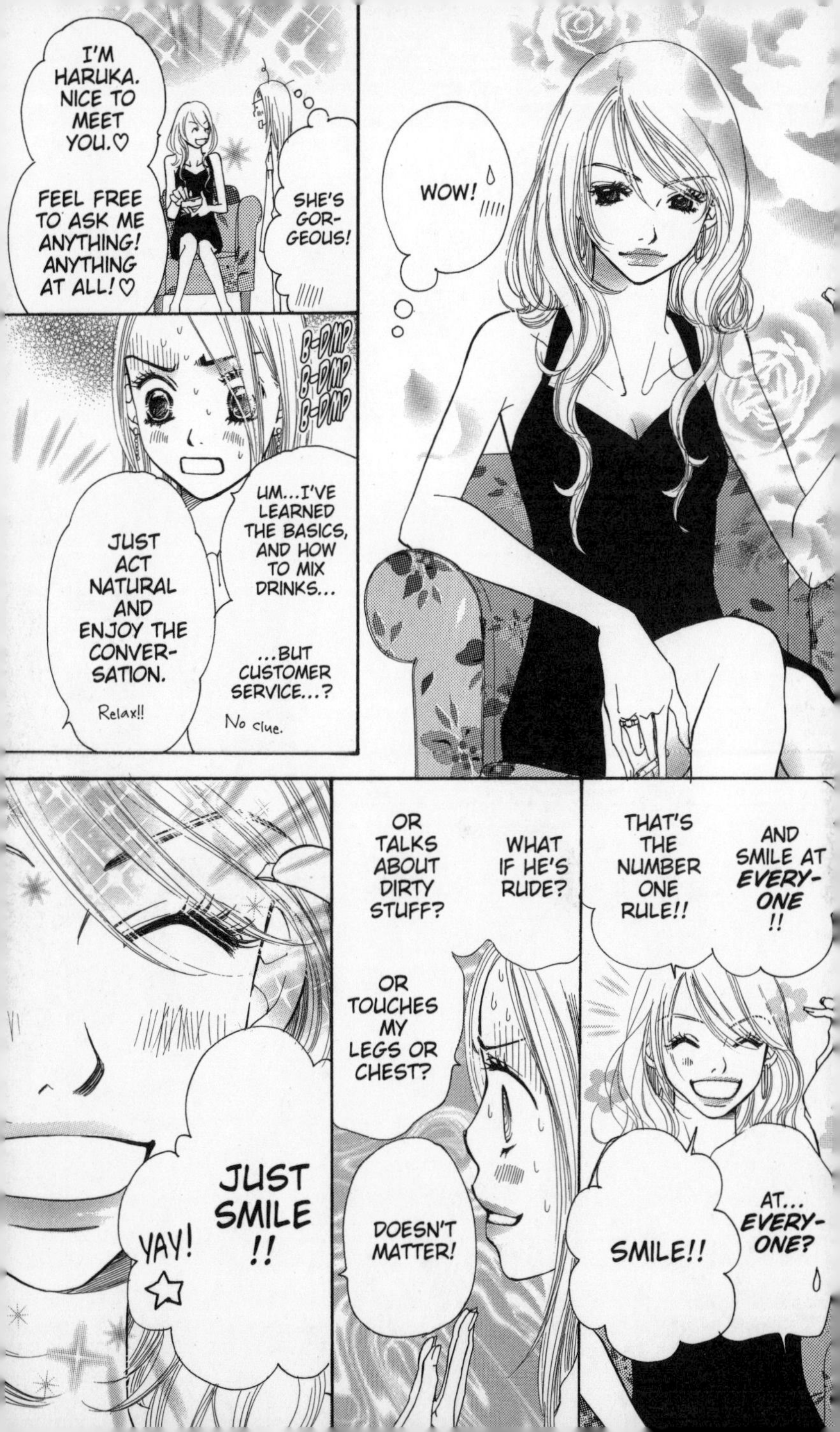
WOW!
SHE'S GORGEOUS!
I'M HARUKA. NICE TO MEET YOU.♡
FEEL FREE TO ASK ME ANYTHING! ANYTHING AT ALL!♡
B-DMP B-DMP B-DMP
UM...I'VE LEARNED THE BASICS, AND HOW TO MIX DRINKS...
...BUT CUSTOMER SERVICE...?
No clue.
JUST ACT NATURAL AND ENJOY THE CONVERSATION.
Relax!!
AND SMILE AT EVERYONE!!
THAT'S THE NUMBER ONE RULE!!
AT... EVERYONE?
SMILE!!
WHAT IF HE'S RUDE?
OR TALKS ABOUT DIRTY STUFF?
OR TOUCHES MY LEGS OR CHEST?
DOESN'T MATTER!
JUST SMILE!!
YAY! ☆

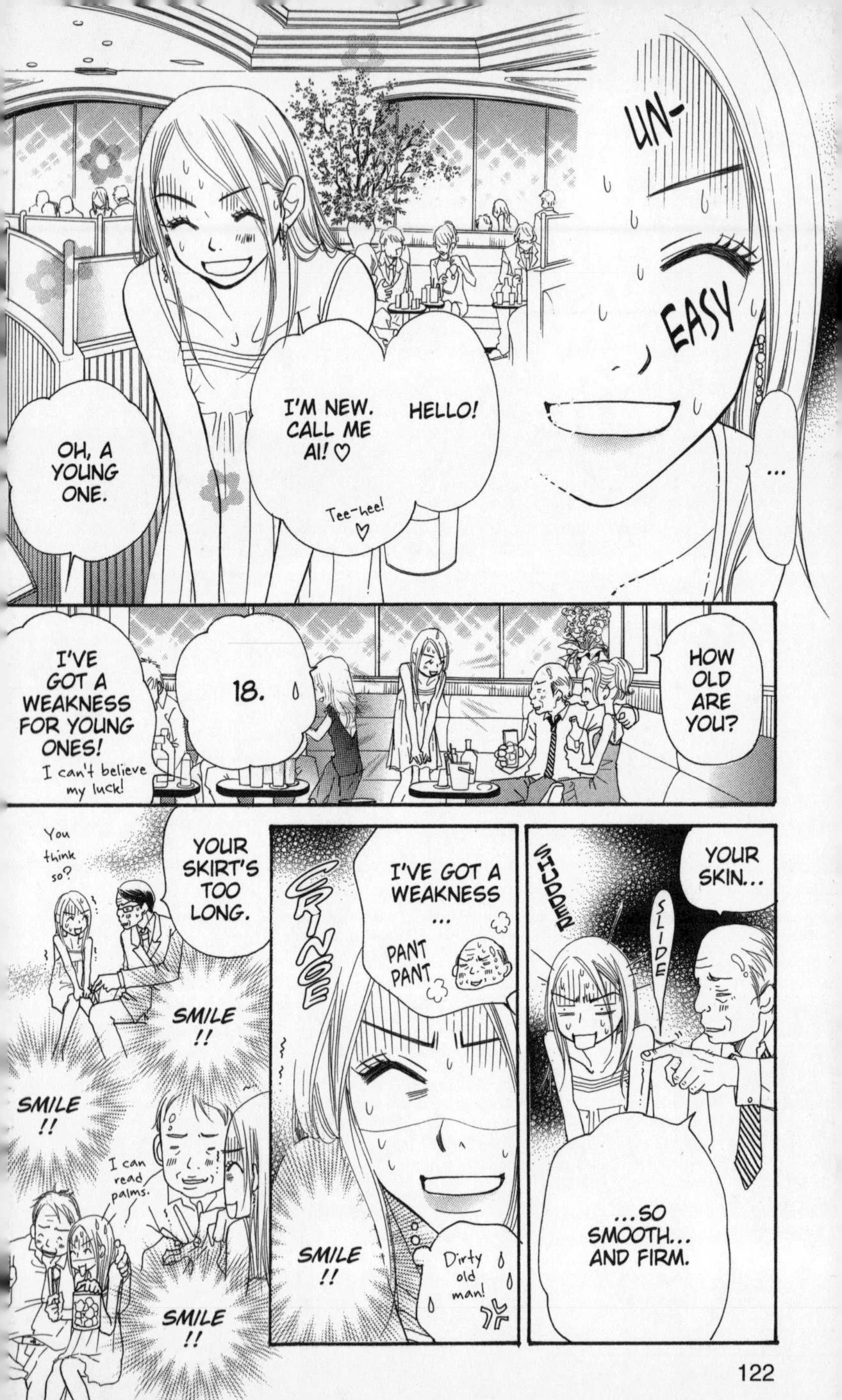
UN-
EASY
...
HELLO!
I'M NEW. CALL ME AI! ♡
Tee-hee! ♡
OH, A YOUNG ONE.
HOW OLD ARE YOU?
18.
I'VE GOT A WEAKNESS FOR YOUNG ONES!
I can't believe my luck!
YOUR SKIN...
SHUDDER
SLIDE
...SO SMOOTH... AND FIRM.
I'VE GOT A WEAKNESS ...
PANT PANT
CRINGE
SMILE !!
Dirty old man!
YOUR SKIRT'S TOO LONG.
You think so?
SMILE !!
SMILE !!
I can read palms.
SMILE !!

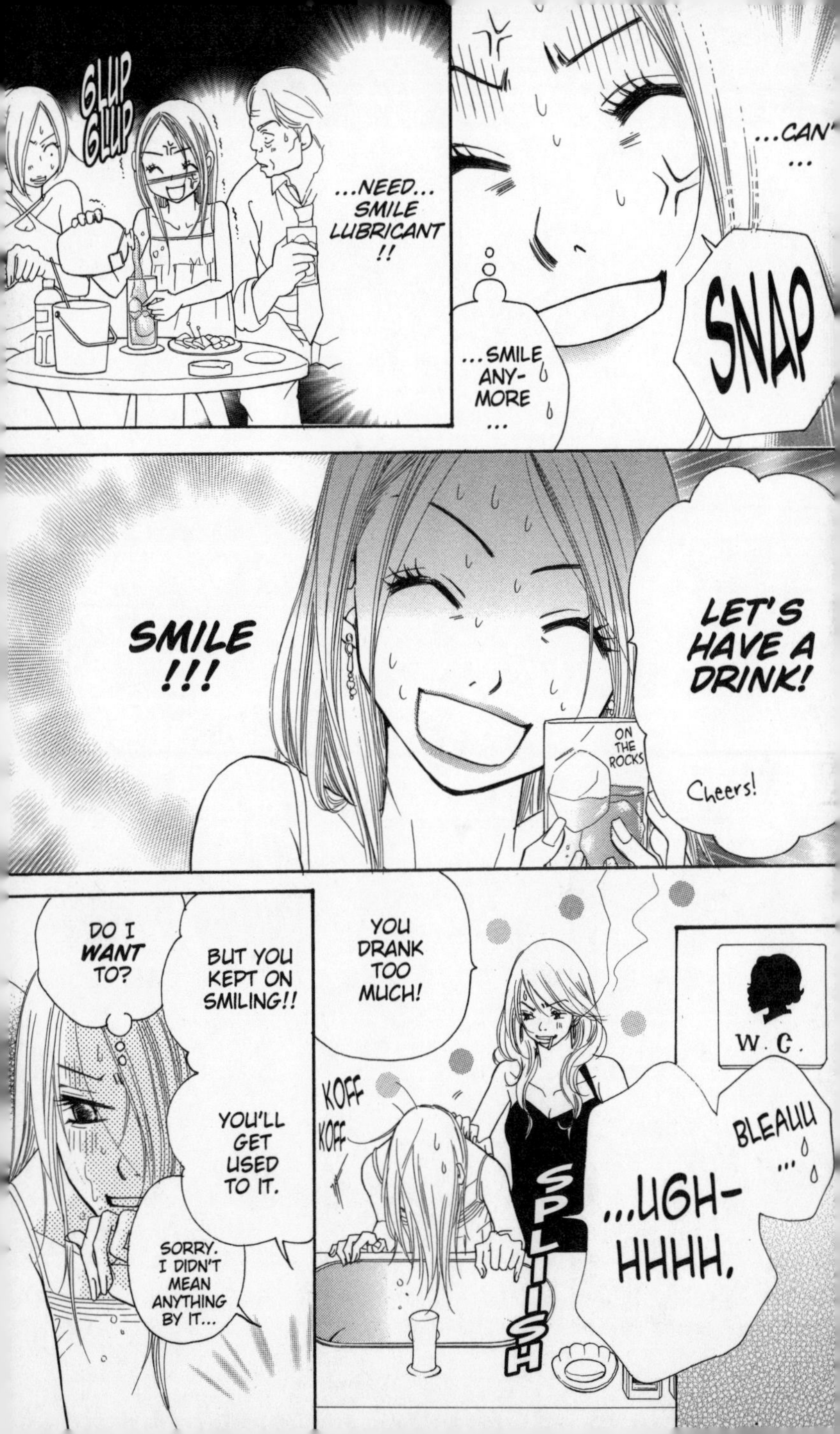

...CAN'
...
SNAP
...SMILE ANY-MORE ...
GLUP GLUP
...NEED... SMILE LUBRICANT !!
LET'S HAVE A DRINK!
Cheers!
ON THE ROCKS
SMILE !!!
BLEAUU ...
...UGH-HHHH.
SPLIISH
W.C.
KOFF KOFF
YOU DRANK TOO MUCH!
BUT YOU KEPT ON SMILING!!
DO I WANT TO?
YOU'LL GET USED TO IT.
SORRY. I DIDN'T MEAN ANYTHING BY IT...

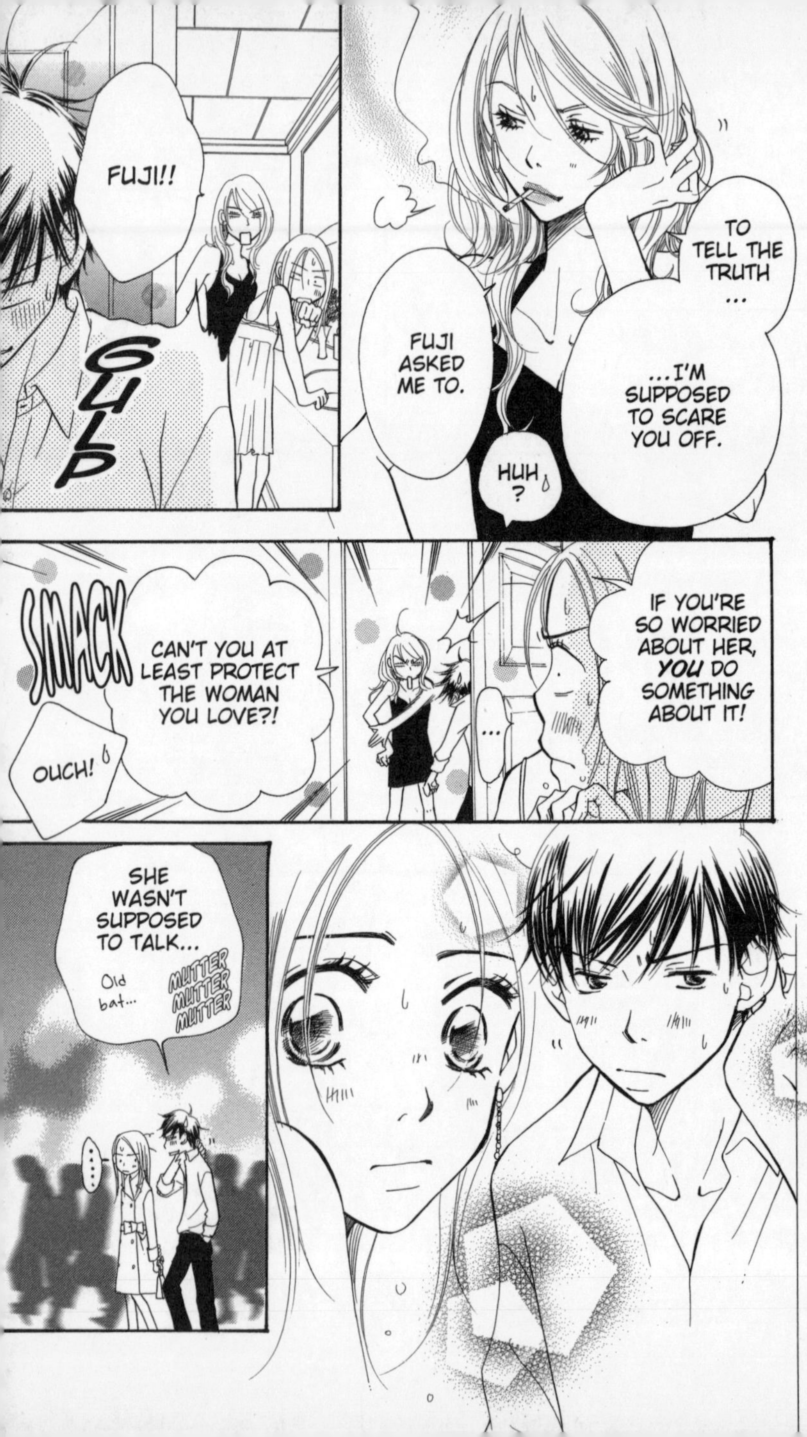
TO TELL THE TRUTH...
...I'M SUPPOSED TO SCARE YOU OFF.
HUH?
FUJI ASKED ME TO.
FUJI!!
GULP
IF YOU'RE SO WORRIED ABOUT HER, *YOU* DO SOMETHING ABOUT IT!
...
SMACK
CAN'T YOU AT LEAST PROTECT THE WOMAN YOU LOVE?!
OUCH!
SHE WASN'T SUPPOSED TO TALK...
Old bat...
MUTTER MUTTER MUTTER
.....

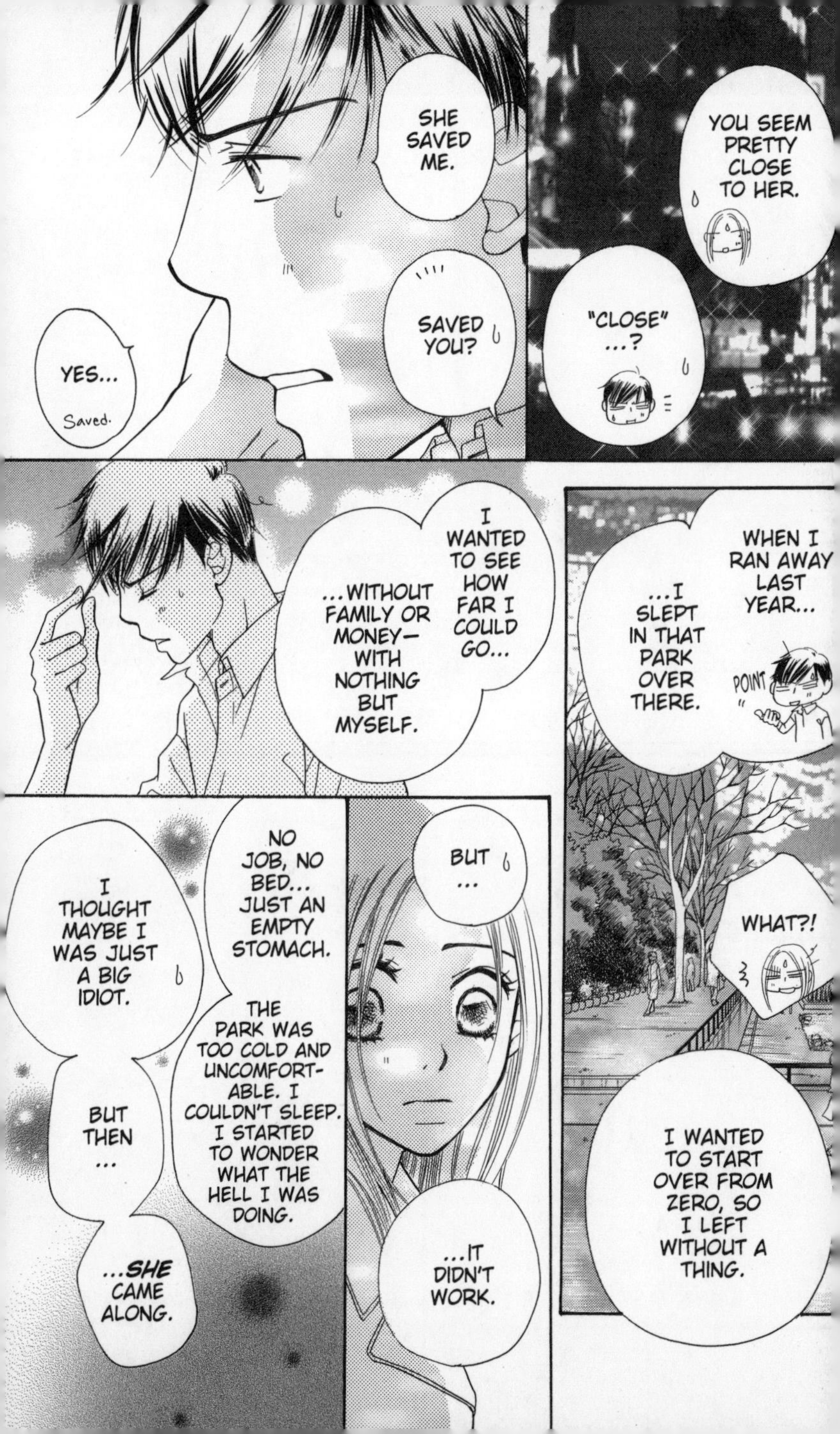
YOU SEEM PRETTY CLOSE TO HER.
"CLOSE" ...?
SHE SAVED ME.
SAVED YOU?
YES...
Saved.
WHEN I RAN AWAY LAST YEAR...
...I SLEPT IN THAT PARK OVER THERE.
POINT
WHAT?!
I WANTED TO START OVER FROM ZERO, SO I LEFT WITHOUT A THING.
I WANTED TO SEE HOW FAR I COULD GO...
...WITHOUT FAMILY OR MONEY—WITH NOTHING BUT MYSELF.
BUT ...
...IT DIDN'T WORK.
NO JOB, NO BED... JUST AN EMPTY STOMACH.
THE PARK WAS TOO COLD AND UNCOMFORT-ABLE. I COULDN'T SLEEP. I STARTED TO WONDER WHAT THE HELL I WAS DOING.
I THOUGHT MAYBE I WAS JUST A BIG IDIOT.
BUT THEN ...
...*SHE* CAME ALONG.

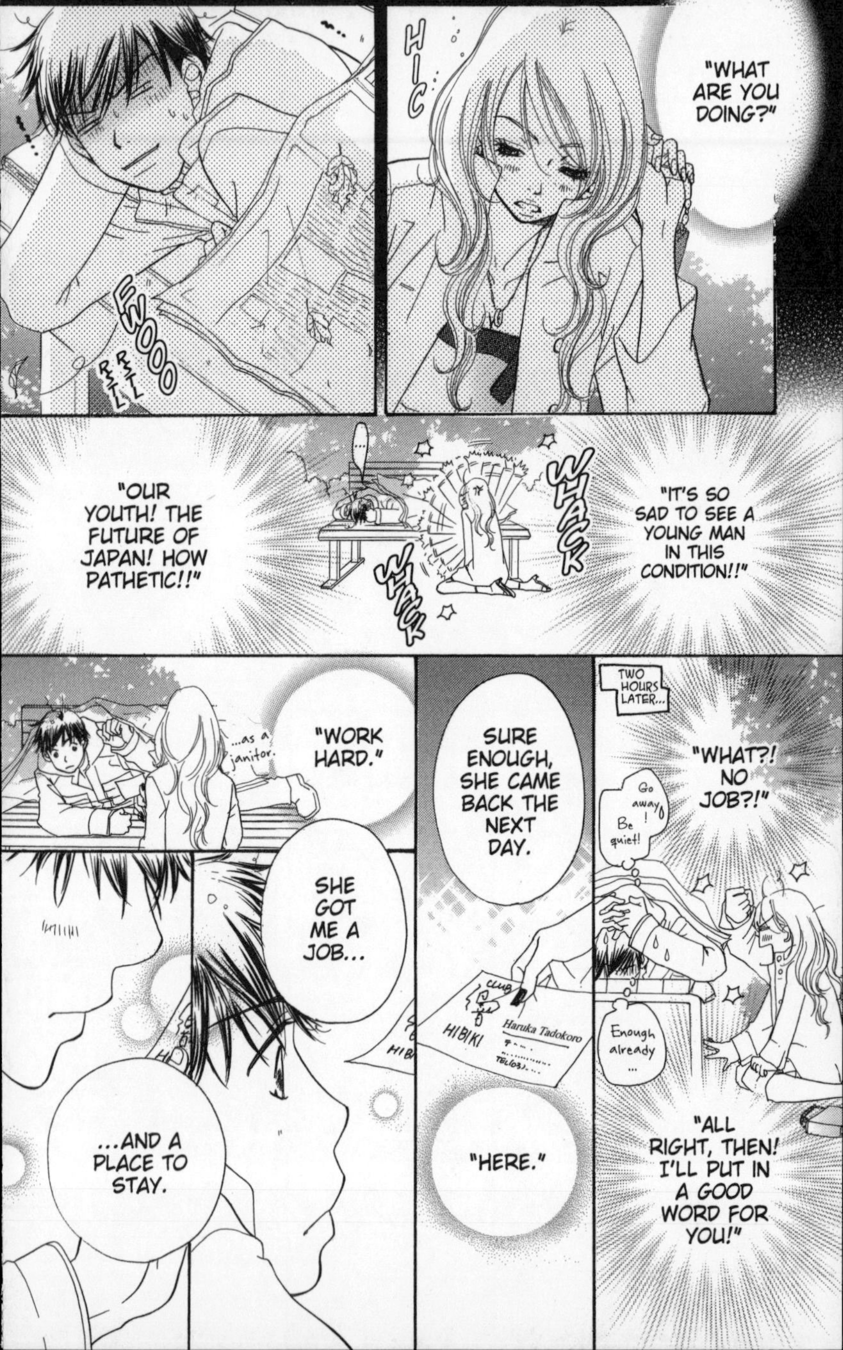
"WHAT ARE YOU DOING?"
HIC...
...
FWOOO
RSTL RSTL
"IT'S SO SAD TO SEE A YOUNG MAN IN THIS CONDITION!!"
WHACK
...
WHACK
"OUR YOUTH! THE FUTURE OF JAPAN! HOW PATHETIC!!"
TWO HOURS LATER...
"WHAT?! NO JOB?!"
Go away!
Be quiet!
Enough already...
"ALL RIGHT, THEN! I'LL PUT IN A GOOD WORD FOR YOU!"
SURE ENOUGH, SHE CAME BACK THE NEXT DAY.
CLUB
HIBIKI
Haruka Tadokoro
"HERE."
"WORK HARD."
...as a janitor.
SHE GOT ME A JOB...
...AND A PLACE TO STAY.

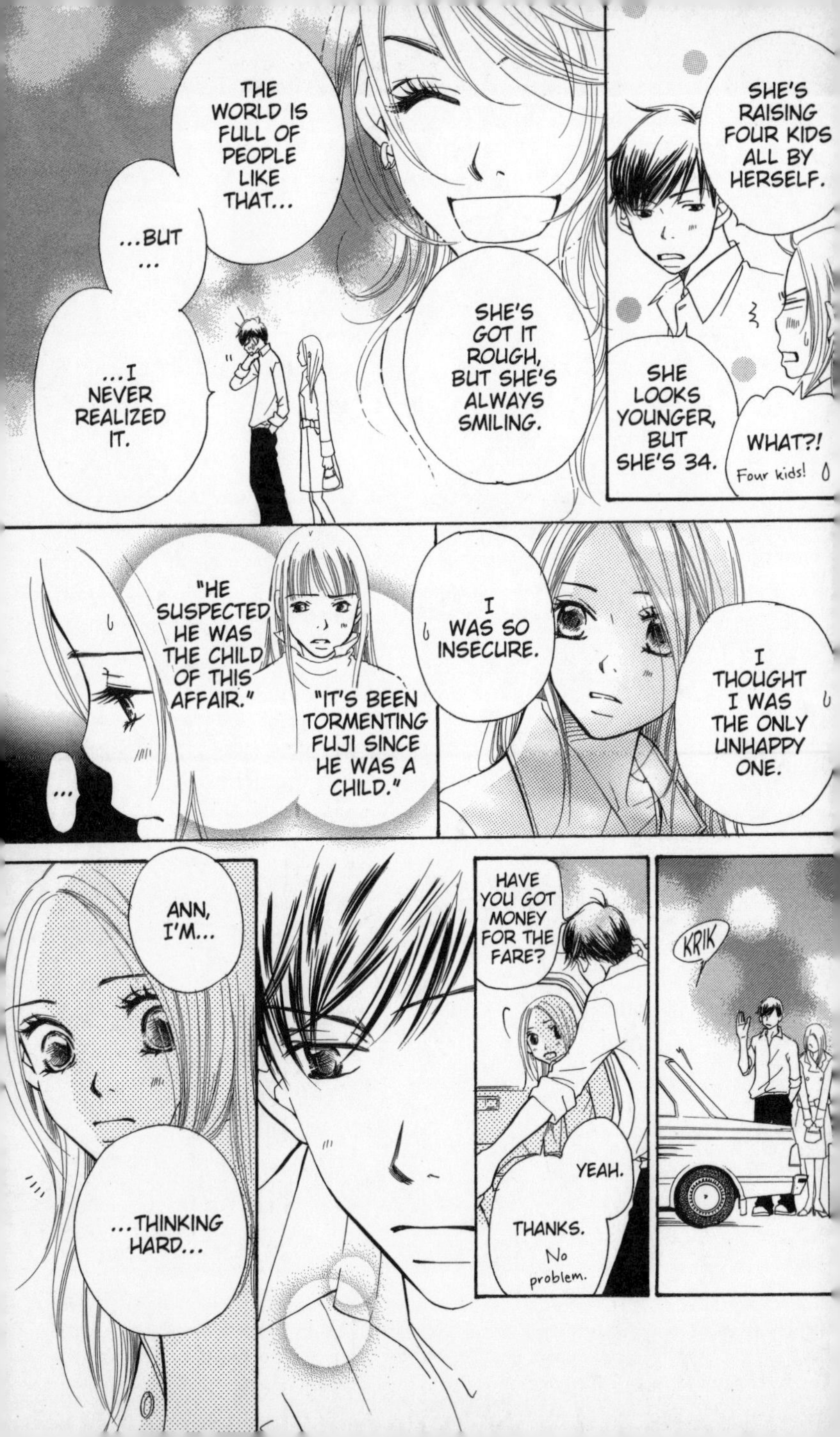
SHE'S RAISING FOUR KIDS ALL BY HERSELF.
WHAT?!
Four kids!
SHE LOOKS YOUNGER, BUT SHE'S 34.
SHE'S GOT IT ROUGH, BUT SHE'S ALWAYS SMILING.
THE WORLD IS FULL OF PEOPLE LIKE THAT...
...BUT ...
...I NEVER REALIZED IT.
I THOUGHT I WAS THE ONLY UNHAPPY ONE.
I WAS SO INSECURE.
"HE SUSPECTED HE WAS THE CHILD OF THIS AFFAIR."
"IT'S BEEN TORMENTING FUJI SINCE HE WAS A CHILD."
...
KRIK
HAVE YOU GOT MONEY FOR THE FARE?
YEAH.
THANKS.
No problem.
ANN, I'M...
...THINKING HARD...

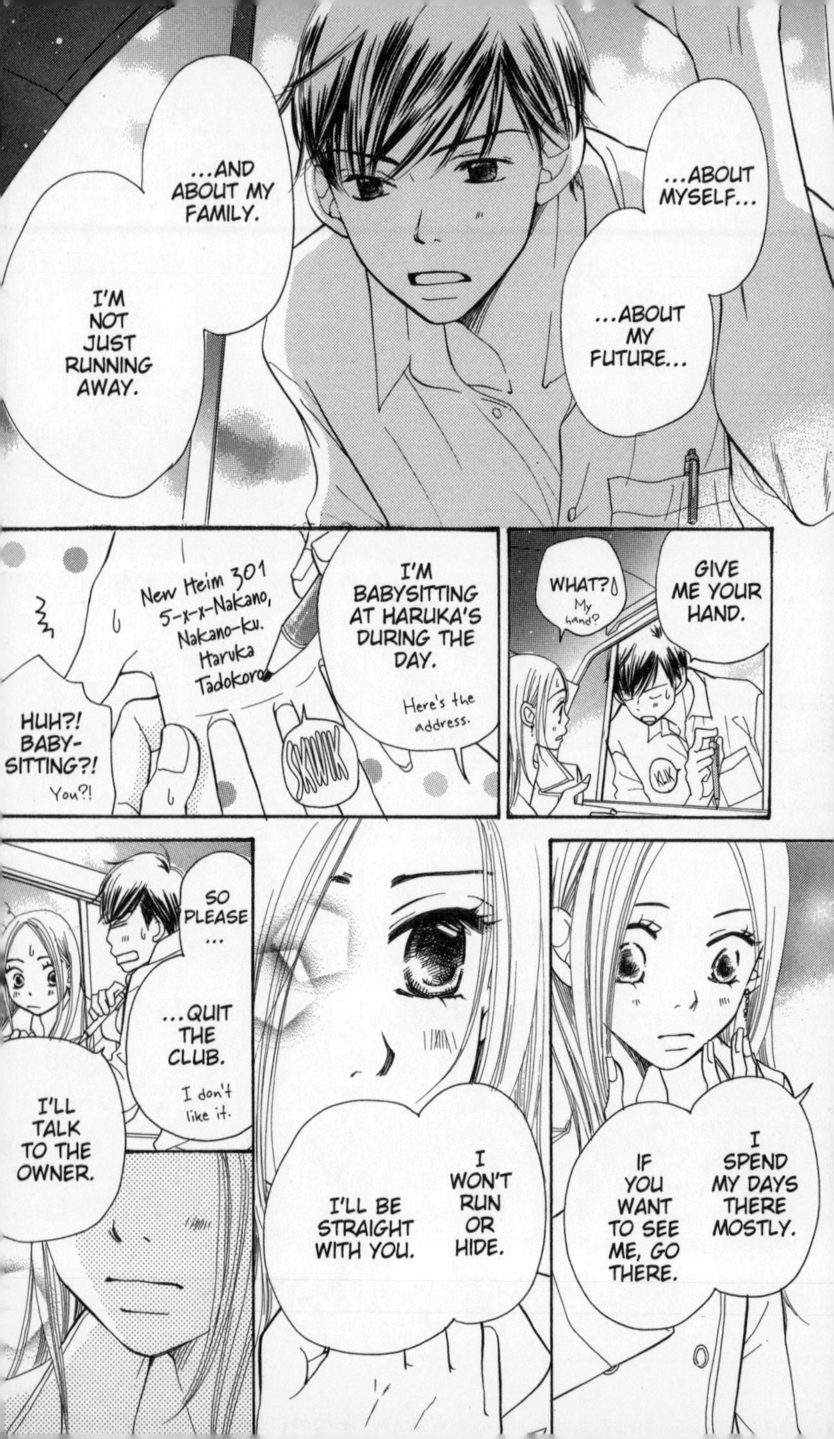
...ABOUT MYSELF...
...ABOUT MY FUTURE...
...AND ABOUT MY FAMILY.
I'M NOT JUST RUNNING AWAY.
GIVE ME YOUR HAND.
WHAT? My hand?
KLIK
I'M BABYSITTING AT HARUKA'S DURING THE DAY.
Here's the address.
SKWIK
New Heim 301 5-x-x-Nakano, Nakano-ku. Haruka Tadokoro
HUH?! BABY-SITTING?!
You?!
I SPEND MY DAYS THERE MOSTLY.
IF YOU WANT TO SEE ME, GO THERE.
I WON'T RUN OR HIDE.
I'LL BE STRAIGHT WITH YOU.
SO PLEASE ...
...QUIT THE CLUB.
I don't like it.
I'LL TALK TO THE OWNER.

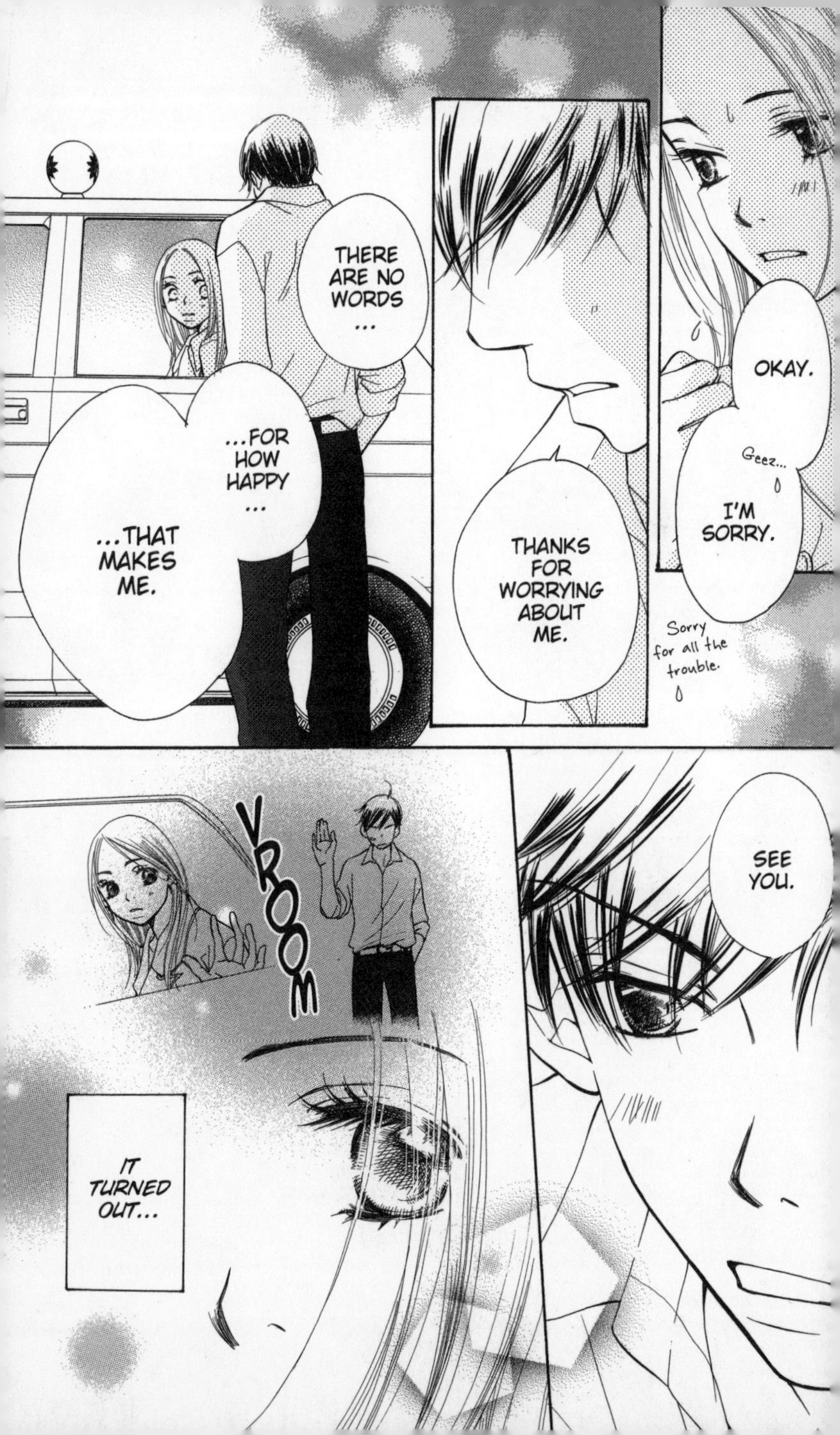

OKAY.
Geez...
I'M SORRY.
Sorry for all the trouble.
THANKS FOR WORRYING ABOUT ME.
THERE ARE NO WORDS...
...FOR HOW HAPPY...
...THAT MAKES ME.
SEE YOU.
VROOM
IT TURNED OUT...

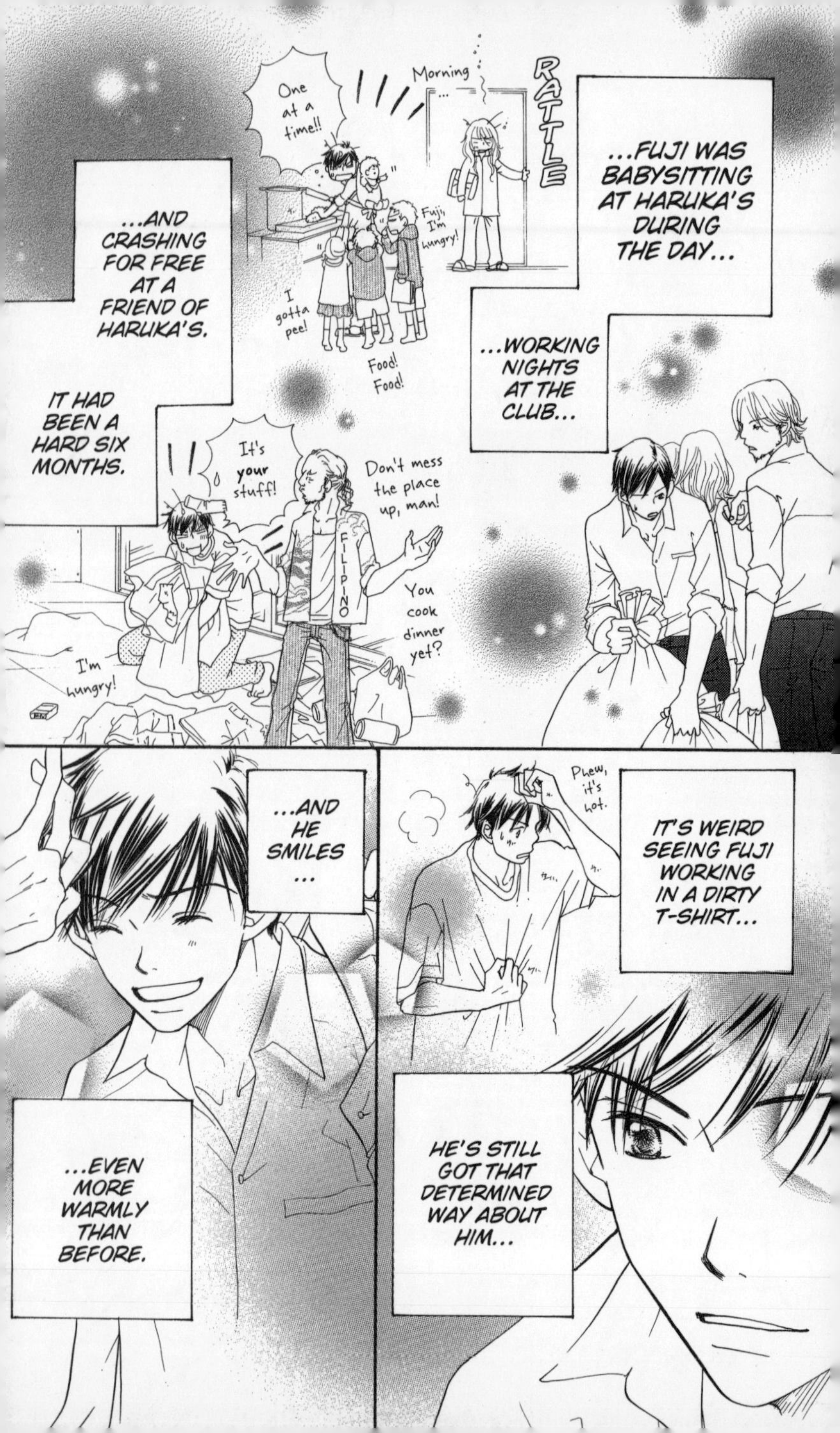
...FUJI WAS BABYSITTING AT HARUKA'S DURING THE DAY...
RATTLE
Morning...
One at a time!!
Fuji, I'm hungry!
I gotta pee!
Food! Food!
...WORKING NIGHTS AT THE CLUB...
...AND CRASHING FOR FREE AT A FRIEND OF HARUKA'S.
Don't mess the place up, man!
You cook dinner yet?
It's **your** stuff!
I'm hungry!
IT HAD BEEN A HARD SIX MONTHS.
Phew, it's hot.
IT'S WEIRD SEEING FUJI WORKING IN A DIRTY T-SHIRT...
HE'S STILL GOT THAT DETERMINED WAY ABOUT HIM...
...AND HE SMILES...
...EVEN MORE WARMLY THAN BEFORE.

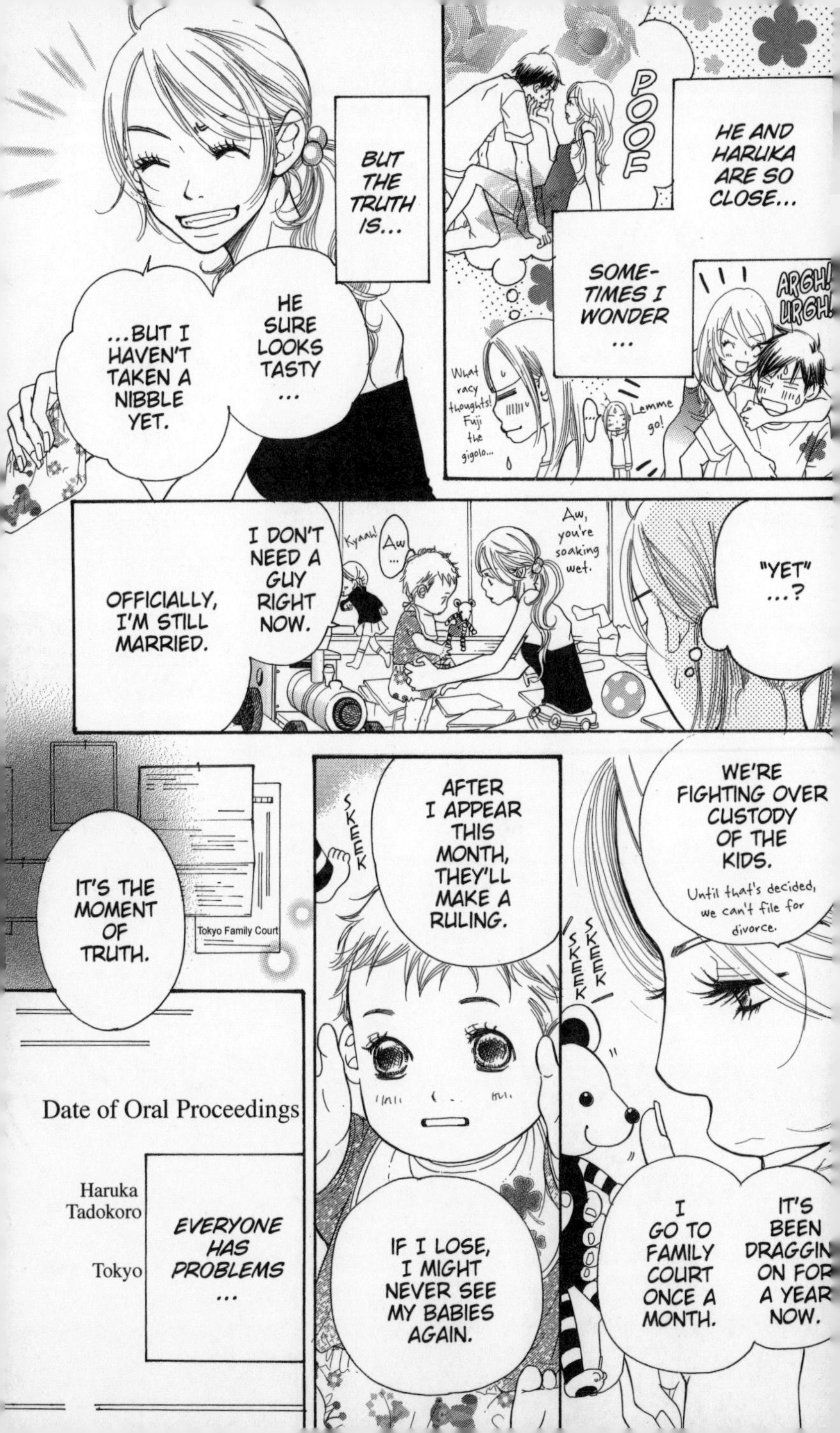
POOF
HE AND HARUKA ARE SO CLOSE...
SOMETIMES I WONDER...
ARGH! URGH!
Lemme go!
...
What racy thoughts! Fuji the gigolo...
BUT THE TRUTH IS...
HE SURE LOOKS TASTY...
...BUT I HAVEN'T TAKEN A NIBBLE YET.
"YET"...?
Aw, you're soaking wet.
Aw...
Kyaaa!
I DON'T NEED A GUY RIGHT NOW.
OFFICIALLY, I'M STILL MARRIED.
WE'RE FIGHTING OVER CUSTODY OF THE KIDS.
Until that's decided, we can't file for divorce.
SKEEK SKEEK
IT'S BEEN DRAGGIN ON FOR A YEAR NOW.
I GO TO FAMILY COURT ONCE A MONTH.
AFTER I APPEAR THIS MONTH, THEY'LL MAKE A RULING.
SKEEK
IF I LOSE, I MIGHT NEVER SEE MY BABIES AGAIN.
IT'S THE MOMENT OF TRUTH.
Tokyo Family Court
Date of Oral Proceedings
Haruka Tadokoro
Tokyo
EVERYONE HAS PROBLEMS...

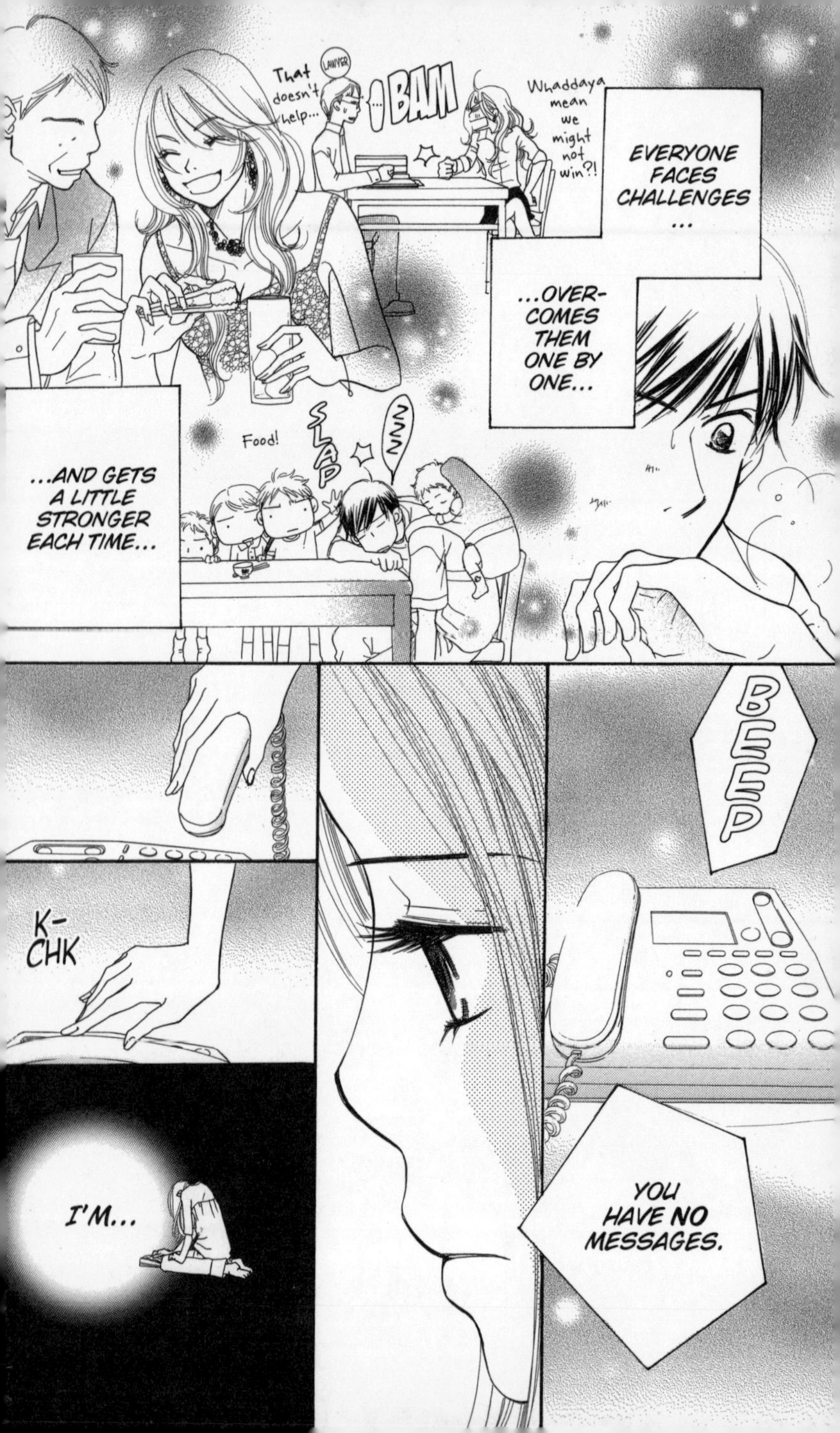
EVERYONE FACES CHALLENGES...
Whaddaya mean we might not win?!
BAM
LAWYER
That doesn't help...
...
...OVER-COMES THEM ONE BY ONE...
ZZZ
SLAP
Food!
...AND GETS A LITTLE STRONGER EACH TIME...
BEEP
YOU HAVE NO MESSAGES.
K-CHK
I'M...

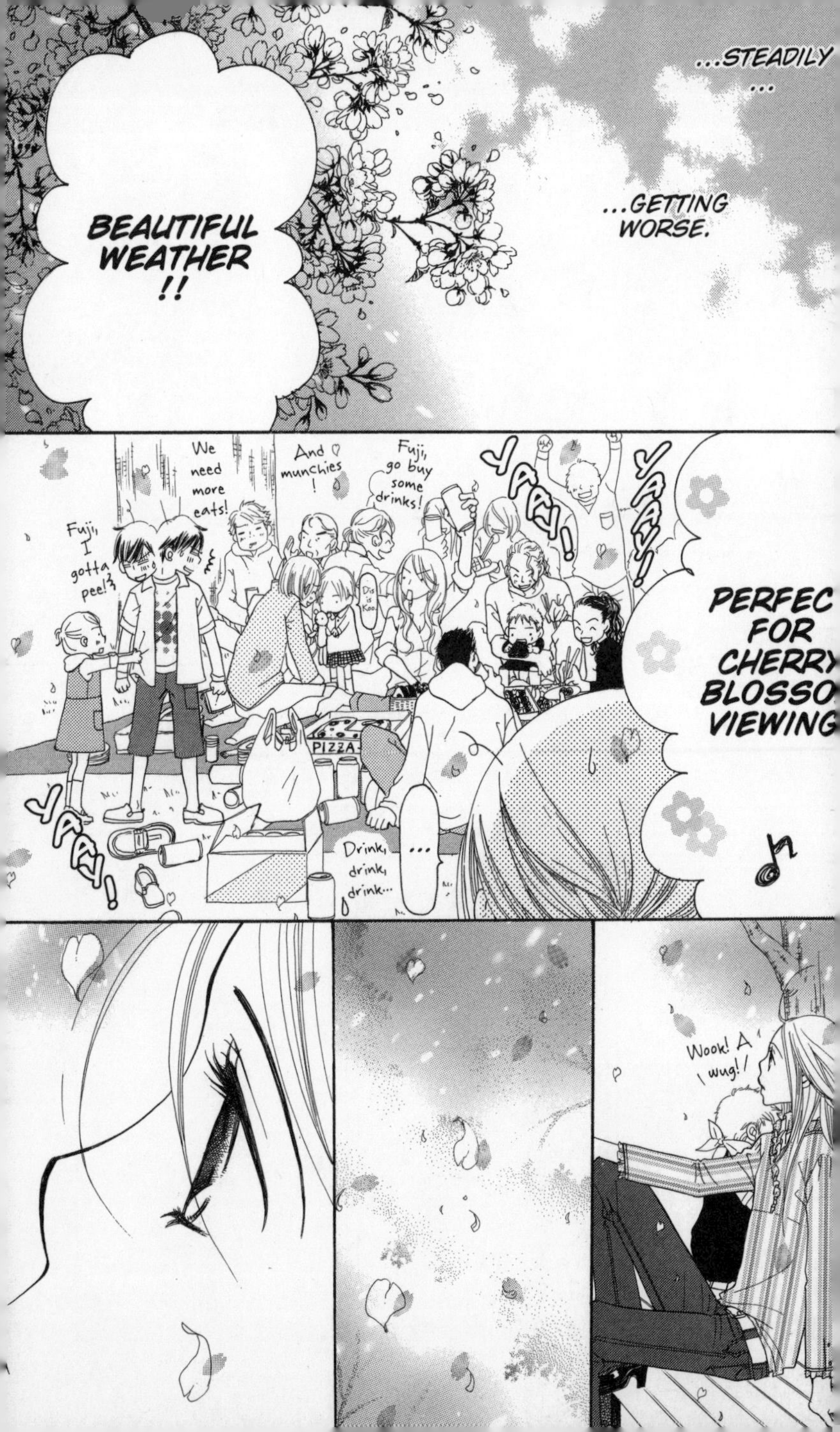

...STEADILY ...
...GETTING WORSE.
BEAUTIFUL WEATHER !!
YAAAY!
PERFEC FOR CHERRY BLOSSO VIEWING
YAAY!
Fuji, go buy some drinks!
And munchies!
We need more eats!
Dis is Koo.
Fuji, I gotta pee!
...
Drink, drink, drink...
YAAY!
Wook! A wug!!

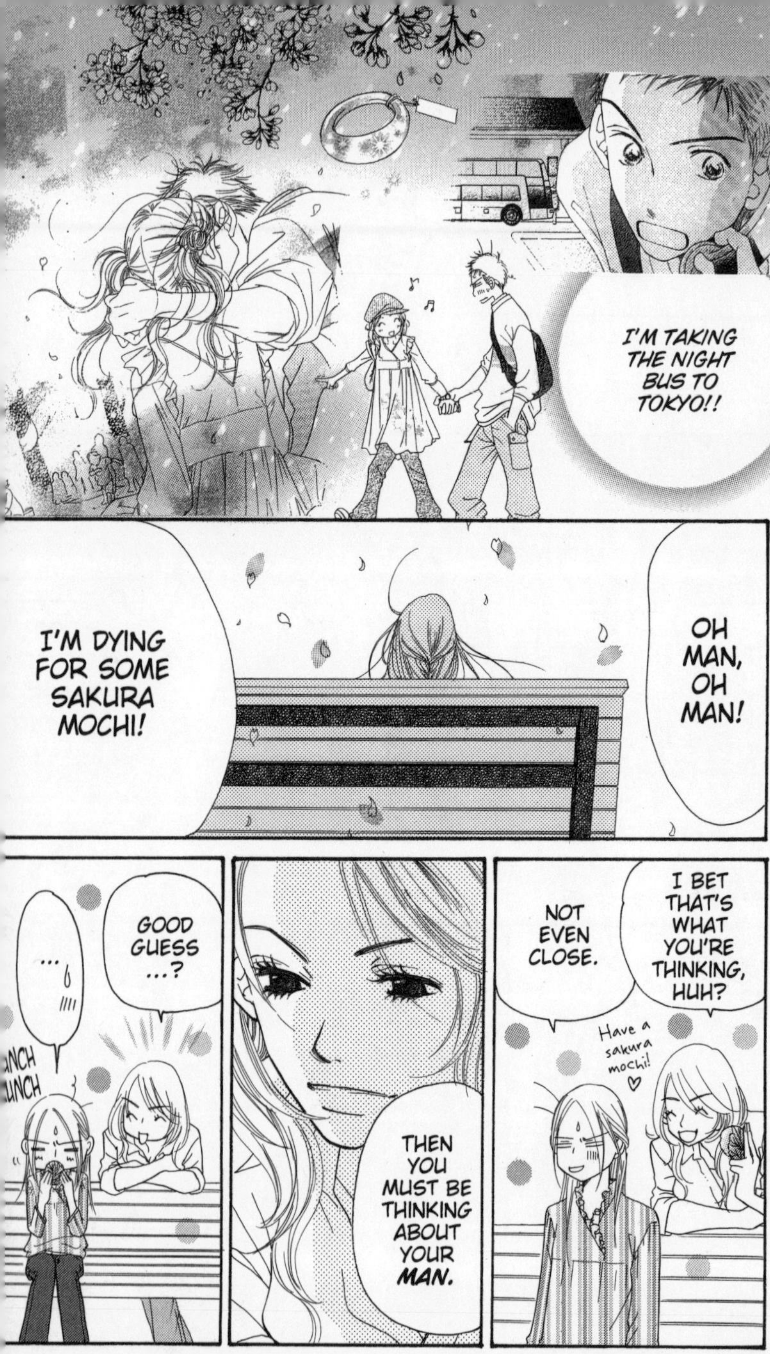
I'M TAKING THE NIGHT BUS TO TOKYO!!
OH MAN, OH MAN!
I'M DYING FOR SOME SAKURA MOCHI!
I BET THAT'S WHAT YOU'RE THINKING, HUH?
NOT EVEN CLOSE.
Have a sakura mochi! ♥
THEN YOU MUST BE THINKING ABOUT YOUR ***MAN.***
GOOD GUESS ...?
...

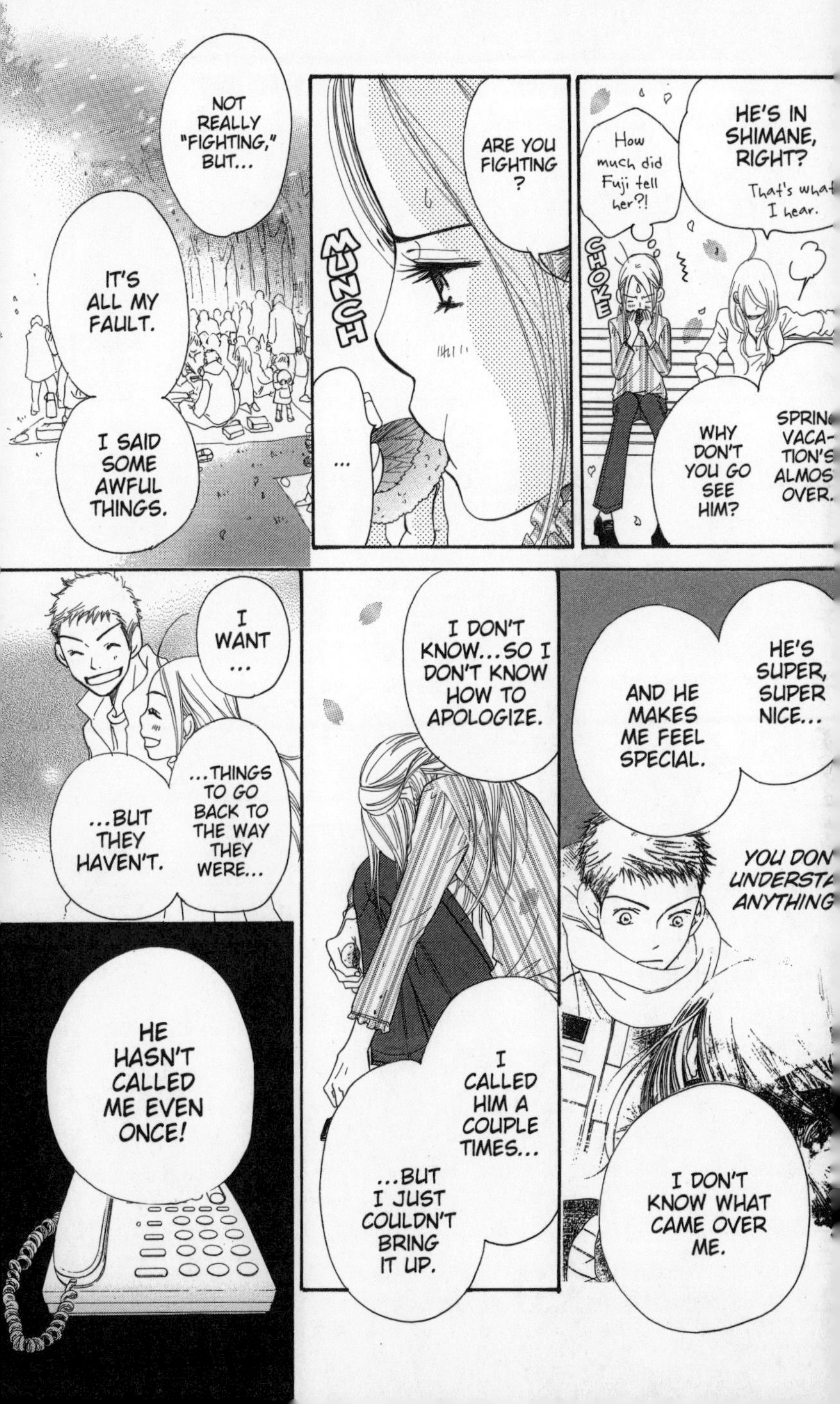
HE'S IN SHIMANE, RIGHT?
That's what I hear.
How much did Fuji tell her?!
CHOKE
SPRIN VACA- TION'S ALMOS OVER.
WHY DON'T YOU GO SEE HIM?
ARE YOU FIGHTING?
MUNCH
...
NOT REALLY "FIGHTING," BUT...
IT'S ALL MY FAULT.
I SAID SOME AWFUL THINGS.
HE'S SUPER, SUPER NICE...
AND HE MAKES ME FEEL SPECIAL.
YOU DON UNDERST ANYTHING
I DON'T KNOW WHAT CAME OVER ME.
I DON'T KNOW...SO I DON'T KNOW HOW TO APOLOGIZE.
I CALLED HIM A COUPLE TIMES...
...BUT I JUST COULDN'T BRING IT UP.
I WANT...
...THINGS TO GO BACK TO THE WAY THEY WERE...
...BUT THEY HAVEN'T.
HE HASN'T CALLED ME EVEN ONCE!

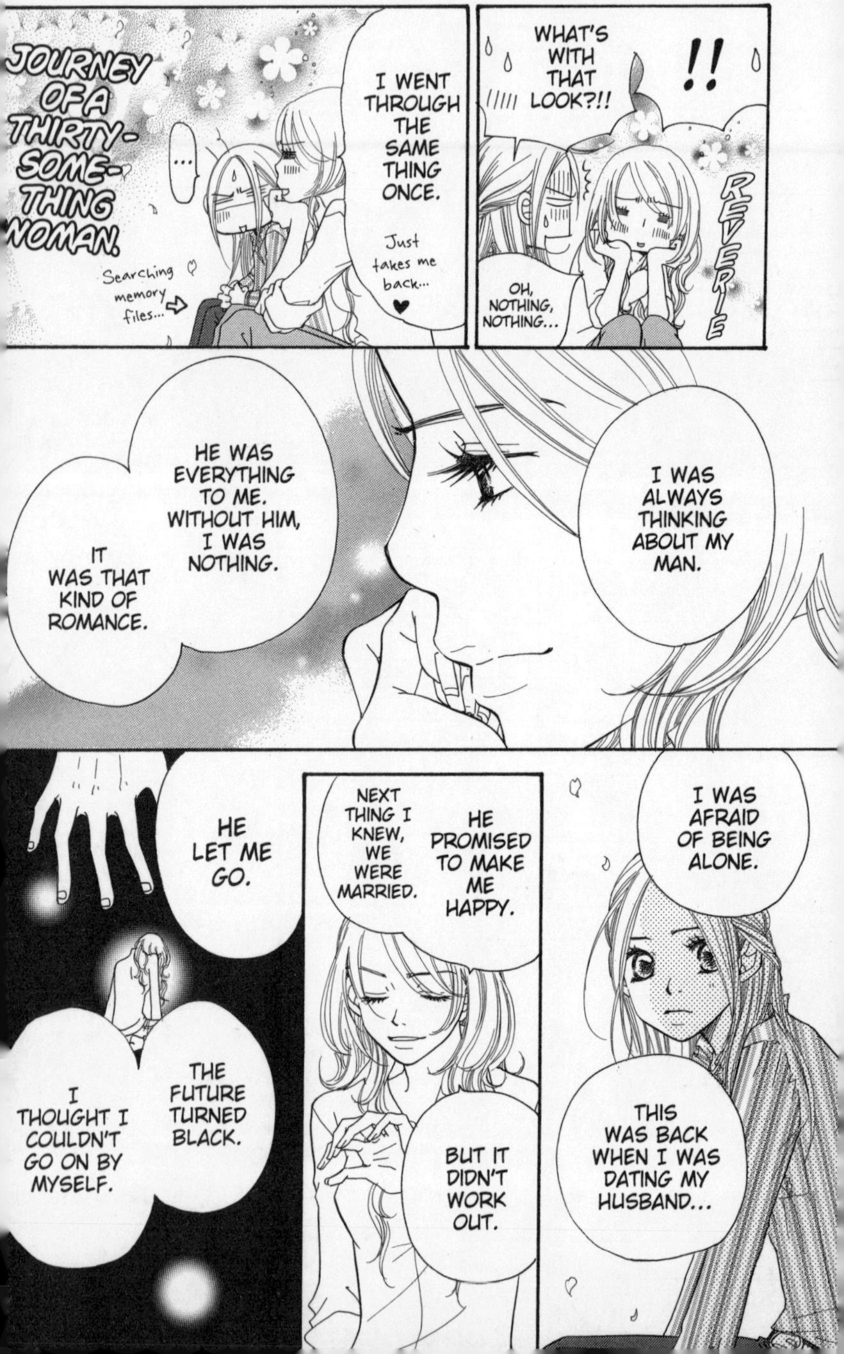
!!
WHAT'S WITH THAT LOOK?!!
REVERIE
OH, NOTHING, NOTHING...
I WENT THROUGH THE SAME THING ONCE.
Just takes me back... ♥
...
JOURNEY OF A THIRTY-SOMETHING WOMAN.
Searching memory files...
I WAS ALWAYS THINKING ABOUT MY MAN.
HE WAS EVERYTHING TO ME. WITHOUT HIM, I WAS NOTHING.
IT WAS THAT KIND OF ROMANCE.
I WAS AFRAID OF BEING ALONE.
THIS WAS BACK WHEN I WAS DATING MY HUSBAND...
HE PROMISED TO MAKE ME HAPPY.
NEXT THING I KNEW, WE WERE MARRIED.
BUT IT DIDN'T WORK OUT.
HE LET ME GO.
THE FUTURE TURNED BLACK.
I THOUGHT I COULDN'T GO ON BY MYSELF.

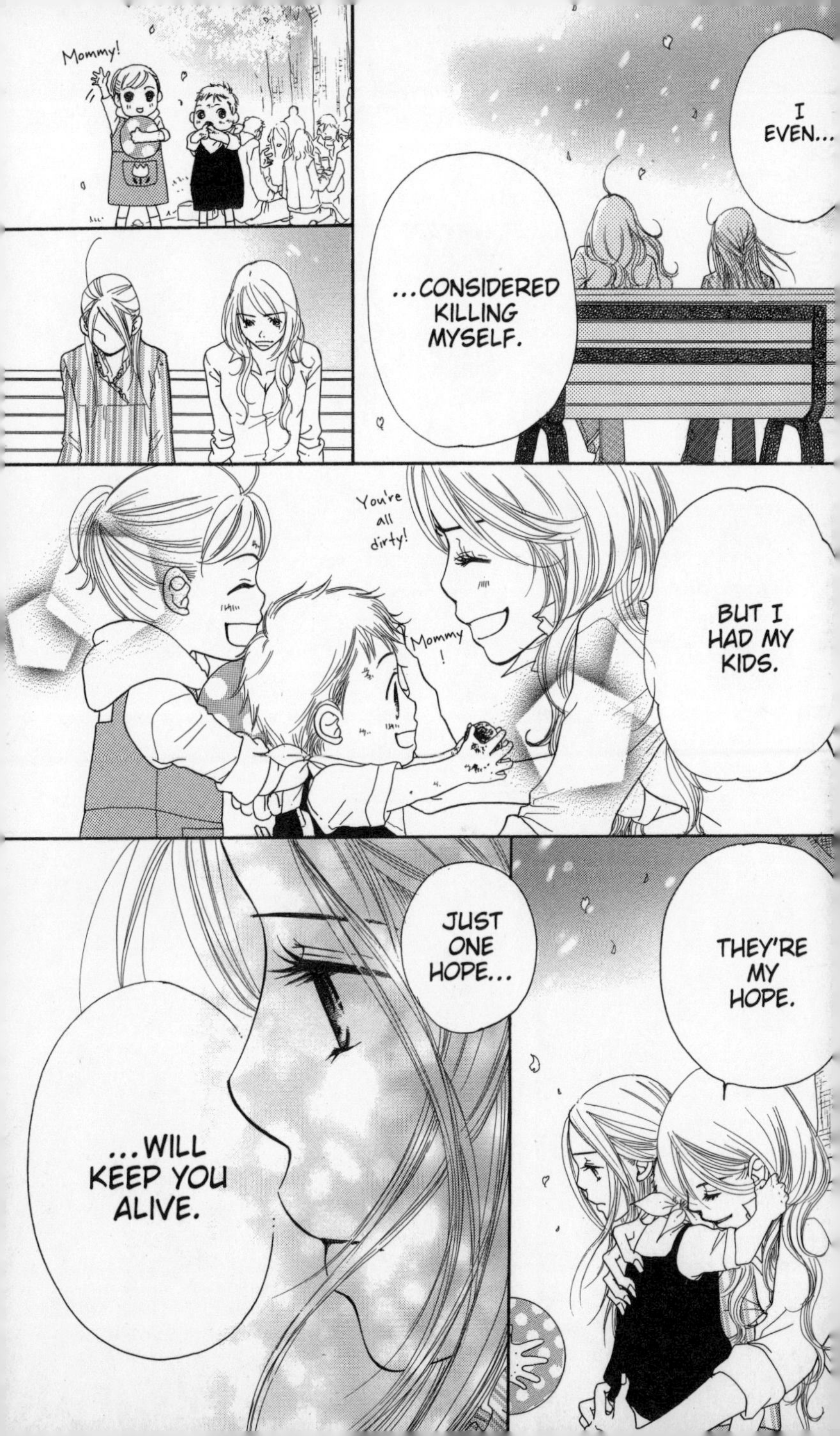
I EVEN...
...CONSIDERED KILLING MYSELF.
Mommy!
BUT I HAD MY KIDS.
You're all dirty!
Mommy!
THEY'RE MY HOPE.
JUST ONE HOPE...
...WILL KEEP YOU ALIVE.

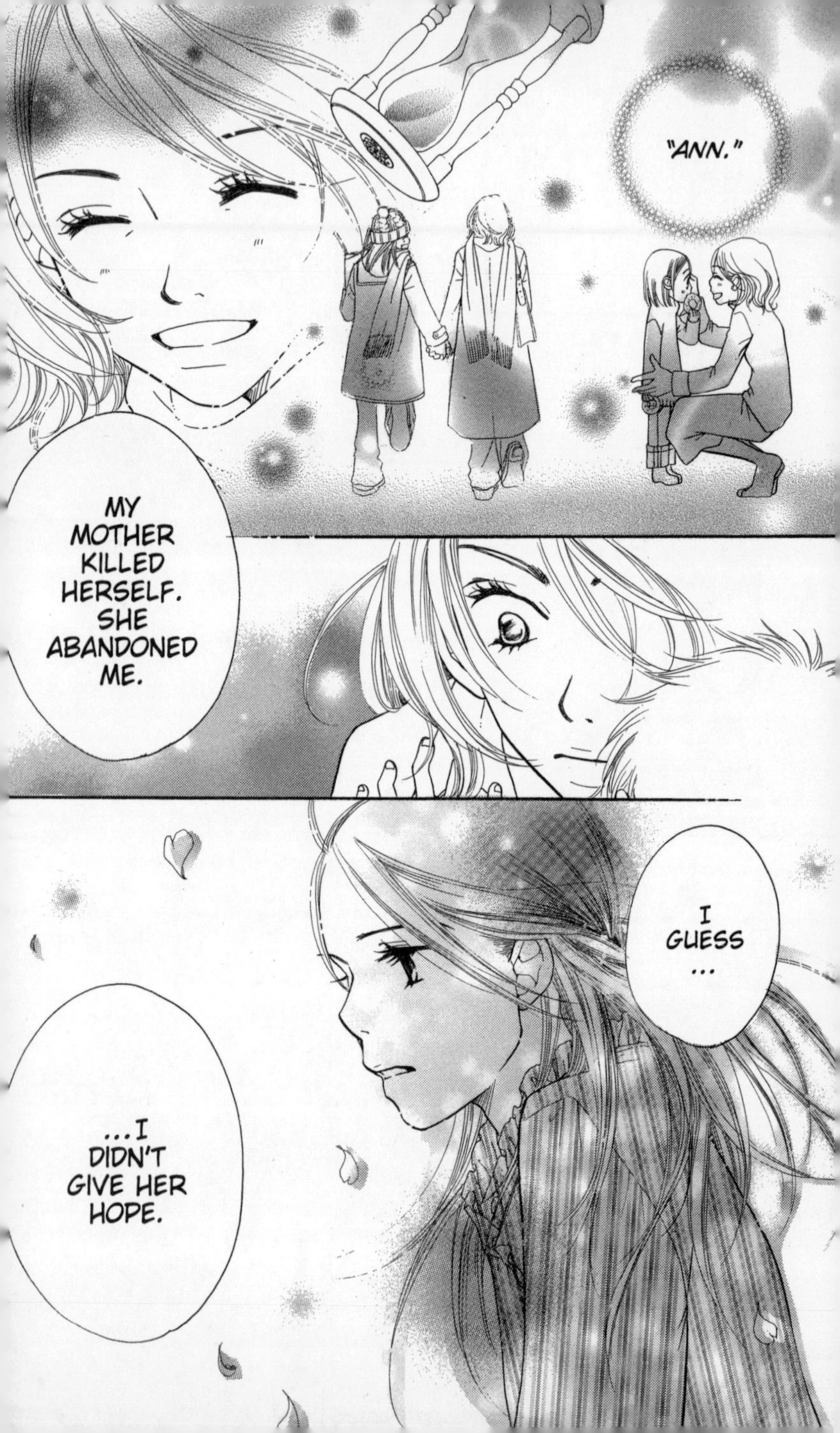
"ANN."
MY MOTHER KILLED HERSELF. SHE ABANDONED ME.
I GUESS ...
...I DIDN'T GIVE HER HOPE.

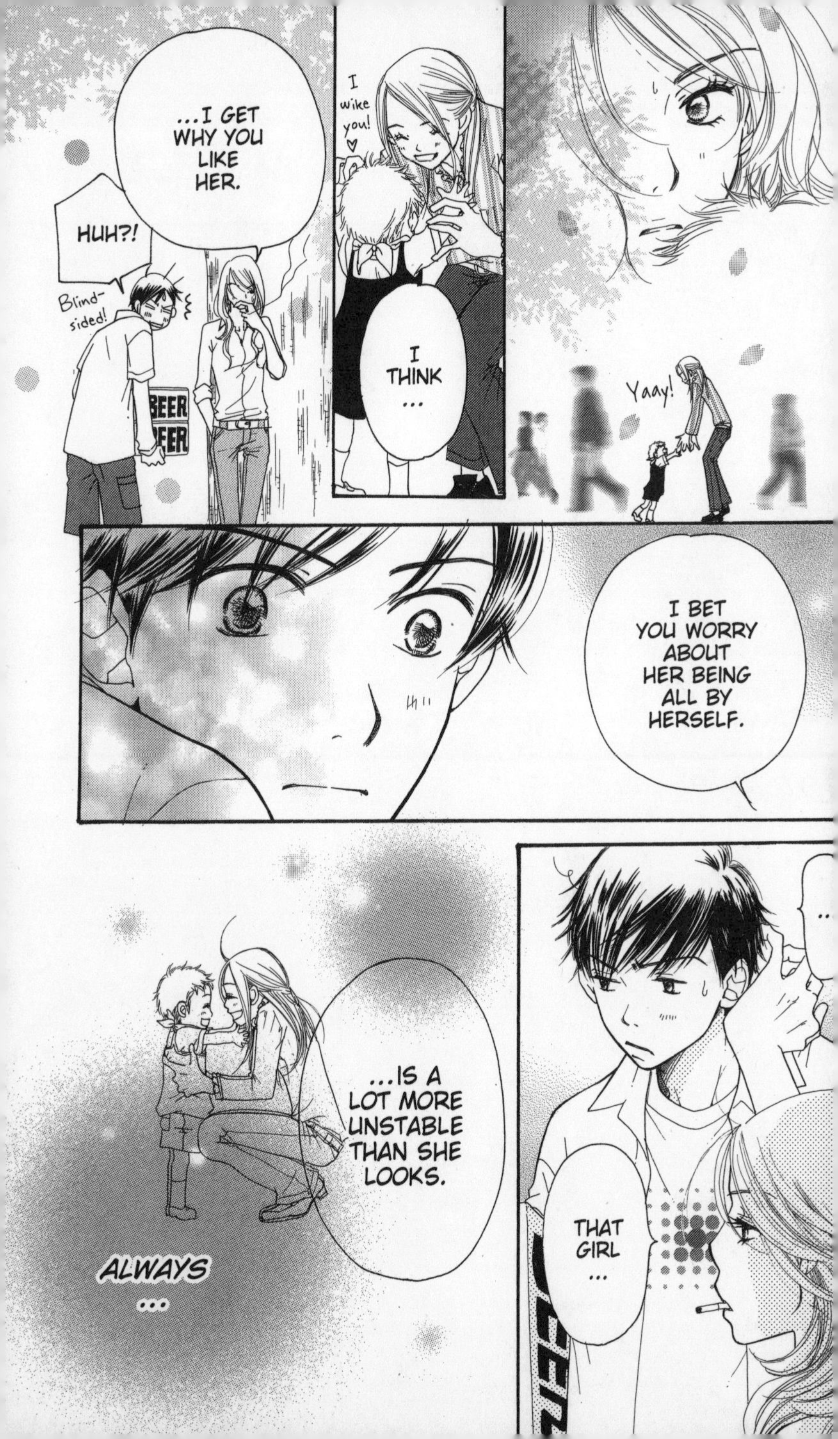

Yaay!
I wike you! ♥
I THINK ...
...I GET WHY YOU LIKE HER.
HUH?!
Blind-sided!
I BET YOU WORRY ABOUT HER BEING ALL BY HERSELF.
...
THAT GIRL ...
...IS A LOT MORE UNSTABLE THAN SHE LOOKS.
ALWAYS ...

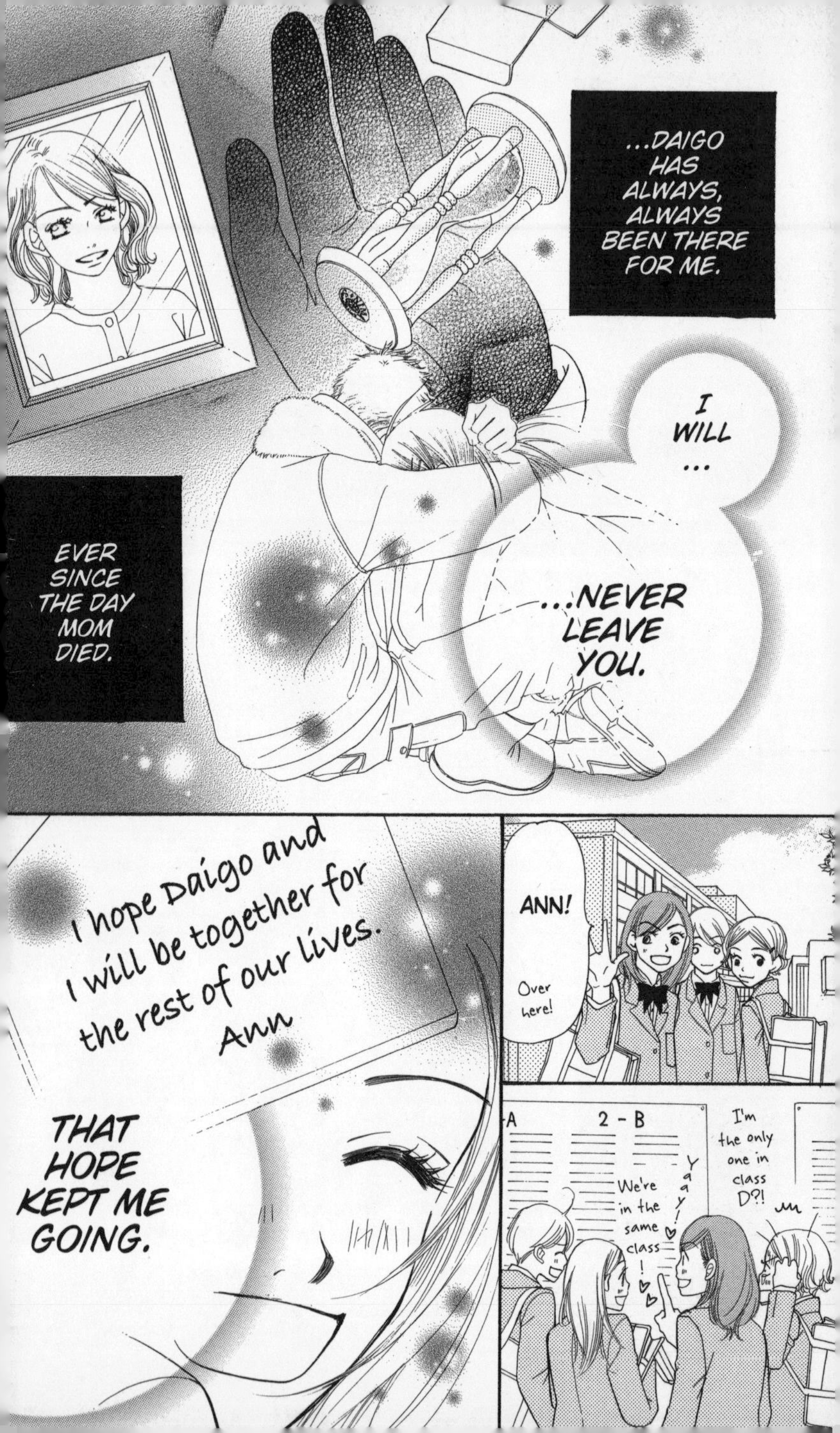
...DAIGO HAS ALWAYS, ALWAYS BEEN THERE FOR ME.
I WILL ...
...NEVER LEAVE YOU.
EVER SINCE THE DAY MOM DIED.
ANN!
Over here!
I'm the only one in class D?!
2 - B
A
Yaay!
We're in the same class!
I hope Daigo and I will be together for the rest of our lives. Ann
THAT HOPE KEPT ME GOING.

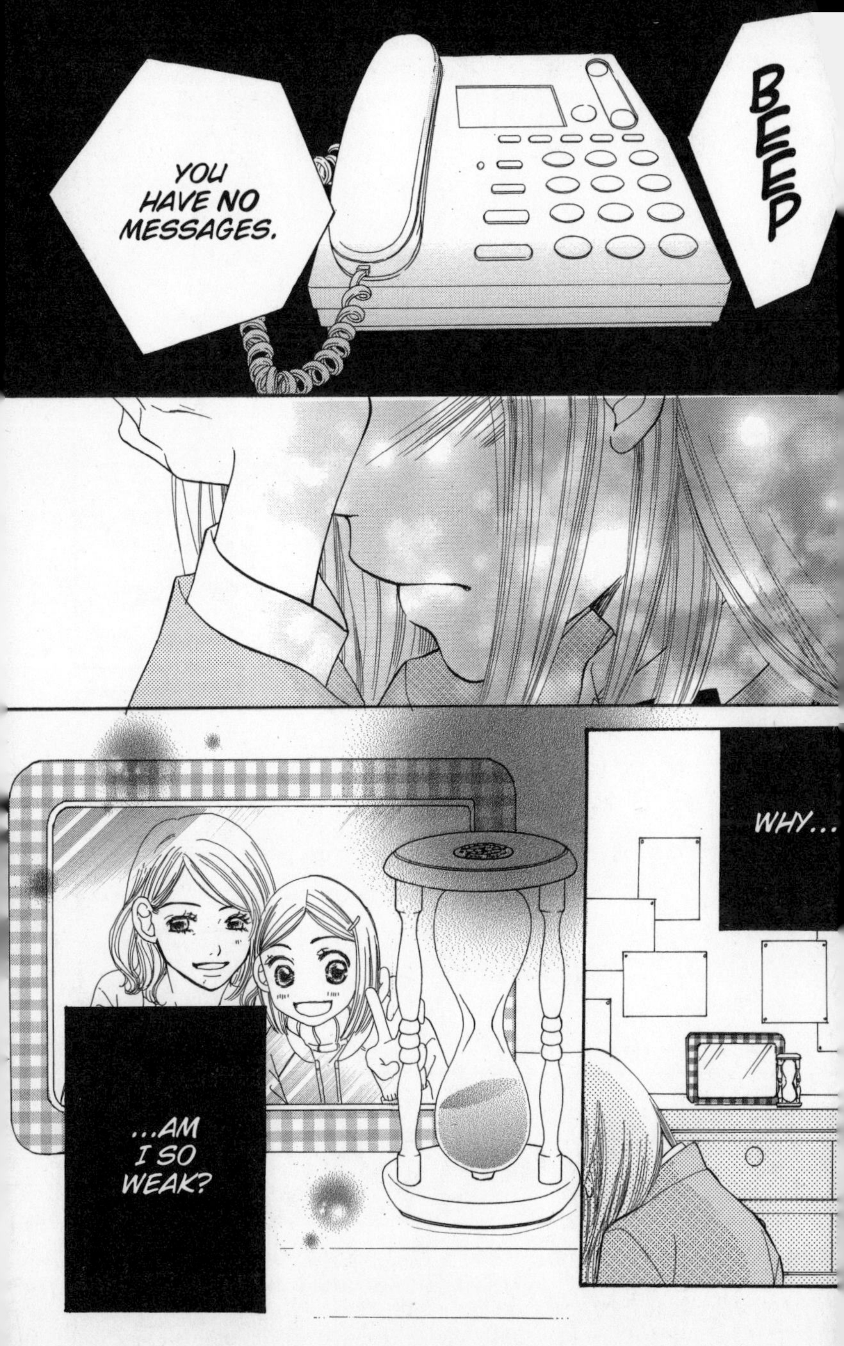
BEEP
YOU HAVE NO MESSAGES.
WHY...
...AM I SO WEAK?

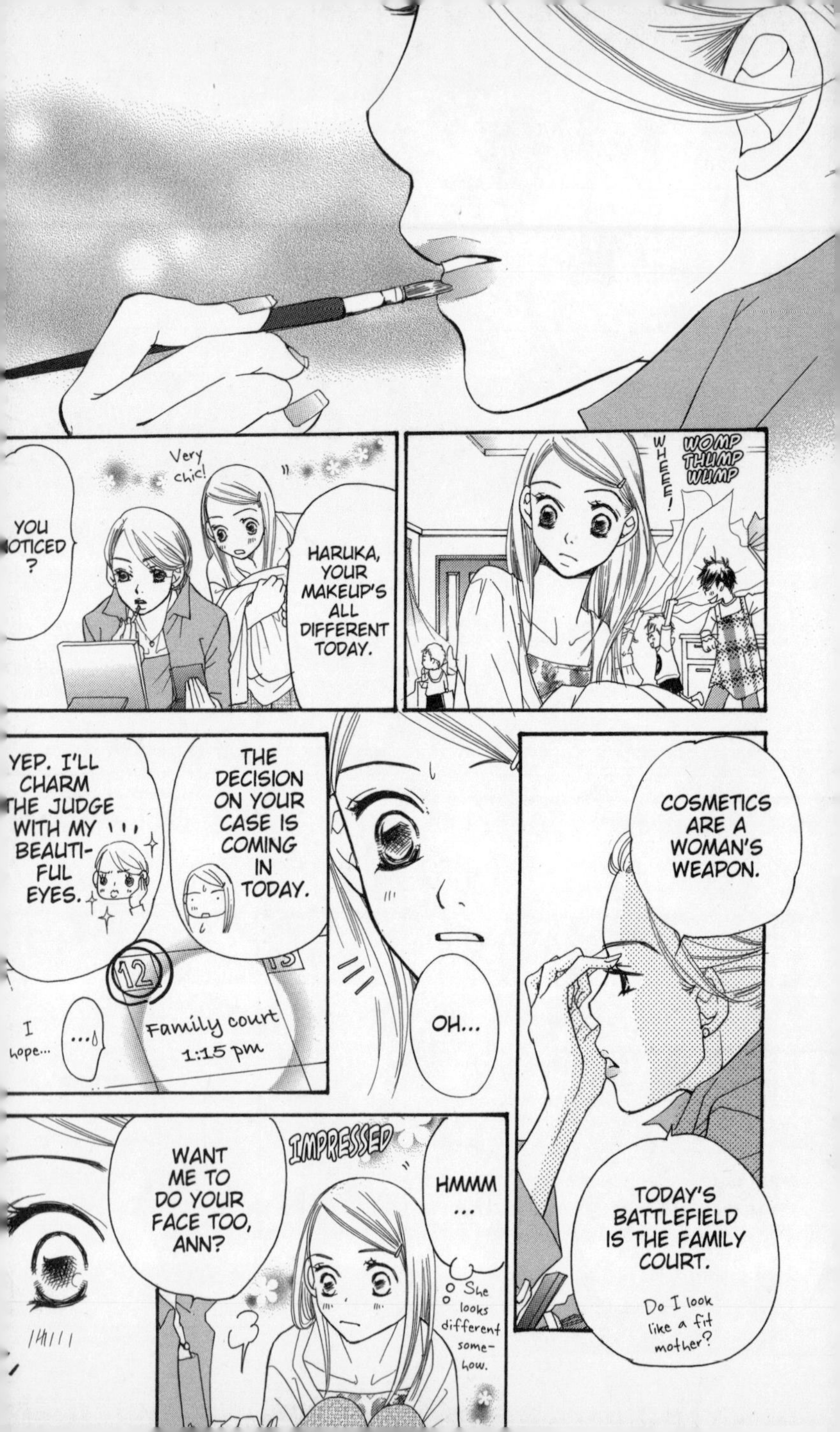
WHEEE!
WOMP THUMP WUMP
HARUKA, YOUR MAKEUP'S ALL DIFFERENT TODAY.
Very chic!
YOU OTICED ?
COSMETICS ARE A WOMAN'S WEAPON.
TODAY'S BATTLEFIELD IS THE FAMILY COURT.
Do I look like a fit mother?
OH...
THE DECISION ON YOUR CASE IS COMING IN TODAY.
YEP. I'LL CHARM THE JUDGE WITH MY BEAUTIFUL EYES.
12
Family court 1:15 pm
...
I hope...
IMPRESSED
HMMM...
She looks different somehow.
WANT ME TO DO YOUR FACE TOO, ANN?

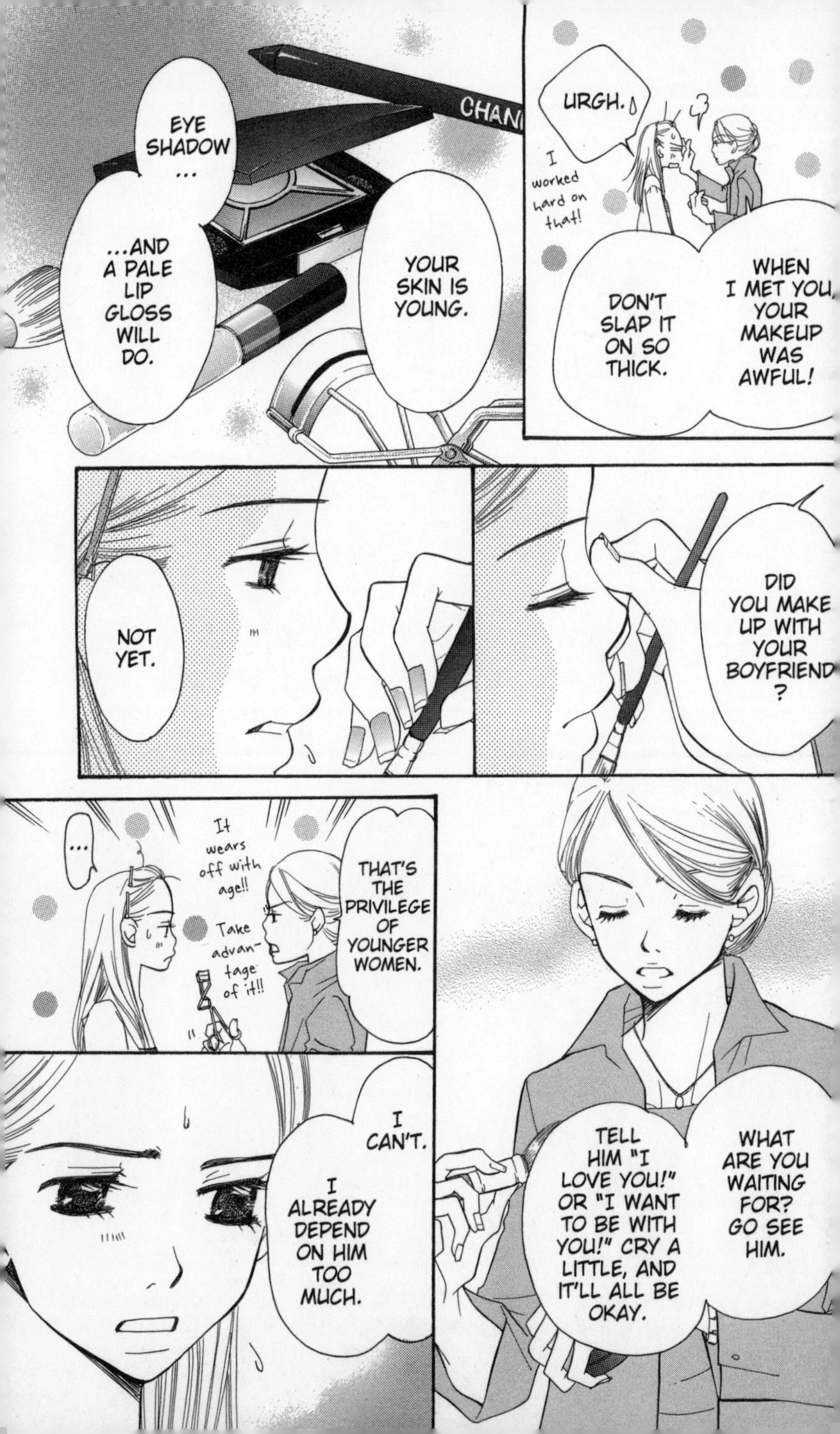
URGH.
I worked hard on that!
WHEN I MET YOU, YOUR MAKEUP WAS AWFUL!
DON'T SLAP IT ON SO THICK.
EYE SHADOW...
...AND A PALE LIP GLOSS WILL DO.
YOUR SKIN IS YOUNG.
CHANI
DID YOU MAKE UP WITH YOUR BOYFRIEND?
NOT YET.
WHAT ARE YOU WAITING FOR? GO SEE HIM.
TELL HIM "I LOVE YOU!" OR "I WANT TO BE WITH YOU!" CRY A LITTLE, AND IT'LL ALL BE OKAY.
THAT'S THE PRIVILEGE OF YOUNGER WOMEN.
It wears off with age!!
Take advantage of it!!
...
I CAN'T.
I ALREADY DEPEND ON HIM TOO MUCH.

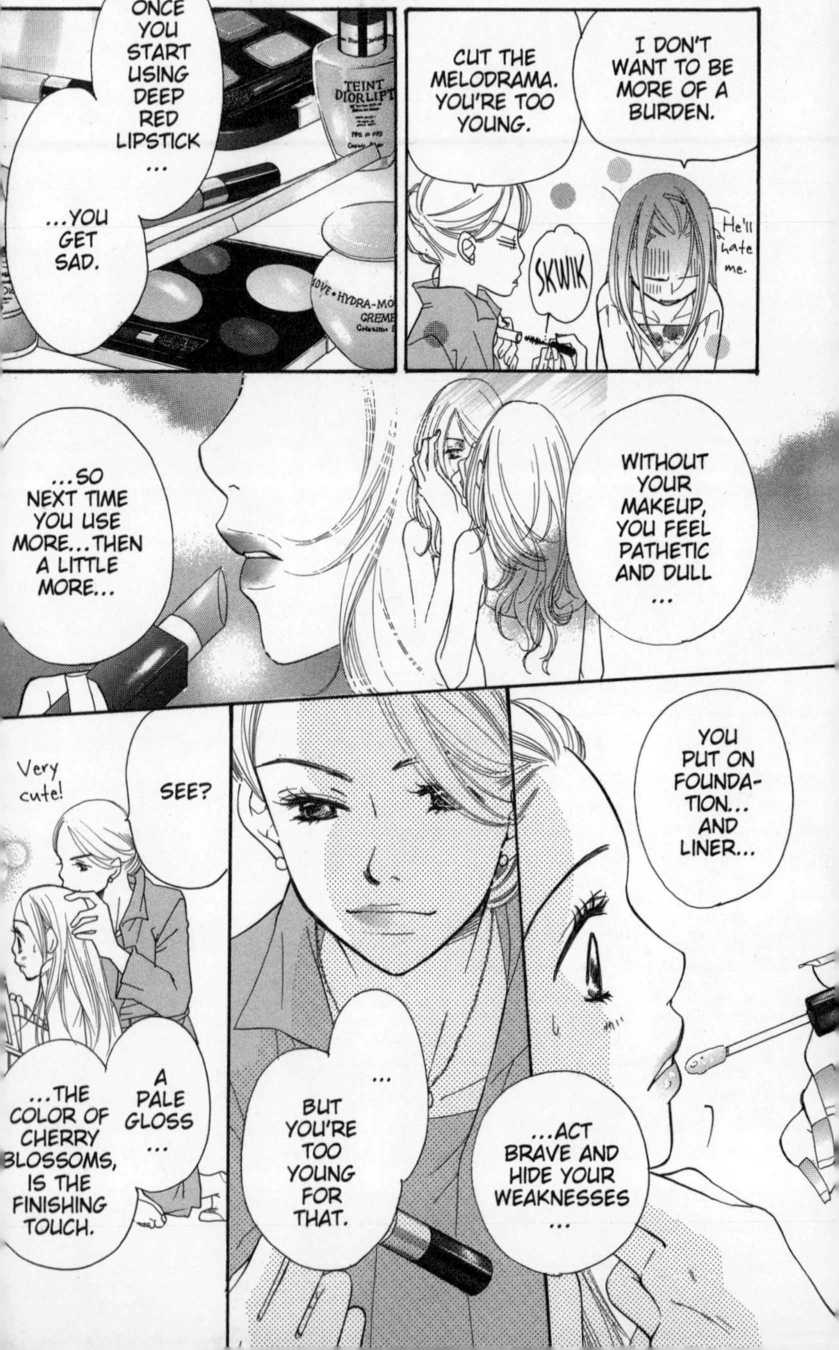
I DON'T WANT TO BE MORE OF A BURDEN.
CUT THE MELODRAMA. YOU'RE TOO YOUNG.
He'll hate me.
SKWIK
TEINT DIORLIFT
ONCE YOU START USING DEEP RED LIPSTICK...
...YOU GET SAD.
WITHOUT YOUR MAKEUP, YOU FEEL PATHETIC AND DULL...
...SO NEXT TIME YOU USE MORE...THEN A LITTLE MORE...
YOU PUT ON FOUNDATION... AND LINER...
...ACT BRAVE AND HIDE YOUR WEAKNESSES...
...
BUT YOU'RE TOO YOUNG FOR THAT.
SEE?
Very cute!
A PALE GLOSS...
...THE COLOR OF CHERRY BLOSSOMS, IS THE FINISHING TOUCH.

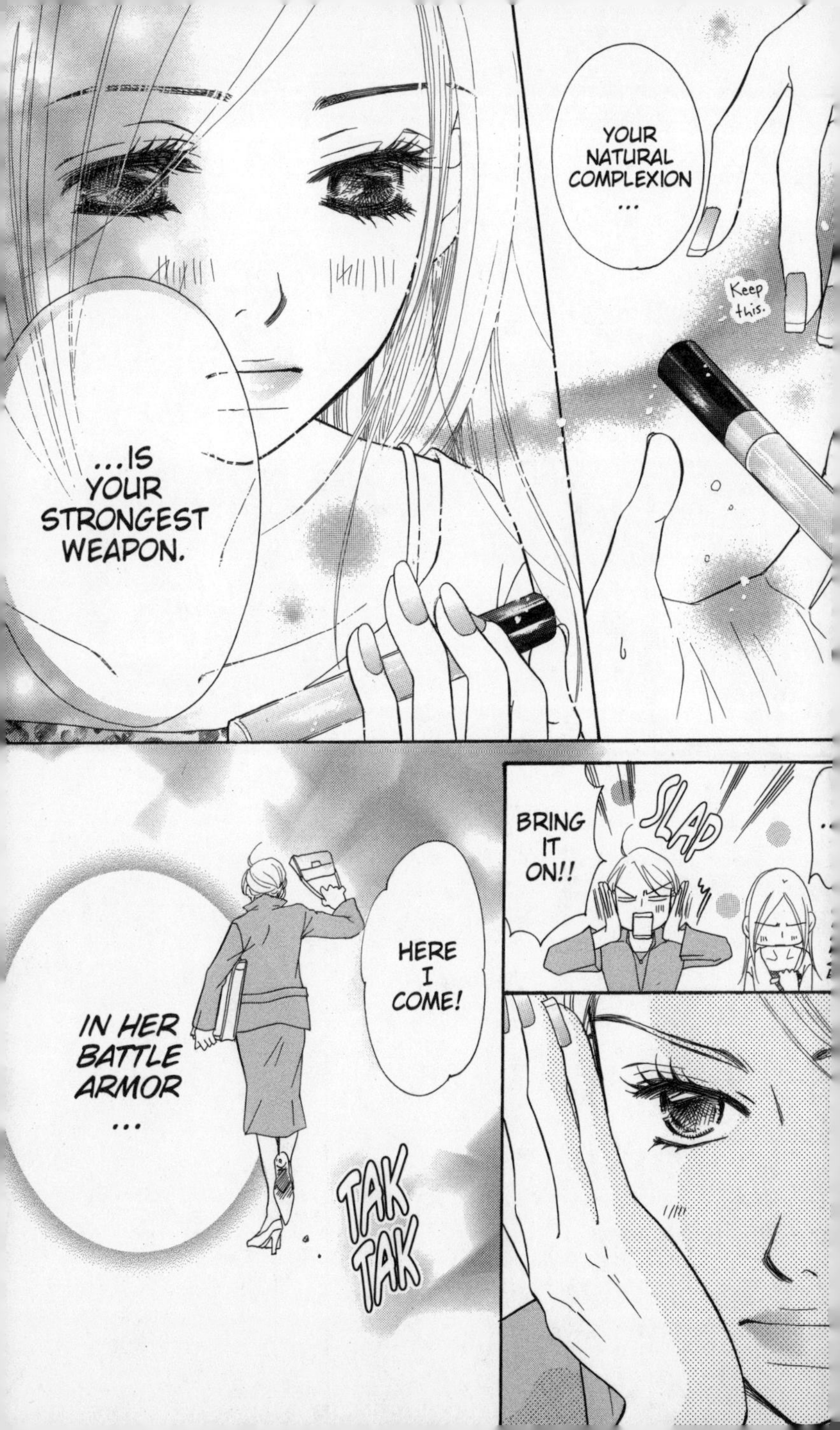
YOUR NATURAL COMPLEXION ...
Keep this.
...IS YOUR STRONGEST WEAPON.
SLAP
BRING IT ON!!
...
HERE I COME!
IN HER BATTLE ARMOR ...
TAK TAK

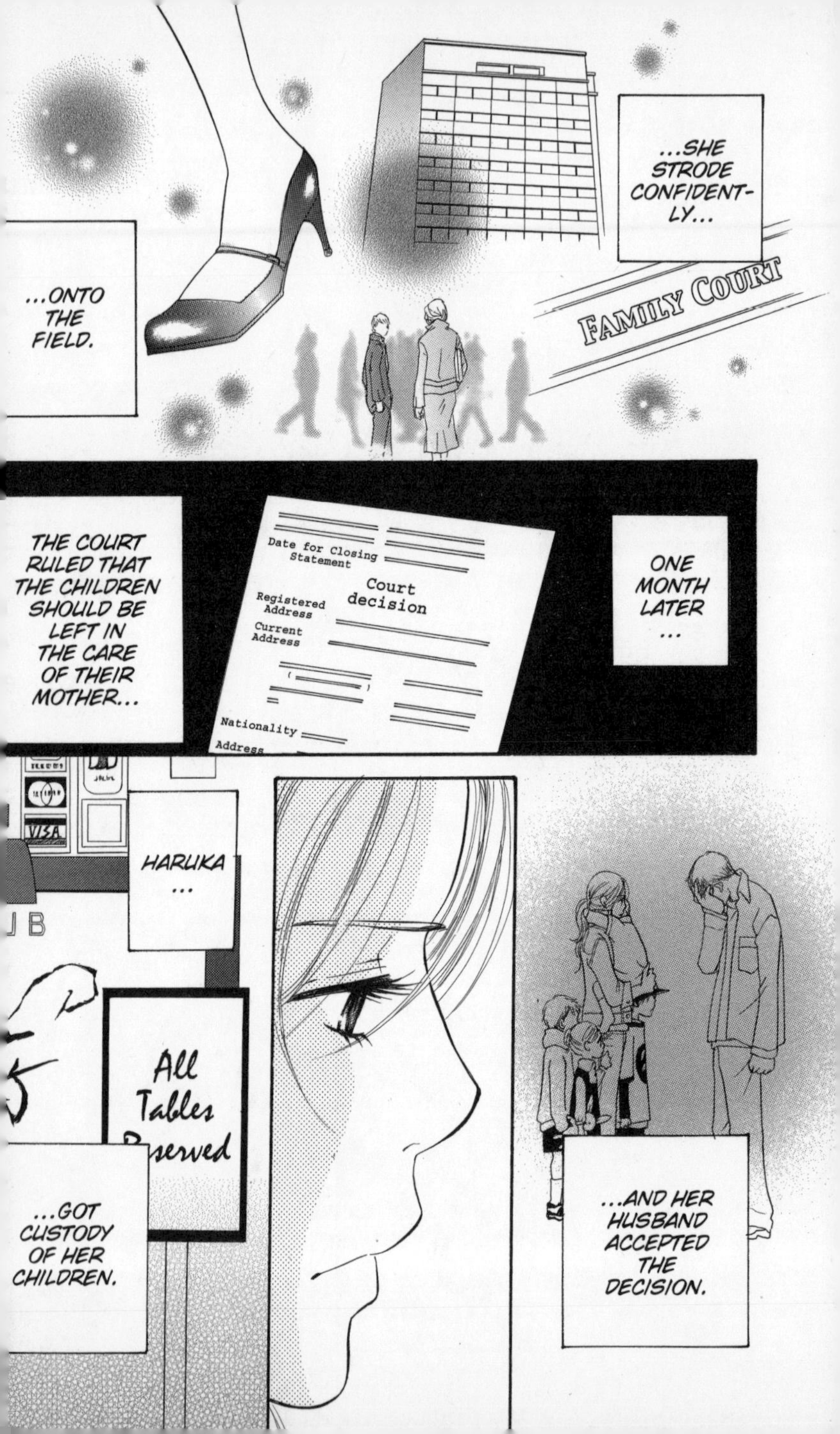

...SHE STRODE CONFIDENT-LY...
FAMILY COURT
...ONTO THE FIELD.
ONE MONTH LATER...
Date for Closing Statement
Court decision
Registered Address
Current Address
Nationality
Address
THE COURT RULED THAT THE CHILDREN SHOULD BE LEFT IN THE CARE OF THEIR MOTHER...
...AND HER HUSBAND ACCEPTED THE DECISION.
HARUKA...
...GOT CUSTODY OF HER CHILDREN.
All Tables

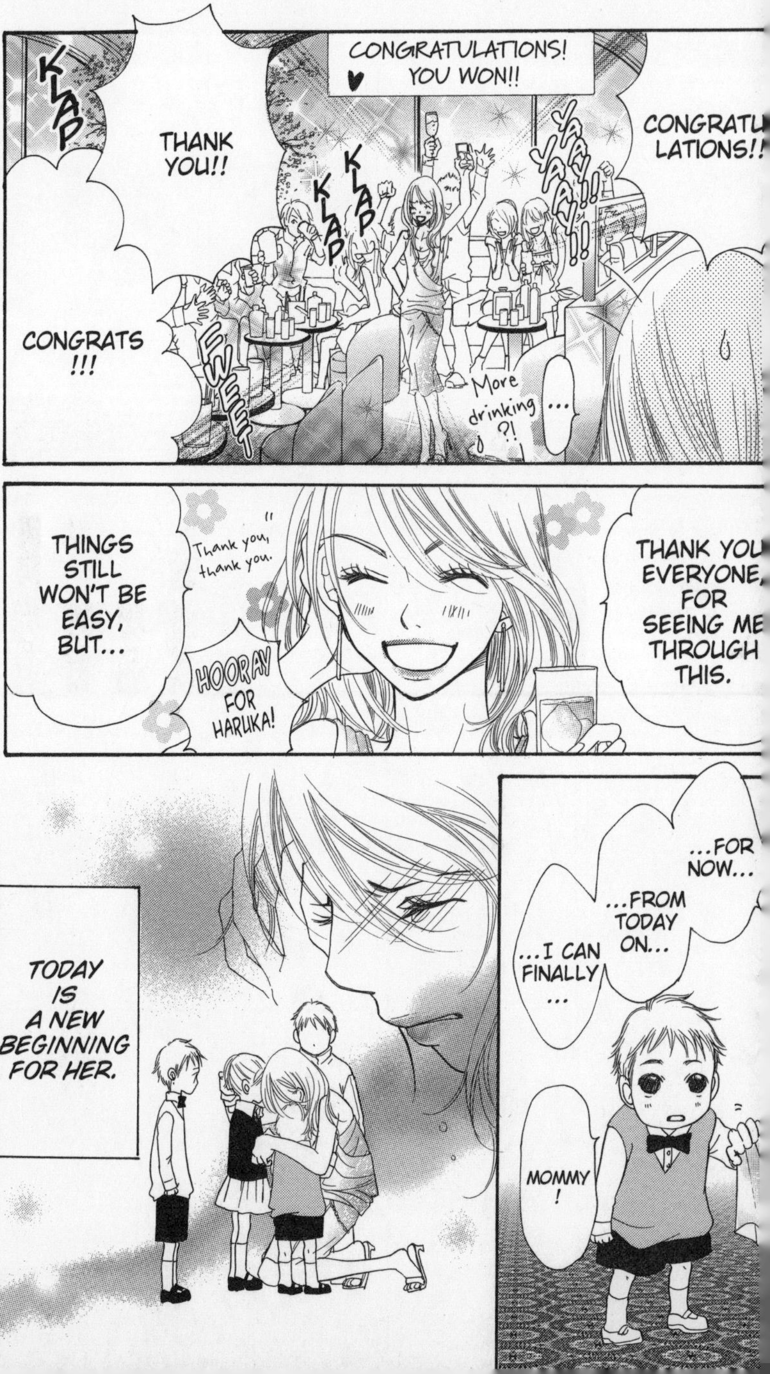
CONGRATULATIONS! YOU WON!!
CONGRATU LATIONS!!
YAAY YAAY!!
THANK YOU!!
KLAP
KLAP KLAP
...
More drinking?!
CONGRATS!!!
FWEET
THANK YOU EVERYONE, FOR SEEING ME THROUGH THIS.
Thank you, thank you.
HOORAY FOR HARUKA!
THINGS STILL WON'T BE EASY, BUT...
...FOR NOW...
...FROM TODAY ON...
...I CAN FINALLY...
MOMMY!
TODAY IS A NEW BEGINNING FOR HER.

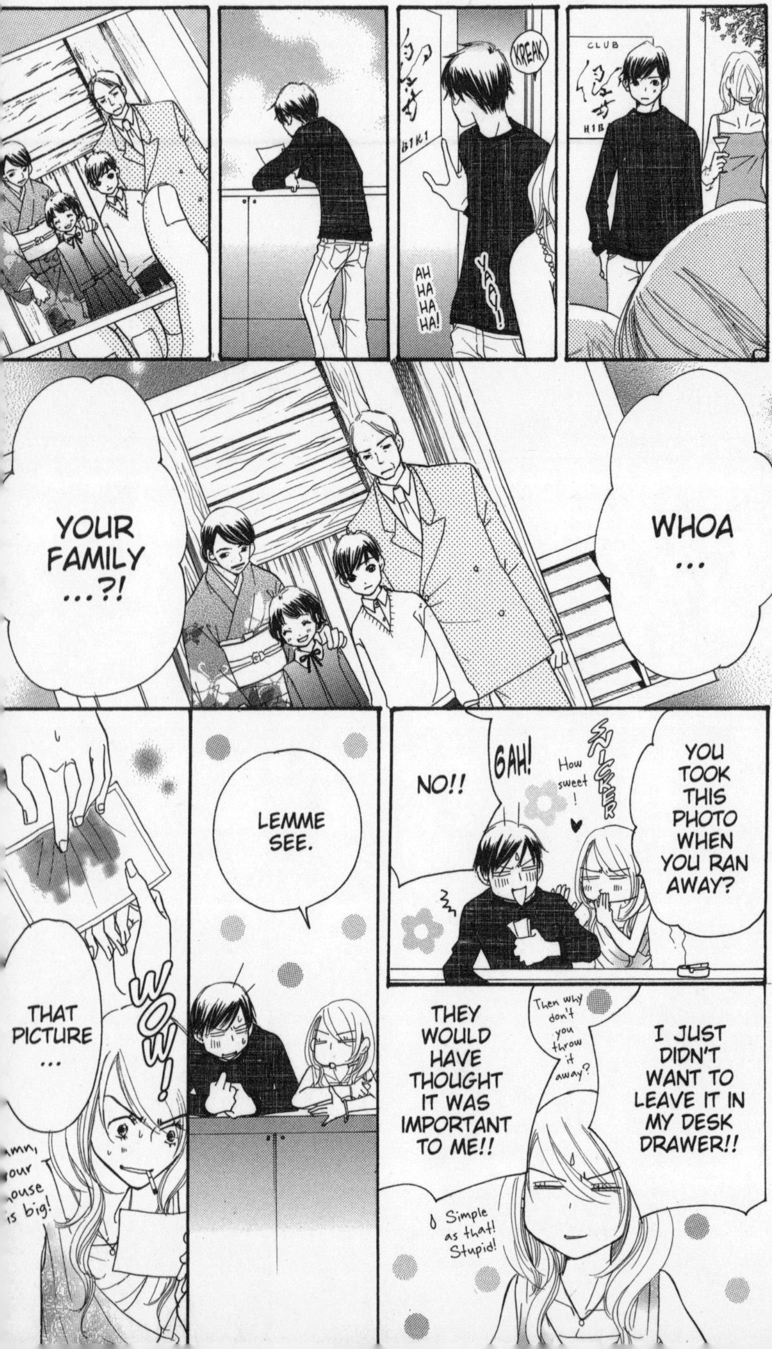
CLUB
KREAK
YAAAY!
AH HA HA HA!
WHOA ...
YOUR FAMILY ...?!
YOU TOOK THIS PHOTO WHEN YOU RAN AWAY?
SNICKER
How sweet!
GAH!
NO!!
LEMME SEE.
I JUST DIDN'T WANT TO LEAVE IT IN MY DESK DRAWER!!
Then why don't you throw it away?
THEY WOULD HAVE THOUGHT IT WAS IMPORTANT TO ME!!
♪ Simple as that! Stupid!
WOW!
THAT PICTURE ...
amn, our ouse is big!

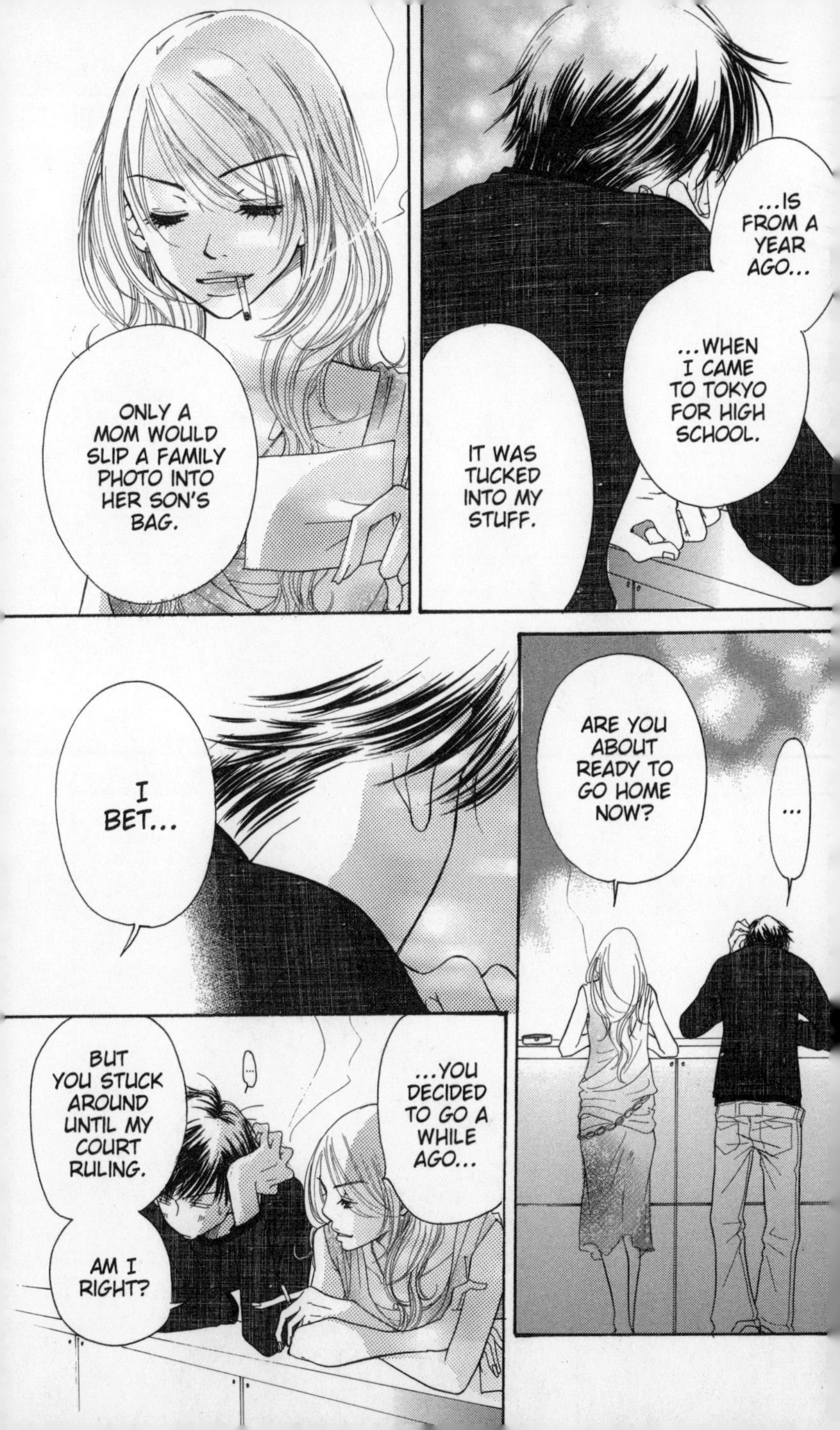
...IS FROM A YEAR AGO...
...WHEN I CAME TO TOKYO FOR HIGH SCHOOL.
IT WAS TUCKED INTO MY STUFF.
ONLY A MOM WOULD SLIP A FAMILY PHOTO INTO HER SON'S BAG.
ARE YOU ABOUT READY TO GO HOME NOW?
...
I BET...
...YOU DECIDED TO GO A WHILE AGO...
...
BUT YOU STUCK AROUND UNTIL MY COURT RULING.
AM I RIGHT?

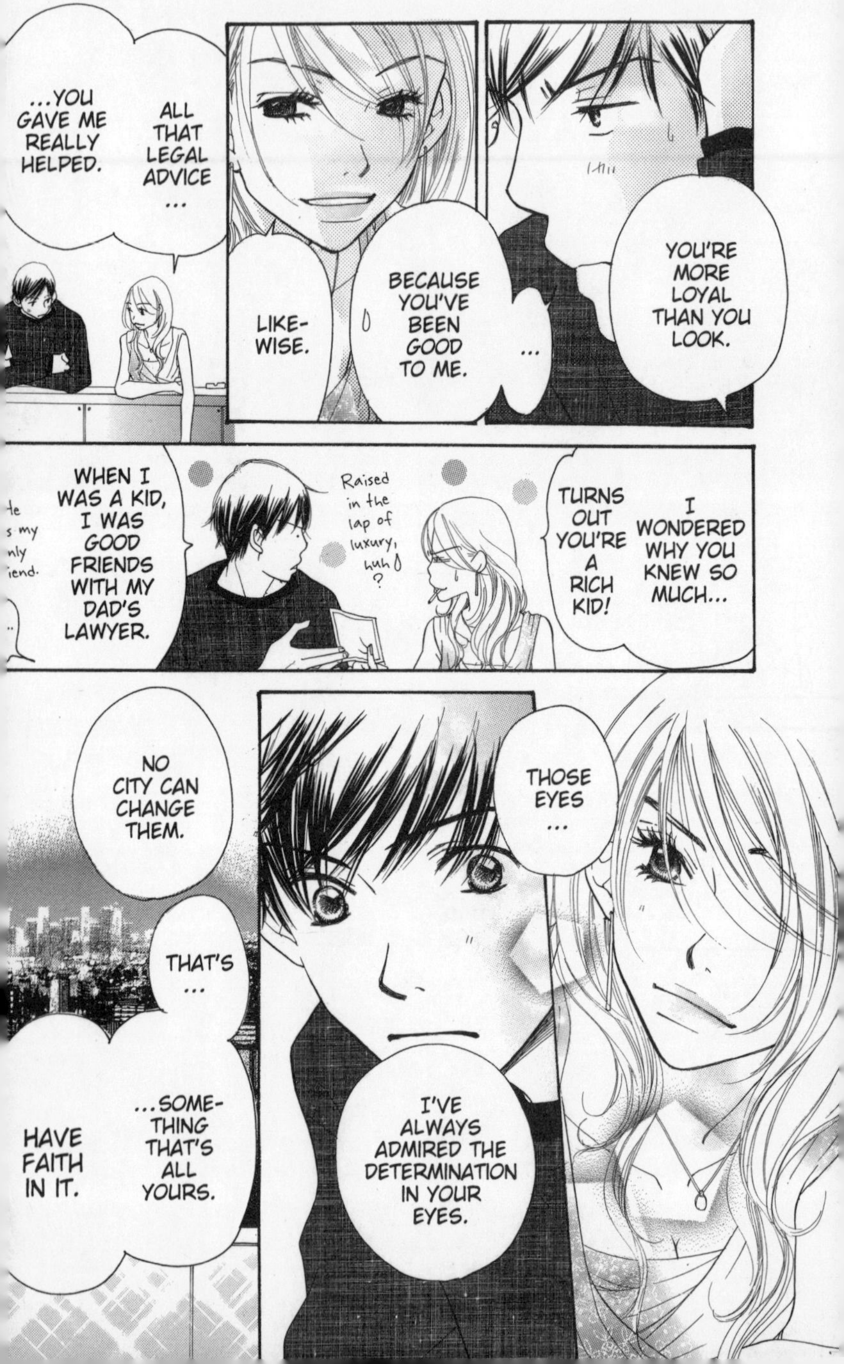
YOU'RE MORE LOYAL THAN YOU LOOK.
...
BECAUSE YOU'VE BEEN GOOD TO ME.
LIKE-WISE.
ALL THAT LEGAL ADVICE...
...YOU GAVE ME REALLY HELPED.
I WONDERED WHY YOU KNEW SO MUCH...
TURNS OUT YOU'RE A RICH KID!
Raised in the lap of luxury, huh?
WHEN I WAS A KID, I WAS GOOD FRIENDS WITH MY DAD'S LAWYER.
THOSE EYES...
I'VE ALWAYS ADMIRED THE DETERMINATION IN YOUR EYES.
NO CITY CAN CHANGE THEM.
THAT'S...
...SOME-THING THAT'S ALL YOURS.
HAVE FAITH IN IT.

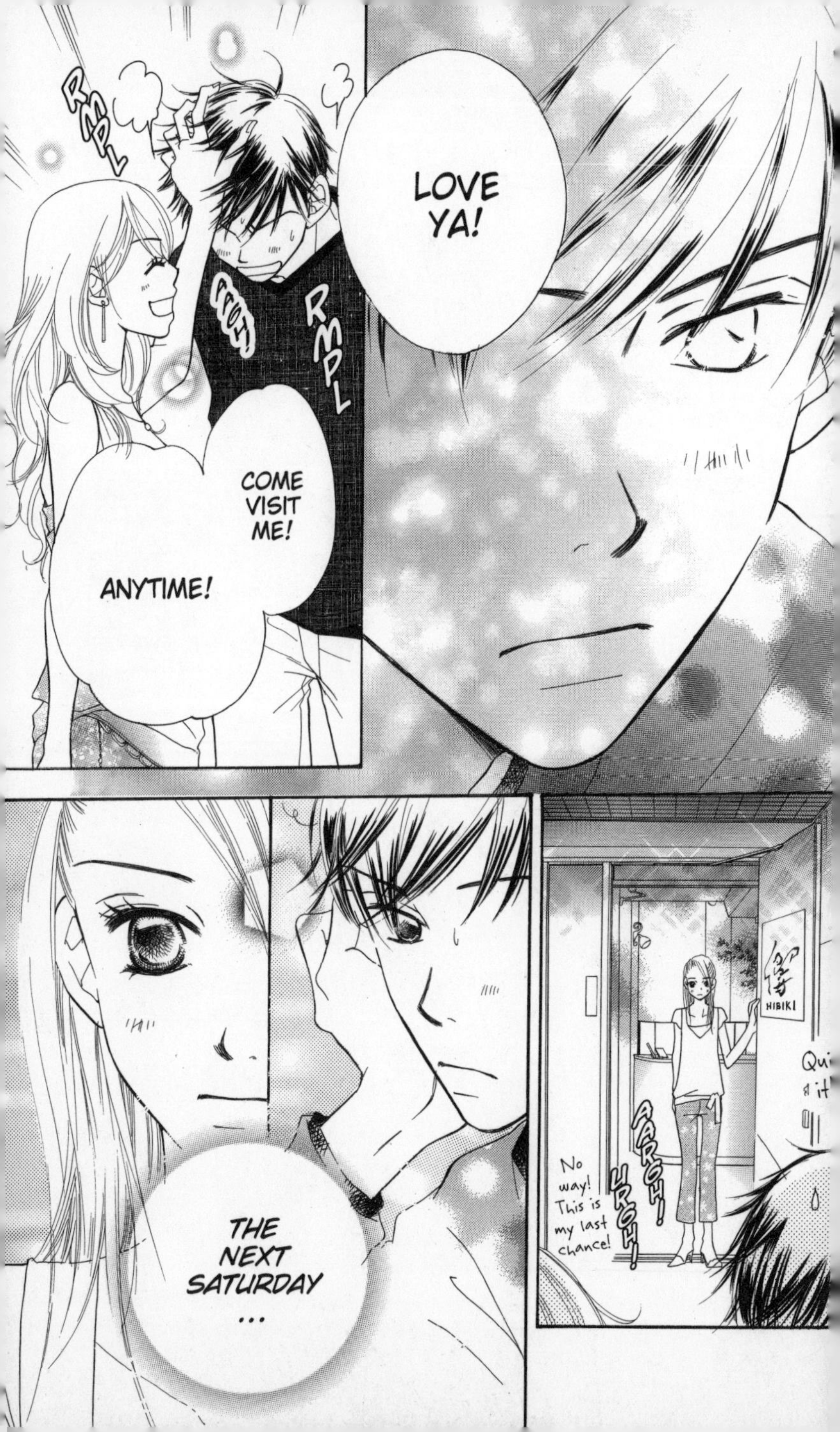

LOVE YA!
RMPL
POOH!
RMPL
COME VISIT ME!
ANYTIME!
HIBIKI
AARGH!
URGH!
No way! This is my last chance!
THE NEXT SATURDAY ...

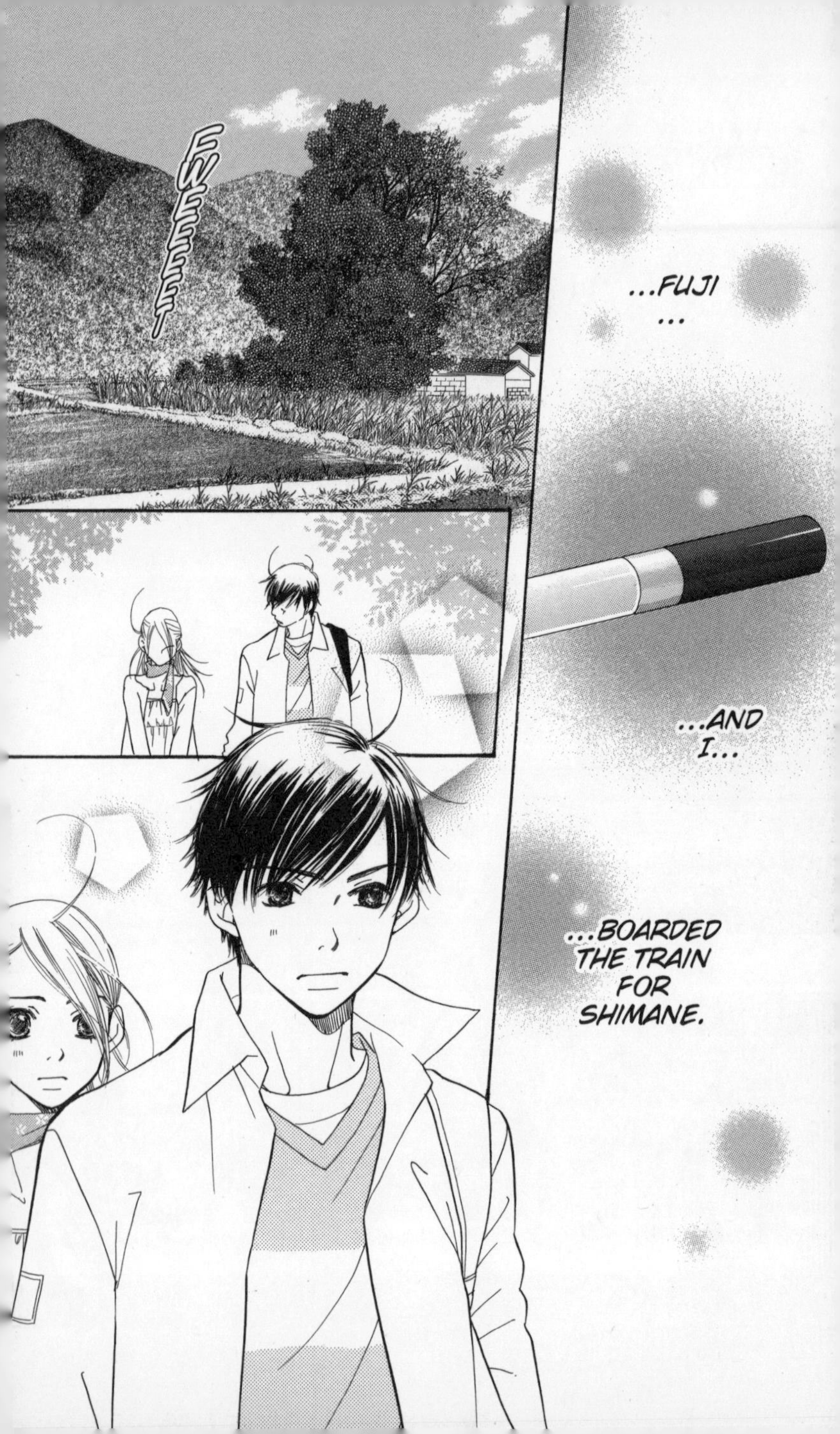
...FUJI ...
...AND I...
...BOARDED THE TRAIN FOR SHIMANE.
FWEEEEET

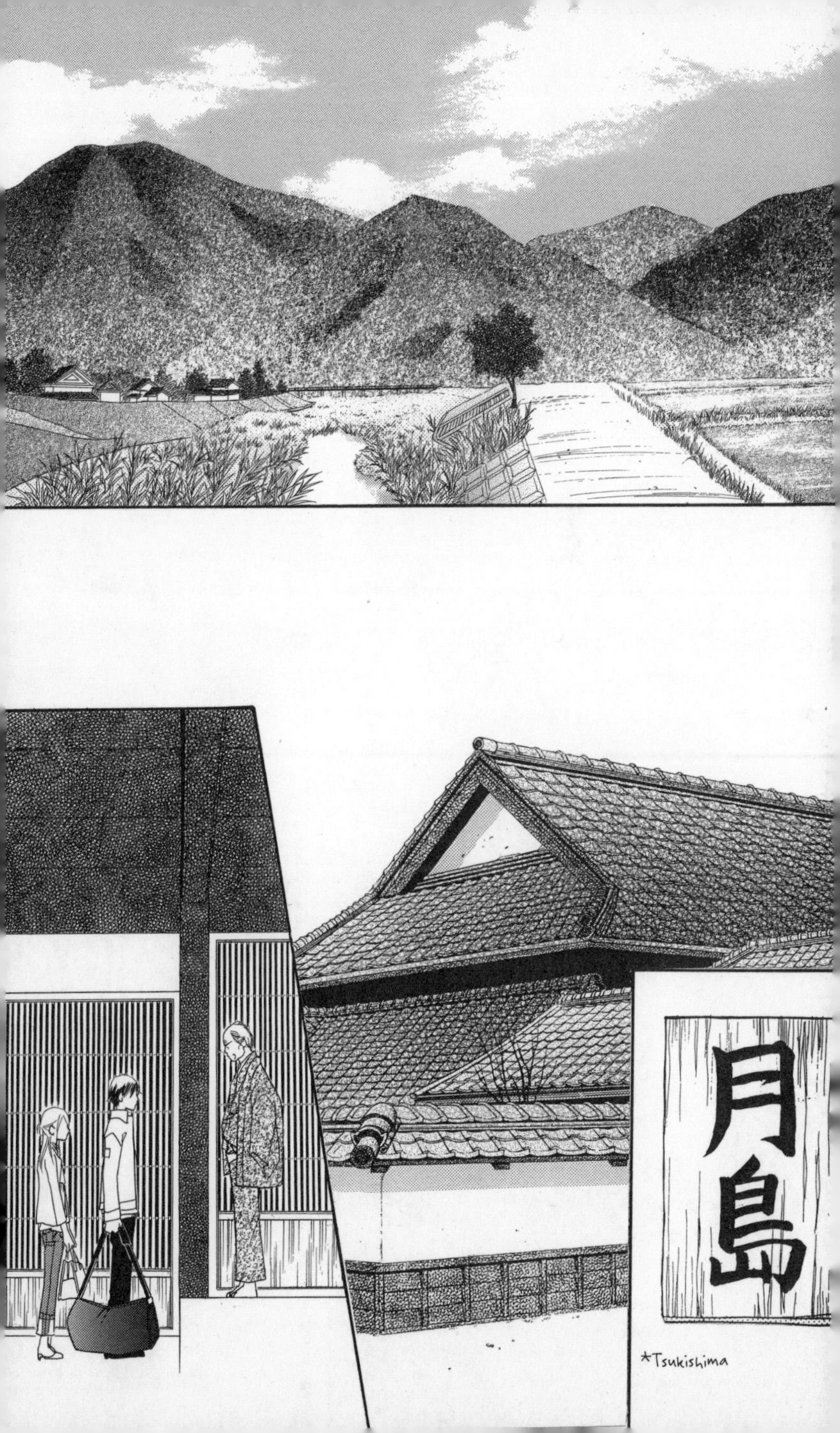
月島
*Tsukishima

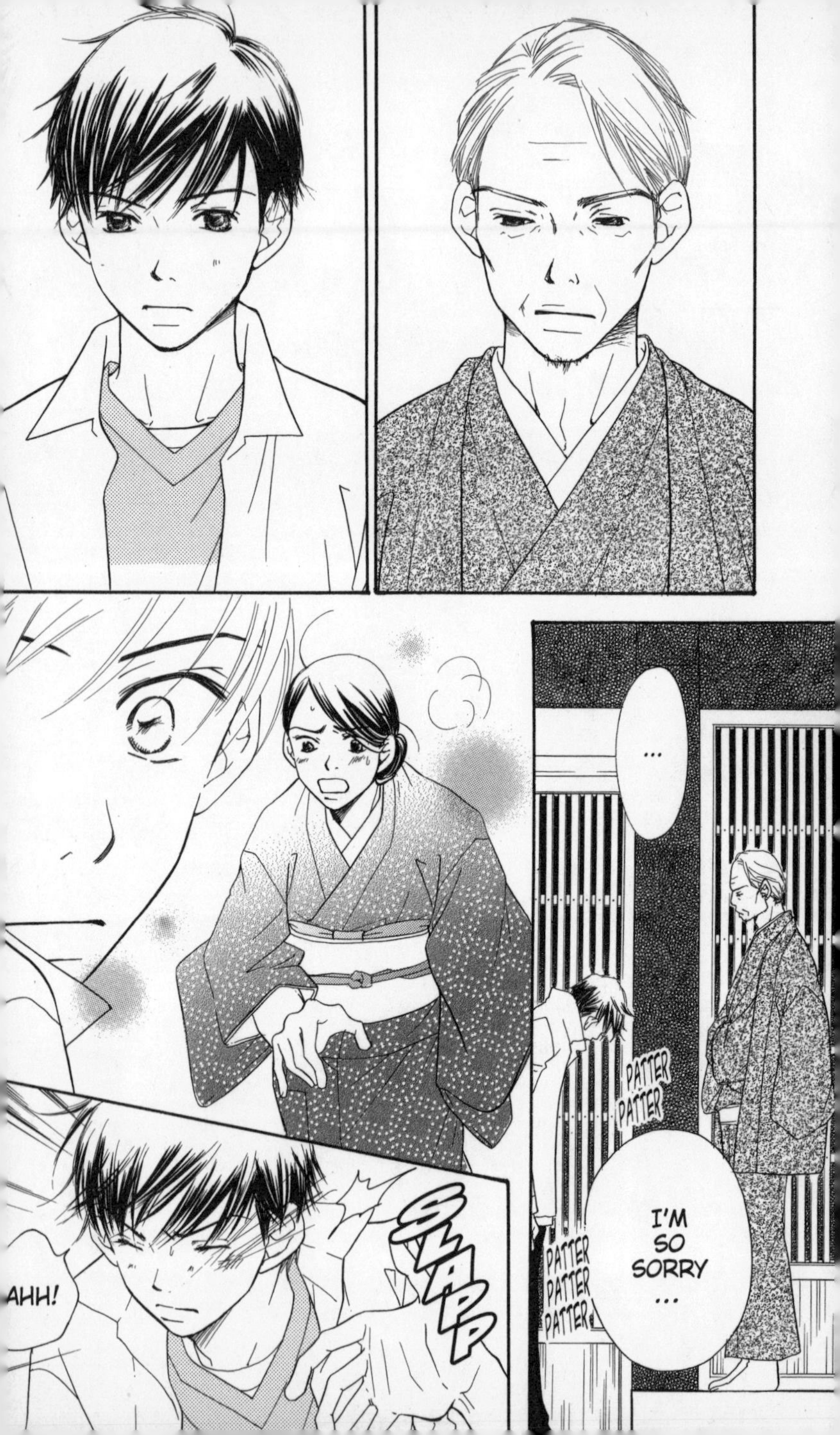
...
PATTER PATTER
I'M SO SORRY ...
PATTER PATTER PATTER
SLAPP
AHH!

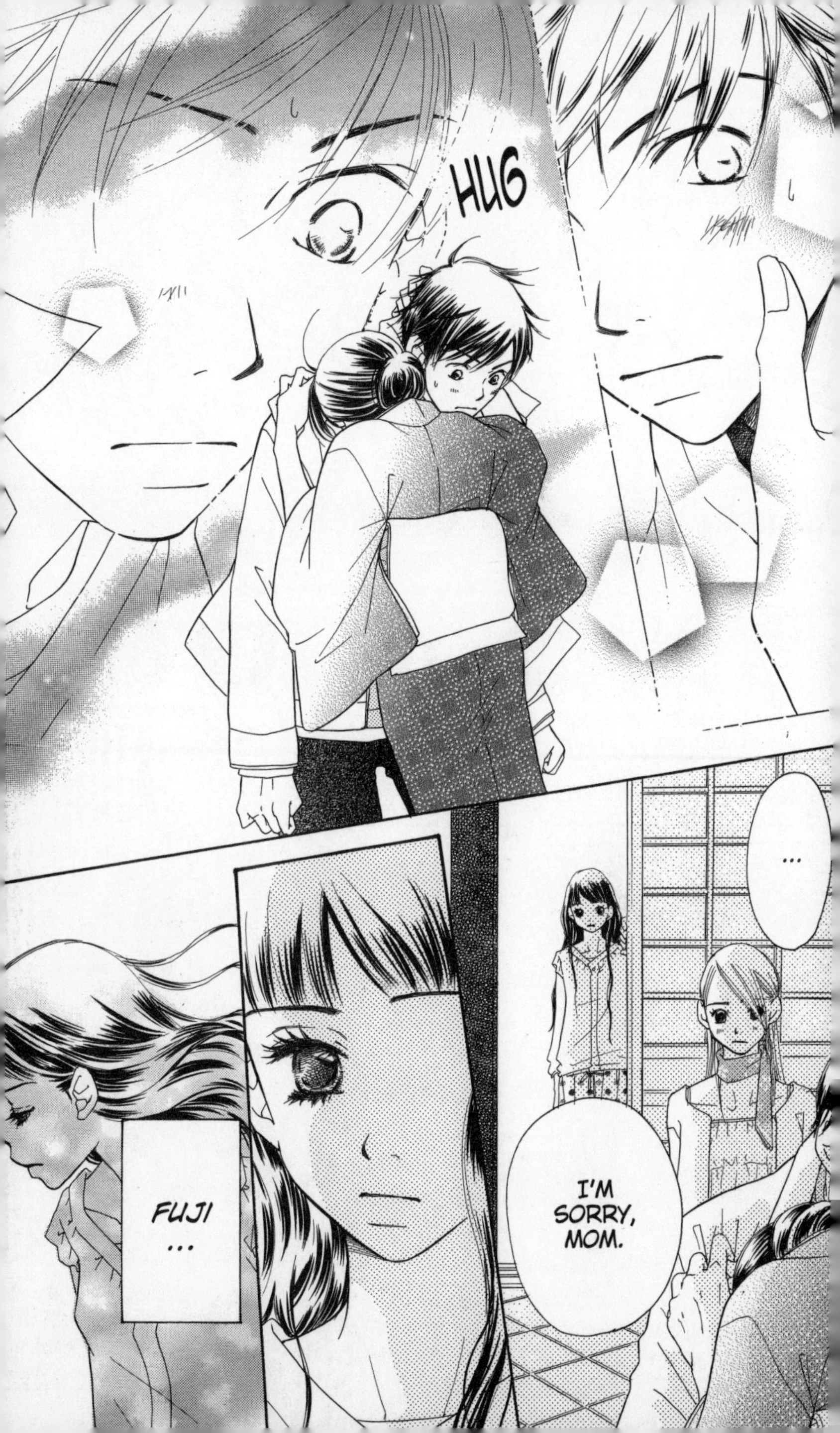
HUG
...
I'M SORRY, MOM.
FUJI ...

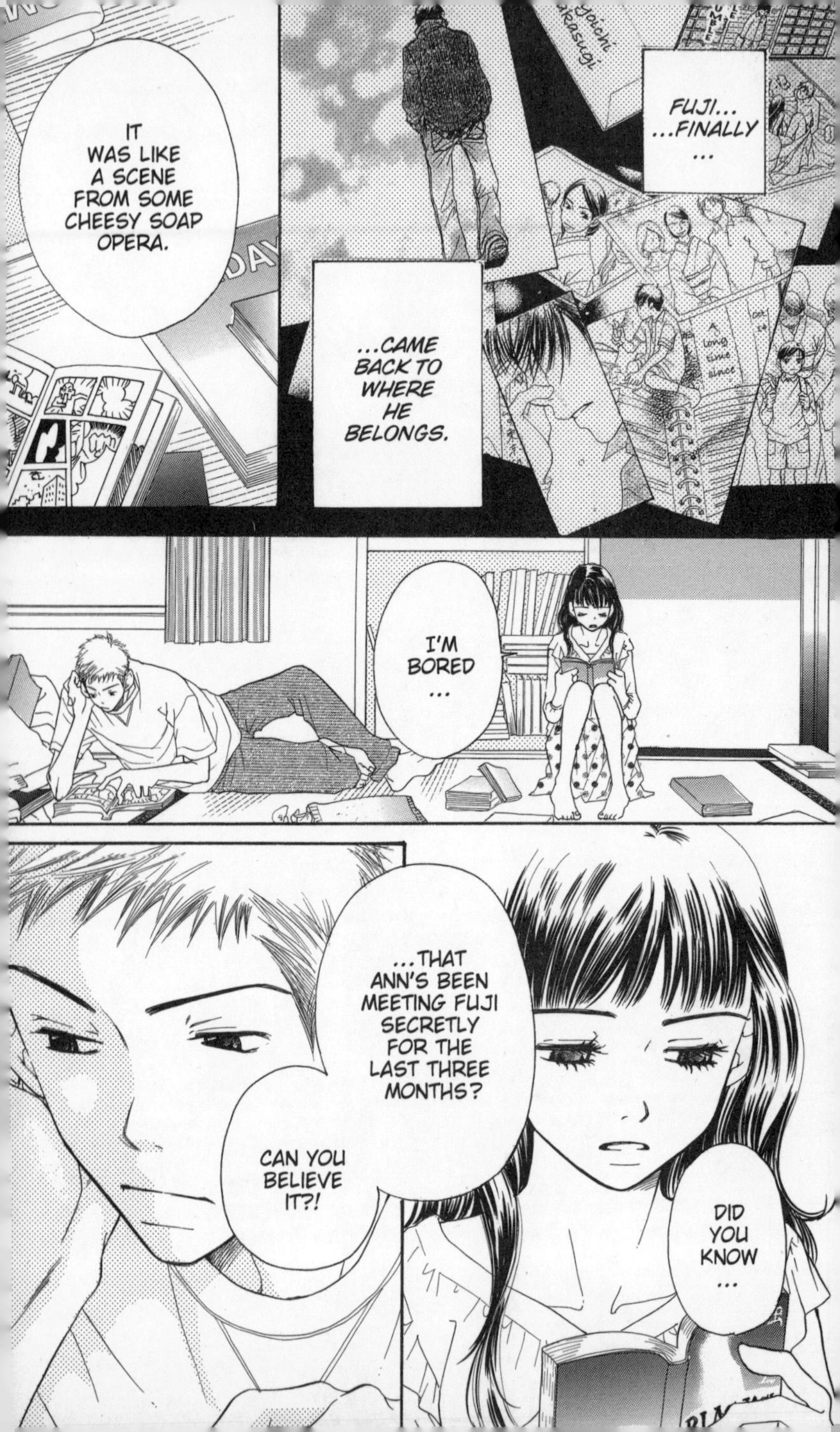
FUJI... ...FINALLY ...
...CAME BACK TO WHERE HE BELONGS.
IT WAS LIKE A SCENE FROM SOME CHEESY SOAP OPERA.
I'M BORED ...
DID YOU KNOW ...
...THAT ANN'S BEEN MEETING FUJI SECRETLY FOR THE LAST THREE MONTHS?
CAN YOU BELIEVE IT?!

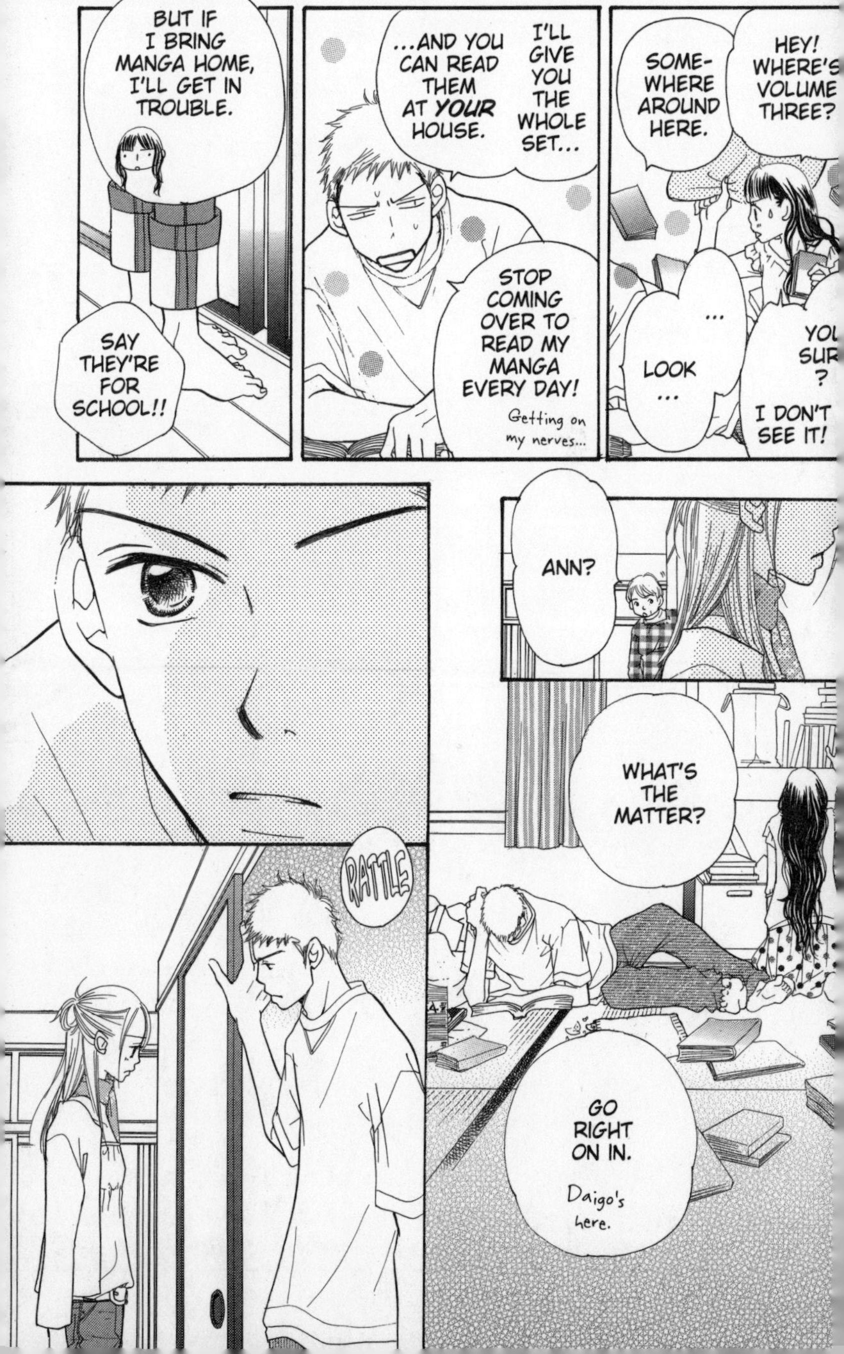
HEY! WHERE'S VOLUME THREE?
SOME-WHERE AROUND HERE.
YOU SUR ? I DON'T SEE IT!
... LOOK ...
I'LL GIVE YOU THE WHOLE SET...
...AND YOU CAN READ THEM AT *YOUR* HOUSE.
STOP COMING OVER TO READ MY MANGA EVERY DAY!
Getting on my nerves...
BUT IF I BRING MANGA HOME, I'LL GET IN TROUBLE.
SAY THEY'RE FOR SCHOOL!!
ANN?
WHAT'S THE MATTER?
GO RIGHT ON IN.
Daigo's here.
RATTLE

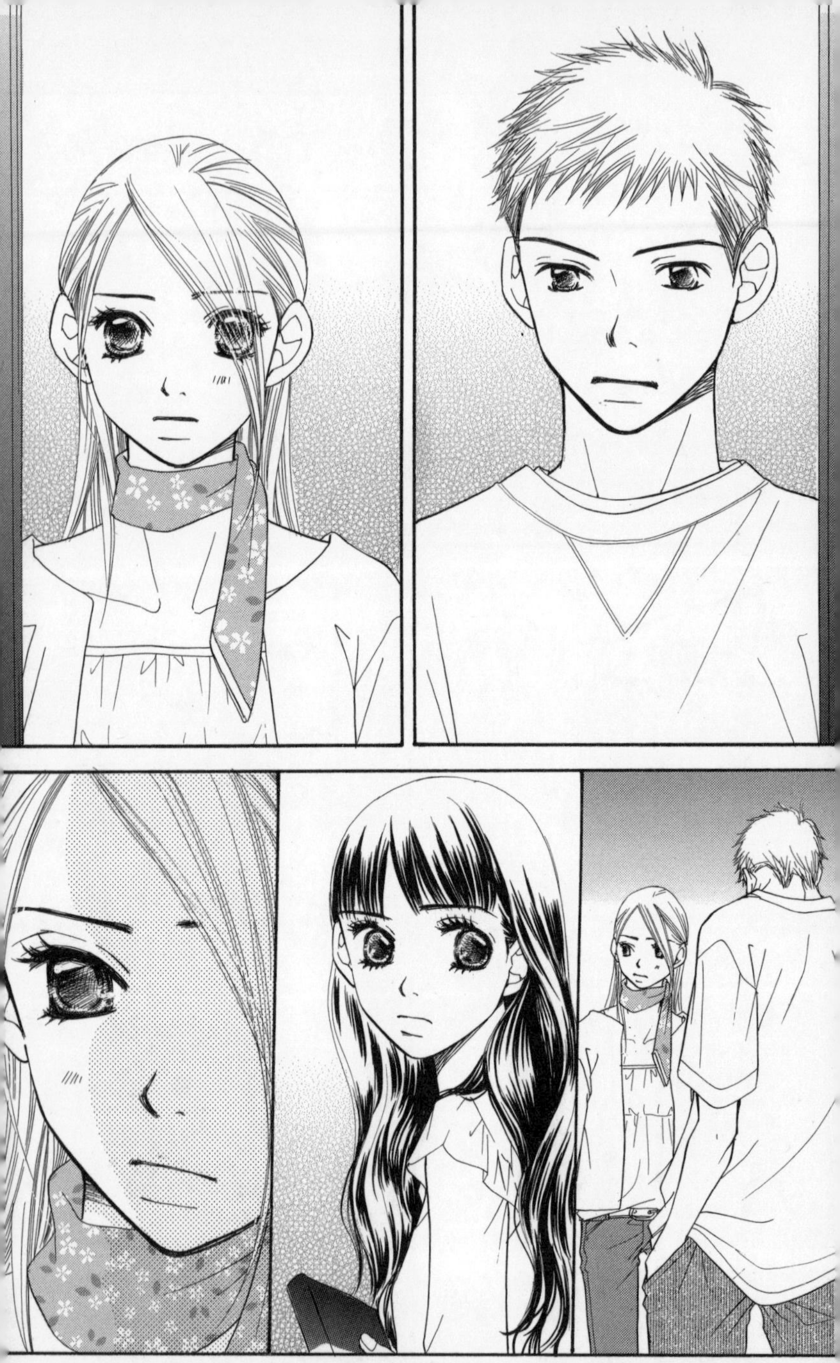

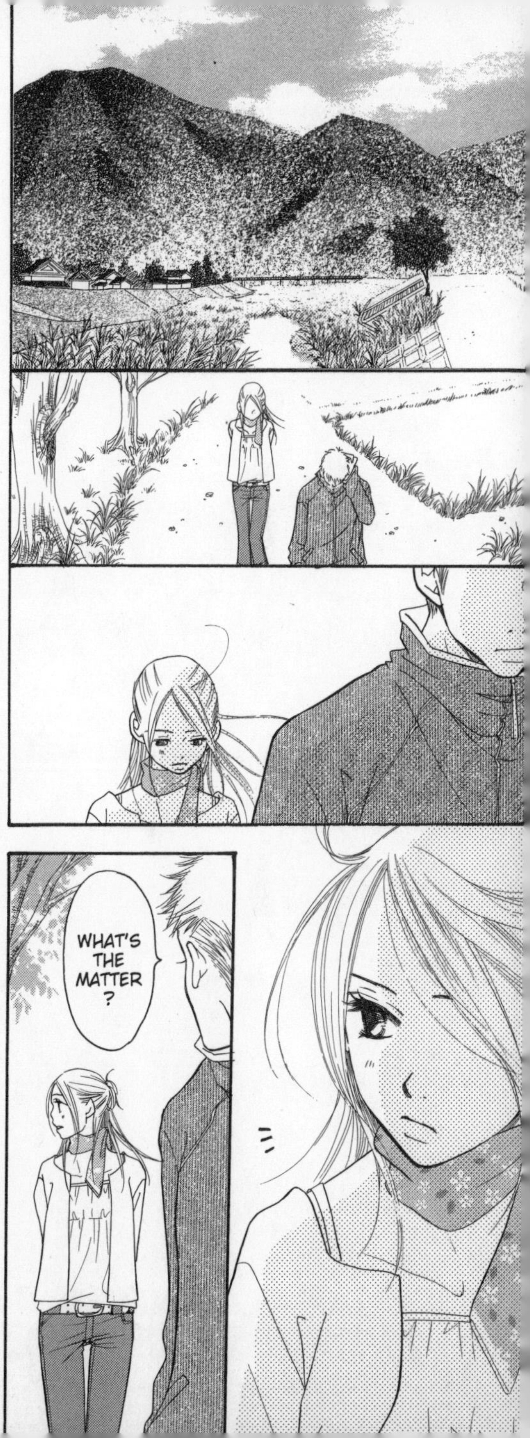
WHAT'S THE MATTER ?

~ Spring, Age 17: Pale Pink

I didn't know much about custody trials and that kind of stuff or about host clubs, so I went around gathering information. I visited the law office where my first manager's husband worked and to the exclusive club where my former manager used to go all the time.

I was nervous at both places, but full of curiosity. They were nice enough to tell me all kinds of things, but unfortunately I wasn't able to use most of it in the story.

I borrowed the name of the club from an actual club that a friend of my friend runs.

Thank you to everyone who helped me!

By the way, my manga has an awful lot of drinking in it, doesn't it? I wonder if that's all right. I mean, even minors are chugging it down!

Thank you for reading! See you in volume 5!

Hinako Ashihara

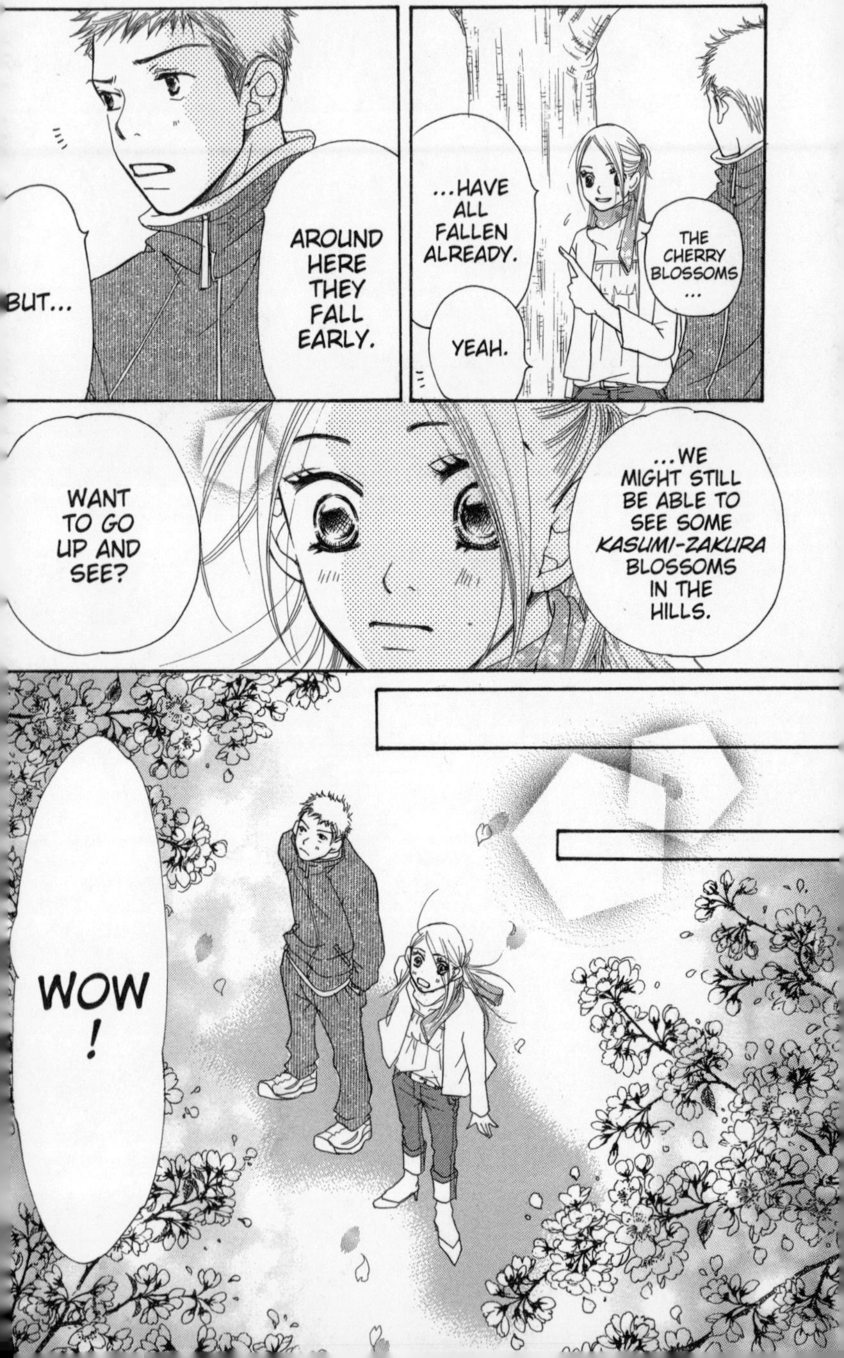
THE CHERRY BLOSSOMS ...
...HAVE ALL FALLEN ALREADY.
YEAH.
AROUND HERE THEY FALL EARLY.
BUT...
...WE MIGHT STILL BE ABLE TO SEE SOME *KASUMI-ZAKURA* BLOSSOMS IN THE HILLS.
WANT TO GO UP AND SEE?
WOW!

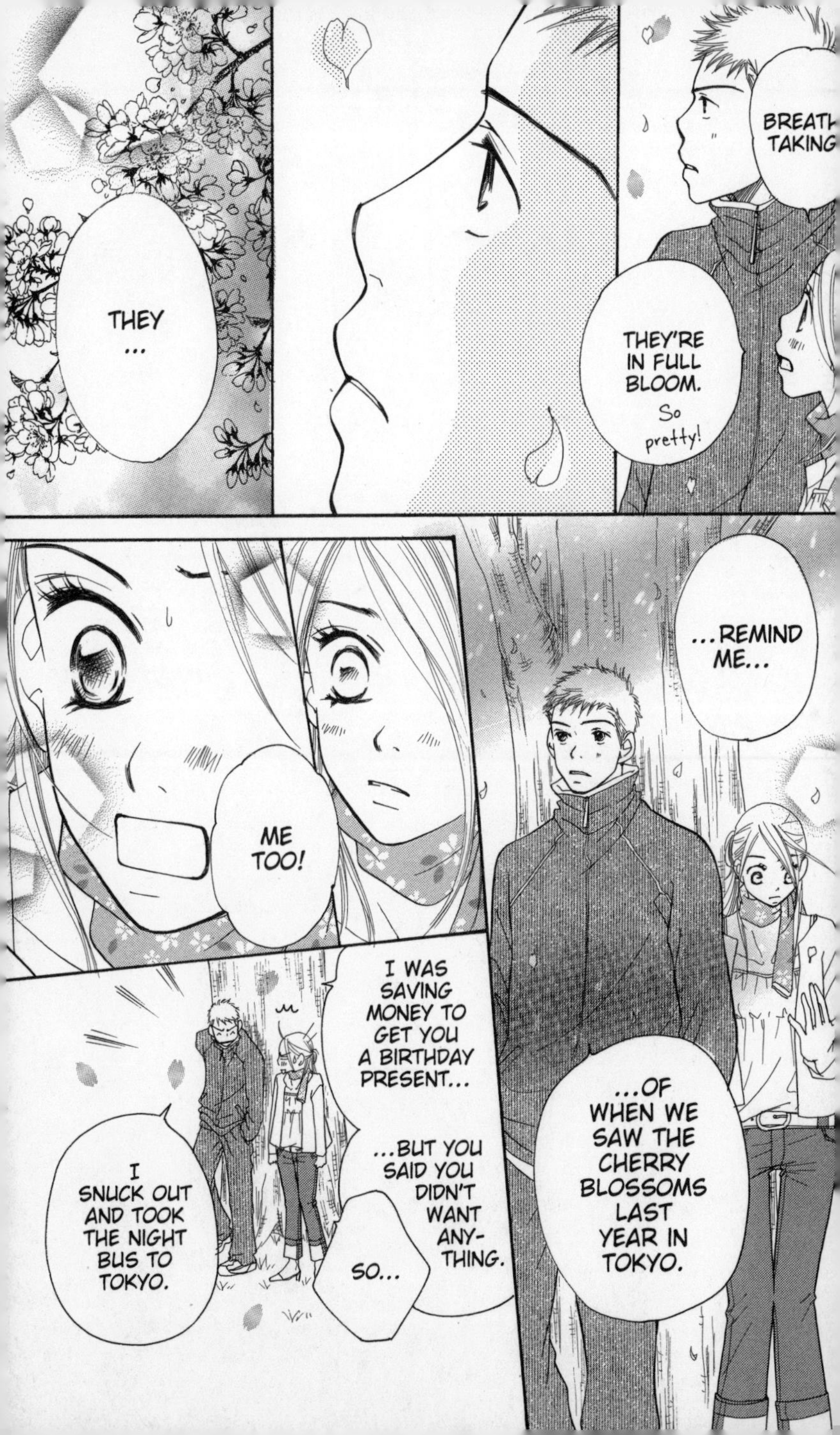
BREATH TAKING
THEY'RE IN FULL BLOOM.
So pretty!
THEY ...
...REMIND ME...
...OF WHEN WE SAW THE CHERRY BLOSSOMS LAST YEAR IN TOKYO.
ME TOO!
I WAS SAVING MONEY TO GET YOU A BIRTHDAY PRESENT...
...BUT YOU SAID YOU DIDN'T WANT ANY-THING.
SO...
I SNUCK OUT AND TOOK THE NIGHT BUS TO TOKYO.

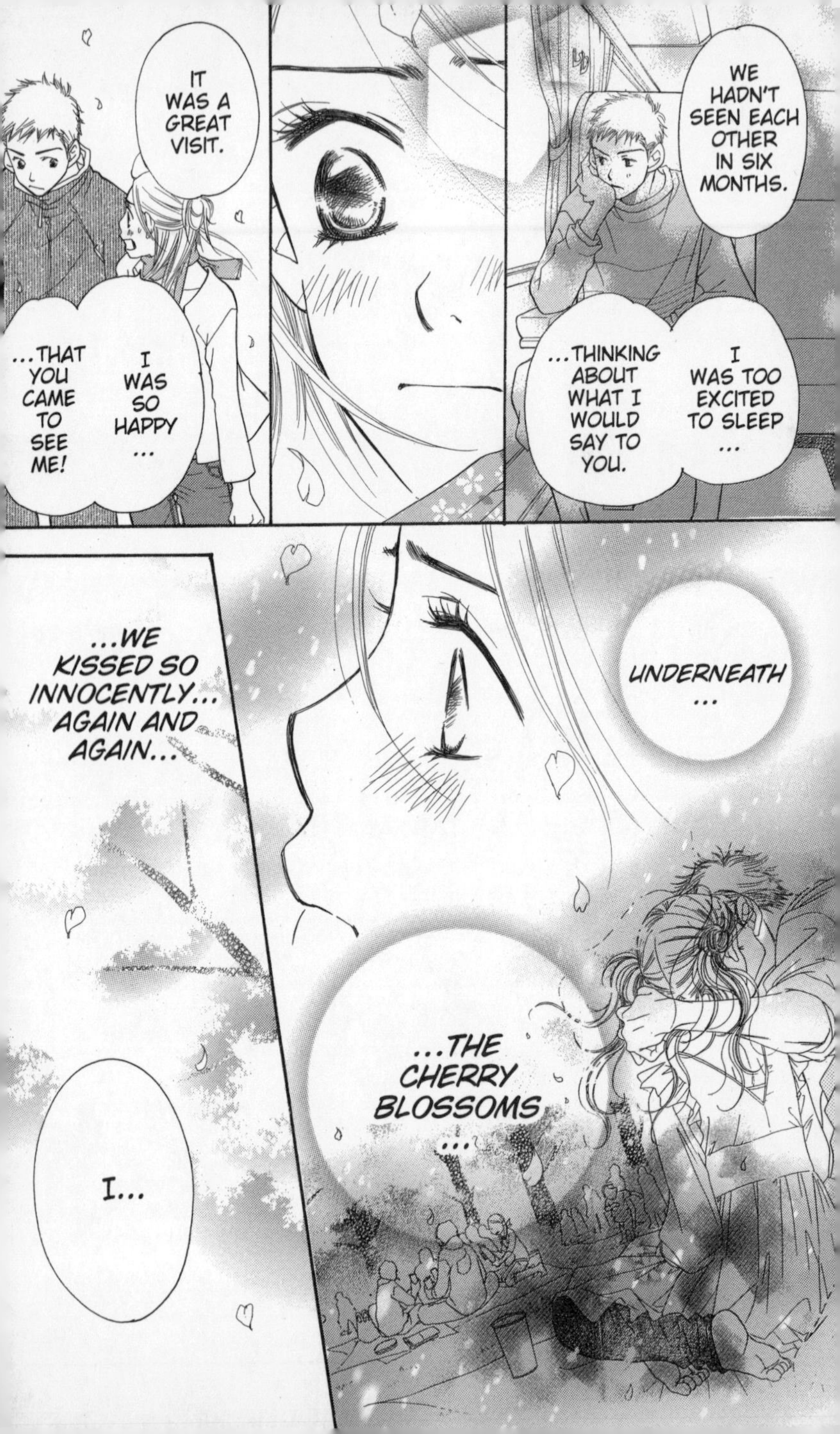
WE HADN'T SEEN EACH OTHER IN SIX MONTHS.
I WAS TOO EXCITED TO SLEEP ...
...THINKING ABOUT WHAT I WOULD SAY TO YOU.
IT WAS A GREAT VISIT.
I WAS SO HAPPY ...
...THAT YOU CAME TO SEE ME!
UNDERNEATH ...
...THE CHERRY BLOSSOMS ...
...WE KISSED SO INNOCENTLY... AGAIN AND AGAIN...
I...

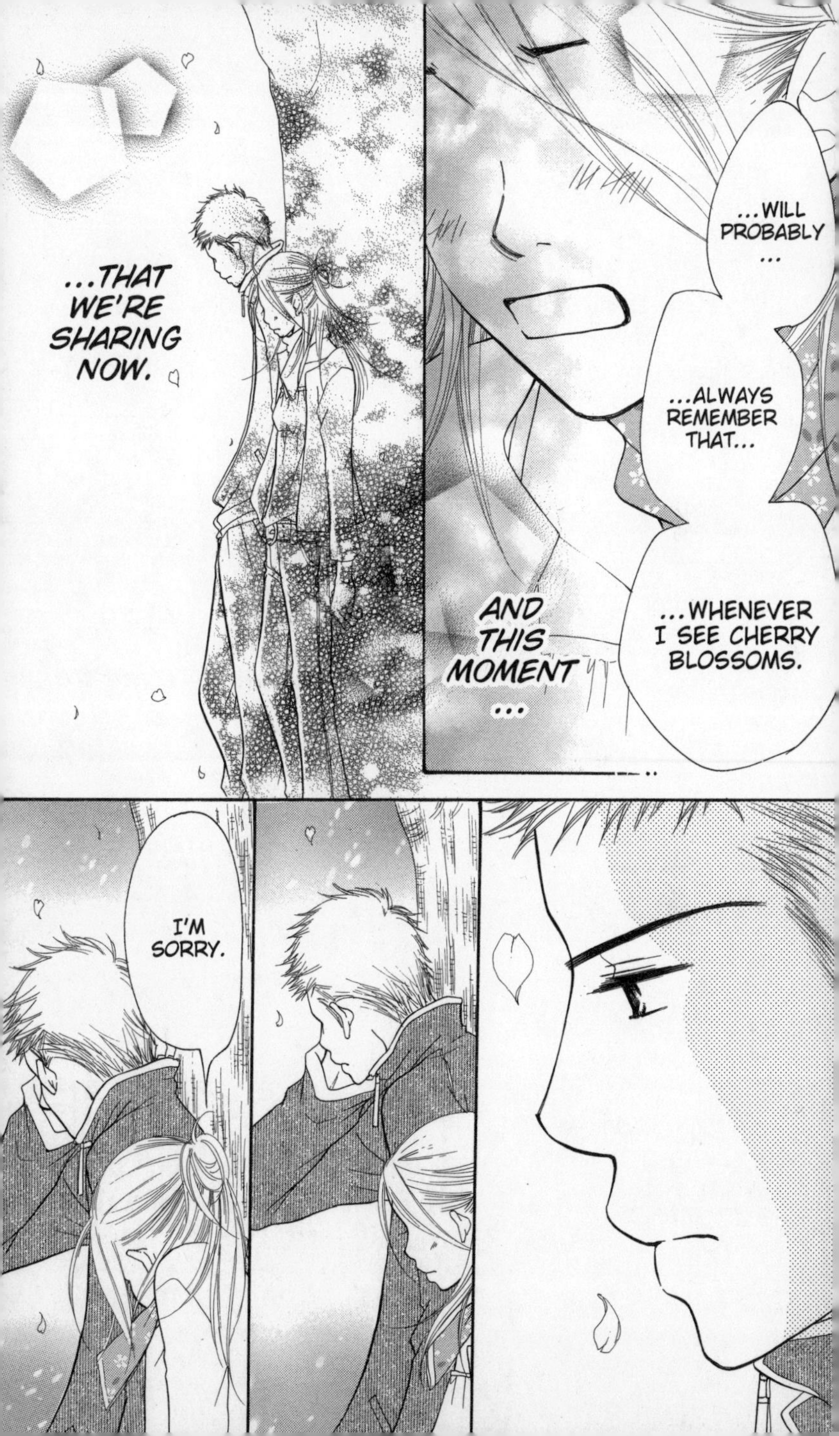
...WILL PROBABLY ...
...ALWAYS REMEMBER THAT...
...WHENEVER I SEE CHERRY BLOSSOMS.
AND THIS MOMENT ...
...THAT WE'RE SHARING NOW.
I'M SORRY.

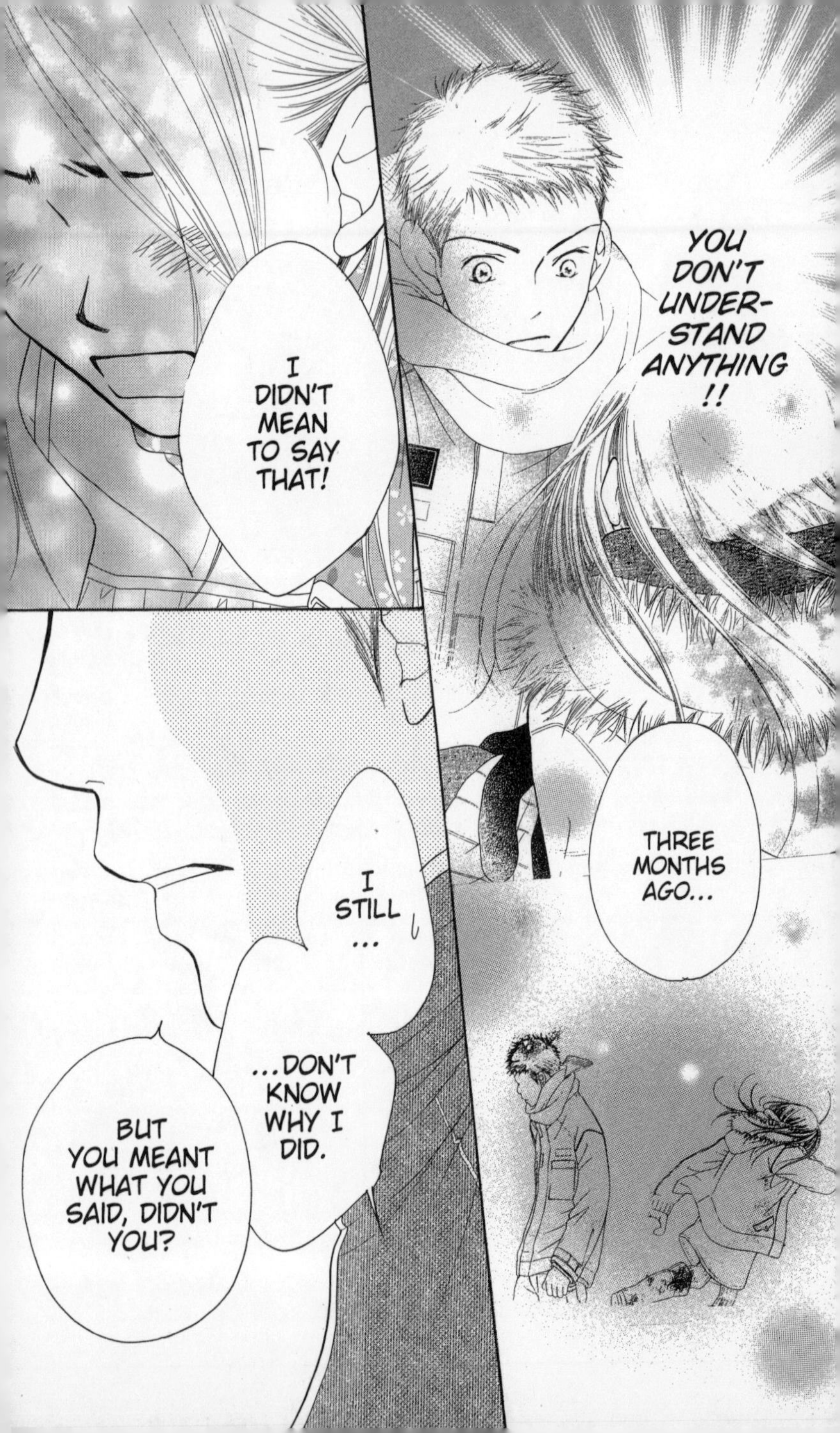
YOU DON'T UNDER-STAND ANYTHING!!
THREE MONTHS AGO...
I DIDN'T MEAN TO SAY THAT!
I STILL...
...DON'T KNOW WHY I DID.
BUT YOU MEANT WHAT YOU SAID, DIDN'T YOU?

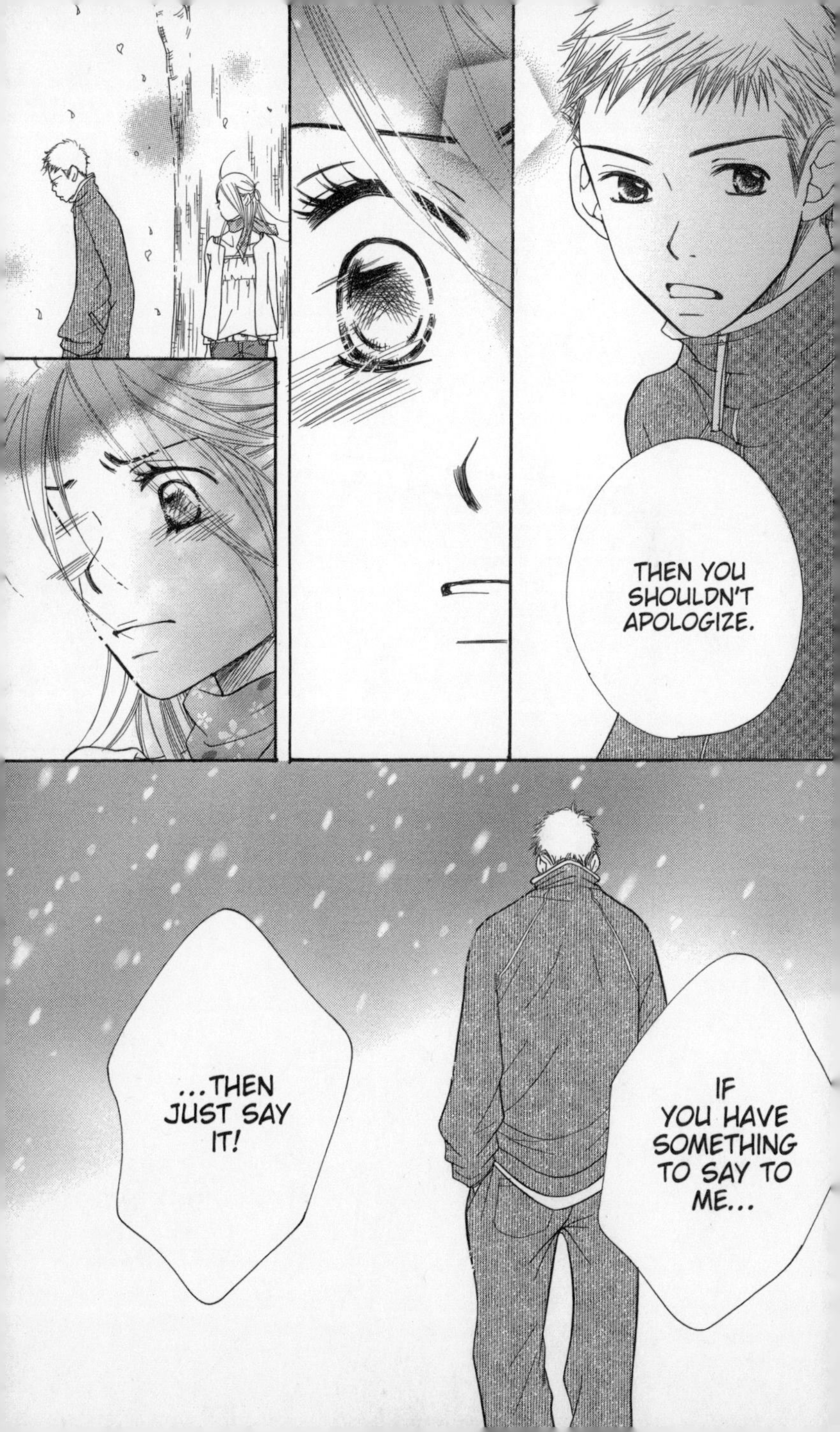
THEN YOU SHOULDN'T APOLOGIZE.
IF YOU HAVE SOMETHING TO SAY TO ME...
...THEN JUST SAY IT!

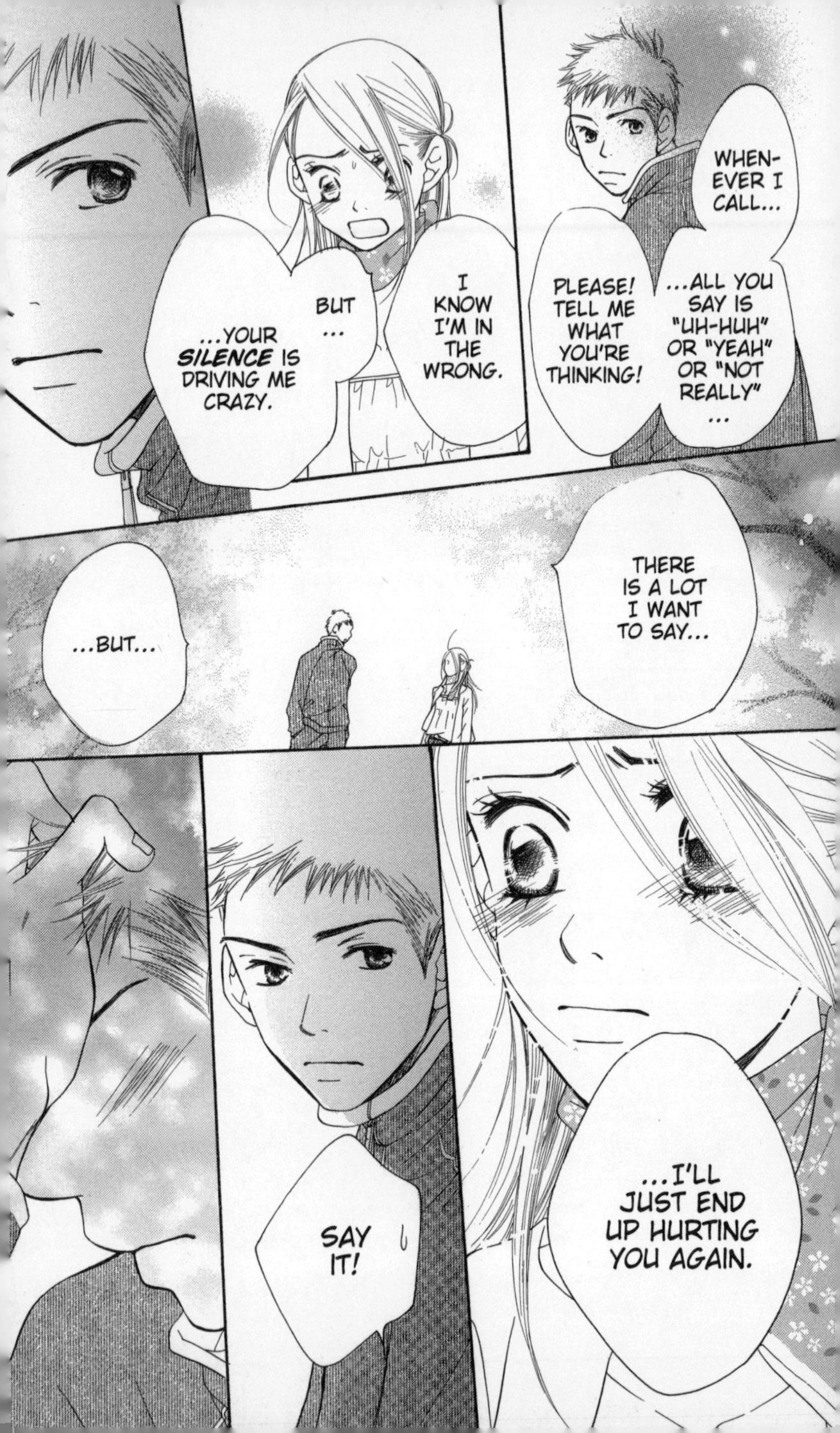
WHEN-EVER I CALL...
...ALL YOU SAY IS "UH-HUH" OR "YEAH" OR "NOT REALLY" ...
PLEASE! TELL ME WHAT YOU'RE THINKING!
I KNOW I'M IN THE WRONG.
BUT ...
...YOUR **SILENCE** IS DRIVING ME CRAZY.
THERE IS A LOT I WANT TO SAY...
...BUT...
...I'LL JUST END UP HURTING YOU AGAIN.
SAY IT!

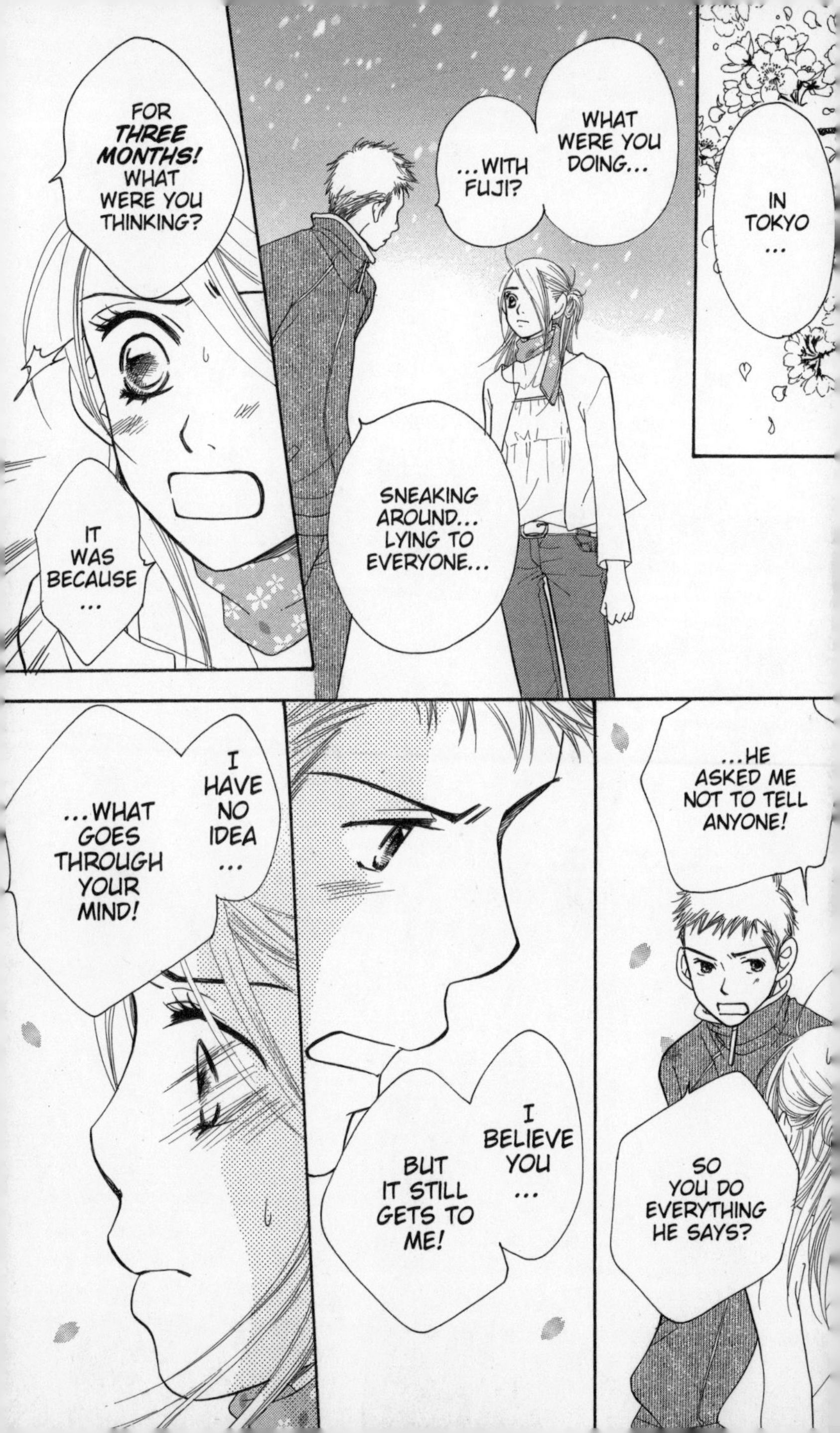
IN TOKYO...
WHAT WERE YOU DOING...
...WITH FUJI?
SNEAKING AROUND... LYING TO EVERYONE...
FOR THREE MONTHS! WHAT WERE YOU THINKING?
IT WAS BECAUSE...
...HE ASKED ME NOT TO TELL ANYONE!
SO YOU DO EVERYTHING HE SAYS?
I BELIEVE YOU...
BUT IT STILL GETS TO ME!
I HAVE NO IDEA...
...WHAT GOES THROUGH YOUR MIND!

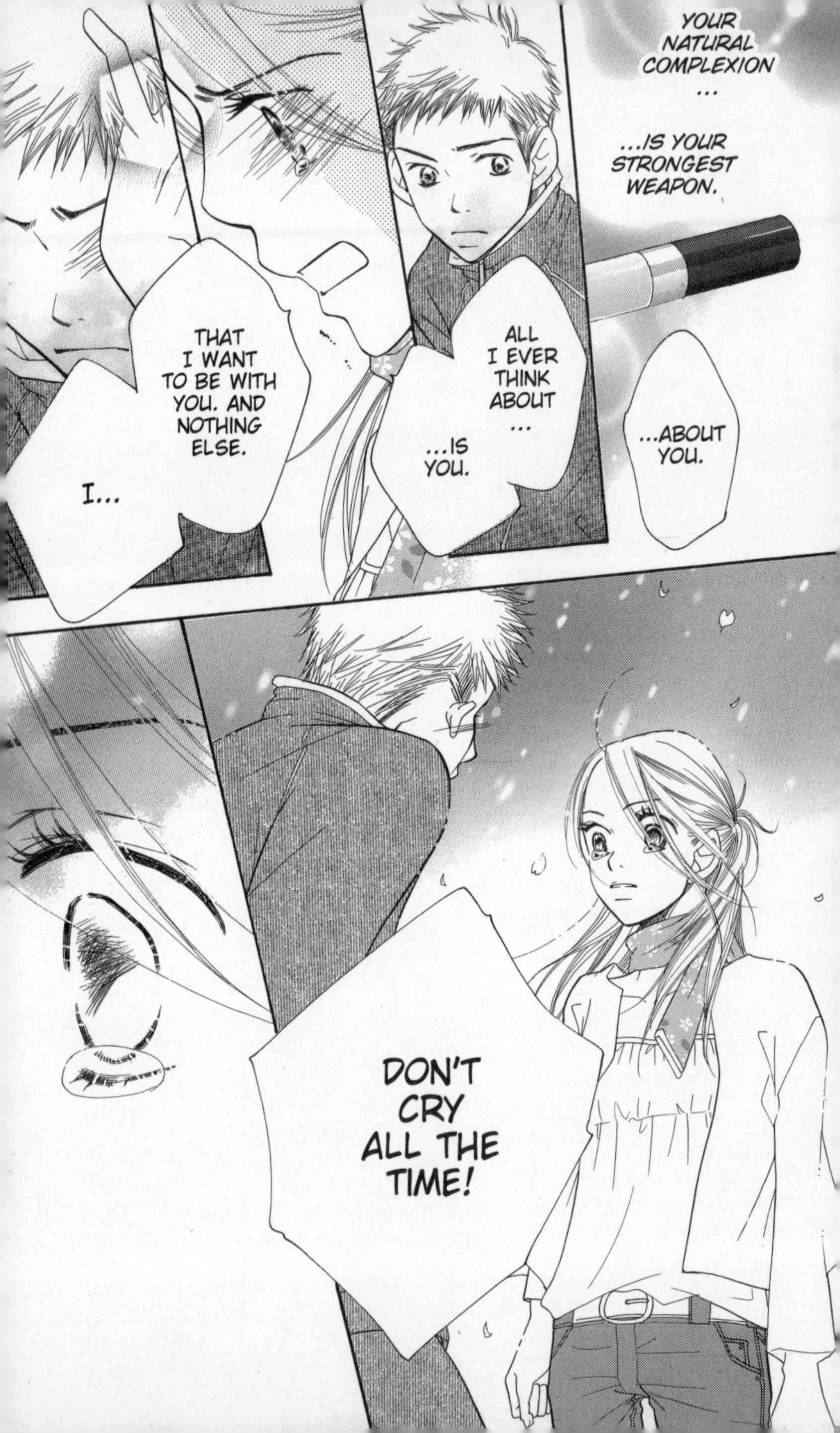
YOUR NATURAL COMPLEXION ...
...IS YOUR STRONGEST WEAPON.
...ABOUT YOU.
ALL I EVER THINK ABOUT ...
...IS YOU.
THAT I WANT TO BE WITH YOU. AND NOTHING ELSE.
I...
DON'T CRY ALL THE TIME!

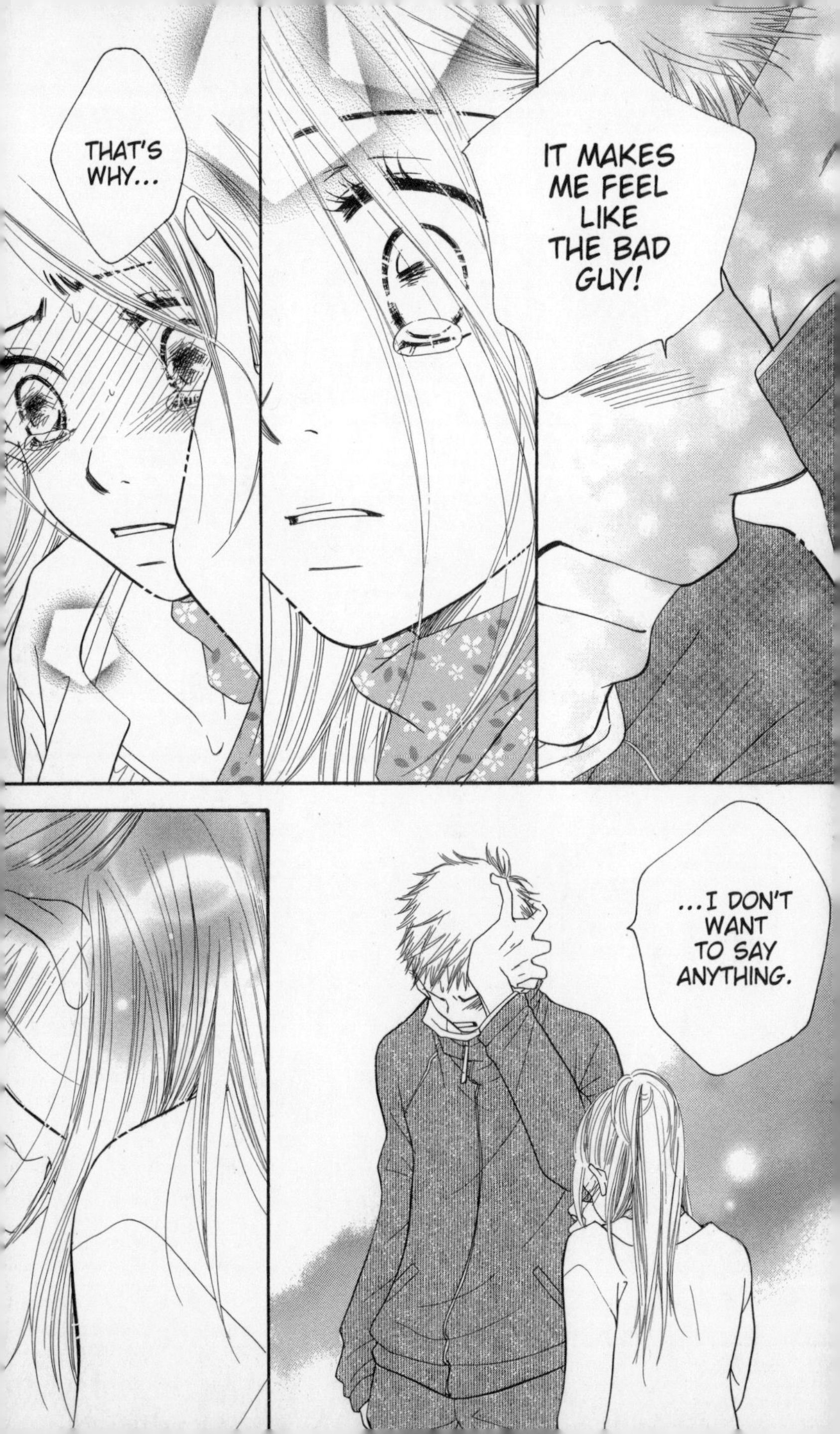
IT MAKES ME FEEL LIKE THE BAD GUY!
THAT'S WHY...
...I DON'T WANT TO SAY ANYTHING.

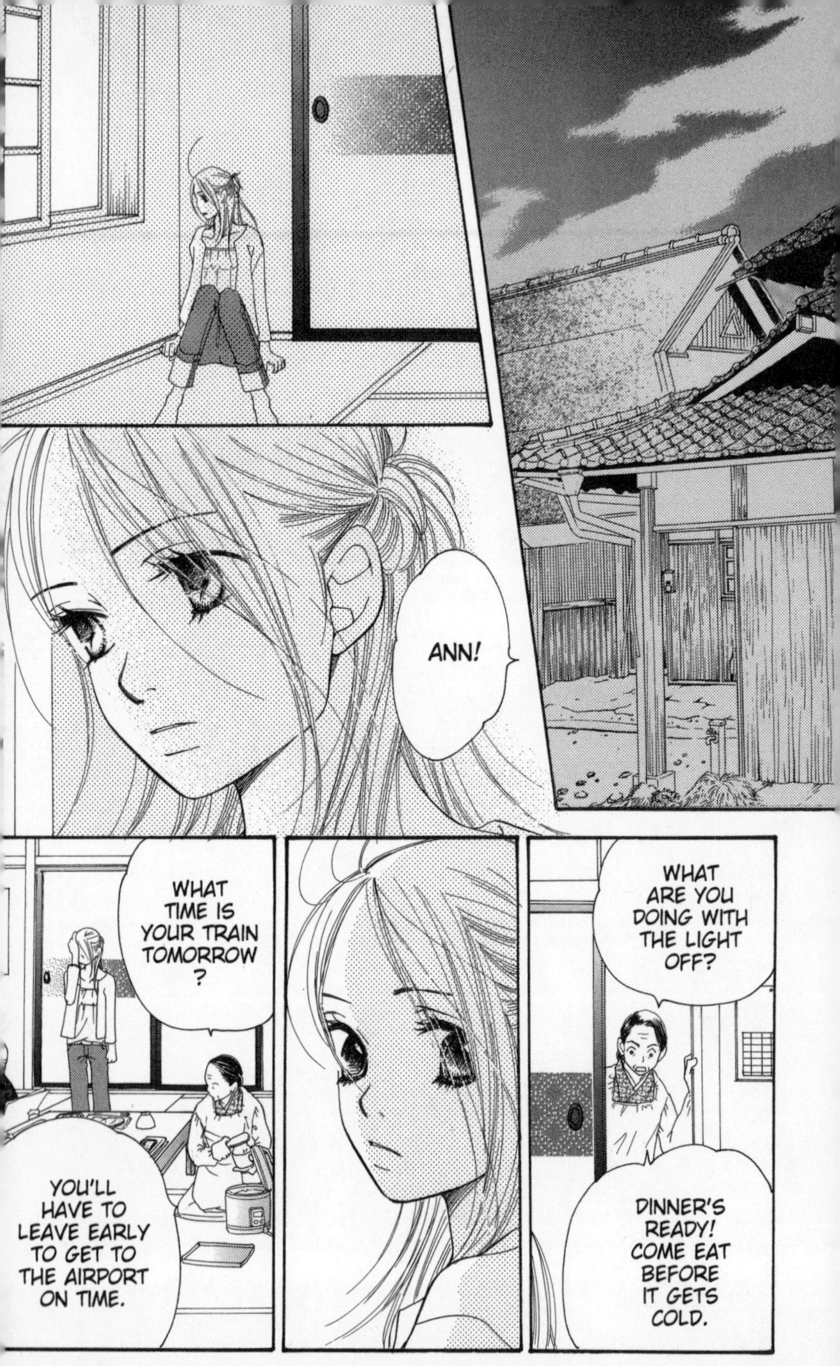
ANN!
WHAT ARE YOU DOING WITH THE LIGHT OFF?
DINNER'S READY! COME EAT BEFORE IT GETS COLD.
WHAT TIME IS YOUR TRAIN TOMORROW?
YOU'LL HAVE TO LEAVE EARLY TO GET TO THE AIRPORT ON TIME.

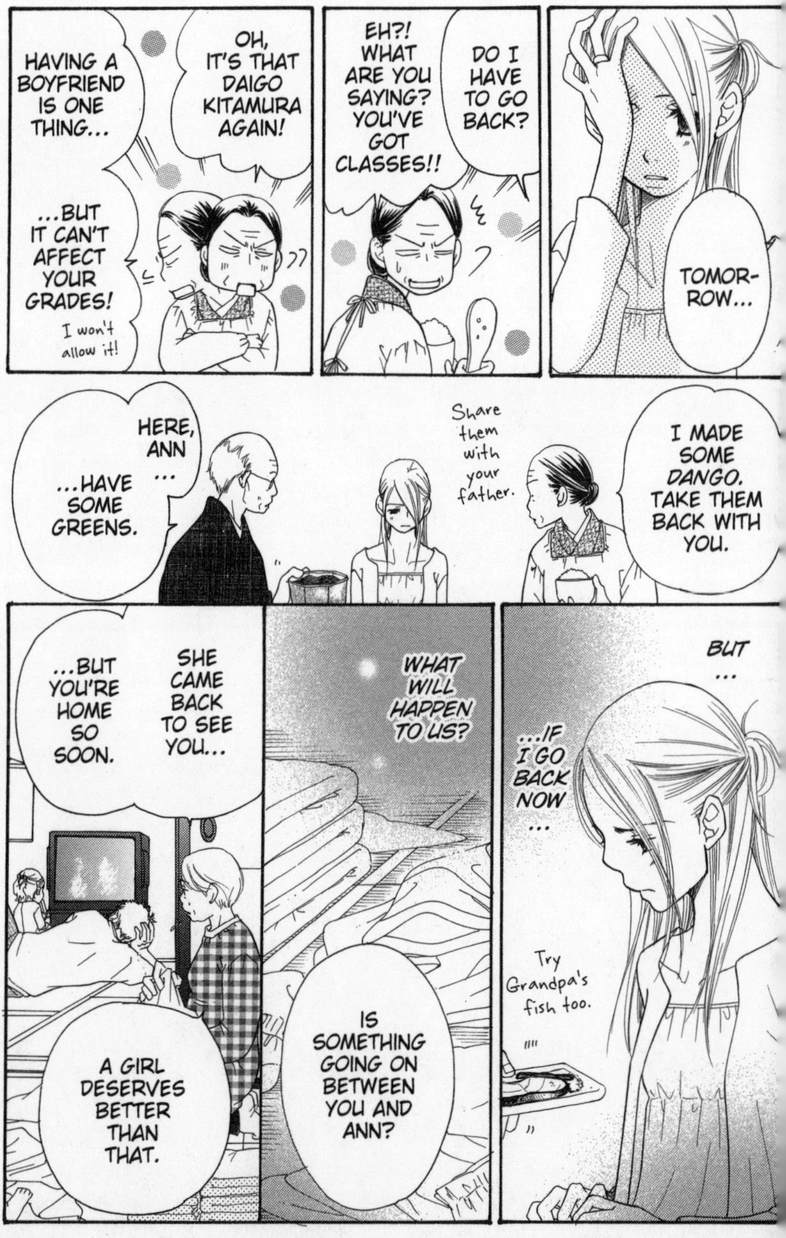
TOMOR-ROW...
DO I HAVE TO GO BACK?
EH?! WHAT ARE YOU SAYING? YOU'VE GOT CLASSES!!
OH, IT'S THAT DAIGO KITAMURA AGAIN!
HAVING A BOYFRIEND IS ONE THING...
...BUT IT CAN'T AFFECT YOUR GRADES!
I won't allow it!
I MADE SOME DANGO. TAKE THEM BACK WITH YOU.
Share them with your father.
HERE, ANN...
...HAVE SOME GREENS.
BUT...
...IF I GO BACK NOW...
Try Grandpa's fish too.
WHAT WILL HAPPEN TO US?
IS SOMETHING GOING ON BETWEEN YOU AND ANN?
SHE CAME BACK TO SEE YOU...
...BUT YOU'RE HOME SO SOON.
A GIRL DESERVES BETTER THAN THAT.

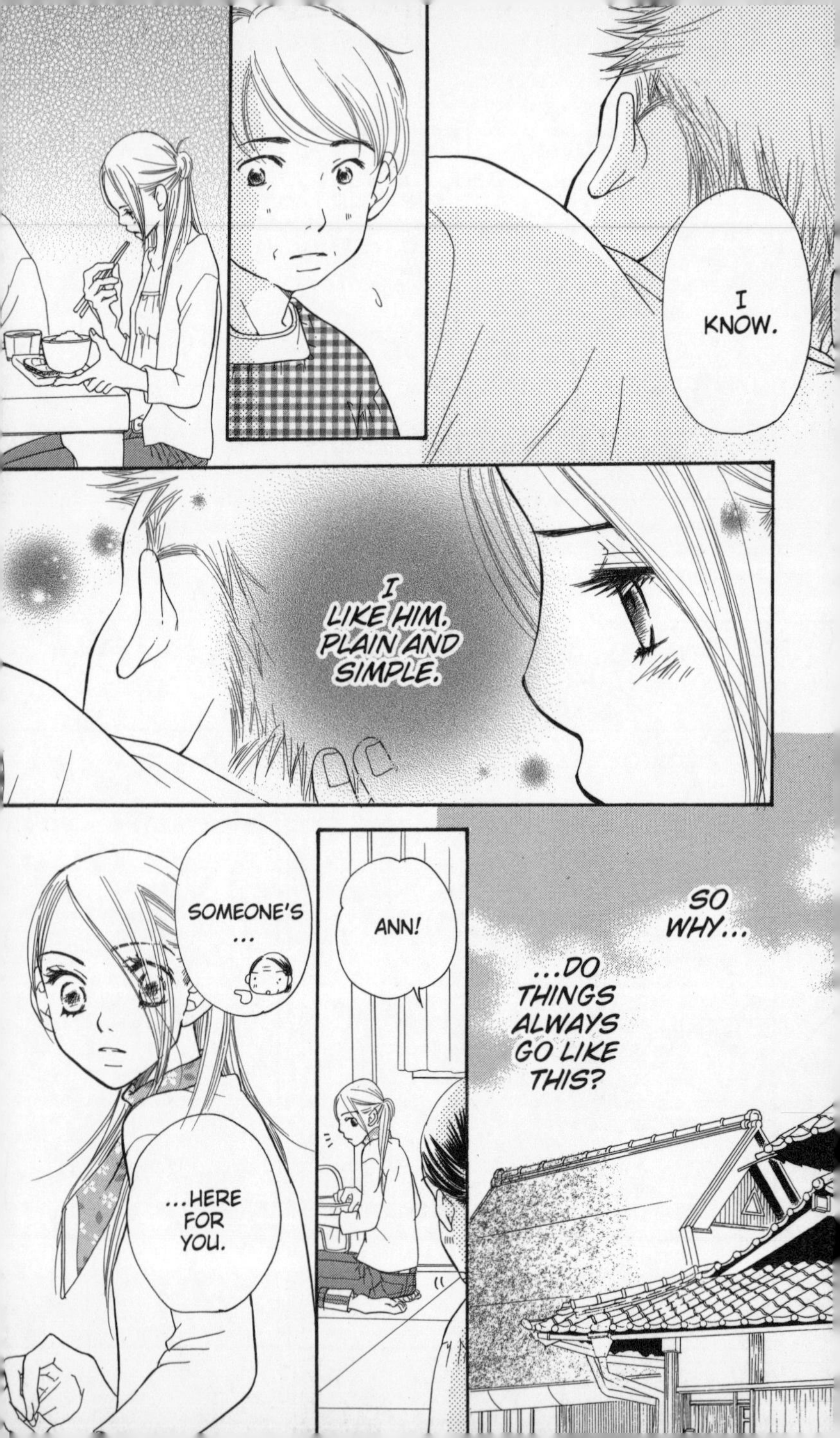
I KNOW.
I LIKE HIM. PLAIN AND SIMPLE.
SO WHY...
...DO THINGS ALWAYS GO LIKE THIS?
ANN!
SOMEONE'S ...
...HERE FOR YOU.

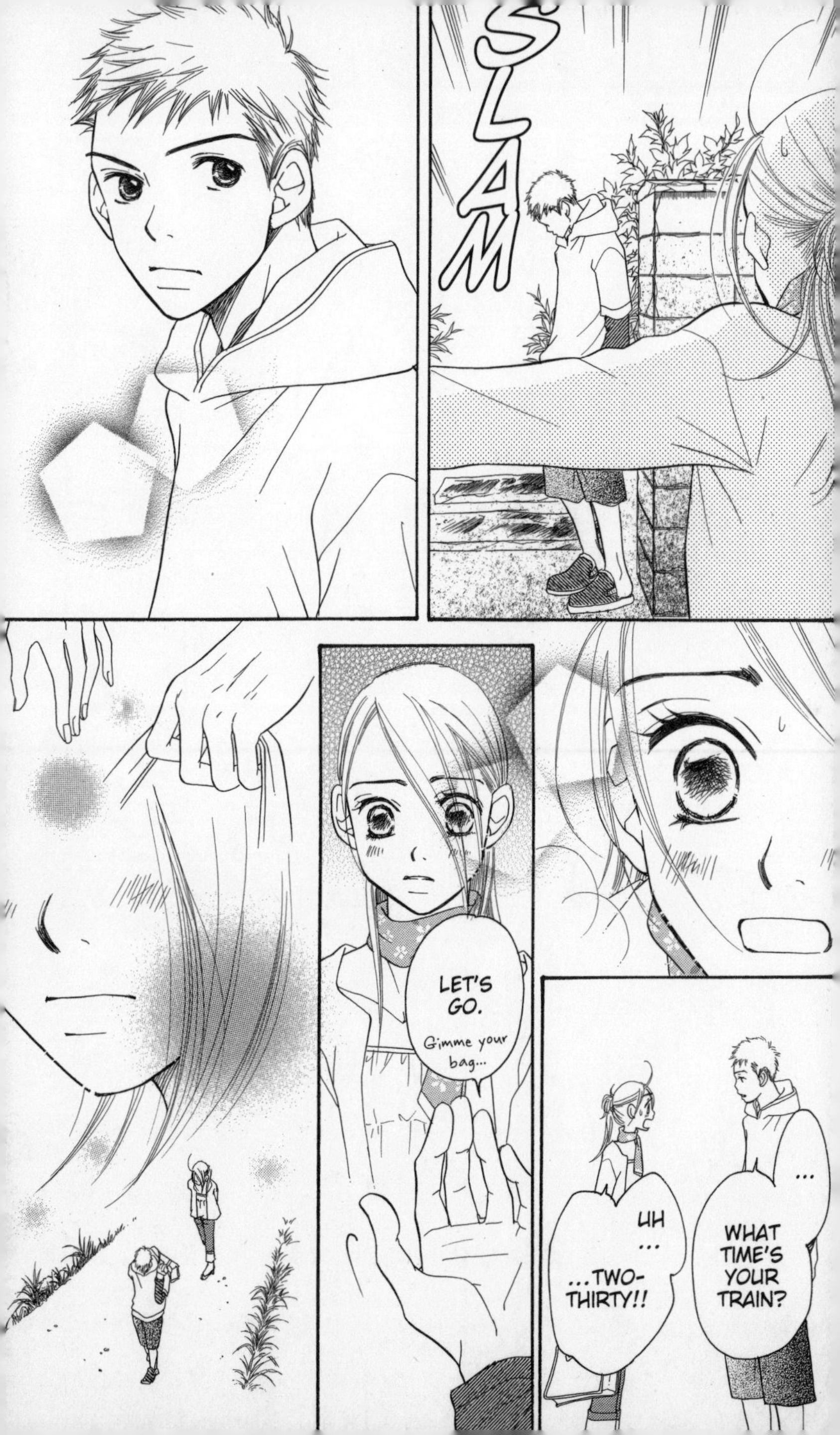
SLAM
LET'S GO.
Gimme your bag...
...
WHAT TIME'S YOUR TRAIN?
UH ...
...TWO-THIRTY!!

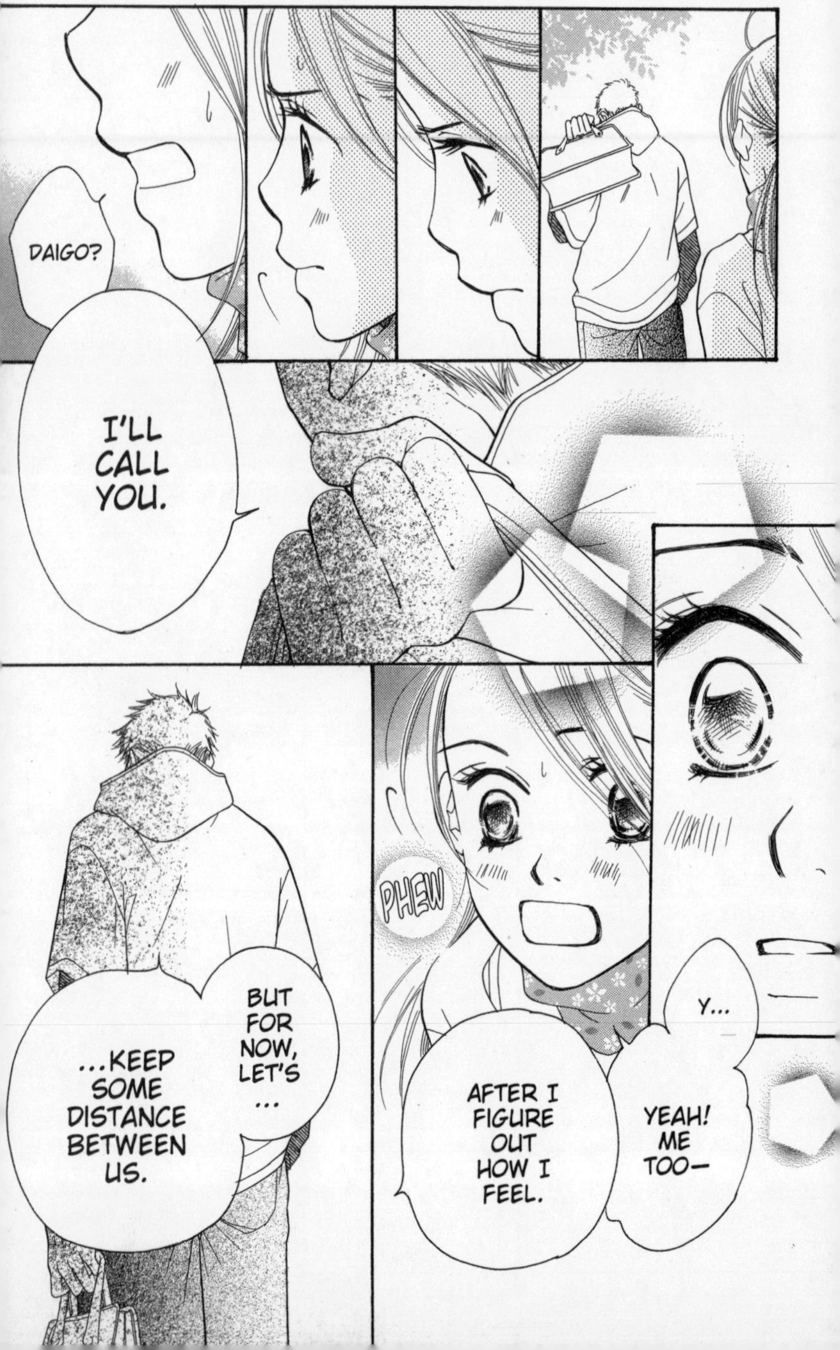
DAIGO?
I'LL CALL YOU.
Y...
YEAH! ME TOO—
PHEW
AFTER I FIGURE OUT HOW I FEEL.
BUT FOR NOW, LET'S...
...KEEP SOME DISTANCE BETWEEN US.

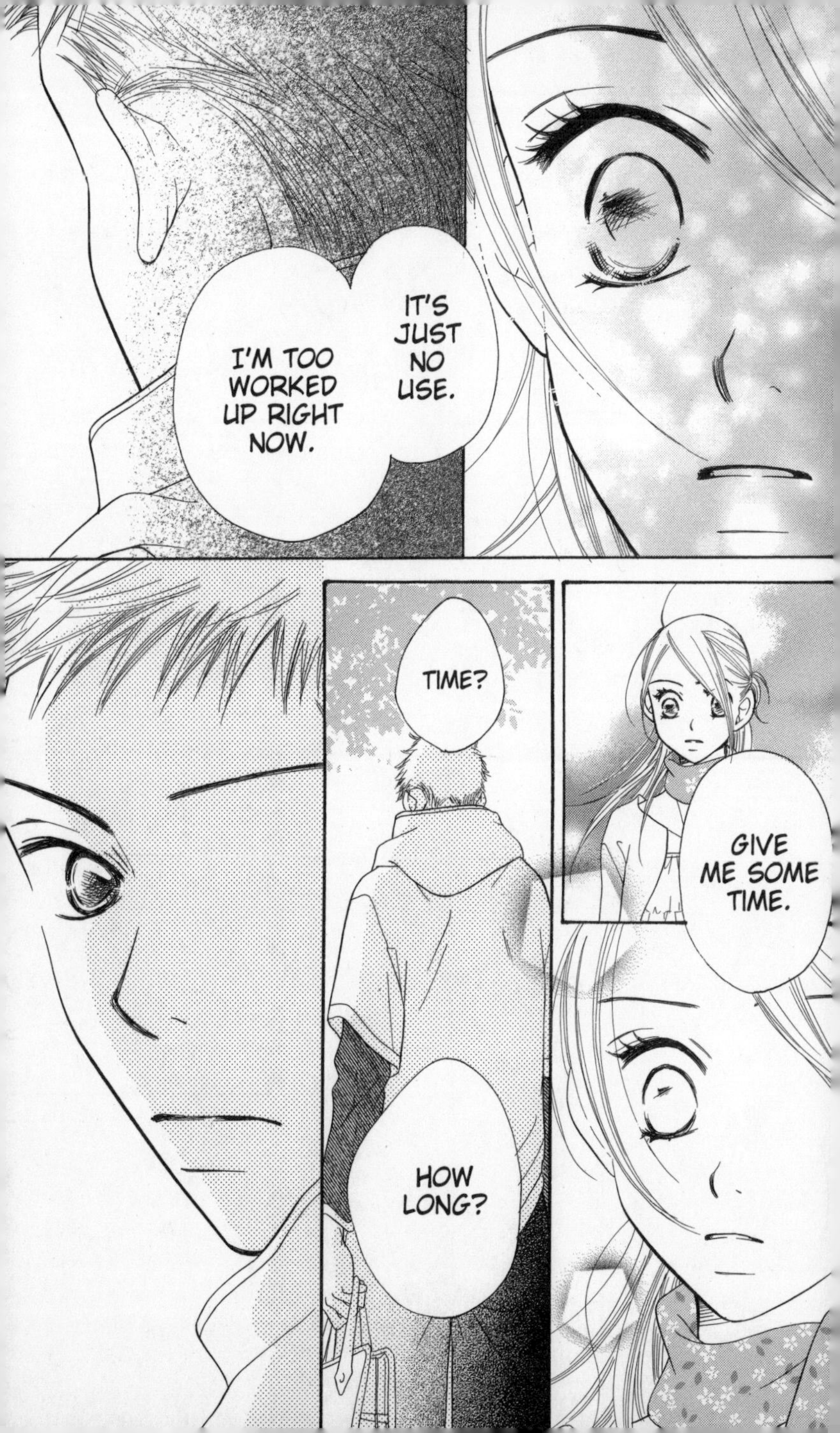
IT'S JUST NO USE.
I'M TOO WORKED UP RIGHT NOW.
GIVE ME SOME TIME.
TIME?
HOW LONG?

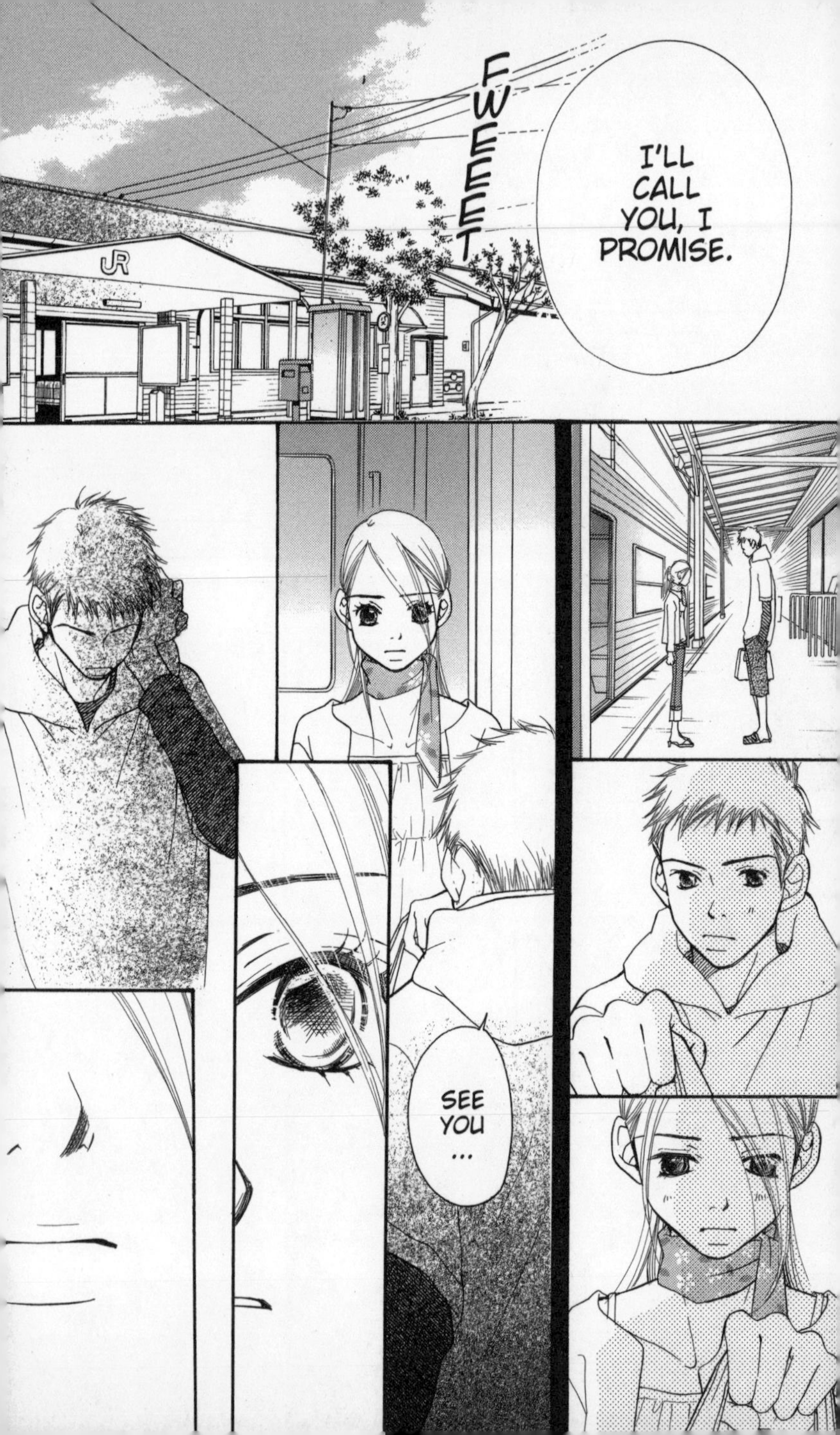
I'LL CALL YOU, I PROMISE.
FWEEET
SEE YOU ...

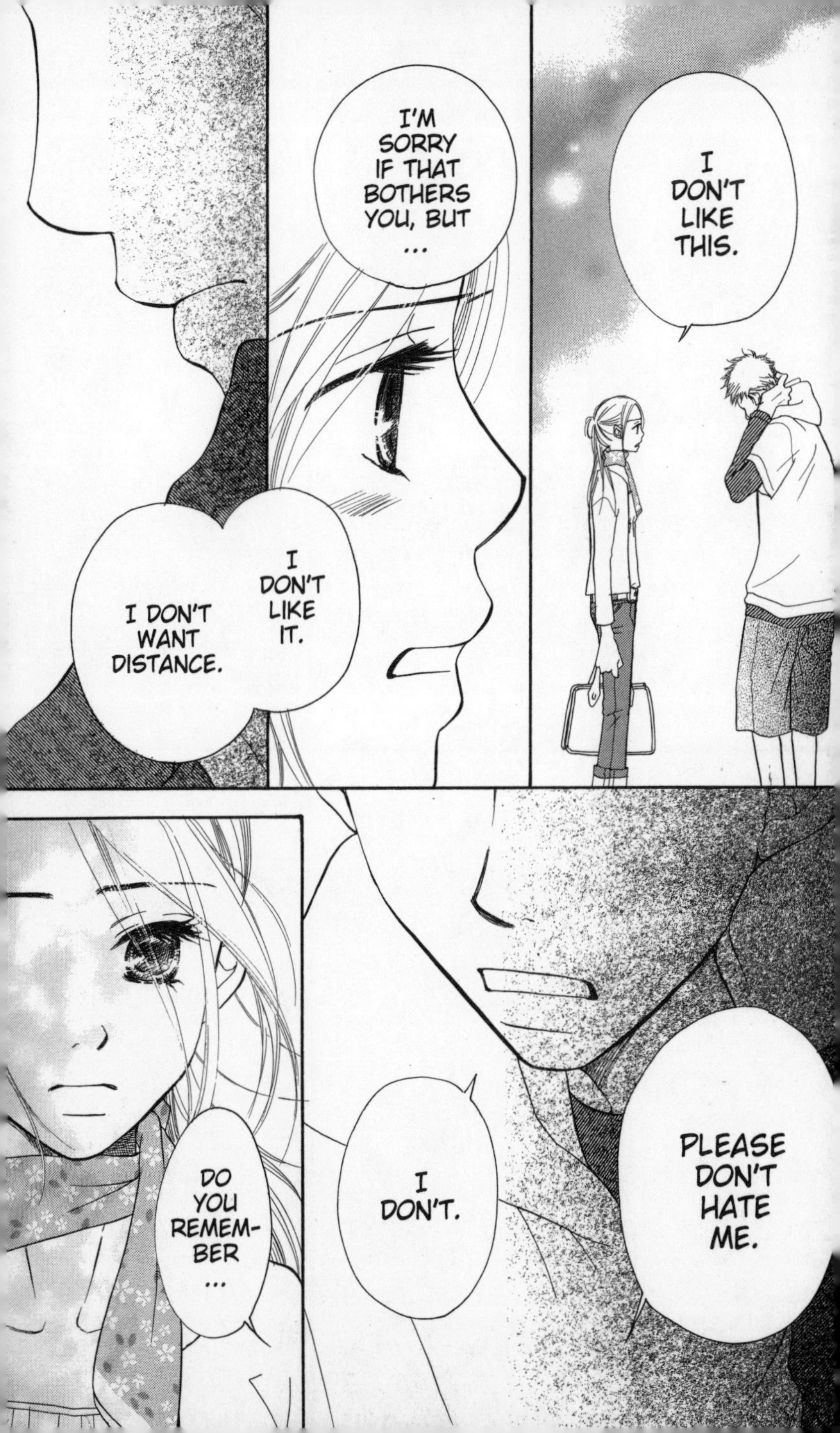
I DON'T LIKE THIS.
I'M SORRY IF THAT BOTHERS YOU, BUT ...
I DON'T LIKE IT.
I DON'T WANT DISTANCE.
PLEASE DON'T HATE ME.
I DON'T.
DO YOU REMEM-BER ...

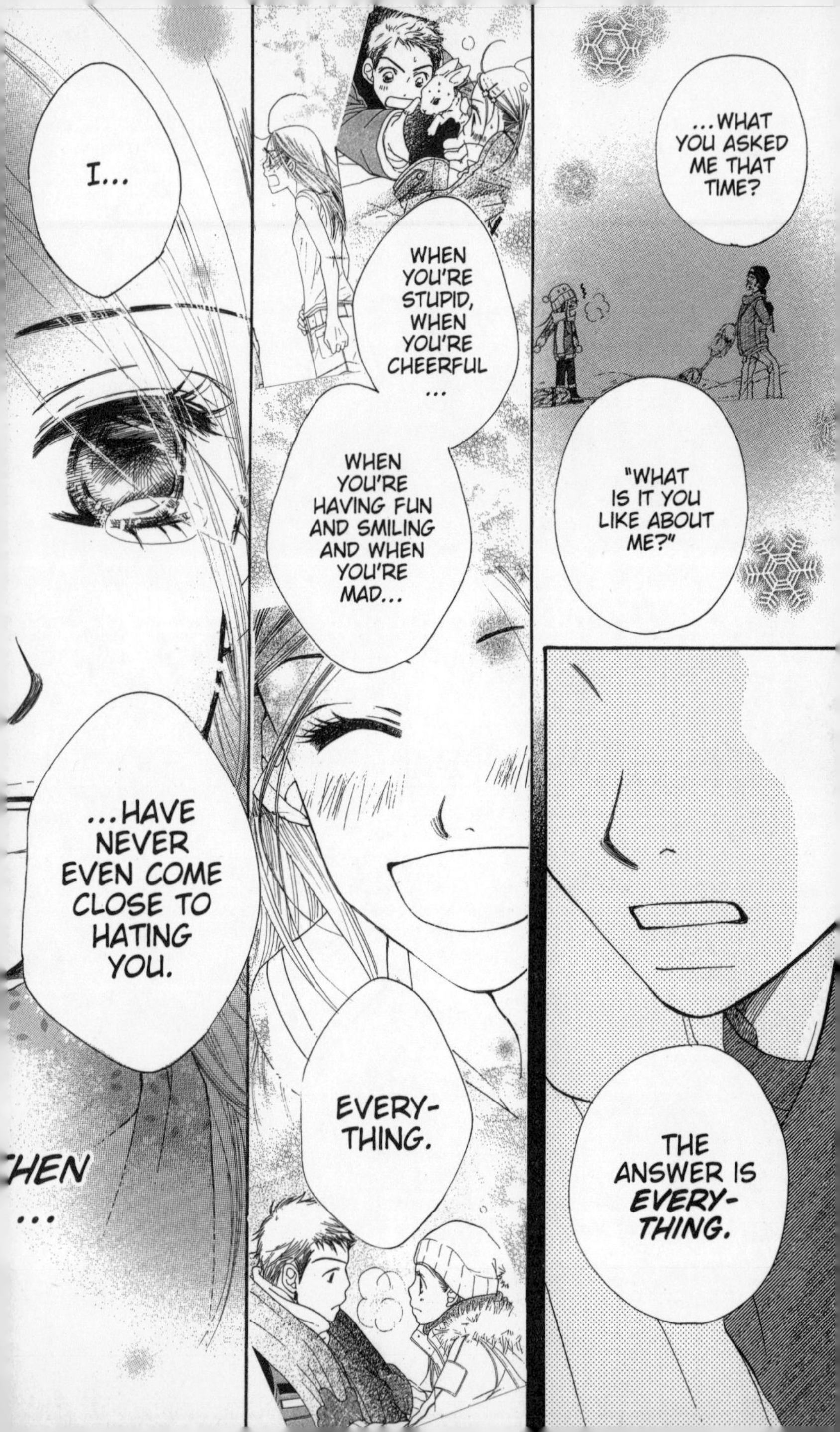
...WHAT YOU ASKED ME THAT TIME?
"WHAT IS IT YOU LIKE ABOUT ME?"
THE ANSWER IS *EVERY-THING.*
WHEN YOU'RE STUPID, WHEN YOU'RE CHEERFUL...
WHEN YOU'RE HAVING FUN AND SMILING AND WHEN YOU'RE MAD...
EVERY-THING.
I...
...HAVE NEVER EVEN COME CLOSE TO HATING YOU.
HEN ...

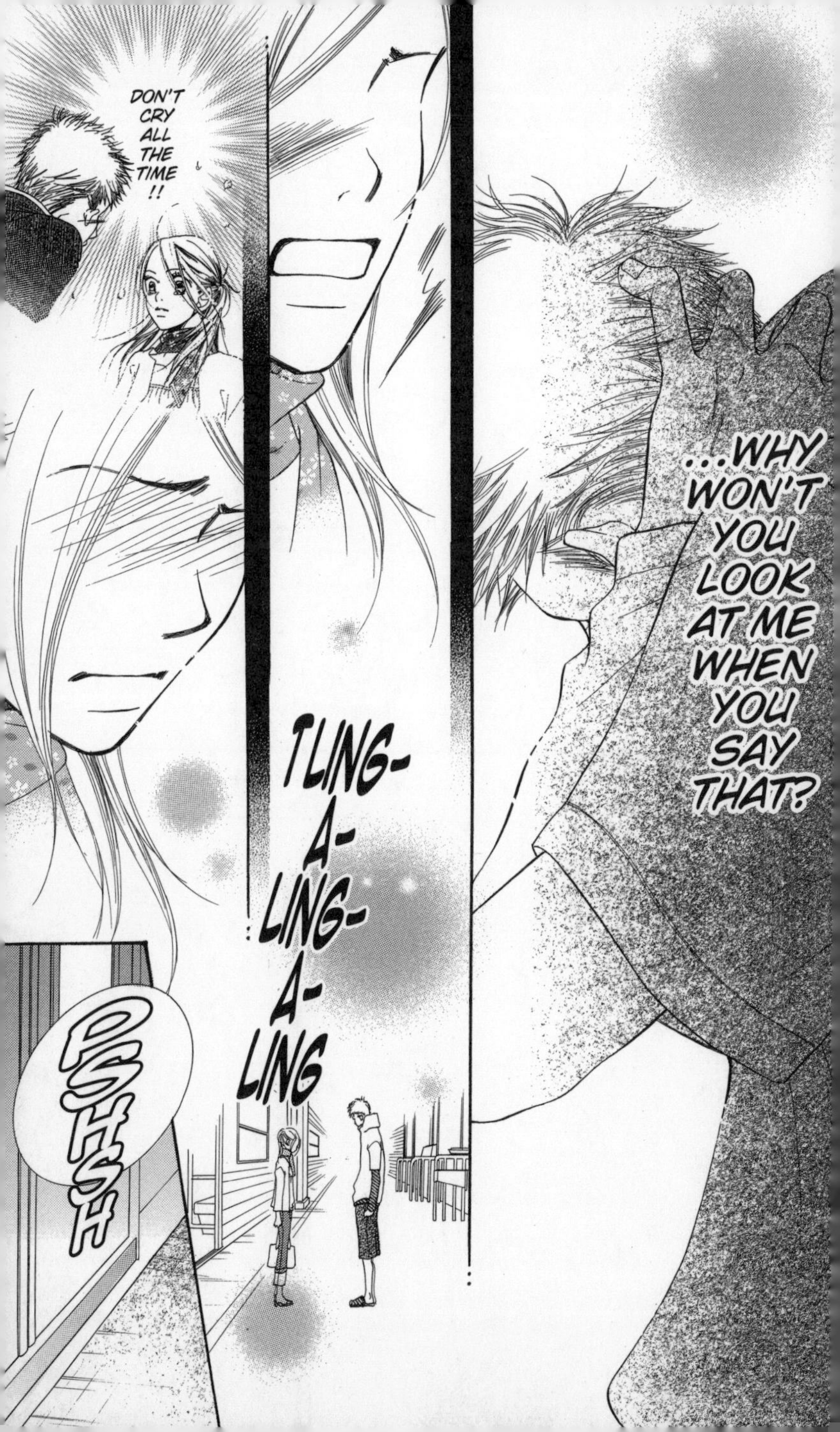
...WHY WON'T YOU LOOK AT ME WHEN YOU SAY THAT?
TLING-A-LING-A-LING
DON'T CRY ALL THE TIME!!
PSHSH

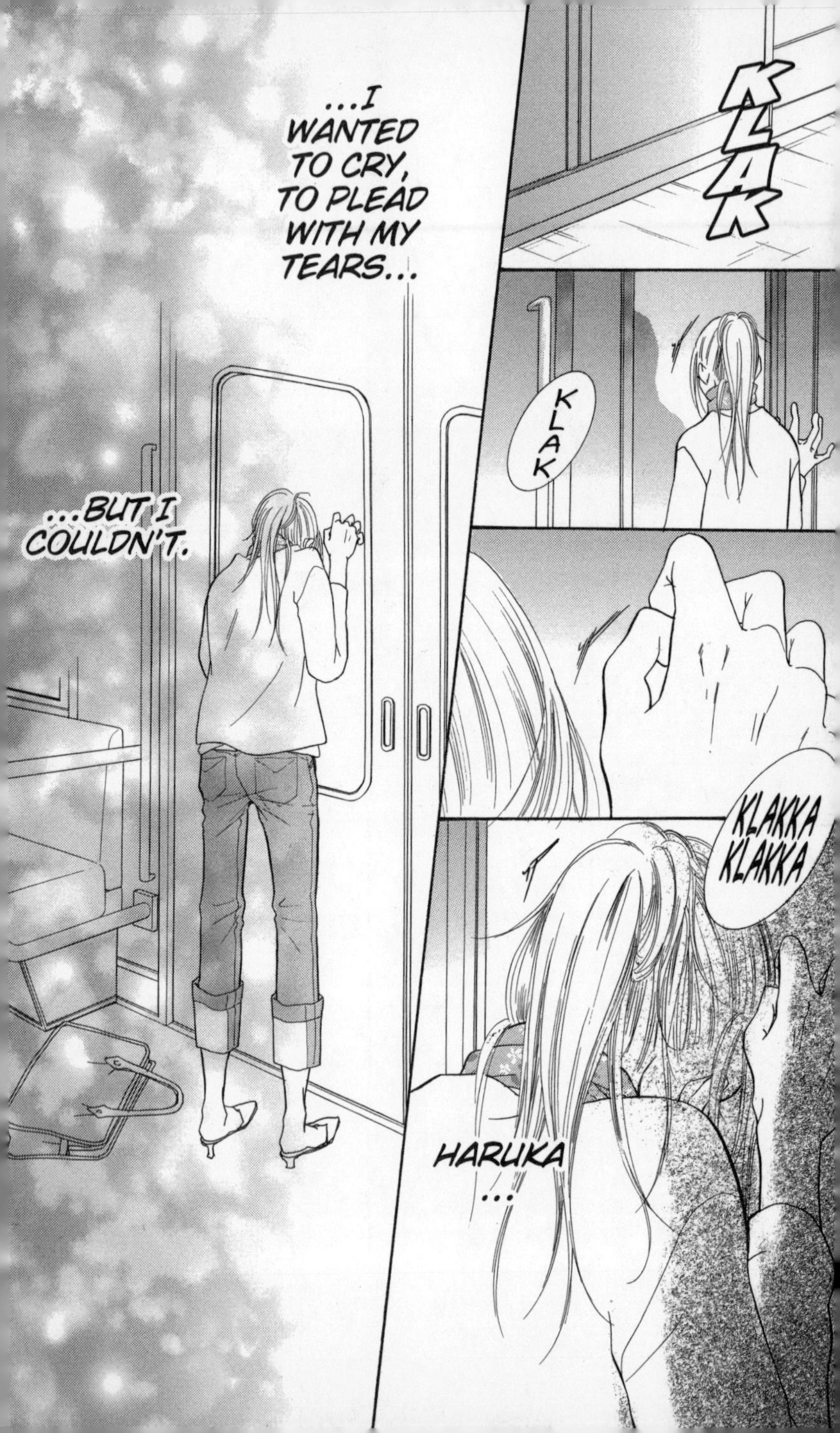
KLAK
KLAK
KLAKKA KLAKKA
HARUKA...
...I WANTED TO CRY, TO PLEAD WITH MY TEARS...
...BUT I COULDN'T.

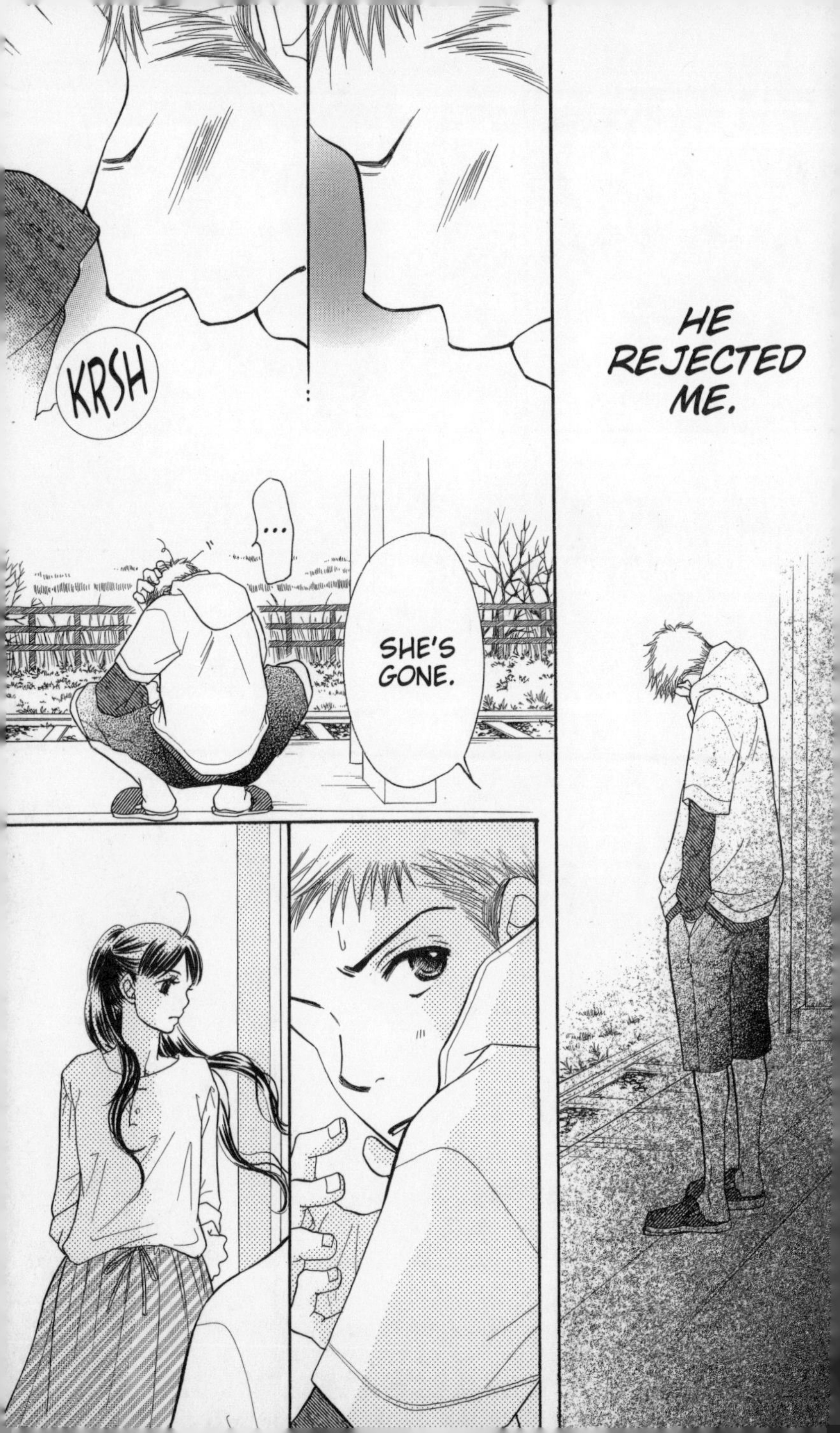
HE REJECTED ME.
KRSH
...
SHE'S GONE.

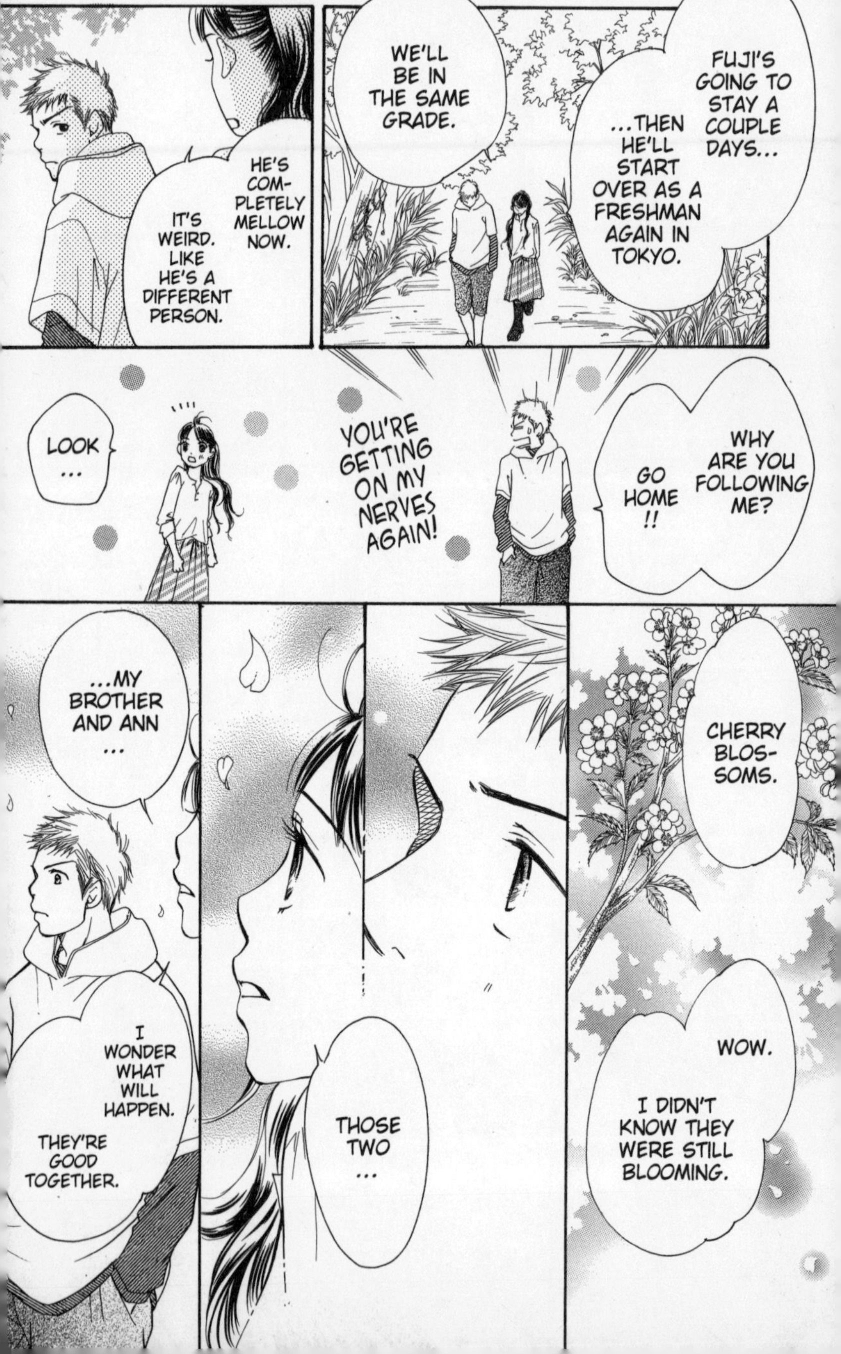
FUJI'S GOING TO STAY A COUPLE DAYS...
...THEN HE'LL START OVER AS A FRESHMAN AGAIN IN TOKYO.
WE'LL BE IN THE SAME GRADE.
HE'S COM-PLETELY MELLOW NOW.
IT'S WEIRD. LIKE HE'S A DIFFERENT PERSON.
WHY ARE YOU FOLLOWING ME?
GO HOME !!
YOU'RE GETTING ON MY NERVES AGAIN!
LOOK ...
CHERRY BLOS-SOMS.
WOW.
I DIDN'T KNOW THEY WERE STILL BLOOMING.
THOSE TWO ...
...MY BROTHER AND ANN ...
I WONDER WHAT WILL HAPPEN.
THEY'RE GOOD TOGETHER.

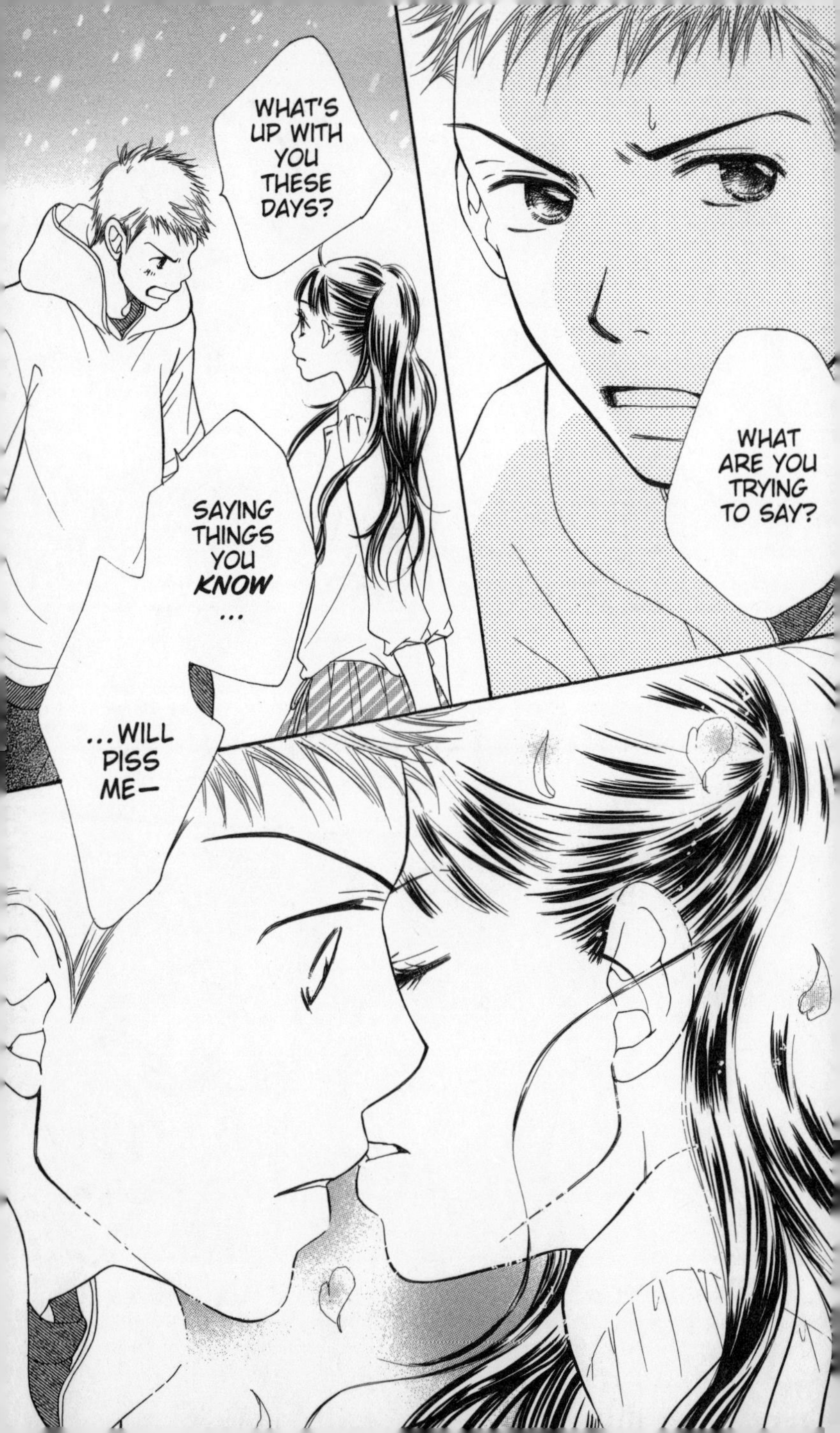
WHAT ARE YOU TRYING TO SAY?
WHAT'S UP WITH YOU THESE DAYS?
SAYING THINGS YOU **KNOW** ...
...WILL PISS ME—

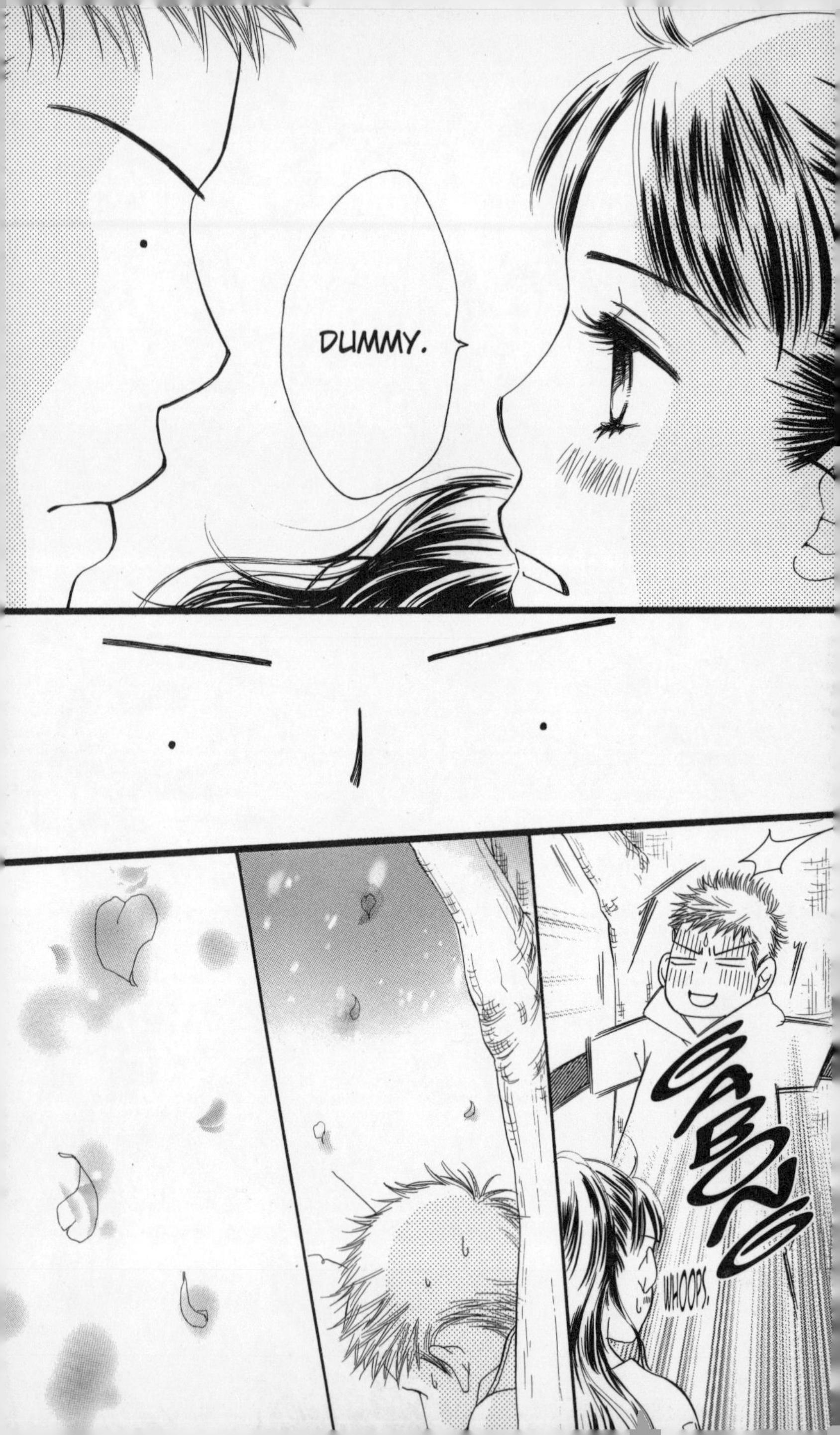
DUMMY.
WHOOPS.

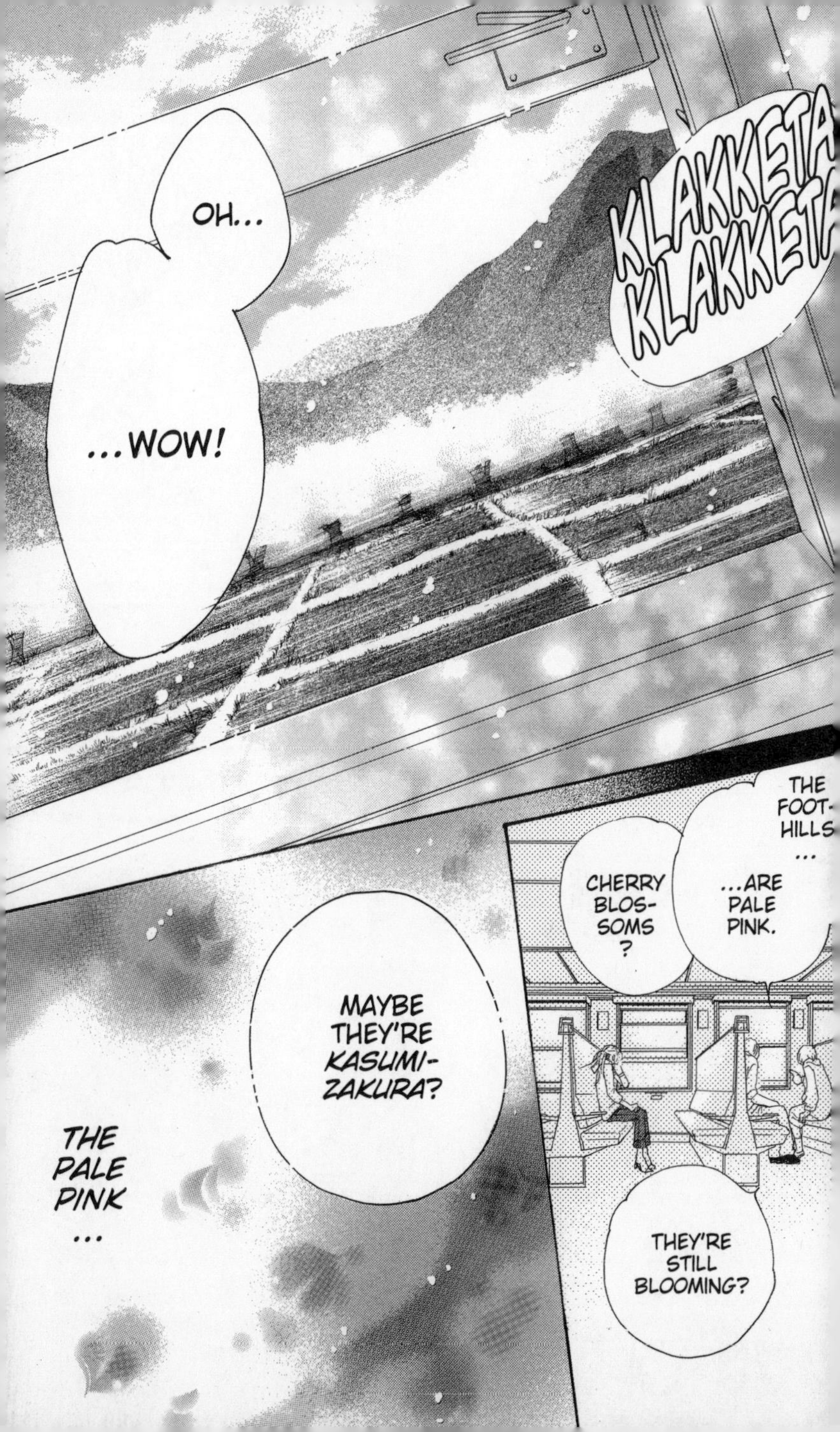
KLAKKETA KLAKKETA
OH...
...WOW!
THE FOOT-HILLS...
...ARE PALE PINK.
CHERRY BLOS-SOMS?
THEY'RE STILL BLOOMING?
MAYBE THEY'RE KASUMI-ZAKURA?
THE PALE PINK...

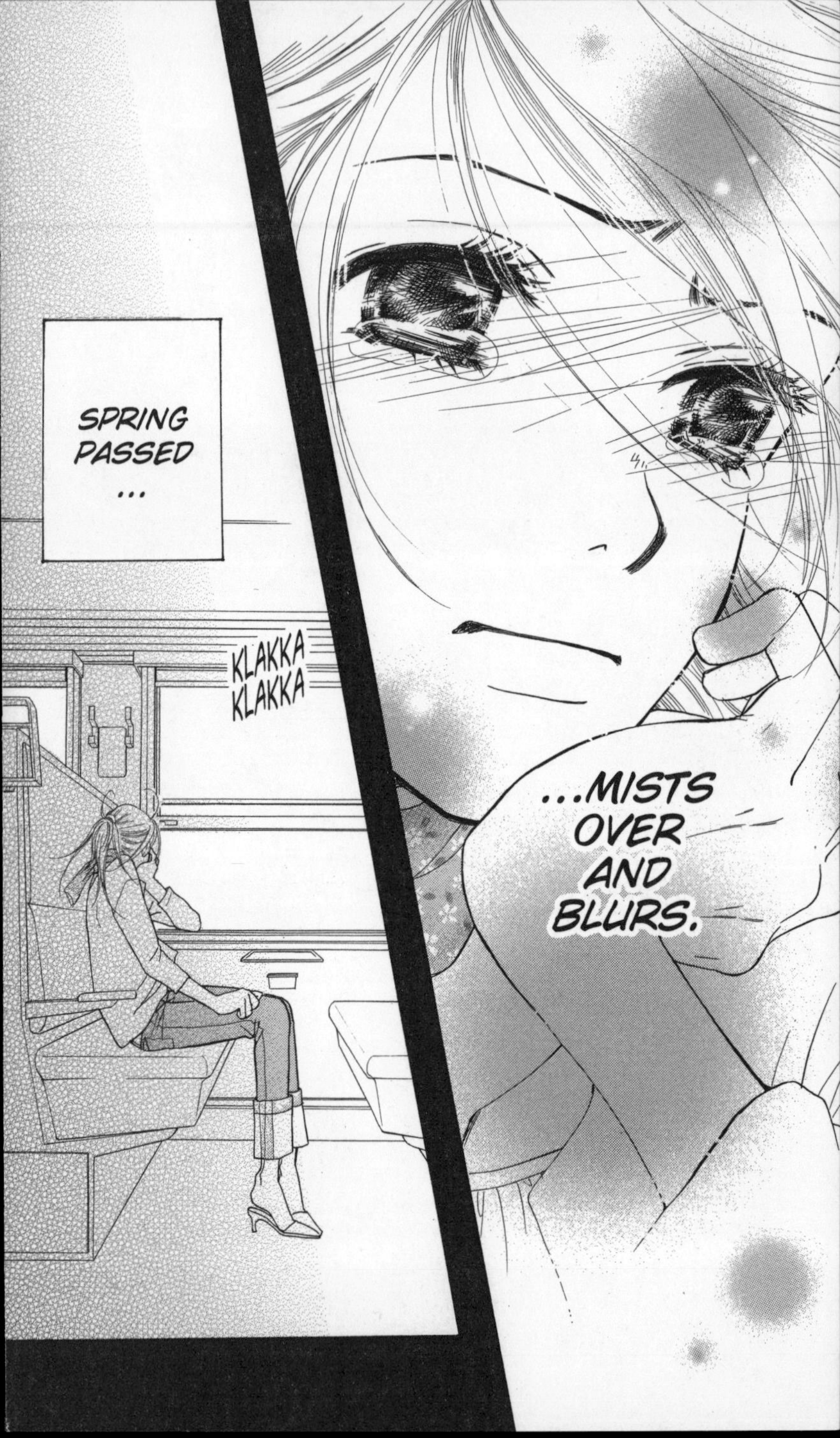
...MISTS OVER AND BLURS.
SPRING PASSED ...
KLAKKA KLAKKA

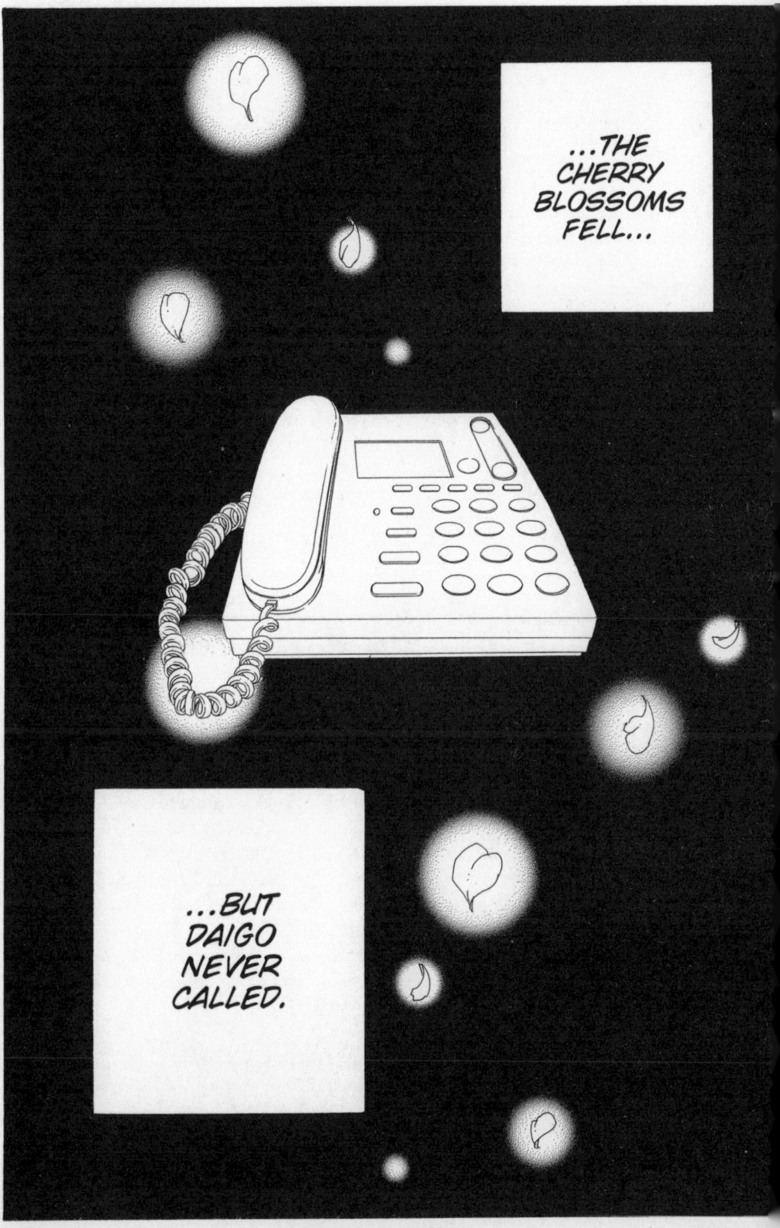
...THE CHERRY BLOSSOMS FELL...
...BUT DAIGO NEVER CALLED.

Glossary

If only adolescence came with an instruction manual. We can't give you that, but this glossary of terms might prove useful for this volume.

Page 4: Snows of Remembrance
Wasure-yuki is literally "forget-snow." It refers to snow in the springtime. Many Japanese people are completely unfamiliar with this word. One possibility is that just when the snows of winter have been forgotten, it snows again. Another possibility is that a snowfall in the springtime is sure to be the last snow, and the snows of winter will with its passing be forgotten. The author herself says she is using the word in an unusual way. See the sidebar on page 67 for more discussion.

Page 12, panel 4: *kogal*
Kogals are teenage girls known for their unusual clothes, platform boots, and excessive makeup. They aren't actually rebellious, but follow current trends together.

Page 14, panel 4: A Christmas Party for Dorks/ Out-with-the-Old-Year Dogsled Race/ Drop-By New Year's Party
Christmas Eve is a big date night in Japan, so usually only single people would attend a Christmas party. In Japan, parties toward the end of the year are called "Forgetting-the-Year" parties. The basic concept is out with everything that has passed and in with a new, hopefully happy, year. But, of course, the fact that a lot of drinking goes on at these parties, leading to some memory loss, is also obvious.

The modifier "Drop-By" for "New Year's

Party" is informal in a way that would be considered impolite under the usual strict rules of Japanese culture. At New Year's parties, everyone tends to dispense with these rules.

Page 17, panel 6: *nabe*
As a traditional Japanese dish, *nabe* is not a typical choice to celebrate a Western holiday. Fried chicken (rather than turkey) and "Christmas cake" (American-style birthday cake with strawberries on top) are more common.

Page 18, panel 2: print club/*puri-kura*
Puri-kura is an abbreviation of *purinto kurabu*, or print club. The word refers to small booths where friends can have their photos taken against a number of bright, fun backgrounds (among other frills), as well as the resulting pictures, which are usually printed as stickers.

Page 39, panel 5: stupid in love
Literally *bakappuru*: *baka* (idiot) + *kappuru* (couple). This refers to couples who are so head-over-heels in love that they act goofy and ridiculous. They themselves don't realize it because they are so wrapped up in each other, but to those around them, their behavior is embarrassing.

Page 41, panel 1: *osechi*
Osechi refers to special foods prepared for the New Year's holidays.

Page 43, panels 3 to 5: original pun

The original joke here is based on Japanese puns. Japanese people call these types of puns "old guy" jokes, because middle-aged to older men like to make them. Others generally consider them extremely boring and groan-worthy. Here is the original play of words in this scene:

Grandpa: Shall I give you an *otoshidama*, Ann? [otoshidama: money given to children by older relatives at the New Year]

Ann: Really?! [FX] I can't believe it!!! [Ann is at the age when many children would have stopped receiving otoshidama.]

Grandpa: Here's a ball. [The *dama* in *otoshidama* comes from *tama*, which means ball.]

Grandpa: Drop it…and you'll get an "otoshidama." [The *otoshi* of *otoshidama* means "year," but here he is making a pun on the word *otosu*, which means "to fall."]

Page 89, panel 4: canned coffee

In Japan, canned coffee is dispensed from vending machines that heat them in the winter and chill them in the summer. The Japanese company Pokka Corp. invented hot can vending machines in 1973. The first canned coffee, Mira Coffee, appeared in Shimane prefecture in 1965.

Heated metal cans are too hot to hold, and plastic bottles let in air, which ruins hot coffee, so in 2000, the company Ito En invented a new type of plastic bottle that keeps out oxygen.

For some reason, English is the language of choice for Japanese canned coffee labels.

Brad Pitt starred in a Japanese commercial for the canned coffee brand Roots. (Which can be seen on youtube.)

Page 110, panel 2: Kabukicho

One of the busiest areas of Shinjuku, Tokyo. An entertainment and red-light district.

Page 112, panel 3: Club Hibiki

Hibiki means "echoes" or "resonance" and can, depending on the situation, be translated as "sound/beat/note/ring," etc. "Echoes" would be closest to the style of name these kinds of places typically have.

Page 112, panel 4: Host

A name for young men who work at "host" clubs" entertaining women customers. A kind of modern-day male geisha.

Page 133, panel 2: *sakura mochi*

Pounded-rice cake wrapped in a cherry tree leaf.

Page 160, panel 3: *kasumi-zakura*

Kasumi-zakura = Prunus Verecunda Koehne. This kind of cherry tree grows wild.

Page 171, panel 4: *dango*

Japanese sweet dumplings made from rice flour.

Page 186, panel 1: *kasumi*

The *kasumi* of *kasumi-zakura* means "mist over/haze/blur," etc.

Profile of Hinako Ashihara

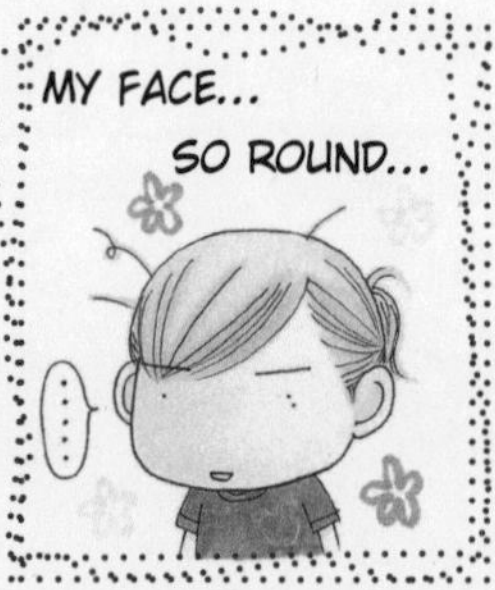
MY FACE...
SO ROUND...
......

I've got a mole under one eye. A friend pointed out that I don't include it when I draw my face. Why? Because it would look like I have three eyes. Well, um, anyway... welcome to volume 4. *Sand Chronicles* is my first series to go past volume 3! Yay!
—Hinako Ashihara

Hinako Ashihara won the 50th Shogakukan Manga Award for *Sunadokei*. She debuted with *Sono Hanashi Okotowari Shimasu* in Bessatsu Shojo Comics in 1994. Her other works include *SOS*, *Forbidden Dance*, and *Tennen Bitter Chocolate*.

SAND CHRONICLES
Vol. 4
The Shojo Beat Manga Edition

This manga volume contains material that was originally published in English in *Shojo Beat* magazine, August 2008~October 2008 issues. Artwork in the magazine may have been slightly altered from that presented here.

STORY AND ART BY HINAKO ASHIHARA

English Adaptation/John Werry
Translation/Kinami Watabe
Touch-up Art & Lettering/Rina Mapa
Additional Touch-up/Rachel Lightfoot
Cover Design/Yukiko Whitley
Interior Design/Izumi Evers
Editor/Annette Roman

Editor in Chief, Books/Alvin Lu
Editor in Chief, Magazines/Marc Weidenbaum
VP, Publishing Licensing/Rika Inouye
VP, Sales & Product Marketing/Gonzalo Ferreyra
VP, Creative/Linda Espinosa
Publisher/Hyoe Narita

Printed in Canada

Published by VIZ Media, LLC
P.O. Box 77010
San Francisco, CA 94107

store.viz.com

PARENTAL ADVISORY
SAND CHRONICLES is rated T+ for Older Teen and is recommended for ages 16 and up. This volume contains mature themes.
ratings.viz.com

Shojo Beat Manga Edition
10 9 8 7 6 5 4 3 2 1
First printing, January 2009